THE GREATEST OF ALL LEATHERNECKS

Major General John Arthur Lejeune,
13th Commandant of the US Marine Corps.
USMC History Division.

THE GREATEST OF ALL LEATHERNECKS

JOHN ARCHER LEJEUNE AND THE MAKING OF THE MODERN MARINE CORPS

JOSEPH ARTHUR SIMON

LOUISIANA STATE UNIVERSITY PRESS
BATON ROUGE

Published by Louisiana State University Press

Manufactured in the United States of America
First printing

DESIGNER: *Mandy McDonald Scallan*
TYPEFACE: *Sentinel*
PRINTER AND BINDER: *Sheridan Books, Inc.*

The maps were created by David Lindroth.

Library of Congress Cataloging-in-Publication Data

Names: Simon, Joseph Arthur, 1939– author.
Title: The greatest of all leathernecks : John Archer Lejeune and the making of the modern Marine Corps / Joseph Arthur Simon.
Other titles: John Archer Lejeune and the making of the modern Marine Corps
Description: Baton Rouge : Louisiana State University Press, 2019. | Includes bibliographical references and index.
Identifiers: LCCN 2019014121| ISBN 978-0-8071-7197-4 (cloth : alk. paper) | ISBN 978-0-8071-7245-2 (pdf) | ISBN 978-0-8071-7246-9 (epub)
Subjects: LCSH: Lejeune, John Archer, 1867–1942. | United States. Marine Corps—Biography. | Generals—United States—Biography. | World War, 1914–1918—Campaigns—France.
Classification: LCC VE25.L45 S56 2019 | DDC 359.9/6092 [B] —dc23

The paper in this book meets the guidelines for permanence and durability of the Committee on Production Guidelines for Book Longevity of the Council on Library Resources. ♾

To Lucienne

CONTENTS

ILLUSTRATIONS

PHOTOGRAPHS

MAPS

PREFACE & ACKNOWLEDGMENTS

John Archer Lejeune (1867–1942), the thirteenth commandant of the US Marine Corps, was a luminary figure in the history of the Marine Corps and in the development of amphibious operations and other advancements for the modern corps. Thus far, a comprehensive biography of this exceptional figure in the history of the corps has not been published.[1] Although Lejeune was commandant almost a century ago, his role in creating a new mission that gave the corps an important place in the American defense establishment is essential for contemporary studies.

Lejeune, with the support of progressive officers in the new Navy of steam and steel (late nineteenth and early twentieth centuries) and a few other visionary Marines, led the corps to evolve from the old mission of acting as colonial infantry in the Caribbean and Western Pacific to a new mission of amphibious landings to support the Navy. Lejeune and other far-sighted Marines developed the Advanced Base Force, a Marine defensive force to occupy and provide a base for the Navy. This base enabled the Navy to defend the homeland of the United States. Later, Lejeune was instrumental in leading the change from the defensive role of the ABF to the offensive mission (amphibious assault) of the Marine Expeditionary Force. In the 1930s this force became the Fleet Marine Force, which captured essential islands and land areas in the Pacific war against Japan during World War II. Lejeune also developed the Marine Corps Schools in the 1920s, which became the intellectual center of the corps. Graduates of the schools were instrumental in writing the *Tentative Manual on Landing Operations* in 1934, a step-by-step handbook on how to conduct amphibious assault. Finally, Lejeune's persistence and pressure on Congress and the Navy to institute selection (promotion) by merit instead of by seniority and to imbed the Marine Expeditionary Force into the fleet eventually became law in the 1930s.

In the following account of Lejeune's life and achievements, I hope to honor Lejeune's legacy. My authorship of this book dates back over fifty years to 1965 when my major advisor, historian Dr. T. Harry Williams, suggested that I research the life and work of Lejeune for my master's thesis at Louisiana State University. At that time, no biographer had written a thesis, much less a book, on Lejeune. To help finance my research, Professor Williams contacted Walter McIlhenny, a member of the family that produces Tabasco hot sauce made from locally grown hot peppers at Avery Island, Louisiana. McIlhenny—who had been a brigadier general in the Marine Corps Reserve and commanded Marines at Guadalcanal and Peleliu, Palau Islands, in World War II—gave the university a grant that made it possible for me to copy the Lejeune papers at the Library of Congress for the LSU libraries.

I corresponded with two of Lejeune's daughters, Eugenia D. Lejeune and Laura T. Lejeune, in Washington, DC, for permission to copy General Lejeune's papers, receiving authorization to copy only his official papers, not his personal letters and papers.[2] These papers and other sources provided enough information to write a partial biography of Lejeune's life from 1867 to 1917 for my master's thesis, but not enough to write a complete study for a PhD dissertation. The entire collection of the Lejeune papers later became available at the Library of Congress. These included the lifetime correspondence between Lejeune and his family, notably the weekly letters to his sister Augustine.

Retirement from higher education administration in 2003 offered me the opportunity to conduct further, more comprehensive research on Lejeune in order to write a complete biography. From earlier research, I was convinced that it was Lejeune's leadership in the Marine Corps that had created the new mission of amphibious assault that resulted in the modern Marine Corps, as evidenced by the corps's performance in the Pacific in World War II. Several scholars have maintained that Lejeune was the most important twentieth-century commandant.[3] Further, the superlative phrase "the greatest of all leathernecks" was often used in reference to Lejeune, most recently in the issuance in 2005 by the US Postal Service of a postage-stamp series honoring Lejeune, John Basilone, Daniel I. Daly, and Lewis B. Puller.[4]

I was concerned that some historians had downplayed Lejeune's pioneering work in developing amphibious operations and the modern Marine Corps in the 1920s. Instead, a few credible historians seemingly gave all of the credit to the corps of the 1930s.[5] My doctoral dissertation provides a thorough analysis of the publications by these writers and their conclusions.[6] Unique to my research is the use of previously unused or neglected archival sources that dispel incorrect assumptions such as those made by these writers, and presents new information that gives due credit to John Archer Lejeune, the originator, instigator, and first developer of amphibious assault as the mission of the modern Marine Corps.

Since work on this book goes back almost five decades, many individuals who supported me are now deceased. Nevertheless, special recognition must go to the late Dr. T. Harry Williams, Boyd Professor at Louisiana State University, who first suggested Louisiana-born Lieutenant General John Archer Lejeune, USMC (Ret.), as the topic for my master's thesis. Williams secured a grant from Brigadier General Walter McIlhenny, USMCR (Ret.), in New Iberia, Louisiana, to purchase Lejeune's official papers from the Library of Congress. I am also grateful to the late Dr. Robert D. Higginbotham of LSU for his time, guidance, and constructive criticism during the preparation of my master's thesis. Later Dr. Higginbotham continued his work as distinguished scholar at the University of North Carolina at Chapel Hill.

The research and writing to earn the PhD from Lancaster University through the University of Cumbria in Great Britain began when I had the honor in 2005 of meeting James Blair Glennon Jr., Colonel USMC (Ret.)—grandson of General Lejeune—and Colonel Glennon's wife, Margaret Wyatte Glennon. The opportunity to interview the Glennons and read the correspondence between General Lejeune and his oldest daughter, Ellie Murdaugh Lejeune Glennon, was priceless. I also had the good fortune of meeting Brigadier General Gordon Donald Gayle, USMC (Ret.), Colonel Glennon's classmate at the Naval Academy (1939), who supported my work and provided me lodging at his home in Washington, DC, during the many months that I researched archival materials on General Lejeune at the Library of Congress, the National Archives and Records Administration in Washington and College Park, Maryland, and the Alfred M. Gray Research Center at Quantico, Virginia.

I am grateful for the assistance and direction of Sonia Mason, Dr. Robert Poole, Dr. Thomas Mills, Dr. Douglas Ford, Alan Farmer, Dr. Chris Read, Dr. Sam Edwards, and especially Dr. Richard McGregor, all at the University of Cumbria and Lancaster University.

Charles W. Johnson, archives specialist at the National Archives and Records Administration, and Alisa M. Whitley, archivist at the Marine Corps Archives and Special Collections Center at Quantico, were especially helpful, as was Kara R. Newcomer, historian, Historical Reference Branch.

I am also grateful to LeAnn Fawver, archivist at the US Army History Institute, for providing military papers written by General Lejeune when he was a student at the Army War College.

I am honored and thankful for the input and suggestions for my manuscript by Dr. Allan R. Millett, Ambrose Professor of History and director of the Eisenhower Center for American Studies at the University of New Orleans.

In the identification and collection of photographs, the following people were of greatly appreciated assistance: at the Defense Visual Information Distribution Service: Jhanteill Lopez; Lejeune descendants and family: James B. Glennon III and Harry Hull; Louisiana State Library: Charlene Bonnette; LSU Archives: Barry Cowan and Michelle Melançon; LSU Residential Life: Amanda Hawk; National Archives: Holly Reed; Navsource: Gary Priolo; USMC History Division, Quantico: Kara Newcomer; and USNA Public Affairs: Madelyn Darbie.

Special thanks to David Lindroth for the exceptional maps.

I have also been blessed with superb proofreaders, especially my sister, Jacqueline Simon Colthart; my daughter, Teighlor Simon March; and my wife, Lucienne Bond Simon, PhD. Lucienne has spent countless hours, years actually, as proofreader and advocate. Without her assistance and support, this book would not have been possible.

ABBREVIATIONS

(USED IN TEXT & NOTES)

ABF Advanced Base Force
AEF American Expeditionary Forces
AWC Army War College
AWCCA Army War College Curriculum Archives, Military History Institute
CG Commanding General
CinC Commander in Chief
CNO Chief of Naval Operations
CO Commanding Officer
FLEXs Fleet Landing Exercises
FMF Fleet Marine Force
GHQ General Headquarters of the AEF
GPO Government Printing Office
GRC Alfred M. Gray Research Center, Quantico, VA
HAF Marine Corps University, Archives Branch, Alfred M. Gray Research Center, Historical Amphibious Files, Quantico, VA
JFQ *Joint Force Quarterly*
LCM Landing Craft Mechanized
LCVP Landing Craft Vehicle Personnel
MCG *Marine Corps Gazette*
MCS Marine Corps Schools
MEF Marine Expeditionary Force
MGC Major General Commandant
NARACP National Archives and Records Administration, College Park, MD

NARAW	National Archives and Records Administration, Washington, DC
NIP	Naval Institute Press
NWC	Naval War College
ONI	Office of Naval Intelligence
RG	Record Group, National Archives and Records Administration
USN	United States Navy
USNA	United States Navy Archives
USNIP	*United States Naval Institute Proceedings*
VMI	Virginia Military Institute

THE GREATEST OF ALL LEATHERNECKS

INTRODUCTION

John Archer Lejeune was born in 1867 to Ovide and Laura Lejeune on a small cotton and sugar plantation in an area then known as Raccourci, located a few miles north of New Roads, Louisiana, on the Mississippi River in Pointe Coupee Parish. It was a difficult time for the Lejeune family, their neighboring plantation owners and small farmers, as well as for former slaves, living through Reconstruction as imposed by the victorious Union forces that had defeated the South during the Civil War.

Since there was no school in that part of southern Louisiana at that time, Laura Lejeune developed an elementary school for the neighborhood, educating young Lejeune and his older sister, Augustine. Later, he enrolled at his great-uncle James Archer's boarding school near Natchez, Mississippi. At the age of sixteen, Lejeune entered the precollege program at Louisiana State University in Baton Rouge, at that time a military school. He attended LSU from 1881 to 1884 before earning an appointment to the US Naval Academy at Annapolis, Maryland. Lejeune excelled in his studies at Annapolis from 1884 to 1888. In his next two years as a naval midshipman, he survived and earned acclaim for bravery and leadership during the Great Samoan Typhoon of 1889.

Lejeune entered the Marine Corps in 1890, which at that time was a smaller service within the Navy Department. He commanded detachments of Marine guards aboard naval warships during the 1890s, leading a landing party against enemy troops in Puerto Rico during the Spanish-American War of 1898. In the early years of the twentieth century, he led Marines in landing at Panama, 1903–4 and 1906, to secure the isthmus for the canal builders. He also led several larger landings in Cuba and the Philippines during a war scare with Japan, as well as in Veracruz in the war against Mexico in 1914. Lejeune earned a reputation during the decade as an advocate for a new mission for the Marine Corps—amphibious landings to defend distance bases in order to support the "New Navy" of steam and steel in their quest to gain control of the sea against an enemy fleet. This new mission was a radical departure from the outdated charge of the "old corps," which, at that time, provided discipline for unreliable sailors—many recent immigrants—who might mutiny against the ship.

Lejeune turned in an outstanding performance as a student at the Army War College (AWC) from 1909 to 1910 and was the first Marine officer to suggest offensive amphibious operations in a lecture to the Advanced Base Force School in 1915 and to Congress in early 1920. Lejeune had commanded the Army's famed Second Division in 1918, which included a Marine Brigade in World War I, and also in the occupation of Germany in 1919. He was the only Marine to command an Army division in the Great War. Lejeune became major general commandant (MGC) in 1920, serving three terms of office before retiring from the corps in 1929. He led a sharply divided corps to the amphibious mission, developed a modern organization, war planning, the Marine Expeditionary Force (MEF), and the Marine Corps Schools (MCS), and organized the first maneuvers utilizing amphibious assault. As superintendent of the Virginia Military Institute (VMI) from 1929 to 1937, Lejeune remained committed to the Marine Corps of the 1930s, supporting from retirement the corps's further development of the mission of amphibious assault that was successfully utilized in World War II. Lejeune died in 1942 at the same time the Marine Corps was fighting Japanese forces on Guadalcanal in the Solomon Islands.

Since Lejeune's career occurred within the context of the Marine Corps and the development of amphibious operations, I will provide a brief review of the evolution of the corps and the history of amphibious operations. While there is no dearth of scholarship on these two subjects, for the most part books on the Marine Corps focus on the war against Japan in the Pacific from 1941 to 1945. These books satisfy the general reader with narratives of bloody victories, individual heroic actions, and Marine valor. Shortly after World War II, many people thought that major amphibious operations were developments of the war.[1] Nothing could be further from the truth. Landings from the sea in wartime date from antiquity.

While this book begins in the mid- to late nineteenth century and with

Lejeune's entry into the Marine Corps in 1890, a brief review of the corps from its origin will be helpful for the reader to understand the evolution of the organization. This overview begins in 1775 and focuses on the commandants and their priorities during their tenure.[2] In the early years (American Revolution up to the Civil War), the Marine Corps was a very small organization, often regarded as unnecessary by the Navy, its leadership consisting of political appointees fighting among themselves for power and prestige.

The story began with the creation of two battalions of marines[3] by the Second Continental Congress on November 10, 1775, during the American Revolution. Although marines served mainly on a small number of continental and state-funded sailing ships and were generally overwhelmed by the Royal Navy, there were several landing operations. One successful amphibious operation involved a group of marines landing without British or Loyalist resistance at Hanover Sound on Providence Island in the Bahamas on March 3, 1776, seizing the governor's residence and Fort Montagu.[4]

The Marine Corps was officially established by Congress on May 28, 1798, and consisted of 33 officers and 832 enlisted Marines. Relations between sea captains and the leaders of the Marine detachments aboard were often poor, because—with the exception of using Marines in battle to provide small-arms fire and boarding parties—no one really understood the purpose of the Marines. Marines nevertheless fought well aboard naval ships during the Quasi-War with France, 1799–1801, and during the Barbary Wars off the coast of North Africa.[5] Marines landed in Tripoli in 1804 and 1805 and won acclaim by capturing Derna, the Tripolitan port west of Alexandria, Egypt.

Under Commandant Franklin Wharton, 1804 to 1818, Marines engaged the Barbary pirates in Tripoli, fought with the Army against the Spanish, pirates, Indians, and fugitive slaves in New Orleans in 1805–6, but—even though fighting with the militia—were unable to prevent a much larger British force from capturing and burning the Capitol in Washington during the War of 1812. They did, however, serve in small numbers with Andrew Jackson's army of five thousand men that defeated British forces attacking New Orleans in 1815.[6]

The Marine Corps and Navy experienced great changes during the period from 1820 to 1859. In the 1820s and 1830s Marines continued the tradition of fighting as riflemen from the top masts aboard wooden sailing ships during close engagements with enemy ships, leading boarding parties to subdue the crew of the enemy vessel or protecting their own ship from enemy boarding, and providing discipline for untrustworthy sailors, often recent immigrants who could not find other jobs and who had a high rate of desertion. In the 1840s and 1850s, new technology introduced steam-powered, propeller-driven, iron-reinforced ships with superior cannon that had a longer range and more accuracy. With greater distance and more destructive fire between fighting ships, Marines performed more landing missions ashore and often manned the ships' great guns. Marines joined the Army in fighting Seminole Indians in Florida and the Creek Indians in Georgia and Alabama from 1836 to 1838, often landing from the fleet to fight Seminoles in lengthy riverine operations. More importantly, Marines served with distinction landing from the fleet along the coasts of California and eastern Mexico during the Mexican War in 1846–47. In most cases, the Marines were commanded by a naval officer with a Marine officer as second in command.[7] These operations were directed by the US government to displace the Indians and Mexicans and open up new territory for an increasing population of American settlers eager to acquire this land.

During the Civil War, the Marine Corps was still a small service rendered ineffective by poor leadership. The corps was dominated by petty jealousies and squabbling between the commandant and senior officers, resulting in the defection of many aggressive and talented younger officers to the Confederate Marines. The corps fought only once ashore with the Union Army that was defeated at the battle of first Manassas and later lost many Marines in a doomed night amphibious assault with a naval regiment on Fort Sumter, Charleston Harbor, in 1863. At this time, the Army developed an amphibious division during the war and conducted several successful landings such as the Fort Fisher Campaigns, 1864–65.[8]

The Marine Corps entered a dark period called the "postwar doldrums" due to public apathy toward the entire military establishment after the Civil War. This public and governmental disinterest in the military lingered to 1876.[9] Because of the corps's uneven performance during the Civil War, the commandant, Brigadier General Jacob Zeilin, had to face criticism from the Navy and Congress. There was also a congressional attempt to abolish the Marine Corps. Consequently, Zeilin had to spend an inordinate amount of time defending the corps, securing the support of naval officers who admired the corps, and citing the accomplishments of the Marines to Congress. At the same time, a large majority of Zeilin's Marines were deployed aboard warships displaying the growing military strength of the United States around the world. From 1866 to 1876, Marines landed in China, Formosa, Japan, Nicaragua, Uruguay, Mexico, Korea, Panama, and Hawaii. In fact, six Marines received the Medal of Honor for storming ashore against Kanghwa-do in the Han estuary in Korea under the protection of naval guns.[10]

At about this time, progressives in the American military saw the need for reform in the Army and the Navy. For the Army, the era of fighting Indians during the movement of settlers westward had passed. In addition, because of the terrible carnage suffered by soldiers during the Civil War through frontal charges against modern rifles and artillery, the service had to develop new strategies and tactics. Similarly, the Navy saw a need to develop newer, more powerful ships to compete with European nations for world trade—abandoning the passive mission of defending the American coastline with obsolete and sluggish iron-clad monitors and commerce raiding on the high seas by single warships—and pursued a new doctrine of fleet engagements to win control of the sea. William T. Sherman, commanding general (CG) of the Army between 1869 and 1883, and Rear Admiral Stephen B. Luce led professional reform in the Army and Navy by creating a comprehensive educational system in both services. Emulating the great powers of Europe, Sherman was not satisfied with having only one military educational institution (West Point). He revived the Artillery School and encouraged the development of an Engineering School of Application, founding an Infantry and Cavalry School of Application at Fort Leavenworth. He influenced progressive officers to form schools for field artillery and cavalry, the Signal Corps, Hospital Corps, and an Army Medical School, including the Military Service Institution in 1878 for officers who desired to acquire specialized knowledge. For the Navy, Luce became the driving force behind the creation of the US Naval Institute in 1873, the Office of Naval Intelligence (ONI) in 1882, and the Naval War College (NWC) in 1884, leading to the development of the new Navy of steam and steel. Because of these advances, the Navy would motivate the Marine Corps toward modernization and the creation of the amphibious mission.[11]

During these changes in the late nineteenth century, the US government aspired to become a world power. When he was president of the US NWC, 1886–89 and 1892–93, Alfred Thayer Mahan argued that naval power had to be evaluated in a global context in which navies engaged the enemy to win command of the sea. With a fleet as an offensive weapon, a nation could concentrate its power at a decisive point such as at an advanced naval base near the enemy fleet, destroy the commercial trade of the enemy, and develop effective lines of communication and links to the home country. Mahan's ideas—which only partially influenced the development of the "new" American Navy—were inspired by his understanding of Great Britain's control of the sea lanes in the seventeenth and eighteenth centuries as presented in his best-known book, *The Influence of Sea Power upon History, 1660–1783,* published in 1890.[12]

For the first time, from 1897 to 1909, the US Navy was able to project American power in the Pacific while helping to shape foreign policy along with the Department of State. With the acquisition of American territory across the Pacific as the result of the Spanish-American War and the development of trade in the Far East, especially with China, the United States entered into a trading and political rivalry with Japan.[13]

Unfortunately, the leadership of the Marine Corps was resistant to adopting a new mission of large-scale amphibious operations as demanded by progressives in the Navy. The commandants who led the Marine Corps during the early period of Lejeune's career—Charles G. McCawley (1876–91), Charles Heywood (1891–1903), and George Frank Elliott (1903–10)—resisted the Navy's plan to remove Marine ship's guards from warships in order to place larger groups of Marines in transports to land and capture naval bases abroad to allow the Navy to win control of the sea. These commandants still believed that the Marine guards were necessary to protect naval officers from mutiny by the sailors.[14]

The Navy, the American government, and progressives in the Marine Corps gradually overcame the resistance of the Marine Corps's leadership to large-scale landing operations from transports. First, the Navy landed Marines and sailors from transports protected by warships to thwart a rebel uprising and preserve free transit across the Isthmus of Panama in 1885. The naval force ashore was not a permanent expeditionary force, but a group put together that included over twelve hundred men, two battalions of Marines under Major Charles Heywood, a Navy bluejacket artillery force, and crew members of ships lying offshore.[15] Second, the Greer Board, appointed by the Secretary of the Navy in 1889 to study the mission of the Navy and Marine Corps, saw no need for the corps except perhaps for large-scale missions, and voted to remove Marine guards from warships.[16] Third, the newly created Navy Board led by Admiral George Dewey recommended in 1900 that the Marine Corps develop a permanent Advanced Base Force (ABF) to support the Navy by defending naval bases overseas. Finally, the Navy and progressives in the Marine Corps were highly impressed when a Marine battalion supported by the fleet landed from a transport during the Spanish-American War to establish a naval base for the fleet close to the land fighting in Cuba in 1898. This meant that the fleet did not have to return to the United States to refuel.[17]

While the Marine Corps landed to secure bases in the Caribbean in the early twentieth century, the corps spent almost two decades developing the ABF, a Marine force empowered to defend naval bases outside the continental United States against enemy fleets. At the Culebra Maneuvers located near Puerto Rico in 1914, the Marine Corps demonstrated that the ABF could defend the island in a war game against an amphibious assault from Marines and sailors from the fleet.[18]

The American invasion of Mexico at Veracruz in 1914 was led by Marines landing from the Navy's Atlantic Fleet. The invasion was prompted by President Woodrow Wilson's displeasure over the rise of a Mexican dictatorship during that country's Civil War and by the desire of the United States to secure Mexican oil fields which were deemed important should the United States participate in the war in Europe. While the invasion proved that the Marine Corps could successfully assault a defended Veracruz, the invasion proved to be of no value to the United States and also created ill will between the two countries for many years.[19]

In the latter years of the nineteenth century and the early years of the twentieth, the Navy developed War Plan Orange—war against Japan—a plan to protect new overseas possessions won from Spain after the Spanish-American War. The Navy and the Marine Corps gained the important responsibility of protecting the Philippine Islands, Guam, and Puerto Rico from possible invasion by either Japan or Germany. In addition, the United States annexed Hawaii in 1898 despite the strong protest of Japan. By the end of the nineteenth century the American Navy had developed a two-ocean fleet and achieved naval parity with Britain, the world's preeminent navy, after the Washington Naval Conference of 1922.[20]

Leaders of the Marine Corps wanted to participate in the Great War against Imperial Germany in 1917 and 1918, but had no amphibious mission because the British Navy had already won control of the Atlantic except for the German submarine threat. In addition, the American Army did not want the corps's participation in the war in France, wanting instead an "all-Army show." Pressure from the secretary of the Navy and President Wilson, however, forced the Army to accept a brigade of Marines in the Army's Second Division. In this conflict, the Marines earned great acclaim in battle and in the American press, but suffered heavy casualties despite their small numbers. The War Department felt that this adulation was unfair to their soldiers, for the Army had provided the great bulk of troops in the war.

During the interwar period, 1919 to 1941, the Marine Corps moved from a mission of defensive amphibious operations to offensive amphibious assault; developed a new organizational structure to facilitate war planning, intelligence, education, training, aviation, and amphibious operations; and incorporated the concept of combined operations in combat. To promote the concept of offensive amphibious operations, the corps renamed the ABF to the MEF in the 1920s and to the Fleet Marine Force (FMF) in the 1930s.[21] In the early 1920s the corps adopted the Navy's War Plan Orange, a strategy to defeat Japan in a Pacific war, a plan that was developed for over forty years.[22] The value of amphibious operations as developed by the Marine Corps was not fully realized until the Navy accepted the concept. This was due in large measure to the conflict within the Navy between senior admirals who continued to support the primary role of the battleship in wartime ("big-gun admirals") and the naval visionaries who saw the potential of airpower, the aircraft carrier, the submarine, and amphibious operations. This problem was not solved until shortly before World War II. In that war, the use of aircraft, the aircraft carrier, the submarine, and amphibious assault led by the Marine Corps in the Pacific proved to be much more important than the battleship.[23]

Amphibious assault by Marines and the Army would not have been possible without the civilian development of workable landing craft because the Navy was never able to develop a functional landing craft. In 1964, General Dwight Eisenhower was interviewing historian Stephen Ambrose about the prospect of Ambrose becoming an editor of his official papers. Eisenhower asked him: "I notice you are teaching in New Orleans. Did you ever know Andrew Higgins?" Ambrose replied, "No sir, he died before I moved to the city." "That's too bad," Eisenhower replied. "He is the man who won the war for us. . . . if Higgins had not designed and built those LCVPs [Landing Craft Vehicle Personnel] we never could have landed over an open beach. The whole strategy of the war would have been different."[24]

The subject of amphibious operations is an important component in the study of Lejeune's career and the Marine Corps. Amphibious warfare did not begin with the Marine Corps or with the failed Allied assault at Gallipoli in 1915. The first recorded account of amphibious warfare occurred during the war between the Greeks and Persians in 480 and 479 BC at Marathon in Greece when the Persians landed approximately ten thousand infantry from six hundred warships propelled by rowers. The landing of Persian soldiers was unopposed by the Greeks, and the fighting was conducted on land using conventional tactics. According to one historian, the war was won by Greece because the tactics of land fighting were already well developed while naval warfare at this time was still evolving.[25] Persian warships landed troops primarily to capture enemy supplies.[26]

Other important, albeit primitive, landings occurred at Hastings, England, in 1066; with Mongol attempts to invade Japan in 1274 and 1281; and landings by the Spanish fleet from 1538 to 1594.[27] Of all the important military philosophers and strategists in the nineteenth century, Antoine-Henri, Baron de Jomini, was one of the very few to write about sea power and amphibious operations. Jomini remarked that ancient historians wrote much more about the extensive "debarkations" or amphibious operations of the ancients—the Persians, Phoenicians, Greeks, Carthaginians, and Romans—than Jomini's contemporaries did about amphibious operations during his lifetime, operations such as the Anglo-Russian expedition to Holland in 1799, or General Sir Ralph Abercromby's amphibious operation in Egypt in 1801. With the publication in 1838 of his volume *The Art of War,* Jomini both validated the concept of amphibious landings as a proper component of military strategy and doctrine and summarized the major amphibious operations from ancient times up until his day, even laying down rules (doctrine) for amphibious operations that are still used today.[28]

Marine Corps historian J. D. Hittle agreed with Jomini that amphibious operations had a long history of development and that some early ship-to-shore operations such as the Nordic invasions, the Crusades, and early French and British expeditions were "helter-skelter affairs," having nothing in common with the practiced, meticulously planned, and well-executed Aboukir Bay landings supervised by British generals Abercromby and John Moore at the beginning of the nineteenth century.[29]

Great Britain had successful amphibious campaigns and landed forces without opposition in the Egyptian campaign of 1882 and at the Punitive

Expedition to China in 1900. In the Great War, 1914 to 1918, Great Britain conducted small amphibious assaults against German submarine bases in Belgium, the most successful a night assault on Zeebrugge.[30] The British, however, had not developed an amphibious strategy for large-scale operations in the early twentieth century and were not prepared to assault Gallipoli in 1915. The campaign was politically driven, suffered from inadequate preparation and planning, and had a poor command structure. Unfortunately, the failed Allied amphibious assault at Gallipoli led Great Britain to lose interest in developing amphibious capability during the interwar period. As a consequence, Britain failed to respond effectively when the Germans invaded Norway in 1940.[31]

It was the US Marine Corps that benefited the most from the Allied failure at Gallipoli by beginning an extensive study of the reasons for the failure. These studies helped prepare the Marine Corps for conducting successful amphibious assault missions against Japan in World War II. Even before the studies on Gallipoli began in 1921,[32] however, MGC John A. Lejeune had adopted the amphibious assault mission for the US Marine Corps as part of War Plan Orange in 1920. During his nine years as commandant, 1920 to 1929, Lejeune developed a new structure at USMC Headquarters to facilitate war planning and intelligence gathering, conducted four Civil War reenactments to teach combined operations, planned three ship-to-shore landings with the fleet to practice amphibious maneuvers, worked to convince the Navy of the importance of the amphibious assault and to include the MEF as a part of the fleet, and lobbied Congress to permit selection by merit. Finally, Lejeune inspired his successors to continue work in the 1930s to refine the new mission.[33] Consequently, the corps was fundamentally prepared for war when the Japanese bombed Pearl Harbor on December 7, 1941. Two understrength divisions—the First Marine Division and the Army's First Infantry Division—formed I Corps (Provisional), US Atlantic Fleet, under the command of Holland Smith, and were practicing amphibious landings at the recently established base at New River, North Carolina, later named Camp Lejeune.[34]

1
EARLY YEARS IN LOUISIANA

Louisiana-born John Archer Lejeune was the beneficiary of a distinguished lineage. The exemplary qualities repeatedly shown by Lejeune as a Marine—perseverance, tenacity, resilience, integrity, a sense of honor, resourcefulness, vision, and ambition—are apparent in his ancestry. Shortly after King George's War, 1744–1748, Lejeune's great-grandfather Jean Baptiste Lejeune, who was born in Bretagne, left France and located in Acadia (Nova Scotia), Canada.[1] He and his two brothers rallied to the French standard during the French and Indian War in North America (1754–63) and fought under the Marquis de Montcalm on the Plains of Abraham, overlooking Quebec. Vanquished but unsubdued after British General James Wolfe's triumph, the Lejeunes chose to leave Canada by traveling down the St. Lawrence River and across the Great Lakes. After lingering briefly in Kaskaskia, Illinois, they led twenty men down the Mississippi River and settled in the Fausse Rivière district of Louisiana.[2]

Jean Baptiste would live a long, full life in Louisiana. Eventually, at the venerable age of 105, he fell off his horse after visiting a doctor for a tooth extraction and died from blood loss on April 10, 1854.[3]

Jean Baptiste's son, Joseph, married Augustine Le Moyne (later changed to Lemoine).[4] Augustine traced her lineage to Charles Le Moyne, a Frenchman awarded two seigneuries in Canada in the 1670s.[5] He was an interpreter, soldier, businessman, and father of numerous sons, three of whom attained distinction in early Louisiana: Pierre Le Moyne d'Iberville, Jean Baptiste Le Moyne de Bienville, and Antoine Le Moyne de Châteauguay. Joseph and Augustine lived in lower Pointe Coupee Parish when their son Ovide was born on August 31, 1820.[6]

Unfortunately, Joseph died in 1821 and Augustine died about 1826, leaving Ovide—John Lejeune's father—an orphan. Ovide remembered his mother as "determined, strong-willed, but very unselfish and kind."[7] A guardian and tutor, Alexandre Labry Jr., assumed responsibility for the young boy until Ovide went to school in Cape Girardeau, Missouri.[8] In 1837, Ovide left for what was supposed to be a brief visit to Pointe Coupee Parish. Independence, however, proved too invigorating a force for the seventeen-year-old to suppress, so, instead of returning to Missouri, he transferred to a boarding school in Baton Rouge, studied business in New Orleans, and later obtained a position with a local commission merchant.

Ovide's fortunes prospered, especially after returning to Raccourci to raise sugarcane on land inherited from his parents.[9] Romance followed success. As described by his son John A. Lejeune, in 1857 Ovide, "the tall, black-haired, black-eyed bachelor," met sixteen-year-old Laura Archer Turpin, a native of Mississippi who was visiting her uncle Dr. John G. Archer at Longwood Plantation. The Archers, close friends and neighbors of Ovide, welcomed his visits. The reason was obvious: "My father was immediately attracted to my mother," wrote John, "and they were married."[10] The wedding took place on June 14, 1859, at the Presbyterian Church near the Turpin home in Jefferson, Mississippi.[11]

Like Ovide, Laura Archer Turpin descended from prominent families. Her parents were Joseph A. Turpin, born in Jefferson, and Maryland native Laura Archer. The Turpins were French Huguenots who fled to England after the revocation of the Edict of Nantes by Louis XIV in 1685, which terminated the protection of Protestants in France and renewed the persecution of Protestants by Catholics and the government.[12] The Turpins migrated to the American colonies early in the eighteenth century and established homes in the section presently known as Queen Anne's County, Maryland. Part of the family left Maryland in 1808 and settled in the Territory of Mississippi.[13]

The Archer line stemmed from Dr. John Archer (May 5, 1741–September 28, 1810) of the Harford County area of Maryland, the first medical doctor in the American colonies. Dr. Archer graduated from the Medical School in Philadelphia in 1768.[14] Archer was also a popular Presbyterian minister, a major in the Revolutionary War, a judge, an elector-at-large, and a Jeffersonian Democrat in Congress. Born on a cotton plantation near Natchez, Mississippi, on December 6, 1840, Laura Archer Turpin was reared in accordance with strict Presbyterian traditions. After completing her education in Baltimore, Laura returned home, where she met Ovide Lejeune of Raccourci.

John Archer Lejeune adored his parents: "My father was absolutely fearless. . . . he was of tireless energy, fiery in spirit, but . . . [had] the kindest heart of any man I ever knew." Laura Lejeune "always exercised perfect self-control, was gifted with excellent judgment, was charitable in word and deed, and beloved by the community."[15] The couple was hardworking and like many plantation owners enjoyed moderate financial success in pre–Civil War Pointe Coupee Parish.

The majority of the population in the parish and in Louisiana as a whole consisted of slaves of African descent, owned primarily by plantation families. Much of the white population was small farmers and sharecroppers who did not own slaves and earned a subsistence living. Living conditions for residents of rural areas outside of New Orleans were fairly primitive. The state government of antebellum Louisiana—as compared to the governments of the more prosperous northern states—provided few social services and little in the way of public education or infrastructure such as roads and railroads.[16] In spite of these poor conditions, the literature of the early and mid-twentieth century often romanticized the antebellum South. One writer, for example, noted that during this period the Pointe Coupee area was "rich in tradition, legend, and history. Here developed the aristocratic French and Spanish cultures, while east of the Mississippi River, amid the Tunica Hills of West Feliciana Parish, surged the societies of the Anglo-Saxon land barons. Over time these divergent cultures met and gradually blended."[17]

The Lejeune plantation—Old Hickory—was acquired by Ovide Lejeune in 1850 at Old River, Louisiana. Old Hickory was an integral part of the parish, alternately and successfully producing sugarcane, cotton, corn, and assorted vegetables. The year 1860 was likely the most successful one economically for the Lejeune family. The value of Ovide's real property was $130,000, while the value of his personal property was $45,000. The Lejeunes owned 700 acres of improved (cultivated) land and 850 acres of unimproved property valued at $62,000, with farming implements and machinery worth $50,000, plus a good number of horses, mules, sheep, and swine. The plantation produced Indian corn, wool, peas, beans, Irish and sweet potatoes, cane sugar, molasses, and cotton ginned into four-hundred-pound bales.[18]

According to figures given by Joseph Karl Menn, the Lejeune plantation had seventy-seven slaves and thirty-two slave dwellings, making Ovide Lejeune a small plantation owner.[19] It is difficult to determine the market value of the Lejeune slaves. Ovide probably received these slaves as part of the purchase of Old Hickory and did not put a value on them. In general, however, the price of a "prime field hand" in 1860 was $1,800.[20] This probably meant young men. The Lejeune plantation had thirty-three male slaves between the late teenage years up to the age of fifty-five who would have worked in the fields, assuming all were healthy. There were twenty-four females between the ages of sixteen and fifty who would have labored in the fields as well. There were also several slaves in their sixties and seventies, as well as a few children from the ages of three to seven years old and five babies.[21] The way of life of southern planters such as Ovide Lejeune, overseeing an active plantation dependent on slave labor, would end as a result of the Civil War and the Congressional Reconstruction that followed from 1867 to 1877.[22]

Ovide Lejeune strongly opposed the secession of Louisiana from the Union, but when the state became part of the Confederacy, the forty-one-year-old planter spent over $10,000 of his own money to raise a troop of local cavalry. While Laura Lejeune and her infant daughter Augustine waited alone at Old Hickory, Captain Lejeune led his troop to supplement the First Louisiana Regiment of Cavalry commanded by Colonel John Sims Scott from East Feliciana Parish. They rode with the Army of the Tennessee in Alabama, Tennessee, and Kentucky. Three of Laura Lejeune's brothers served in the same army. One brother, White Turpin, was killed at the Battle of Franklin, Tennessee. Ovide's wartime service was cut short in 1862 when recurring pain due to hemorrhoids became a disability, forcing him to resign his command of Company I and to request an exemption from military duty.[23]

Located west and east of the Mississippi River and bordered on the south by the Gulf of Mexico, Louisiana was more vulnerable to federal invasion than many of the other Confederate states. Commodore David Farragut's Union naval force sailed from the Gulf of Mexico up the Mississippi River and fought past two Confederate strongholds, Fort Jackson and Fort St. Philip (that included an assorted Confederate naval fleet and forty or fifty fire rafts) to capture New Orleans. Thus, the South's largest port surrendered early in the war on May 1, 1862, without a shot being fired.[24]

Baton Rouge soon fell, followed in 1863 by Vicksburg and Port Hudson, leaving only the north-central part of Louisiana and the northwestern sections that were situated on the Red River under Confederate control. Thus, unlike the other Confederate states, Reconstruction began in south Louisiana in 1863.[25]

While Pointe Coupee was relatively distant from the main areas of battle from 1862 until the end of the war, small roving expeditions of Confederate and Union soldiers as well as deserters from both armies regularly raided the rich plantation region along the Mississippi River and north of the Red River, taking and destroying property and livestock. In addition, Union forces in these areas destroyed property and buildings as well as confiscated crops in an effort to destroy the South's ability to wage war.[26]

Into this austere post–Civil War and Reconstruction setting—arguably one of the darkest periods for the old southern aristocracy—arrived John Archer Lejeune on January 10, 1867. He was named after his attending physician, great-uncle Dr. John Archer. Soon after Lejeune's birth, Ovide was forced to declare bankruptcy, selling Old Hickory and accepting employment as manager and overseer of the Taylor sugar plantation in lower Pointe Coupee Parish.[27] But Ovide, now called "Captain Lejeune" by the other nearby planters, remained ambitious. With good credit his only resource, he repurchased Old Hickory in 1872 by assuming its heavy mortgage.[28]

As in pre–Civil War days, agriculture dominated the parish economy. Planters employed freedmen as farmhands by issuing periodic supplies against a predetermined share of their crops. Most planters worked their tenants on a "half-hand" or "one-fourth-hand" basis, the percentage depending upon the quality of the crop and the dependability of the farmhand. In turn, total plantation yield was pledged to New Orleans commission merchants, who sold farm implements and provisions to the planter on credit.[29] One prominent neighbor of the Lejeune family was Ovide B. LaCour, the largest landowner in Pointe Coupee. LaCour's general store, located a mile from Old Hickory, was the gathering place for the area's sharecroppers.[30] Undoubtedly young John Lejeune frequently walked down the dusty, often muddy, trail to the store on errands.[31]

Despite the heavy responsibility of plantation ownership, the Lejeunes received only modest profits. Cotton prices were depressed while supply costs remained high. Captain Lejeune was constantly occupied with multiple duties, such as organizing the hands, supervising their work, managing the cotton ginning and pressing, overseeing the corn processing, and bookkeeping. His reputation for dedication and commitment still survived in the parish into the middle 1960s: "He seemed to be everywhere at once," said an older resident, "maneuvering speedy buggies about the plantation keeping tabs on the workers."[32]

Old Hickory was located near what is now Lacour, Louisiana, one and one-half miles south of Old River and Raccourci Island, and three and one-half miles north of the Mississippi River's New Texas Landing. Within the farm complex and spacious quadrangle were cotton-gin houses, several outbuildings, a garden, and billets for the field hands. Towering above was an impressive array of water oaks and pecan trees. To the southeast lay the cotton, corn, hay acreage, the batture (the alluvial land between the low tide of the Mississippi and the levee), and partially wooded grazing tracts. Assiduous toil did not guarantee fruition, because soon the Lejeunes were forced to relinquish most of Old Hickory, retaining only the quadrangle area, the batture, and seventy-five acres. This loss was probably due to the severe economic downturn that occurred in the United States and Europe between 1873 and 1877, lowering the price of cotton by half and plunging many merchants and planters into bankruptcy.[33] Captain Lejeune sold the remainder of his land to his good friend Ovide B. LaCour, who allowed Lejeune to rent any necessary land.[34]

Financial hardship was only one challenge to the inhabitants of Pointe Coupee Parish. Social turmoil ensued when enslaved black persons received their freedom within a southern culture which at that time believed in white supremacy. Other challenges included the regular flooding from the Mississippi River overflows in the lowlands that claimed lives and destroyed property, and the absence of primary schools for the area's young people.

Reconstruction and the guarantee of freedom and legal equality to African Americans was a bitter pill to swallow for many white southerners, who continued to consider blacks an inferior race. Former Confederates and many other whites fought the establishment of black equality in the South every step of the way during Reconstruction, especially during Radical Reconstruction beginning in 1867. While some historians maintain that few real accomplishments occurred during the era of Radical Reconstruction in Louisiana, others note that "to the Republicans' lasting credit, a decade and a half later 34,642 Negroes received the rudiments of an education."[35] Although the Republican Reconstruction governments in Georgia, Alabama, Arkansas, and Texas were partially successful in financing more comprehensive and integrated railroad systems and a more diversified economy, the program was marred by corruption.[36] There was also corruption and self-serving in Republican-led Louisiana, and the grand design of the Radicals to build railroads and develop country towns, law enforcement, and schools outside of New Orleans rarely went beyond the planning stage. One writer did note, however, that the Republicans had some difficulty building schools and railroads while dodging Rebel bullets.[37]

The general social upheaval together with a lack of law enforcement in some locations led to violence in parts of the South, including Pointe Coupee. Thefts occurred at Old Hickory. The Lejeune family lost fourteen head of cattle in 1876. As Lejeune himself recalled, "In our section the local officials, including those sworn to enforce the laws and prosecute criminals, did not perform their functions."[38]

Ovide Lejeune—ever on alert for the possibility of uprisings and rebellion by freedmen, white criminals, and renegades—was the captain of a Vigilance Committee similar to the Ku Klux Klan. He participated in the trial and hanging of several black men who confessed a plan to murder Dr. William Archer and Ovide himself.[39] A recent book by Gillis Vandal confirms this post–Civil War lynching, concluding that it was influenced by the redefinition of race relationships and the determination of most whites to maintain white supremacy.[40] Vandal writes that five black men were lynched in Pointe Coupee Parish in 1878 because of rumors of a plot to kill the leading white men of the region.[41]

As a young boy growing up during the latter years of Reconstruction, John Lejeune was likely conditioned by his elders at that time to believe in white supremacy. To John Lejeune's credit, however, race relations never became an issue in the Marine Corps during his service in the field, 1900–1918, or as commandant, 1920–1929. The adult Lejeune had an attitude of "sympathetic paternalism" in his work, common to Marine officers of his generation. Lejeune developed a special respect for all Marines, an attitude that disregarded social station and education, leading Lejeune as commandant to develop military and vocational education for all enlisted Marines and Marine Corps Schools for all officers regardless of their background.

Scholarship from the mid- to late twentieth century and the twenty-first century has explored the efforts of Reconstruction to accord African Americans, for the first time in the South, dignity, honor, and equality. Although the entrenched cotton-growing economy of the South had created conditions of lifelong bondage for generations of African Americans, the Union victory over the Confederacy, followed by Reconstruction, attempted to right the wrongs so long imposed on blacks by southern society. In many ways, Reconstruction can be seen as the first civil rights movement in the United States to promote equality between the races; conversely, the civil rights movement of the 1960s may be considered as the second Reconstruction. In fact, the legal strategy for the civil rights movement of the 1960s was based on the constitutional amendments and civil rights acts enacted during Reconstruction.[42]

In a series of actions, Congress disenfranchised former Confederates and abolished slavery (Thirteenth Amendment, ratified 1865); established the Freedmen's Bureau to help freedmen with labor contracts and provide schooling for their children (1865 and 1866); affirmed the right of freedmen to enjoy the full and equal benefits of all federal laws, ending discrimination in state laws (Civil Rights Act of 1866); made native-born freedmen citizens of the United States, giving them equal protection of the law and the vote to all male inhabitants (Fourteenth Amendment, ratified 1868); imposed military rule in the South to enforce freedom for freedmen; established rules for readmission of the ex-Confederate states to the Union and required these states to guarantee the vote to black men (Military Reconstruction Acts, 1867); prohibited racial discrimination in voting rights for black men in all states in the nation (Fifteenth Amendment, ratified 1870); and outlawed racial discrimination in public accommodations, transportation, and juries (Civil Rights Act of 1875).[43]

Aside from racial tensions, the high water which frequently flooded the countryside continued to pose threats to Pointe Coupee residents, including the Lejeune family. Early Raccourci, virtually surrounded by the Mississippi River and the Old River, had no protective floodway levees and lock systems, while the prewar shallow levees were entirely neglected during the war and Reconstruction. Young John Lejeune never forgot the portentous tolling of plantation bells in the quiet of night, the ominous signal of high water. These deluges destroyed crops and soil, swept away property, and frequently drowned children, the aged, and the infirm. Again Ovide Lejeune was called forward and, by common consent, assumed charge of four miles of levee. When the swollen rivers and bayous threatened the land, every able-bodied man hauled mules, tools, and carts to Old Hickory where, under Captain Lejeune's supervision, they struggled day and night against the elements until the danger subsided. "My father had many narrow escapes," wrote his son, "as he did not leave the scene of the crevasse as long as it was possible to rescue the helpless, and he did not hesitate to wade through the torrent of rushing water to nearby houses and to carry in his arms the sick and the little children to a place of safety."[44]

Inadequate educational facilities presented additional difficulties for John Lejeune and other young people of Pointe Coupee. Public schools were almost nonexistent in the parish, and Raccourci had no schools at all. Laura Lejeune assumed the work of community education and began teaching Lejeune's sister Augustine, or "Teeney,"[45] when the girl reached seven. Her instruction varied from the basics of grammar to piano lessons. When the need arose, the Lejeune home welcomed all interested pupils. The first day brought two students, but gradually the news spread until daily attendance averaged forty-five. Even boarders arrived, young girls who lived too far away to commute. When Teeney reached eighteen, she became the assistant teacher, specializing in piano instruction. The school blossomed into a permanent institution and lasted twenty years.[46]

Before long, the Lejeune School also flowered into the local social center. Sarah Archer, wife of Dr. John Archer, arranged and supervised children's dances, songfests, games, amateur theatricals, hayrides, and May parties. Both women left lasting impressions in the parish. Laura Lejeune was remembered as "a charming woman" who assumed complete responsibility for the children in the area and delighted in bringing them together for Sarah Archer's parties. Typical was a message sent to little Mary Brown LaCour: "We will pick you up at twilight, in a hay wagon, to take you to a dance."[47] While Mrs. Lejeune provided scholarly direction, Mrs. Archer gave organization, purpose, and discipline to the school center. "She was quite a leader," recalled one resident, "the executive type," who provided discipline in the school for Mrs. Lejeune, a milder woman. They were "good women with a purpose, not easily forgotten."[48]

Religion, like education, played an important role in life in Pointe Coupee. The Archers and Lejeunes were regular communicants of St. Stephen's Episcopal Church, the only Protestant church in the parish. John Lejeune was confirmed there. John and Augustine rode horses to services when the roads were passable along Old River's levee. John attended Aunt Sarah's

Sunday school in the afternoon, while his mother, who had received permission from the nearest priest, prepared her Catholic students for their first communion and instructed them in catechism.[49]

At the age of seven, John entered his mother's school. "She was a thorough, painstaking, and patient teacher," he recalled, "and I received under her tutelage an excellent grammar school foundation for my future education."[50] He even learned to play the piano. Lejeune learned to write by repeatedly duplicating "copy book" sentences worded by his mother. The sentences also provided lessons in ethics, for each line contained popular nineteenth-century moral platitudes.[51]

Lejeune's early days were not monopolized by the classroom. Ample time remained for outdoor games and farm chores. His duties included tending chickens and turkeys and caring for the livestock. Dawn often found him two miles from Old Hickory, driving the cows from their remote grazing fields over a wooded path in order to get them home for an early milking. After school he would climb pecan trees, striking down the nuts with a bamboo pole. He earned his first dollar during summer vacation, picking cotton and breaking corn alongside field hands.

Yet this "unsophisticated country boy" enjoyed his youth. He acquired a lasting fondness for horseback riding and, with a shotgun given to him by his father, rode endless miles through the Raccourci lowlands in pursuit of game. Often he arrived home at dusk, bearing strings of bass caught during lazy vacation afternoons at Old River.[52]

Lejeune spent his early adolescent years in isolation. No railroads and few roads disturbed the tranquil countryside. Only steamboats linked Raccourci with the outside world. He witnessed the twilight period of the Mississippi River steamboat era, for later railroad development plus the Civil War had diverted river traffic eastward instead of to New Orleans. Although steamboating declined rapidly after 1880, practically disappearing from western rivers, it was still Pointe Coupee's lifeline, providing colorful pageantry for the simple rural folk.[53] As Lejeune later recalled, few boys who saw the spectacle would ever forget the majestic *Natchez* landing near Old Hickory, with rugged Captain Leathers tolling the bell, or the colorful *Robert E. Lee, Pargaud,* and *Edward J. Gray,* steaming downriver from Cincinnati or St. Louis to New Orleans. At high water, these spectacular vessels with crimson stacks and shrill whistles appeared to float above the trees, when viewed from the three-and-one-half-mile distance of Old Hickory.[54]

Night captured the picturesque riverboats at their romantic best. Twinkling like a carnival, the boats permeated the rural air with sounds of music, gambling, dancing girls, and gaiety.[55]

Despite his many duties, Ovide Lejeune found time to train his only son. Since honey commanded a premium price, father and son studied all the available literature on bee culture and converted ten bee colonies into twenty modern hives. With the assistance of a young farmhand, they extracted honey during the spring and summer, sealed it into barrels, and shipped it to New Orleans merchants. Captain Lejeune delighted in his young son's comradeship. By 1880, Ovide was sixty years old, and eager to pass on the lessons learned from his years of practical experience. Ovide had returned from his service in the Civil War with considerable admiration for West Point officers. He was particularly fond of Robert E. Lee, who embodied, in his opinion, the ultimate in gentlemanly stature. John Lejeune was taught to revere the academy officers, especially General Lee, possessor of "the noblest qualities of which human nature was capable."[56] Like his father, most of the local men had served the Confederacy, and young John never wearied of hearing their war tales.

Young Lejeune's early reading included books about the thrilling exploits of his heroes, leaders such as Robert E. Lee, Nathan Bedford Forrest, Albert Sidney Johnston, Joseph E. Johnston, and P. G. T. Beauregard. His favorite books included *Surry of Eaglenest* and *Mohun* by John Esten Cook. Eventually his interests swelled over into the Napoleonic wars. He read, studied, and nearly memorized John Stevens Cabot Abbott's *Life of Napoleon Bonaparte* and Joel Tyler Headley's *The Lives of Napoleon's Marshals* before his thirteenth birthday. French generals Michel Ney, Andre Massena, Joachim Murat, Nicoles Jean Dien Doult, and Jean Lannes were exalted by Lejeune second only to Confederates.

Ovide Lejeune had high moral values and impressed his philosophy of righteousness upon his son. He did not tolerate bullying or abuse or insulting language and believed that absolutely no insult was acceptable. "If any boy or man insulted me," wrote John Lejeune, "I should knock him down." Further, said his father, "if the boy or man should be your size, use your fists, but if he be bigger or stronger than you, use a whip, a stick or a club." "To deceive anyone," he continued, "was a cowardly act, and any dishonorable act was despicable." A Lejeune, both men believed, would always remain above reproach, but should his character be challenged, the challenger would learn the error of his accusation. "My father," recalled his son many years later, "was truly a man *sans peur et sans reproche.*"[57]

The thoroughness of Ovide Lejeune's instruction was soon tested. Near Old Hickory lived a drunkard known simply as "Jack." Probably for lack of better humor, the Lejeune family teasingly began calling its youngest member "Jack." The name was unacceptable to John Lejeune, and he announced he would answer only to "John." The day of reckoning arrived early in the morning that followed the announcement, when Captain Lejeune pounded on his son's door and boomed, "Get up, Jack!" After Ovide's repeated calls were not acknowledged, Ovide entered, but his son stood his ground and "John" emerged victorious.[58]

Even John Lejeune's humor reflected his sense of propriety. One boyhood tale he enjoyed sharing was of an elderly friend from Bayou Lettsworth who was attempting to sell his land. When an interested stranger appeared one day seeking good farmland secure from overflows, the old gentleman showed him his land, promoting its great fertility. When the ground dipped lower, the apprehensive buyer inquired about water stains on the lower two feet of the trees. "Nothing but hogs scratching themselves on the bark," shot back the honest old face, pointing out nearby hogs feeding on acorns. Soon, however, the ground dropped even lower and the tree discoloration rose about fifteen feet. "Damnedest, tallest hogs I ever heard of," snickered the stranger. "Needless to say," concluded John Lejeune, "there was no deal."[59]

Lejeune's boyhood idol was young Dr. William Bisland Archer. He was impressed by his cousin's "buoyant spirit, a heart full of ambition and a love of the bright things of life." He was also fond of his great-uncle, Dr. John Archer, who enjoyed giving advice to the youngster. "When it comes to marriage, John," he advised, "don't marry in haste, choose a good woman. When you're ready, be sure to marry the 'kit' of a good 'cat.'"[60] Pointe Coupee lost a devoted public servant and Lejeune his idol when William Archer died on October 6, 1878, at the age of twenty-five. He had volunteered to treat yellow fever victims at Greenwood, Mississippi, and contracted the dreaded disease himself.[61]

With bewildering abruptness, the decade of the 1880s introduced John Lejeune to a new world. Laura Lejeune was ambitious for her only son and recognized the importance of education for his future. Accepting the limits of her own education, which had terminated at sixteen, Laura enrolled John in his great-uncle James Archer's boarding school near Natchez. A

Yale University graduate, Archer was a dedicated educator of superior intelligence.

John Lejeune joined his eight fellow student boarders at Oakwood early in January 1880.[62] It was a difficult adjustment for the rather shy Lejeune, who experienced great loneliness at Oakwood. "To be with strangers was torture," he recalled, fighting to overcome a strong case of motherly dependence. Since John was naturally quiet and pensive, he found it even more difficult to develop self-assurance and aplomb in the company of strangers. Probably because of this discomfort, he found classroom instruction "unexciting and monotonous."[63] James Archer was an excellent teacher and disciplinarian who stressed formal drill and provided the boys with a thorough preparatory education. Regular church attendance and occasional trips into Natchez in the Archer family carriage provided welcome relief from the tedious routine of school days. Lejeune also enjoyed exploring the hilly Mississippi countryside with his classmates. One excursion uncovered a three-tiered Indian mound which, according to tradition, contained a chieftain's burial ground on the top tier, while the lower two provided a weapons arsenal for protection against hostile spirits. Closer investigation unearthed arrowheads and bones, remnants of an ancient culture which inspired Lejeune to begin a lifetime hobby of archaeology. He later spent hours alone studying and daydreaming about the ancient Indian civilizations that existed before Columbus.[64]

The outstanding event during Lejeune's Oakwood days was a visit aboard the ship *Alliance,* an American man-of-war docked on the Mississippi River at Natchez. After lunching in Natchez with his Aunt Pamela Chamberlain, Lejeune and his fellow students boarded the old wooden, steam-driven sailing vessel. When docked at a port, it was a naval tradition for the officers to host a social for the local citizens, especially the young women. (This was how Lejeune met his future wife years later at a party hosted aboard ship at Portsmouth.) The deck and gun batteries of the *Alliance* were brilliantly polished for an upcoming dance, while overhead flew an impressive array of colorful flags hung from recently scrubbed masts, yards, and awnings. Friendly sailors took an interest in the boys and guided them throughout the ship, often pausing to reveal the methods used to climb the rigging, weigh anchor, and fire the great nine-inch smooth-bore muzzle-loading main battery.

After the tour, the boys gathered together and listened to an old sailor's exciting tales of high seas and foreign ports. “It was like being in another world,” wrote Lejeune. “I never dreamed . . . that my path . . . would lead to such strange places and . . . thrilling adventure.” Later Lejeune noted that one young officer, attired in light blue trousers with a red stripe different from the uniform of the other officers, was First Lieutenant George F. Elliott, the Marine Corps officer aboard ship who commanded the Marine detachment. This was Lejeune’s first meeting with the man who later became a Marine Corps commandant.[65]

Although young Lejeune had developed intellectually and socially at Oakwood, he hoped to attend a larger, less isolated institution. Upon expressing this desire to his parents during the summer of 1881, they accepted his decision and began a search for a more suitable school. Dr. Stevenson Turpin, Laura Lejeune’s oldest brother, who lived at Bayou Lettsworth, suggested Mississippi’s Starkville Military Institute, later to become Mississippi State University. The surgeon was a good friend of Starkville’s president, General Stephen D. Lee, for both men had served together on General J. B. Hood’s medical staff shortly after the Battle of Nashville in December 1864. Dr. John Archer, however, recommended Louisiana State University in Baton Rouge. Since both schools had military programs with approximately equal fees, the decision was left to John. “I selected the Louisiana State University for the reason that, inasmuch as I expected to continue to live in Louisiana after the completion of my education, I considered that it was important for my success in life to have the opportunity to be associated at college with the boys from the state in which I had planned to reside.”[66]

Ovide Lejeune accompanied his fourteen-year-old son on the steamboat journey downriver to Baton Rouge, where the university was located in a building that had formerly housed the State Institution for the Deaf, overlooking the Mississippi River. As the pair walked about and observed the cadets clad in West Point–style uniforms of gray with blue caps, John Lejeune was deeply impressed by the military atmosphere of the school. Father and son called on the president of LSU, Colonel William Preston Johnston, son of Confederate General Albert Sidney Johnston, and registered at the office of Treasurer Harney Schofield.[67]

The expenses for John Lejeune to attend LSU were no light burden for the Lejeune family. The monthly cadet fee of sixteen dollars covered board, room, washing and mending, fuel and lights, and medical services. In addition, each cadet had to provide his own textbooks and regulation uniforms, costing approximately fifty-five dollars per year. Since most of the younger men attending the university possessed insufficient education to enter the freshman class, a preparatory department had been established several years before. Like all "freshfish"—the name given to the new arrivals by the older cadets—Lejeune was tested by Colonel Samuel W. Robertson to determine whether he belonged in the "lower prep" or "upper prep" class. The commandant of cadets placed Lejeune in the upper prep class, where he had three choices of curriculum: the classical or liberal arts, the agricultural, or the mechanical. Lejeune selected the classical course, consisting of classes in English grammar and composition, elementary rhetoric, arithmetic, algebra, elementary geometry, elementary freehand drawing, Latin, and Greek.[68]

Lejeune was still developing physically when he officially registered at LSU on October 3, 1881. He was a short, stocky young man, standing five feet, one and a half inches tall, and was the university's 1,028th cadet.[69] At this time, Lejeune acquired the military discipline that, in one form or another, would endure for the rest of his life.

Cadet Lejeune shared a large, eleven-man room, monitored by Cadet Captain Armand I. Lasseigne. The room contained only the barest essentials: small study tables, chairs, individual washstands, and trunks for personal clothing. There were no beds. After tattoo roll call (the tattoo signals that all light in squad rooms be extinguished and that all loud talking and other disturbances be discontinued within fifteen minutes, at which time taps should follow), the cadets rolled out thin cotton mattresses on the heavy plank floors to sleep on. At reveille the mattresses were rolled up and hooked on the walls. The building's bathing facilities consisted of foot tubs in the basement. During cold weather the cadets hauled up scuttles of coal to their room for the open grate fires. Lejeune lived on the fifth floor his first year and regularly carried up heavy buckets of water and coal. This exercise, he claimed, was instrumental in building up his powerful back, arms, and legs. Each student alternated as the room orderly, held responsible for room discipline, cleanness, and maintenance by school officials, and expected by fellow cadets to sustain the winter fire. A roommate, Cadet Henry Kahn of Natchitoches Parish, remembered when he and Lejeune as freshmen were called by the fife and drum to alternate as marchers to lead others to classes in the rooms of Nicholson, Boyd, McCullough, Thomas, Magruder, Sewell, and Robertson.[70]

While the expressed purpose of LSU was to educate civilians, not professional soldiers, Lejeune considered the outstanding characteristic of the university to be its military spirit.[71] Although the authorities were more concerned with academic success, the martial milieu—based on the systems of West Point, Annapolis, and the Virginia Military Institute—was complete.[72]

The taboo list was clear to the highly regulated cadets. No cadet could vacate his room during study hours, alter his musket, consume liquor or tobacco, participate in any "game of chance," duel, form combinations against school authority, wear long hair, or allow dogs, horses, cooking provisions, or valets in his quarters. In addition, the cadet was to wear his uniform at all times, regularly attend his parents' choice of church, and abstain from all vicious, immoral, and irregular conduct. Surprisingly, swimming in the Mississippi River—which had powerful and dangerous undercurrents—was prohibited only for those wearing insufficient clothing to satisfy police regulations. Routine duties were exceedingly demanding, for over one hundred demerits per term meant immediate dismissal.[73] Even conscientious John Lejeune received fifty demerits one term.[74]

Young Lejeune's fascination with Civil War personalities sharpened during his student days at LSU. From his assigned seat in the mess hall, he overlooked the life-sized portrait of General William T. Sherman, generally considered as the first president of LSU. In reality, Sherman was in 1860 the superintendent of the Louisiana State Seminary of Learning and Military Academy, located near Alexandria, Louisiana, the predecessor of LSU. Lejeune was especially stirred by the imposing painting of Generals Robert E. Lee and Stonewall Jackson that hung in the library, pictured on horseback shortly before the Battle of Chancellorsville. Much later, when Lejeune became superintendent of VMI in 1929, he wrote Colonel Thomas D. Boyd, president of LSU, to inquire where he could purchase such a picture.[75]

Lejeune admired many of his teachers at LSU. James W. Nicholson, head of the Mathematics and Mechanical Department, appeared to Lejeune to be "a mathematical genius." "He told us," related Lejeune, "that he was a self-educated mathematician, and I never knew a teacher who had as great a gift for making an abstract subject easy and simple to the students." Another favorite of Lejeune was his English professor: "To know Thomas D. Boyd was to admire and to love him." Most classmates, including two future governors of Louisiana, Henry L. Fuqua and John M. Parker, shared Lejeune's view.[76]

Cadet Lejeune commenced his second year as a freshman, entering the four-year classical course that led to the bachelor of arts degree.[77] His textbooks included Otto's *French Grammar,* Hart's *Composition and Rhetoric,* Davis's *Geometry,* Gildersleeve's *Latin Grammar,* Jones's *Latin Exercises,* Goodwin's *Greek Grammar,* and White's *First Lessons in Greek.* There was also instruction on Cicero's *Orations* and studies of Caesar and Virgil. He continued practicing the piano and maintained his dedicated attitude towards education as instilled by Laura Lejeune. He wrote often to his mother, informing her of his classwork and his opinion of the professors and textbooks. Commenting on a teacher, he wrote: "Professor Thomas has resigned and Professor McGouder, a teacher at some school in Texas, has taken his place. I hear he is a very smart man, but I hardly think he is Mr. Thomas's equal. The latter has gone to Europe to perfect himself." Cadet Lejeune even kept tabs on family friends enrolled at LSU, becoming disappointed when they fell behind in schoolwork. For example, he wrote, "Willie Burton is studying under the charge of a [cadet] officer by the name of Prescott, who is one of the best students in the building, and I know he will make him study so that he can study himself."[78]

The once shy country boy adapted well to his new school, thanks no doubt to the year and a half he spent at Oakwood that had seasoned him for dormitory life. He developed friendships with numerous students, especially those in "Calcasieu Parish," a second-floor room housing twelve cadets from that area. He continued regular church attendance and remained in close touch with his family, despite a short Christmas vacation that prevented a holiday at Old Hickory during his second year.[79]

Lejeune began his third or sophomore year in October 1883, continuing language studies in Latin, Greek, and French, and beginning studies in Roman, Greek, and French history as well as in analytical geometry and higher algebra.[80] During Lejeune's three years at LSU, when classes were over during the day, military training began for the cadets. Lejeune acquired his first soldierly training at the university, participating in daily drill, dress parades, guard mounting, and formation practice up to battalion level. These activities closely followed the military tactics and drill advocated by Emory Upton of West Point.[81] Lejeune became cadet second lieutenant his third year, no small honor for a sophomore. As a company grade officer he became proficient in drill and ceremonies, knowledge that required considerable practice and study. Christmas of 1883 found him home at Old Hickory, proudly wearing his lieutenant's shoulder straps.

The cadet corps added a martial and colorful dimension to Lejeune's academic experience at LSU from 1881 to 1884. The corps and honor companies customarily competed with other universities and state militia units in New Orleans, Tuscaloosa, Auburn, and Charleston. The corps contributed pomp, dignity, and a certain amount of splendor on special occasions such as George Washington's birthday, university commencement, state holidays, and inaugurations.

Despite the close supervision of the students by the administration, Lejeune felt that *esprit de corps* was high—stressing duty, honor, and patriotism. Formal written examinations utilized the honor system. There was even occasional entertainment at the school—monthly cadet "hops," church picnics, and social gatherings arranged by the citizens of Baton Rouge.

Although young Lejeune enjoyed his three years at LSU, he understood that the expenses were a burden for his family. During these years, Ovide Lejeune, who had a very high opinion of the US Military Academy at West Point, worked to secure an appointment for his son when he reached the required age for admission. Congressman Judge E. T. Lewis informed Ovide that there was no vacancy at West Point, although there was an opening at the Naval Academy, and he offered it to John Lejeune. "I had scarcely heard of Annapolis," recalled Lejeune, "and had seen only one naval vessel. But I took the appointment, which was for the class of 1888, with the view chiefly of getting a good education."[82] Lejeune resigned from LSU early in April 1884 and went home to study for the Naval Academy's entrance examination.

Young John Lejeune did reasonably well academically at LSU. Out of approximately seventy students for 1883 in his class, he ranked seventh in Greek, eleventh in Latin, thirty-third in French and rhetoric, and thirty-fifth in mathematics.[83] Although his educational achievements were considerable, Lejeune felt he profited most by developing physical fitness and a sense of military discipline.[84] From the standpoint of the university, Lejeune's three years were long enough for him to leave an impression on the cadet corps: "All I heard," wrote a student who entered LSU in 1885, "was what John Lejeune, Armand I. Lasseigne . . . Walter Bynum and Julius F. Arial did that formed LSU tradition."[85]

John Lejeune returned to Old Hickory to find a family eager to help him prepare for the Annapolis entrance exam. He could not have known that his departure from Louisiana would be permanent and that family days in Louisiana were over. These early years had been important in molding young Lejeune. Pointe Coupee itself, rural and sequestered, offered him a chance to rely on himself to a degree that sometimes was not possible in urban America. His family's influence was also of great importance. Laura Lejeune bequeathed tolerance, patience, humility, and a healthy respect for education. The Archer family offered superior intelligence coupled with a flair for scholarly endeavor. The Turpin family provided the strengths of perseverance, resourcefulness, courage, and ambition. Ovide Lejeune left his mark—courage, character, leadership ability, and a strong sense of honor. And even though Ovide had fought for the Confederacy, he longed for the nation's reunification. Further, although Lejeune's formative years had been spent within the turmoil of Reconstruction, John Lejeune remained sheltered from the residual bitterness that frequently made its way into the southern personality.

Louisiana State University provided Lejeune with an essential broadening influence by exposing him to group competition and association within a military atmosphere. Thus, family, environment, and military schooling planted the seeds for Lejeune's future success.

2
A NAVAL CADET

John Lejeune's success as a naval cadet would be no accident: his ambition and marked ability had been noted by relatives before he left for Annapolis. "He is seventeen years old," wrote his uncle J. A. Turpin of Louisiana to a cousin in Maryland, "and a very promising boy. He will make his mark in the world if he lives. If you have an opportunity—I would like you to see him."[1] Matured by nearly five years of boarding school and LSU and eager to do well at Annapolis, Lejeune arrived early in May 1884 and presented himself to the superintendent, Captain F. M. Ramsey. He felt ill at ease as he registered, for, unlike himself, most candidates were from large cities. In addition, the entrance examination was a substantial obstacle. Generally only half of the candidates became cadets, and those who were unsuccessful returned home bearing all their travel expenses personally. Lejeune viewed failure as an unbearable humiliation.[2] Thus, it was a nervous group of young men who stood at attention in front of the gunnery building, grimly awaiting the results of the examination. While the academy band played the customary martial music, the names of the fortuitous few were read out, including the name of John A. Lejeune.[3] Afterwards, the band struck up "Home Sweet Home" in an attempt to lighten the disappointment of the rejected candidates as they gathered their bags for departure.[4]

Plebe Lejeune's first duty was to assemble with classmates in Captain Ramsey's office to take an oath of allegiance and agree to serve the US Navy for eight years, "unless sooner discharged."[5] Unfortunately for Lejeune, the distribution of cadet uniforms was delayed, forcing the plebes to continue wearing the clothes they had brought from home. Since Lejeune had packed only his LSU cadet uniforms of Confederate gray, minus the cadet second lieutenant's shoulder straps, he attracted the attention of several upperclassmen who were hopefully awaiting any excuse to bully a plebe. Eager to remain inconspicuous, the other plebes avoided Lejeune like the plague. Lejeune was experiencing a bad day when, suddenly, a huge young man with a Cumberland accent and a mouth full of tobacco appeared on the scene. "Y'all don't appear to like that uniform," said Midshipman Carlo B. Brittain of Pineville, Kentucky. "Let me tell you something, it was good enough for my old man and it's good enough for me. I reckon anybody who declares war on that uniform or anybody who wears it declares war on me." This intervention quickly terminated the hazing party, beginning a friendship between Lejeune and Brittain that lingered until 1923, when Rear Admiral Brittain died aboard the flagship of the Atlantic Fleet.[6]

Soon thereafter the plebes acquired their various necessities and marched to their temporary quarters, the old sailing frigate *Santee,* which was anchored in mud along the dock. Lejeune had to sling his hammock and sleep on the gun deck—not the most pleasant place—where every morning an old smooth-bore cannon fired morning reveille, followed by the loud boatswain's pipe and command, "All hands! Up all hammocks!" Days aboard the *Santee* were filled with mariner duties such as boat drill, swimming exercises, and the setting up and lowering of sails. The routines aboard a similar ship, the *Dale,* required each plebe to go aloft every morning, scramble over the crosstrees, and hurriedly climb down from the rigging hand-over-hand and drop into the sea. Lejeune and his fellow plebes managed to find some time for fun after hours by catching soft-shell crabs from the pier and sailing small cutters in Chesapeake Bay. Highlighting the period was an inspection of the *Santee* by President Chester A. Arthur, who spoke at the graduation exercises.[7]

Lejeune and members of the fourth class accompanied the first and third classes on a summer cruise aboard the venerable *Constellation,* which embarked on June 9, 1884, with 109 naval cadets under the command of N. H. Farquhar and executive officer Lieutenant Walton Goodwin.[8] These summer midshipman cruises were almost identical to eighteenth-century sailing voyages, for even in 1884 the conditions were much the same. The cadets slept below deck on hammocks under extremely crowded conditions, without benefit of ice, fresh meat or vegetables, cold storage, electricity, or ventilation. The ship was illuminated by oil lamps. During rough seas when the ports were closed and the hatches battened down, the air became unfit to breathe. The voyage began in a storm that found most plebes, including Lejeune, unable to hold down any meals for several days. "At first we were afraid we were going to die," he recalled, "and then, after a while, we were afraid we were not." The drinking water for the cadets came from the hot, dark water discolored by the ship's rusted water tanks, while their primary diet was salt meat and fish, hardtack and baked beans.[9]

The plebe class acted as seamen on the cruise. Lejeune and his classmates stood long watches day and night; hauled on ropes; climbed aloft whether the sea was calm or stormy to loosen or furl the sails; reefed the topsails; sent down the yards; and drilled on the old, nine-inch, smooth-bore, muzzle-loaded, cast-iron cannon. The upperclassmen, who served as cadet officers, assumed the additional task of teaching the fourth class naval yore. Although it was against regulations, the third, or sophomore class, traditionally expected certain feats of memory from the plebes. Any plebe who rebelled or showed too much "gall" quickly earned the rancor of the entire third class, which denied the plebe rations and access to certain sections of the ship, forced him to eat soap, drink vinegar, chew paper, or stand on his head. If the plebe still showed improper respect, he was compelled to fight the third class's "champion," a large, strong brute who rarely lost a match. The plebes generally conformed to tradition: if one informed the authorities, he was placed in "conventry," or isolation, by the upperclassmen.[10] Each day was long and the work physically exhausting, developing Lejeune and his fellow plebes into young men in top physical condition. Usually the plebes worked side-by-side with hardy bluejackets, representatives of the old sailing Navy, who gave good advice and respected the youth and inexperience of the new classmen.

On July 16, 1884, the *Constellation* docked at Portsmouth, Virginia, where the cadets formed an infantry battalion commanded by Ensign William F. Fullam, participating in the reception ceremonies honoring the Greely Relief Mission.[11] Lejeune would remember his first meeting with Ensign, later Rear Admiral, Fullam, the man who devoted the greater part of his career attempting to force Marine guards off of naval warships.

When academic work began on October 1, the fourth class moved into better quarters on the upper floors of the "new building," where Lejeune shared a room with another cadet. The room contained one large study table illuminated by a gaslight, two small iron bedsteads, two iron washstands, and two wardrobes—all Civil War–era relics.[12] Lejeune's classes were small, six or eight students in each, in which the students received instruction in English, history, algebra, geometry, French, and Spanish. The students were required to pass monthly and semiannual exams or be released from the academy.[13]

While academic study occupied about three-quarters of Lejeune's time, practical exercises, which came after 4:00 p.m. and on Saturday mornings, supplemented classroom instruction. The plebes learned fleet tactics by maneuvering eight small steam launches about Chesapeake Bay and manning the *Wyoming,* an old steamship, on which each cadet alternately served as fireman, mechanic, engineer, seaman, and gunner. In addition, the naval cadets fired the great guns, howitzers, and mortars; conducted infantry drill ashore, including practice with small arms, swords, and bayonets; and learned signaling afloat, navigation, marine surveying, steam engineering, gymnastics, ballroom dancing, sailing, sail-making, and the mechanics of ordnance such as the dismantling, assembling, and firing the rapid-fire guns. Unfortunately, the academy had no modern ordnance pieces except a 37 mm Hotchkiss, a Gatling, and a small Gardner gun, which made it necessary to practice with the obsolete Civil War–era Parrott gun. It was not unknown for the ancient muzzleloaders to explode in the faces of unwary cadets. Even the marine engines were sadly outdated.[14]

Lejeune found the academy more demanding than LSU, but his hard work paid off. By March 1885, out of a class of seventy-two, he stood second in English, history, French, and Spanish, and thirty-ninth in algebra and geometry.[15] Since social privileges were gained by good conduct, Lejeune was careful to steer clear of trouble, accumulating fifty-eight demerits out of a maximum allowable of one hundred.[16] In almost all of his correspondence with his sister, Lejeune focused on his classes and subjects, striving diligently to remain in the top 10 percent of his class. While Lejeune was always ranked in the top of his class in subjects such as English, history, and foreign languages, he usually ranked in the middle in math, chemistry, physics, and drawing. He did improve in the latter classes as he moved from the plebe to the third, second, and first classes.

The upperclassmen delighted in hazing, and it was not long before the word "sir" dominated the fourth-classman's vocabulary. One midshipman, John G. Berry, who was particularly fond of Longfellow's *Evangeline,* discovered that plebe Lejeune was from Louisiana and of Acadian descent. Since Lejeune's name was similar to that of Evangeline's lover, Gabriel La

Jeunesse, his chore was to memorize and recite the poem in front of the "wags," or upperclassmen. After spending hours on this task, he successfully recited part 1 of the poem. "Very well, Mister," came the disgusted reply, "do not bore me further. But, if any upperclassman ever asks you your name, you are to reply, Gabriel La Jeunesse." This name quickly caught on and Lejeune became "Gabe" to his friends throughout his career.[17]

All apprenticeships must end, however, so when the new class of plebes arrived in May 1885, Lejeune considered himself a third-classman, exempt from hazing. One morning while he and several friends were walking to class, an upperclassman approached the smaller Lejeune and ordered him to straighten his hat. When Lejeune ignored this order, the midshipman grasped him, commencing a furious fistfight that was shortly broken up by a nearby officer. While each cadet received a few demerits and words of reprimand, Lejeune had made his point—no longer would he accept subordinate treatment.[18]

As a new third-classman, Lejeune sailed on his second summer cruise on the *Constellation* under Commander C. L. Huntington and executive officer Lieutenant R. R. Ingersoll, June 16 to August 27, 1885. In addition to receiving practical instruction under sail, his class became proficient with the sextant and compass, and learned to fix the ship's position by time sights of the sun, moon, planets, and stars. Every Monday featured great-gun practice in which the midshipmen plotted projectile fall on a vertical plane using polar-distortion diagrams.[19]

While Lejeune's second academic year was a continuation of his first year, his third year included trigonometry, analytical and descriptive geometry, chemistry, history, advanced French, Spanish, English, and mechanical drawing. As a second-classman he worked in the ordnance, maintenance, and repair shops during the summer of 1887 instead of taking the annual summer cruise. In September, Lejeune first met Commander W. T. Sampson, superintendent of the Naval Academy, a man destined to later gain fame in the Spanish-American War.[20]

Life at the academy was not all work. Granted liberty on Saturday afternoons, midshipmen often went into town, marched in Washington, DC, on official occasions, and attended a series of dancing "hops" given on holidays by class committees.[21] In addition, whenever Lejeune received leave, he visited his Archer and Turpin relatives in Maryland.[22] Although Lejeune was not an outstanding athlete, he made the football squad's second team and developed an enthusiasm for the sport that lasted more than fifty years.[23] He was also an avid follower of the academy's baseball team.[24] Lejeune was not large enough to make the football squad's first team. At his physical exam in May of 1886, Lejeune weighed just 135 pounds and was five feet, seven inches, tall. Despite his small stature, however, he was strong, proving during his yearly physical that he could pull 300 pounds behind him as he walked forward.[25]

Midshipman Lejeune's first class participated in the summer cruise of the *Constellation* in 1887, during which navigation and command skills were stressed. Lejeune maintained cross-bearing charts which were checked daily by officers, except on Saturday, at which time he was orally examined by the executive officer to ascertain his general aptitude grade. Unlike the first three years at the academy, which were devoted to general education, the instruction of the senior or first class stressed technical subjects such as astronomy, navigation and surveying, ordnance and gunnery, seamanship, shipbuilding, naval tactics, and physiology and hygiene.[26]

On June 8, 1888, thirty-five of the original plebe class (from 1884) of ninety-five received diplomas from Secretary of the Navy William C. Whitney, a man highly respected by the naval cadets. Lejeune finished thirteenth in his class[27] but reflected on his academy years with mixed emotions. Since he had been raised and educated by a moral, churchgoing, genteel, and honorable family, Lejeune was undoubtedly shocked by some of the behavior of a few naval cadets and administrators. In a letter to his sister, Lejeune noted that "this place cannot be considered the most moral place in the world." Since hazing was particularly severe during Lejeune's days at the academy, he wrote, "I wouldn't be surprised if several upperclassmen get 'bilged' for hazing."[28]

Young Lejeune picked up a few questionable habits at the academy. For example, he noted that "on Saturday I must say I have quite a fine time, when there is nothing else to do I turn in and read a novel. I always read the trashiest. . . . I have become also a lover of the 'soothing weed.' I never indulge, however, except on Saturday and Sundays for during the week the inspector is around too frequently, and if he chances to smell a whiff of smoke in one's room, you are down for ten demerits."[29] One day Lejeune was caught smoking. For his transgression, he had to leave his quarters in the new building and bunk on the rustic and uncomfortable ship *Santee* for thirty days.[30]

Although strict discipline was necessary to prepare the naval cadets for careers in the military, it often seemed to Lejeune to be mostly harassing and impersonal. Demerits flowed freely from upperclassmen to the younger cadets for inconsequential infractions. According to Lejeune, "I was reported once for neglect of duty in allowing my section to make a noise (seven demerits) and was also reported again for disobedience of orders in not signing a certificate that we had to sign before taking an exam (seven demerits). I forgot all about the certificate until it was too late to save myself from getting reported, as I did not sign until after dinner was over."[31]

Later, Lejeune realized that "naval life was much more enjoyable than I had anticipated it would be during my four long years at the Naval Academy," for although the education was comprehensive, the discipline effective, and individual class standing determined solely by achievement, the school was "a great machine." "I missed the human appeal," he wrote years later. "Too much reliance was placed on compulsion, rather than leadership and inspiration by the cadre. Only once was the class addressed by an officer."[32] Lejeune's experience at the Naval Academy most likely influenced his style of leadership as reflected in his years of command in the Marine Corps. Lejeune would become known as an inspiring and visionary leader who relied on the distinguished history and achievements of the corps to motivate his Marines.

Finally, Lejeune found the most enjoyable part of his time at Annapolis to be the opportunity to associate with intelligent and capable young men. In turn, he was well respected and admired by his classmates. Perhaps the best insight into the character of Midshipman Lejeune can be gained from his roommate of three years, Edward L. Beach. He remembered "Gabe" as a man of "keen intelligence, character, and integrity, a true gentleman."[33] The class of 1888 included many men of future prominence who respected Lejeune, such as Curtis D. Wilbur (chief justice of the Supreme Court of California and secretary of the Navy under President Calvin Coolidge), Admiral Charles F. Hughes (chief of naval operations [CNO]), Admiral Henry A. Wiley (commander in chief [CinC] of the US Fleet), Rear Admiral Ashley H. Robertson (commandant of the Naval Base of San Diego), Rear Admiral Samuel S. Robinson (superintendent of the Naval Academy), and Major General Eli K. Cole (commanding general [CG], Marine Corps Department of the Pacific).

Graduation, however, was only one step in the highly competitive effort to enter the naval service. Since the Navy had been allowed to stagnate after the Civil War, the Naval Academy program had been extended to six years, mainly to discourage applicants for commissions. After a mandatory two-year cruise aboard a man-of-war, all midshipmen returned to Annapolis for a comprehensive final examination, where only the top percentage of the class filled vacancies in the Navy Line, Engineer Service, or Marine Corps. The remaining cadets were simply given certificates of competency and fitness, honorable discharges, and one hundred dollars in separation pay.[34] Before leaving for a summer at home, Lejeune, Leroy Stafford, Eli Cole, and Henry Wiley applied for duty aboard the *USS Mohican,* scheduled to sail in September 1888.

The summer of 1888 was a crucial time for Lejeune's final decision on his career plans. Somewhat disillusioned with his first years under naval control, Lejeune spoke seriously with his father about resigning from the service. Wisely, Ovide Lejeune recommended that his son complete the two-year cruise before making a decision and, just as important, Ovide laid down the moral rule that guided his son through forty years of government service: duty should always supersede individual pleasure, as it was an honor and privilege to serve the American flag. The young man took this advice, but decided to save each month's salary, plus separation pay, in case he later decided on a civilian career. This was Lejeune's last meeting with his father, for Ovide died of pneumonia just four months later. Ovide's last request was that John accept his mother's deep religious faith (Episcopalian), as Ovide recently had, and become a Mason.[35] Lejeune fulfilled this latter request thirty-one years later by joining the Masons in occupied Germany after World War I.[36]

Pleased to receive his choice of assignment, Lejeune reported to Mare Island, California, to Commander J. B. Coghlan, the *Mohican*'s captain, on September 22, 1888. Lejeune worked during that fall helping to prepare the *Mohican* for sea, spending many off-duty hours with naval officers, friends, and cadets in San Francisco—social occasions that helped greatly in alleviating his shyness around strangers.

On January 14, 1889, naval cadets Lejeune, Stafford, and Wiley received urgent orders to transfer to the *USS Vandalia,* sailing for Samoa because of a German threat to American interests there.[37] The Samoan archipelago consisted of four principal islands situated midway on the ocean route between Hawaii and Australia. Although Imperial Germany, Great Britain, and the United States had agreed to preserve Samoa's autonomy, Germany decided to establish a colonial empire during this era of extreme nationalism in Europe. Germany also wanted to secure coaling rights in Samoa in order to increase its trade with China.

A crisis arose when German sailors captured Molietoa, the Samoan king who was unfriendly to the Kaiser's interests, and established Tamasee, a puppet, in power. When the Samoans rebelled and united behind the American favorite, Mataafa, a relative of the exiled King Laupepa, German ships bombarded several native villages and landed sailors near Apia, the administrative center of the Samoan Islands. The Germans had three modern ships in Apia Harbor, all sail/steam hybrids, including the iron/wood composite gunboat *Adler,* the iron-hulled gunboat *Eber,* and the *Olga,* the most powerful of the three, a twelve-gun, 2,424-ton corvette. Commander D. W. Mullan of the *Nipsic,* the only American ship in Apia harbor, quickly informed Washington of the invasion, whereupon the Navy Department sent the *Trenton*—flagship of Admiral L. A. Kimberly, CinC of the Pacific Station—and the *Vandalia* to protect American citizens and property and to preserve Samoan independence.[38]

Midshipman Lejeune sailed with the *Vandalia* on January 20, 1889, as it departed amid cheers from the large waterfront crowds of Vallejo, California.[39] It was not long before Lejeune became aware that the *Vandalia,* in comparison with modern European ships, was a floating hulk of dubious military value. The ship, typical of the American Fleet of the late 1880s, was an old open-gun, wooden vessel of sail, equipped with auxiliary steam power.[40]

Notwithstanding America's great industrial growth of the late nineteenth century, the Navy had entered a period of obsolescence, merely retaining the hastily prepared turreted iron-clads of Civil War vintage and repairing the old fleet of wooden cruisers. During this period of relative peace, the Navy restored the age of sail, returning to distant cruising patrols in which, for maximum economy, propellers were designed for optimum performance under sail, not steam. Indeed, it became virtually a court-martial offense for a captain to burn coal. Fortunately, progressive naval officers and public opinion encouraged a new naval program, prompting the Garfield administration to prohibit further repair to the wooden fleet and to prompt Congress to fund new steel cruisers. Thus, while the "New Navy" of steam and steel began life in the early 1880s, by 1889 the backbone of the fleet remained the wooden cruisers that ranked twelfth numerically behind those of many economically weaker nations.[41]

When the *Vandalia* coaled at Honolulu on February 2, 1889, the officers and cadets visited the Royal Hawaiian Hotel, where the American minister presented them to King Rex Kalakaua. Honolulu, after San Francisco, was considered the most pleasant port of the Pacific Station, but Samoa, Lejeune heard from the older officers, had "very few attractions." Revealing the discrimination that most naval officers felt towards people of color, Lejeune heard from these officers that "the white people there were of a very poor class, while the natives were semi-barbarous."[42] During this time, Lejeune stayed in touch with his family and regularly wrote long letters home containing as much money as he could spare.[43] His first duty aboard the *Vandalia* was to work under First Lieutenant F. E. Sutton, Commander of the Marine Guard. Since Sutton preferred working with his Marine sharpshooters, he assigned Lejeune to command the Marine-operated pivot cannon on the forecastle. "No doubt," recalled Lejeune in later years, "my experiences with the Marines on the *Vandalia* had something to do with the decision I ultimately made to apply for a commission in the Marine Corps."[44]

The *Vandalia* arrived in Apia harbor on February 22, where it was forced to berth in the rougher water of the outer harbor, due to the earlier arrival of the American ship *Nipsic,* the British cruiser *Calliope,* and the three German ships. In addition, there were at least nine merchant ships crowding the harbor. The harbor was a peaceful-looking V-shaped lagoon about one mile wide and bordered by dangerous coral reefs, of no small concern to seafaring men. Apia was situated on the northern side of the island of Upolu. From the mountains on the island the rivers Vaisingano and Mulivai drained freshwater into the harbor from the point of the V and had, over the years, provided the silt or mud that covered the coral bottom of the lagoon that allowed ships to anchor. Providing both entrance and exit, the harbor's mouth was small, only about 720 yards wide.[45] "These were mighty tense days," recalled Lejeune, "when we were all sleeping on a powder mine. Then, when it seemed certain that there would be trouble, came the great hurricane."[46]

There was no initial indication of severe weather when Admiral Kimberly arrived on the *Trenton* on March 11, 1889. The sea was "placid," and the weather "particularly pleasant." Most of the local people and seagoing traders believed that the typhoon season was over and simply expected heavy rain, which began on March 14. Accordingly, Admiral Kimberly, who was not only skeptical of German intentions but also running low on coal, ordered the American Fleet to raise steam, lower all anchors, and ride out any inclement weather inside the harbor. When the storm reached hurricane force at about 3:00 p.m. on March 15, the *Vandalia* had prepared for heavy seas with raised steam, lowered yards, and housed topmasts, but, unfortunately for the sailors, the movement of the hurricane was slowed by the mountains as it lingered and blew directly into the mouth of the harbor.[47]

The danger was increasing as Midshipman Lejeune stood his watch on the forecastle from midnight to 4:00 a.m. "It was the darkest night I ever experienced," he related years later. "Literally, it was impossible to see one's hand before one's face. The wind was blowing with terrific force, the rain was falling in blinding sheets, and a heavy sea was running. It was the longest four hours I ever spent."[48] At 3:30 a.m. a giant wave crashed over the bow of the *Vandalia* and hurled everyone across the deck, including Lejeune, who was virtually overboard when he grasped out and caught the last rope of the starboard rigging. Many were not so fortunate. Thirty minutes later, despite the *Vandalia*'s efforts to steam full-speed against the two anchors into the face of the hurricane, it lost ground, gradually being pushed backward toward the deadly reefs. Later it was discovered why the anchors would not hold: the rivers overflowing into the harbor had swept the bottom clean of soil, leaving only hard coral. This torrent of mountain water also caused most of the drownings that occurred, meeting the hurricane-swept sea and forming great whirlpools and undertows inside the harbor.[49]

The German vessels crowded into the inner harbor nearer the reefs were in the most immediate danger. The small gunboat *Eber* swept into the *Nipsic,* then turned helplessly broadside to the sea, where it was lifted up by a huge wave and crushed against the reef, drowning all but five of its eighty-one-man crew. At 6:30 a.m. the *Olga* smashed into the *Nipsic* and tore away the American vessel's bowsprit, rail, and smokestack.[50] Taking stock of the impossible situation, Commander D. W. Mullan steamed ashore to save his crew, but the *Nipsic* capsized twenty yards from the American consulate and drowned eight men.[51]

The German ship *Adler* spent a long night avoiding the reef, but was struck by the *Olga,* which splintered the *Adler*'s bowsprit. After the *Adler* lost its last anchor, a powerful swell lifted it onto the western reef, cracking its keel and causing it to roll on its side with the bow facing the shore. Twenty or so sailors were lost to the sea while the remainder lashed themselves to parts of the ship. The survivors "were drenched, cold, and miserable, and some would bear the psychological scars of their experience for the rest of their lives, but they were alive."[52]

Of all the American crews, those on the *Vandalia* probably suffered the most.[53] Aboard the *Vandalia,* John Lejeune had just been relieved of duty in order to obtain dry clothing and rest when, at 4:10 a.m., all hands were called out to batten down the hatches and prevent the sea from extinguishing the boiler fires. By now the *Vandalia* retained little control, and daylight found it sweeping towards *HMS Calliope.* Three times the two vessels collided, whereupon the *Calliope*'s iron sides tore away the *Vandalia*'s wooden lifeboats, gallery, and gig. Sensing that another collision would shatter both ships, Captain Henry C. Kane decided to steam the newer, more powerful British vessel to the open sea. As the *Calliope* fought its way seaward, it passed the *Trenton.* Although helpless with a flooded engine, useless rudder and steering wheel, the crew gave a rousing four-hundred-man cheer of support for Britannia's courage.[54] It was, as the *London Telegraph* wrote, "distressed manhood greeting triumphant manhood, the doomed saluting the saved." Later, Captain Kane said "those ringing cheers of the American Flagship pierced deep into my heart. . . . Every man on board the *Calliope* felt as I did; it made us work to win."[55]

The *Vandalia* was only momentarily relieved, for soon it approached dangerously close to the western reef, necessitating Captain Cornelius M. Schoonmaker's decision to try to maneuver it into the inner harbor. Lejeune and the officers worked desperately to help the hands bring its head to wind, but, while drifting astern, at 10:45 a.m., the *Vandalia* struck the western reef about two hundred yards from shore and immediately began to fill with water and settle. Although raging sea broke over the rails at heights of fifteen feet, several sailors volunteered to swim a line ashore, but were either drowned or pushed back against the ship and crushed. Lejeune's close friend Midshipman Henry Wiley was washed overboard and swept against the wrecked *Nipsic* where, stunned and exhausted, he caught a piece of floating wreckage that was carried near the beach and pulled in by a human chain of Samoans stretched dangerously into the sea. The waves had torn away his clothing and battered him unconscious. Only after great effort was Wiley resuscitated.[56]

A great wave submerged the poop deck at twelve noon and tore loose a Gatling gun, which struck Captain Schoonmaker. "I saw him as he sank," recalled Lejeune, who helplessly watched his captain drown, lying face upward, with his eyes turned towards the sky, and a look of peaceful resignation on his face. Other officers suffered the same fate. Weakened by long exposure to the elements, and too exhausted to resist any longer, Marine Lieutenant Frank Sutton, Paymaster Frank H. Arms, and Pay Clerk John Roche were swept overboard and drowned.[57] At this point, Lieutenant J. W. Carlin, the executive officer, took command and ordered everyone up into the rigging. "We all expected to perish before morning," reported Lejeune, "for it seemed beyond the bounds of possibility for the men in the rigging to endure such terrible strain and cold especially as very few had anything to eat or any sleep for twenty-four hours."[58] Many men simply gave up, accepting death rather than the unbearable strain. "These were hours of physical torture," wrote Lejeune, "with every lacerated spot burning like fire from the effects of the salt water, and my mouth and throat parched and raw from the same cause." Regardless of the pain, the exhausted Lejeune fell asleep standing on the Jacob's ladder, until a seaman woke him and lashed them both to the rigging. This action probably saved Lejeune's life.[59]

Meanwhile, the *Trenton,* making use of the storm sail and placing its men into the rigging to act as sail, managed to drift in toward the inner harbor, but there collided with the *Olga,* which was successfully remaining off the reef. To prevent another, perhaps fatal, collision, the German flagship grounded on the soft mud of the eastern bay, her stern to the wind, saving her entire crew.

As darkness approached, Lejeune witnessed the great bulk of the *Trenton* bearing down on the *Vandalia* and prepared himself for the inevitable collision that would topple the masts and destroy its crew. But certain destruction proved to be salvation. The typhoon swung the *Trenton*'s stern into the *Vandalia*'s side, where a number of lines hurled by sailors soon connected the *Trenton* to the *Vandalia.* The crew of the *Trenton* roared out "three cheers for the *Vandalia,*" hoping to inspire the crew of the *Vandalia* to hang on.[60]

Lejeune was one of the last of the men who had been in the rigging of the mizzenmast for eight hours to climb aboard the *Trenton.* "I followed as quickly as I could, and a few minutes after I had landed safely, the *Vandalia*'s mizzen-mast went by the board." Although the grounded *Trenton* was still in danger, the exhausted Midshipman Lejeune slept soundly until the following morning, Sunday, March 17, when the typhoon mercifully died away.[61]

The calamity demolished four men-of-war, the *Trenton, Vandalia, Adler,* and *Eber,* and claimed 145 lives, 91 from the *Eber* and the *Adler,* 43 from the *Vandalia,* 8 from the *Nipsic,* 1 from the *Trenton,* and 2 from the schooner *Lily.*[62] The typhoon also washed away the prospect of an international incident. Admiral Kimberly arranged a truce while American, German, and British officials met in Berlin and decided that Samoa would remain independent, placing the former King Laupepa back on the Samoan throne. Ten years later, however, the three nations interfered once again in Samoan affairs. Through the Tripartite Convention of 1899, Germany acquired control of the islands lying west of 171 degrees latitude, while the Americans claimed oversight of the islands east of that line.

Ashore, Lejeune worked with the survivors, including Marine Captain Robert W. Huntington of future Spanish-American War prominence, to establish camps and prevent looting. It was during these days that Lejeune first witnessed the animosity that existed between certain Marine and Navy officers. Lieutenant J. C. Wilson, US Navy, the *Vandalia*'s navigator, was especially disdainful of Marines and their function aboard ship. Unfortunately, Lejeune, as a battalion commander of Marines, would serve years later under Wilson's command.

The Navy Department soon vindicated Admiral Kimberly's decision to keep the obsolete fleet in the harbor and wrote letters of appreciation and commendation to several of the survivors. In particular, Midshipmen J. A. Lejeune, L. A. Stafford, and H. A. Wiley of the *Vandalia* received praise: "The gale was terrific and the danger extreme, the ship being on the brink of destruction for fifteen hours. These young officers did their duty in the most commendable manner, distinguishing themselves for coolness, zeal, and pluck."[63] President Benjamin Harrison, in his first annual message to Congress, December 3, 1889, offered similar tributes to the officers and men of the naval disaster.

Lejeune also won the respect of Admiral Kimberly. When the three midshipmen detached from the *Vandalia* on March 27 in order to finish their two-year cruise, Lejeune was entrusted with the disaster report under implicit orders to deliver it personally to the commandant of the Mare Island Navy Yard. On April 27, the Navy assigned the midshipmen to the bark screw gunboat *USS Adams,* which arrived at Honolulu on July 4 in time to witness a revolution against King Rex Kalakaua.[64] Serving as Commander E. T. Woodward's clerk, Lejeune was awakened at 4:00 a.m. by a "ragged, wild-eyed Kanoka native boy." Breathless and very excited, the boy gave Lejeune a crumpled piece of paper from the king. "There is a revolution," it read. "They have captured my palace; I am down at the boat house; what shall I do?" It seems that an American named Wilcox had captured the outbuildings of the king's palace and was directing his followers to toss hand grenades close to the monarch's throne. Lejeune knew that his captain and the king were amicable poker players, so Lejeune woke Woodward and received orders to send Lieutenant C. A. Doyan and the Marine detachment ashore to protect the American legation. Later, Woodward furnished the king with forty thousand rounds of ammunition and sent the ship's battalion of sailors to town as a show of force, while the local militia broke up the uprising.[65]

Later, when the *Adams* returned to Apia, Samoa, in August 1889, Lejeune had the opportunity to meet Robert Louis Stevenson, his wife, and stepson Lloyd Osbourne, who had recently arrived there to live out their years in the Samoan Islands. Although he was suffering from tuberculosis, Stevenson came often to dine with the officers of the *Adams*. "We came to know him well," wrote Lejeune. "Physically, he was little more than a skeleton, but his spirit was undaunted."[66]

Woodward was greatly impressed with the abilities and character of John Lejeune. "He came to this ship with high recommendations from the officers of the wrecked *Vandalia*," wrote the captain. "I have given him every opportunity for instruction in seamanship, navigation, steam engineering, etc.," and "I take pleasure in reporting that he has shown himself to be a capable young officer and that he has great aptitude for the service. His moral character is excellent." Lieutenant Commander J. J. Hunker, who later replaced Commander Woodward aboard the *Adams*, had similar feelings about the young midshipman: "Naval Cadet J. A. Lejeune . . . acted during this period at various times as watch officer, division, and engineer officer. He also had constant practice at navigation. I take great pleasure in testifying to his good character, his attention to duty, aptitude for the service, and excellent intelligence."[67]

Lejeune detached from the *Adams* on March 1, 1890, and proceeded to Annapolis for his final comprehensive examination. His record for the two-year cruise was impressive, most likely due to his performance in the great naval disaster and the thorough cruise journal and navigation notes he had prepared, complete with numerous sight and compass deviation tables and dygograms.[68] Most important, his grade on the comprehensive exam was high, increasing his class position from thirteenth to sixth. Indeed, this distinguished ranking prompted a letter from Senator R. L. Gibson of Louisiana: "I cannot refrain from congratulating you upon the high standing which you have attained. . . . your gallant service at Samoa was brought to my attention by your superior officer, as it afforded me great gratification."[69]

Lejeune's decision to apply for the Marine Corps was not an easy one. While it was a simple matter for him to reject the naval Engineer Corps—"I had no bent for mechanical engineering"—it was difficult for him to decide between the Marine Corps and the Navy Line (Navy officers in command of a ship). He enjoyed occasional sea duty, but did not desire a continuous round of it, a decision most likely influenced by the disaster at Apia. Further, he preferred the military side of naval life, realizing that the days of sail were numbered and foreseeing that the naval officer was becoming more and more the technician. "I realized that whatever ability I had lay in the direction of handling and controlling men rather than in the direction of handling and controlling machinery."[70]

It was not so simple, however, to enter the Marine Corps, for Lejeune soon received a shock. The Academic Board of the Naval Academy felt that Lejeune ranked too high in his class to be assigned to the Marine Corps, and since there was an acute shortage of Navy engineers, he was duly assigned to the Engineer Corps.[71] This decision was unacceptable to Lejeune, who now revealed the polite but tenacious persona that became a trademark throughout his career. In an effort to change the assignment while working through the naval chain of command, he called on every board member, even Captain W. T. Sampson, superintendent of the Naval Academy, but all declined to change the decision. As a last resort, Lejeune called on Commodore F. M. Ramsey, chief of the Bureau of Navigation in Washington, the official who was responsible for the Naval Academy. After Ramsey refused to alter the board's decision, Lejeune talked with Senator Gibson of Louisiana, who secured an interview with Benjamin F. Tracy, secretary of the Navy. Together they stated Lejeune's case and, when the senator mentioned Lejeune's performance during the great typhoon ordeal at Samoa, the secretary rang for Commodore Ramsey and said simply, "Commodore, I want this young man assigned to the Marine Corps."[72] After a quiet summer visit at home in Louisiana with his mother and sister, Lejeune received a letter on July 28, 1890, from Colonel Commandant Charles Heywood of the Marine Corps appointing him as a second lieutenant of Marines.[73]

3
JUNIOR OFFICER YEARS, 1890–1900

It is unlikely that Major C. M. Huntington, commander of the Marine Barracks at the New York City Navy Yard, was especially impressed when he met the reporting twenty-three-year-old Second Lieutenant John A. Lejeune on August 31, 1890. The reason was simple. At first meeting, young Lejeune appeared distinguished neither by personality nor by appearance. Though cordial enough, the new officer was slightly retiring, especially in the company of strangers, and hardly loquacious. Physically, his well-developed chest, shoulders, and frame deceptively gave him a guise of shortness, despite his medium height of approximately five feet, eight inches.[1] Nor was he handsome. Shortly after World War I, an artist named Joseph Cummings Chase painted portraits of general officers in occupied Germany. After Chase had finished Lejeune's painting, the general commented, "I certainly am an ugly one." To this the artist replied, "Do you want it to look any different?" "No," said General Lejeune, "I like it that way."[2]

This opinion of himself was overly harsh. Beneath a thatch of thick, straight, black hair combed down in bangs lay a ruggedly cut nose flanked by soft but alert deep-set brown eyes and long prominent ears—a face reinforced by a resolute jaw and set within a seamed and weather-beaten look that gradually aged into the color of old mahogany. Eventually his visage earned him the nickname "Old Indian," so dubbed by the enlisted men fighting under Lejeune in World War I.

Lieutenant Lejeune spent his first two months as a student in the junior officers' orientation course at the Marine Barracks at the Brooklyn Navy Yard, which specialized in infantry drill and Marine duties aboard ship, a far cry from the more comprehensive military education received by Army officers. For young Marine officers, even as late as 1890, few American publications on tactics and strategy were available. Only by association with Civil War veterans could young Marine officers acquire practical knowledge.[3] When Lejeune asked his superiors for recent military literature, they told him to "memorize the drill manual—that's all you need to know."[4] The fact that Lejeune received no formal military education between his two-month course in 1890 and his enrollment in the Army War College, 1909–10, probably accounted for his enthusiasm for and establishment of the Marine Corps Schools in the 1920s.

In retrospect, Lejeune had no idea that he was joining a small military service which was an anachronism at risk in a wave of naval reform. The leaders of the "old" corps in which Lejeune entered still favored an outdated mission that had evolved during the days of sail, completely at odds with the changed mission of the "new" emerging Navy of steam and steel. In the days of sail, Marines had acted as emergency landing parties; enforced discipline and military standards of character with unreliable bluejackets, mostly aliens; served as naval guards and sentinels; helped repel the assaults of enemy borders; and, as sharpshooters in the rigging, picked off enemy officers at close range.[5]

After the Civil War and into the late nineteenth century, progressive leadership and an awareness of changing conditions in the United States and Europe led the US Army and Navy to institute professionalism in those services. With the end of the expansion of the western frontier and the rise of big business and industries that looked abroad for new markets, as well as to prepare for the possibility of war, William T. Sherman, CG of the Army between 1869 and 1883, and Rear Admiral Stephen B. Luce led professional reform in the Army and Navy by moving away from missions of fighting Indians and defending the coastline through the creation of a more comprehensive educational system in both services. With the goal of avoiding the horrendous carnage from frontal attacks that characterized the Civil War and emulating the great powers of Europe, Sherman—who wanted more schools in addition to West Point—reestablished the Artillery School and developed schools of engineering, infantry, cavalry, signals, hospital, and medicine, including the Military Service Institution in 1878 for officers who desired more specialized education. Admiral Luce led the Navy in creating the US Naval Institute in 1873, the Office of Naval Intelligence in 1882, and the Naval War College in 1884. These schools supported the development of the new Navy of steam and steel.[6] Officially beginning in 1889, the American Navy abandoned the policy of coastal defense through the use of ancient Civil War monitors as well as commerce raiding on the high seas by single warships. Instead, the Navy established a new doctrine of concentrating the fleet to destroy the enemy fleet in order to win control of the sea.[7]

Another voice for the creation of a new Navy was Alfred Thayer Mahan, who as president of the US NWC, 1886–89 and 1892–93, argued that naval power had to be utilized against possible enemy nations with strong navies to win command of the sea. Thus the American Fleet became an offensive weapon concentrated at a decisive point near an advanced naval base to destroy an enemy fleet. Further, the American Fleet could also destroy the commercial trade of an enemy while creating safe lines of communication with the home country. Mahan's ideas had some influence on the development of the "new" American Navy. Mahan's ideas were based on his study of Great Britain's development of a fearsome navy and her consequent control of the sea lanes in the seventeenth and eighteenth centuries, making Britain a world power. Mahan's concept of sea and world power was published in 1890 in his popular book *The Influence of Sea Power upon History, 1660–1783.*[8]

Progressives in the new Navy no longer saw the need for Marine guards aboard ship, wanting to remove them from warships and place them instead aboard transports. This prompted the Marine Corps to develop a new mission of amphibious operations to project naval power ashore.[9] Fundamentally, the emerging modern Navy no longer needed Marine sharpshooters located in the masts and rigging to fire down on the enemy or to board or repel boarders from enemy ships. Steam power had replaced sails, and future naval engagements would take place miles apart using long-range cannonades. Also, the sailors of the new Navy were primarily native-born, not immigrants who often needed Marine discipline to prevent mutinies against the captain and officers.

Several examples illustrate how progressives in the Navy rejected the corps's old mission and wanted a mission of ship-to-shore landings from transports to protect American interests abroad as well as to secure naval bases outside the United States. In 1885, early in the transition to a new Navy, President Grover Cleveland and Secretary of the Navy William H. Whitney sent Marines and sailors to the Isthmus of Panama in transports to maintain passage through the isthmus. This action was meant to end an uprising by rebels in Panama against the government of Colombia—an anti-government movement that threatened American business interests. Rather than landing small detachments of Marine guards from warships as in the past, naval officers landed Marine battalions from transports protected by naval warships. This new type of landing was initiated by Whitney, Rear Admiral James E. Jouett, and Commodore John G. Walker of the powerful Bureau of Navigation. Walker saw this operation as "a perfect opportunity . . . to strengthen the Navy and to promote an active foreign policy."[10] Walker represented many naval officers who recognized the economic and strategic importance of a future canal in Panama and were suspicious of European navies that were active in the Caribbean.[11]

Commander Bowman M. McCalla, an aggressive naval officer, led the operation, and followed the orders of Walker rather than his immediate superior, Jouett. In this large sea-to-shore maneuver with Marines and sailors who were landed from transports, McCalla and Walker demonstrated a new type of amphibious operation for the Marine Corps which resulted in the landing of more Marines.

In his report, McCalla praised the Marines as "highly efficient and admirably disciplined," but criticized them for using the tactics of a "bygone day." McCalla felt that "Marine officers needed advanced professional training in the employment of artillery and machine guns . . . that Marines wasted too much time on shore in barracks." McCalla recommended summer maneuvers for the entire Marine shore establishment in conjunction with the fleet and the Army. Moreover, McCalla criticized the Navy for not having its own transports to carry future naval expeditionary brigades, proposing that the fleet practice more realistic landing operations.[12]

Another incentive for Marines to abandon their obsolete mission and develop a landing mission was the 1889 recommendation of the Navy's Greer Board, which proposed to remove Marine guard detachments from Navy warships. The board was not sure what the Marine Corps should do, but one member of the board thought the corps could be used in large expeditions such as the Panama landing in 1885.[13] The Greer Board, established by progressive Secretary of the Navy Benjamin Franklin Tracy, took on the task of examining ship organization, fleet tactics, and landing operations, thereby rejecting Marine Commandant Charles G. McCawley's recommendations to keep Marines aboard ship as guards and to man the secondary batteries under Marine officers.[14]

The results of the Greer Board's decision angered Marines, especially when the *Army and Navy Journal* claimed that while the "Marine Corps is credited with being a reliable body of men . . . it has been asleep for the past 50 years." When Tracy rejected the Greer Board's decision and kept Marine guards aboard warships, the issue "colored all Marine-Navy relations for the near future."[15]

The old guard of the Marine Corps was fighting a battle it was destined to lose, for President Benjamin Harrison endorsed a vigorous foreign policy of American trade, especially in the Caribbean, South America, and the Pacific. Harrison also wanted a more powerful Navy to implement his expanded interpretation of the Monroe Doctrine, which declared that the American continents were "not to be considered as subjects for future colonization by any European power."[16] Consequently, Tracy recommended to Congress an oceangoing battleship Navy to carry war to the enemy's own shores. This recommendation concurred with a new American naval policy that rejected a defensive posture and supported the doctrine of controlling the seas. Tracy asked for a fifteen-year construction program to build twenty battleships for two fleets—twelve ships for the Atlantic and eight ships for the Pacific.

At the same time, Navy Lieutenant William F. Fullam convinced many naval progressives that it was time to remove Marines from warships. As an alternative, Fullam suggested, Marines could be placed in transports for large amphibious operations. In fact, Fullam spent his entire naval career trying to remove Marines from warships. In his first article in the US Naval Institute's *Proceedings,* Fullam claimed that Marines acting as ships' police undermined the morale of sailors. "The sailor is debased, and his interest and pride in the service are lessened. . . . the marine is brought under elevating influences, his manliness is appealed to, and his efficiency is obtained at the expense of the sailor."[17] In a later article, Fullam suggested "there should be at least six permanently organized battalions of marines, two on the Pacific coast and four on the Atlantic—one at Boston and Portsmouth, a second at New York, a third at Philadelphia and Washington, and a fourth at Norfolk, Port Royal, and Pensacola. There should be a transport on each coast ready to transfer these battalions to any threatened point."[18]

Unfortunately, the movement by Navy progressives and the American government to utilize Marines in a more efficient manner in an increasingly competitive world and naval environment had little effect on the leadership of the old corps. Commandants Charles G. McCawley, 1876–91; Charles G. Heywood, 1891–1903; and George Frank Elliott, 1903–10, still preferred the old mission of Marines acting as ships' guards, watchmen over naval property, and enactors of small ship-to-shore expeditions to protect Americans and property abroad.[19] Commandant Heywood, however, developed positive reforms within the corps, reforms later carried out by Commandants George Barnett and John A. Lejeune. Taking advantage of a rapidly growing Navy, these commandants requested more Marines to man the secondary batteries aboard the new steel ships. Thus, most Marines were bound by the past, trying to hold on to the traditional missions, resistant to the ideas of the Navy's reformers that large amphibious operations should be the primary mission for the corps.[20]

Although McCawley never visualized an amphibious mission for the corps, several actions that occurred during his tenure indirectly pointed the corps in that direction. First, while McCawley, as well as commandants before him, had long advocated that the Marine Corps receive graduates of the Naval Academy, it was progressive naval officers who brought the concept to fruition.[21] The Congressional Appropriation Bill of August 5, 1882—best remembered for its authorization of armored ships and the beginning of the "New Navy"—dictated that Naval Academy graduates fill vacancies in the entry grades of the Navy line, Navy Engineer Corps, and Marine Corps. Consequently, between 1882 and 1898, all of the new lieutenants in the Marine Corps were graduates of Annapolis.[22] This had far-reaching consequences for the corps. Some of these graduates of the Naval Academy during this period—men such as John A. Lejeune, George Barnett, Eli K. Cole, John Russell, Ben Fuller, Wendell Neville, and Dion Williams—would later help to pioneer the development of amphibious operations as a new mission for the Marine Corps. Five of these Marines became commandants.[23]

Heywood, who succeeded McCawley as commandant on February 10, 1891, and served until 1903, resisted the ideas of reformist naval officers. To his credit, however, Heywood began training Marines in techniques that would later help them develop an Advanced Base Force. In trying to keep pace with the Navy's rapid technological developments, in 1891 Heywood established the first formal military training school for new officers and men entering the corps, the School of Application of the United States Marine Corps in Washington, DC. The ten-month course focused on infantry tactics, naval gunnery, torpedoes (mines), high explosives, electricity, field service and modern tactics, field entrenchments, and medical hygiene. There was even a reference to landing operations: "Noncommissioned officers will be instructed also in the duties of guards when embarked, landing and campaigning with the Naval Brigade and the best formation for fighting against superior numbers armed with inferior weapons."[24] Heywood also worked to increase the size of the corps, build up the morale of enlisted Marines, firmly establish the mission of Marines aboard ship, and augment the professionalism of the officer corps. Heywood's primary interest was to establish a corps of officers and men that could man the secondary battery aboard ship: the six-inch rifled guns as well as the smaller-caliber quick-firing cannon and machine guns. Sailors would continue to operate the thirteen-inch and eight-inch guns of the main battery of the new steel warships.[25]

The old Marine Corps and new Navy remained at odds over mission for two decades of the late nineteenth century and the early years of the twentieth century. It was the American government and the new Navy that forced the Marine Corps to adopt the new mission of large landing operations. It is ironic that the leaders of the corps during this period did not recognize the significance of the amphibious mission, for Marines had landed from Navy warships all over the world since the force's inception in 1775 to "show the flag," fight in wars, and open up new markets for foreign trade.[26] Not all Marines, however, discounted the Navy's demand for a new amphibious mission. For example, First Lieutenant George Barnett, an 1881 graduate of the Naval Academy and future commandant, believed "the chief role of the Marines both on shore and at sea must be considered as an expeditionary force for use in any part of the world and not merely as a collection of watchmen."[27] Even as a young officer at this time, Lejeune also felt it was becoming unnecessary for Marines to police sailors aboard ship. Yet Lejeune did believe that withdrawing Marines from the ships meant, "in my opinion, the ultimate abolition of the Marine Corps." Throughout his career Lejeune encouraged a close Navy–Marine Corps relationship of mutual need, so that the corps's existence was interrelated with that of the Navy.[28]

Lejeune's first duty station was at the Navy Yard, Norfolk, Virginia, Marine Barracks, where he spent eleven months training enlisted men. When off duty he met and courted his future wife, Ellie Harrison Murdaugh, daughter of Judge Claudius W. and Eugenia Dixon Murdaugh of Portsmouth, Virginia. The "romance of my life"[29] was suddenly interrupted on

September 27, 1891, when Lejeune was ordered to sea duty for a three-year cruise to command the Marine Guard aboard the *Bennington,* one of the Navy's newest steel gunboats.

The *Bennington* joined Rear Admiral John G. Walker's Squadron of Evolution in October and sailed for Montevideo, Uruguay, because of the "*Baltimore* Affair" of August 1891. In this incident, revolutionaries in Valparaiso, Chile, believing that the United States was aiding the opposition party, killed two unarmed American sailors on liberty from the *USS Baltimore.* In response, the *Baltimore* landed Marines to protect American lives and property, while the United States prepared to go to war. But the government of Chile apologized in January 1892, paid an indemnity, and the matter was resolved diplomatically.[30] Later, the *Bennington* sailed for Gibraltar, Barcelona, Toulon, Cadiz, and Genoa to participate in the four-hundred-year celebration honoring the expedition of Christopher Columbus and the discovery of America. Soon after, the *Bennington* towed the reproduced caravel *Pinta* from Huelva to Havana, Cuba. During these two years, Lejeune's Marines practiced landings, staffed the sentry and orderly posts, acted as guards of honor during ceremonies, and manned the secondary battery—the one-, three-, and six-pound rapid-fire cannon and the Gatling and Hotchkiss revolving machine guns. On February 26, 1892, Lejeune was promoted to first lieutenant.[31]

In his first cruise as a Marine officer, Lejeune experienced a few problems. From mistakes he made and from mistakes he would observe in others, Lejeune later began to believe in "second chances." On the *Bennington,* Lejeune experienced discrimination against Marine officers because of the naval custom that required junior Marine officers to dine in the inferior steerage mess, apart from the naval officers.[32] This problem, however, was the least of Lejeune's troubles on this ship. Lejeune was officially chastised by his captain for inattention to duty aboard the *Bennington.* Commander Royal B. Bradford, captain of the *Bennington,* "a strict disciplinarian and somewhat of a martinet,"[33] rated Lejeune poorly in his Report of Fitness of Officers for the three-month period from October 1, 1891 to January 1, 1892. Commander Bradford reported that Lejeune's "attention to duty was not good" and the "efficiency of men under his special control was not good." Bradford continued: "The men under this officer are not trustworthy as Sentries and are not tidy and soldierly in appearance. The Officer is apparently too indolent and lacking in zeal; he does not give the personal attention to his men that he should; the result is a want of efficiency in the Guard."[34]

Lejeune did not challenge this fitness report. In a letter to the secretary of the Navy, Lejeune wrote, "I would respectfully state that I have no statement to make in regard to the report of Commander R. B. Bradford as to my fitness."[35] In a harsh letter of reprimand, Marine Commandant Heywood wrote to Lejeune that his fitness report "has occasioned much regret on my part. . . . this report has greatly disappointed me both as regards you, and the fact that the Corps has been so poorly represented on board the *Bennington,* and your record as an officer will be greatly affected unless you pay closer attention to your duties."[36]

This unfavorable report apparently galvanized Lejeune to act more assertively as commander of the ship guard, for Bradford's later fitness reports on Lejeune revealed an improved performance. Lejeune's professional ability and attention to duty became "tolerable" in Bradford's fitness report on June 30, 1892,[37] and later "good," in January 1893 and June 1893.[38] Bradford even mentioned in January 1893 that Lejeune had abilities as a linguist or translator: "Reads French easily and speaks it fairly."

While Lejeune kept his opinion of Bradford to himself and never mentioned the captain's name in his autobiography, he expressed his feelings in a letter to his sister when Bradford left the *Bennington*: "All of us that remain [on the *Bennington*] will be delighted to see him leave as he is heartily disliked by every man and officer on board."[39] Much later, writing in his autobiography, Lejeune criticized his unnamed former commander indirectly by speaking highly of his new commanding officer (CO): "There [New York Navy Yard] our commanding officer was relieved by Commander Charles M. Thomas, and in all my forty-five years of service I have never seen a more complete or rapid transformation in a ship or shore command," for, in a week, "the little *Bennington* had become a happy home for officers and men alike. Commander Thomas was a taut Captain too, but somehow he instantaneously captured the imaginations and the hearts of his subordinates so that it was a joy to work for him and we strove mightily for a word of commendation from him."[40]

Perhaps due to his experience of receiving a poor fitness report during his first three months on the *Bennington,* Lejeune eventually came to believe in "second chances." Much later, in the early 1930s, when Lejeune was superintendent of the VMI, he told Colonel A. A. Vandegrift that "every young officer is entitled to one mistake."[41] Lejeune expressed this opinion when Vandegrift was visiting his son, a student at VMI. Lejeune probably knew that Vandegrift had been court-martialed in 1909 by Colonel Eli K. Cole, a classmate and friend of Lejeune, for his "rebellious" attitude and late return to duty at the School of Application at Parris Island, South Carolina. Vandegrift, who thought his career in the corps was ruined, changed his attitude and eventually proved to Cole that he was a good Marine: "Rather than point out what I felt and still feel was injustice, I swore I would eventually show Colonel Cole that he was wrong. . . . I succeeded in this before the old man died in 1929."[42]

Lejeune detached from the *Bennington* in August of 1893, was reassigned to the Norfolk Navy Yard for four years, and married Ellie Murdaugh on October 23, 1895.[43] When his shore duty expired in 1897, he received orders to command the Marine guard on the new cruiser *Cincinnati,* one of the finest and fastest of the new fleet.[44] While the *Cincinnati* joined the South Atlantic Squadron that was cruising off South America, Lejeune commanded a larger Marine Guard, but was challenged when the executive officer, Lieutenant Commander R. M. Barry, who was active in the strong movement to remove the Marines from the ships, rejected the traditional Marine role aboard ship and assigned Lejeune and his Marines to very minor duties. A wiser and more mature Lejeune rose to the challenge, talking with and writing to Captain Colby M. Chester about how his Marines could be greatly useful to the ship. The Marines could free up sailors by manning the secondary battery and be available as a landing force should a need arise. Consequently, Chester assigned Lejeune's Marines to man the secondary battery and appointed Lejeune intelligence officer for the South Atlantic Squadron.[45]

Unlike Lejeune's first fitness report on the *Bennington,* his fitness reports were all marked "excellent" while Lejeune was stationed at the Marine Barracks at the Navy Yard in Norfolk, Virginia,[46] 1893 to 1897, and all marked "excellent" while serving as commander of the Marine Guard and Fleet Intelligence Officer aboard the *Cincinnati,* 1897–99.[47] Lejeune was aboard the *Cincinnati* when the United States went to war with Spain in 1898.

The United States went to war with Spain because of reports in the American press of Spanish atrocities against Cubans and the refusal of Spain to stop its campaign of pacification in Cuba or to renounce its colonies in the Caribbean and Pacific. In addition, Cuba was positioned directly in the path of the shipping lanes from Europe to the Isthmus of Panama—a strategic concern for the United States, which for decades had entertained the idea of developing a canal to join the Atlantic and Pacific fleets. The United States was not particularly concerned about Spain, a declining power, but feared the growing power of the German Fleet and the Kaiser's quest for colonies and coaling stations in the Caribbean and Pacific.

After the declaration of war on April 29, 1898, Spain sent a squadron of three armored cruisers, one battleship, and three destroyers under the command of Admiral Pascual Cervera from the Portuguese Verde Island westward towards Cuba. Unlike the Army, which was not prepared for war, the Navy—since 1895, through the joint planning of the ONI, the NWC, and various temporary strategy boards—had developed several plans for a possible war with Spain. While the US Fleet concentrated in the Caribbean waiting for the Spanish Squadron to appear, the Asiatic Squadron under Commodore George Dewey steamed into Manila Bay on May 1 and destroyed the outmatched and obsolete Spanish Pacific Fleet. The Marine Guard under Marine First Lieutenant Dion Williams from the cruiser *Baltimore* landed and captured the Spanish base of operations at Cavite, but lacked enough manpower to force the surrender of the Spanish land forces in order to occupy Manila. Dewey would have to wait for the organization and transit of Army forces to arrive from the United States to accomplish this.

Since the Army forces at Tampa, Florida, commanded by General William Shafter, were not ready to land in Cuba, Rear Admiral William T. Sampson asked Secretary of the Navy John D. Long to deploy a battalion of Marines to serve with the fleet at Key West. Acting quickly, Marine Commandant Heywood in two days pulled together, under the command of Lieutenant Colonel Robert Huntington, the First Battalion of Marines, which included 631 enlisted men, 21 officers, and 1 surgeon, organized into five infantry companies and one company of artillery.[48]

Having eluded Sampson's North Atlantic Squadron and Commodore William S. Schley's Flying Squadron, Cervera's small Spanish fleet entered the harbor of Santiago de Cuba on the southern coast of Cuba on May 18, 1898. Secretary Long ordered Sampson to blockade Santiago and seize Guantanamo Bay, located about forty miles east of Santiago, in order to establish a coaling station (advance base) for the fleet. Aboard the transport *Panther*, Huntington's battalion landed without initial enemy resistance at Guantanamo Bay on June 10 under the overall command of Commander

Bowman McCalla aboard the *Marblehead.* The Spanish force of 400 to 500 troops at Guantanamo Bay—with an estimated force of 6,000 Spanish troops guarding Santiago—first conducted minor skirmishes against the Marines. Later, however, the Spanish attacked in force, beginning "100 hours of fighting."[49] Thanks to about 50 Cuban insurrectionists who joined the Marines—Cubans who were familiar with the terrain and the enemy camp six miles south near the village of Cuzco—Huntington took the offensive and sent two companies to destroy the water well at Cuzco, the only source of water for the Spanish. At Guantanamo the Marines held firm, fighting off greater numbers of Spanish forces amid many enemy counterattacks.

Even though the Army under Shafter later landed at Daiquiri, only eighteen miles southeast of Santiago Bay on June 22, marched and encircled Santiago City, and did the bulk of the fighting against the Spanish in two costly battles—San Juan Hill and El Caney—the Marine Battalion received more publicity at home, thanks to the Marines being the first infantry to fight in Cuba. This fact generated excellent publicity for the corps, especially from news reporters such as Stephen Crane in the *New York World.*[50] In addition, due to strict health standards, the Marines suffered only a 2 percent casualty rate from sickness.[51]

The Spanish lost their small fleet when Shafter's Fifth Army bearing down on Santiago City prompted Cervera's armored cruisers to steam out of the harbor at 9:30 a.m. on July 3, into the semicircle of American warships that gave chase and pounded away for over four hours, leaving all Spanish ships sinking, burning, or aground.

The Spanish-American War had significant ramifications for the Marine Corps, Navy, and Army. First, the Navy-Marine Corps amphibious operation at Guantanamo Bay had had an objective different from previous Marine landings during the Mexican War, the American Civil War, and Panama in 1885. For the first time, the intention of this landing was to secure a naval coaling station or advance base for the Navy. This allowed the American Fleet to refuel closer to the land fighting and the Spanish Fleet instead of having to steam away to Key West, a distance of over 250 miles. While the Navy had theorized for years about this concept, now forward-thinking Marines could envision a possible new wartime mission for the corps. The success of Huntington's battalion in establishing an ABF for the Navy demonstrated that the Marine Corps could have a new mission in supporting the new Navy.

The effectiveness of naval gunfire ashore was another lesson learned at Guantanamo Bay. It allowed the Marines to land, establish a base camp, repel the Spanish assaults, and destroy the water well at Cuzco. Naval shelling forced the Spanish out of their entrenchments and limited their defense at Cuzco. Naval gunfire also helped the Marines hold their position at Guantanamo Bay despite continuous Spanish counterattacks.[52]

In addition, there was no guiding hand or centralized planning board to coordinate the Army's and Navy's actions during the conduct of the war. The main issue was a disagreement between Shafter and Sampson over objectives. Shafter's goal was to capture the city of Santiago. He asked Sampson to have the fleet enter the mouth of Santiago Bay and steam up the winding, narrow channel to bombard the city. Sampson was not prepared to do this. His objective was to destroy the Spanish ships still located inside the bay. Sampson and Long did not want to risk the armored ships that would be exposed to minefields located at the entrance to the bay and the Spanish cannon situated on the heights overlooking the entrance. For support, Sampson asked Shafter to move the Army south to destroy the gun batteries on the eastern bank of the entrance to the bay (Morro Heights).

At the same time, Huntington's battalion of Marines—reinforced by Marines from the fleet—would destroy the gun batteries on the western heights (Socapa Heights). With the Spanish cannon destroyed and the minefields removed, the Navy could then move up the channel, destroy the Spanish Fleet, and bombard the city. Shafter refused Sampson's request to move his Army south because it would have weakened his forces attempting to capture the city of Santiago. Thus, both commanders were more concerned about the dangers and purposes of their respective forces and differed on overall objectives and strategy. This led to disagreements and hostility not only between the commanders, but also between the secretaries of the Navy and War Department. Later, the Army refused the Navy's offer of Marines to join the Army in the campaign to capture Puerto Rico. Commandant Heywood was quick to point out to Secretary Long that the Navy should use Marines rather than the Army in joint operations because the Marine Corps was part of the naval service. Since the senior naval officer present was always in overall command in amphibious operations, there was never a problem of conflict of authority. There were, however, often problems of command relationships when the Navy and the Army worked together.[53]

Another lesson learned by Navy and Marine Corps was that Marines in transports should accompany the fleet during wartime operations. Admiral Dewey remarked to Dion Williams that had he commanded a force of 2,000 Marines he could have forced the surrender of the Spanish Army and occupied Manila. Dewey also felt he could have occupied the adjacent country and cleared the way for an Army expeditionary force to occupy the entire Philippine archipelago. He believed that better coordination between the Army and the Navy would have allowed the Army to arrive much earlier in the Philippines, perhaps preventing the native insurrection for Philippine independence and the bitter warfare that cost the United States lives, time, and treasure.[54]

The success of Huntington's battalion in Cuba earned Marines greater respect from the Navy and Congress, resulting in increased appropriations to enlarge the corps. The Navy used these Marines to help defend the new possessions in the Pacific, especially the Philippines and Guam, and to support the Open Door policy in China. Consequently, the corps grew from 77 officers and 2,900 men in 1897 to 332 officers and 9,521 enlisted men by 1908, three times the numbers before the war with Spain.[55]

Finally, the Navy and Marine Corps identified internal coordination problems that needed to be resolved. For example, the transport carrying Huntington's battalion was a hastily converted banana boat that was much too small and cramped for the Marines, thus lowering morale. Commandant Heywood therefore asked the Navy for real transports dedicated for use by the Marine Corps. In addition, ineffective communication between the naval transport commander and the Marine assault-force commander hindered the corps's amphibious operation. In a problem that would linger until World War II, transport commanders often interfered with and restricted the authority of the Marine commander aboard ship and on land in a way that put amphibious operations at risk.[56]

Aboard the *Cincinnati,* Lejeune was aware of the significance of the Guantanamo Bay landing. Much later, he wrote that "the fact that this [Huntington] battalion was the first United States force to effect a permanent lodgement on shore in Cuba, and the success of its military operations there brought the Marine Corps into greater prominence and caused the Navy to appreciate more fully its value as an expeditionary force . . . in a naval overseas campaign."[57]

Lejeune led an amphibious landing at Puerto Rico when the Navy escorted Lieutenant General Nelson A. Miles's Expeditionary Army in the seizure of Puerto Rico from the Spanish. Arriving on August 7, 1898, to blockade San Juan, Captain Chester learned that some 800 Spanish troops had recaptured Fajardo on the east coast and were advancing on San Juan to apprehend some American sympathizers. Prior to the arrival of the *Cincinnati,* the *Amphitrite* landed 34 sailors on August 6 to protect the sympathizers sheltered at the San Juan lighthouse and to delay the Spanish advance. At a prearranged signal, the *Cincinnati* played her searchlights on the coast and along with the *Amphitrite* and *Leyden* laid down high-explosive shells in the path of the adversary. Together with a stubborn effort by the sailors in the lighthouse, the naval barrage repulsed the Spanish assault. At dawn, Lejeune led the ship's guard of 30 Marines from the *Cincinnati* and 30 bluejackets from the *Amphitrite* to relieve the exhausted sailors on shore. Lejeune maneuvered his landing boats successfully through the dangerous reefs that had previously grounded Navy Lieutenant Charles N. Atwater's party of sailors, advanced cautiously with his men through the rugged countryside of dense high brush and cactus, determined that the enemy had retreated, had his men dig in to form a defensive line, and protected the orderly withdrawal of the sailors and refugees to the *Leyden.* When the estimated 120 Spaniards still in the vicinity declined to press the issue, Lejeune closed the lighthouse, raised the American flag, and re-embarked his men aboard the *Cincinnati.*[58]

"It was work well done," wrote Captain Chester; "the refugees were soon on board the *Leyden* and transported to Ponce, Puerto Rico."[59] In a letter to the secretary of the Navy, Chester highly commended Lejeune: "He was sent in command of a force of men to the relief of a landing party from the squadron beleaguered by the enemy in the lighthouse . . . the force being released from a dangerous situation with very creditable results. I consider him to be one of the best officers in the Marine Corps, and believe he will fill any position assigned to him with credit to himself and to the service." Lejeune was awarded the Sampson and Spanish Campaign medals for his service in the war.[60]

Like the Marines at Guantanamo Bay, Lejeune learned the value of naval bombardment of the shore in support of landings. Lejeune also learned the mechanics of naval bombardments afloat as his Marine gun crew exchanged fire with the Spanish battery located in northern Cuba at the earthworks of Punta Gorda.[61] For his service in supervising the secondary batteries during the action, Lieutenant Lejeune was commended by Captain

Chester in an official report to the Navy secretary: "In charge of his division, Lieutenant Lejeune took an effective part in the engagement with the shore batteries at Matanzas, Cuba, April, 1898, where he displayed marked courage under fire, and handled his men well."[62]

The final years of the nineteenth century and the beginning of the twentieth century brought fundamental changes for the United States and John Lejeune. Bad news awaited Lejeune when the *Cincinnati* docked at Havana. There in January 1899 he learned that his mother had fallen downstairs while visiting relatives in Port Gibson, Mississippi, and was not expected to live. "It was the saddest period of my life," recalled Lejeune. He buried Laura Lejeune beside Ovide in the churchyard of St. Stephen's Church.[63] Shortly thereafter, in May of 1900, Lejeune visited Louisiana to sell the old family home to Ovide LaCour and to accompany his sister Augustine (Teeney)—now left with no immediate family in Louisiana—to live near Lejeune in Bel Air, Maryland.[64]

There was also good news for Lejeune, for his family increased in size with the birth of his first daughter, Ellie Murdaugh Lejeune, on August 18, 1896. Family was sacred to Lejeune, even more important than the Marine Corps.[65] Unlike many young Marine officers who also served aboard naval warships for many years and remained unmarried for life or married at an older age, Lejeune married at a young age and was deeply involved in the life of his family. Further, on March 3, 1899, Lejeune was promoted to the rank of captain.

With the Treaty of Paris, as ratified in February of 1899, Spain agreed to relinquish Cuba as a possession, and ceded the Philippines, Puerto Rico, and Guam to the United States. In addition, the United States formally annexed the Hawaiian Islands. Suddenly the young nation acquired an overseas empire that stretched from the Antilles to the Philippines and found itself more heavily involved in the European rivalry for trading concessions in China. These circumstances placed a new and great burden on the Navy, the first line of defense, to protect these distant new territories.

Anticipating new demands on Marine Corps manpower to defend the possessions, Commandant Heywood asked Secretary Long on November 9, 1898, for a corps of 6,000 Marines, an increase of 1,268 over its force during the war. Many senior and junior Marine officers supported Heywood in his effort to increase the size of the Marine Corps through the Naval Appropriation Bill of 1899. Lejeune proved to be an apt politician as well as a Marine by using his family connections to support the corps in Congress. In a letter to his sister, Lejeune wrote, "Thank Dr. [Albert] Batchelor for me, for his very successful efforts in behalf of our bill: everyone worked hard for it, and no opposition to the Marine Corps developed in the Senate."[66] It is probable that Dr. Batchelor influenced Representative Adolph Meyer from Louisiana, the leading Democrat on the House Naval Affairs Committee. Meyer offered an amendment to the Naval Personnel Bill that incorporated the changes and additions to the Marine Corps as recommended by Heywood. After the full House of Representatives agreed to the amendment, the Senate passed the bill a month later. President William McKinley signed the bill into law on March 3, 1899.[67]

Captain Lejeune finished his sea tour as commander of a larger ship guard on the modern battleship *Massachusetts.* In a letter he wrote: "I will have much more to do than on the *Cincinnati,* as I have sixty Marines, and they man a large and important part of the battery—four six-inch guns and two six pounders. . . . it is a very strict ship, but everyone seems contented and fond of the ship."[68] Some months later, Lejeune wrote, "this is a comfortable, happy ship."[69] Even so, Lejeune faced discrimination as a Marine officer aboard this ship from naval officers of his own rank. During these days the question of precedence in rank between Marine and Navy officers of the same grade became a hotly contested issue.[70] Since there were several Navy full lieutenants aboard the *Massachusetts* who felt they "ranked" a Marine captain, Lejeune determined to settle this issue once and for all, writing on October 28 and November 6 to the Navy Department's judge advocate general requesting a definite ruling on the question. Because of Lejeune's persistence, the Navy Department, in letters of November 1 and 13, made a decision: Navy and Marine officers of comparable rank had equal authority unless one possessed an earlier date of commission or entered the service before. Further, to avoid future problems, the Navy Department instructed the Bureau of Navigation to include all Marines on the common order of rank list published in the official *Navy Register.*[71]

Lejeune's first ten years as a junior officer in the Marine Corps had not been spectacular nor, for that matter, dissimilar to that of his fellow officers. He had served in generally the same positions and, because of the policy of promotion by seniority, had received promotion at approximately the same time. Yet there remained a basic difference. John Lejeune had no idiosyncrasies like those of Percival Pope, no flamboyance like that of

Littleton W. T. "Tony" Waller, and none of the showmanship displayed by young Smedley Butler.[72] But, in spite of this, he impressed all he met. Outwardly quiet, conservative, and unassuming, Lejeune was at the same time an enormously ambitious career officer, whose energies focused not on himself, but on the welfare and expansion of the Marine Corps. With the establishment of his growing family, Lejeune became dedicated to the corps and developed the reputation for being a reformer who supported the new mission of the Navy while demanding equal treatment and recognition for Marines within the naval service.

4
BUILDING A REPUTATION, 1900–1910

At the turn of the twentieth century, it was apparent that the defense of the new American possessions won from Spain in the Caribbean and Pacific demanded better cooperation, planning, and respect between the Army and the Navy. Disagreement between the services over the conduct of the Caribbean campaign had especially strained the relationship between the Departments of War and the Navy. Consequently, because of the recommendations of Admiral Henry C. Taylor and the fact that most secretaries of the Navy were political appointments and lacked knowledge of war planning, Secretary John Davis Long signed General Order 544 on March 13, 1900, creating the General Board of the Navy. An advisory body, the board was to conduct war planning; to recommend to the secretary the nation's probable enemies, the manner in which future wars should be fought, and the best way to prepare for war; and to develop proposals relative to naval bases, ship strength, and the strategic disposition of the fleet.[1] In addition, President Theodore Roosevelt in 1903 created the Joint Army and Navy Board—composed of members of the General Board and the Army's general staff—to coordinate American defense.

Admiral George Dewey, who headed the Navy Board for seventeen years, added prestige to the General Board, while Taylor provided a strong guiding hand during its early years. One of the board's first recommendations confirmed the amphibious mission of the Marine Corps: "The plans of a naval campaign in Asiatic waters in case of war in which the United States might become engaged, involve the defense of a Naval Advanced Base where supplies can be collected for the use of the fleet." The board deemed it "desirable that the Commandant of this base should have a sufficient force with him, independent of the crews of the fighting vessels. . . . for this purpose it is suggested that the Marines would be best adapted and most available for immediate and sudden call."[2]

As a first step, the General Board requested that Marine Commandant Heywood prepare detailed descriptions of his plans for the defense of the Naval Advanced Base, to include the construction of improvised earthworks; the mounting of large defensive artillery; the installation of field telegraph, telephone, range finders, signal stations, and searchlights; and the placing of mines and torpedoes for harbor defense. In addition, the General Board, supported by Secretary Long, asked Heywood to instruct the Marine Corps in the development of the defense and to prepare a force of 1,000 men with stores of food, supplies, and ammunition in order to act independently for two months. Finally, the board recommended that the corps maintain a continuous force of at least 400 specially trained Marines in a battalion to "meet the possible demand for it at any time."[3]

As a result of these directives, in May 1901, in the first formal effort to train Marines to operate as a Naval Advanced Base, Heywood ordered Major Henry C. Haines, on staff at the NWC, to take charge of a small detachment of Marines at Newport, Rhode Island, home of the Navy Torpedo Station and the NWC. Haines was to instruct these Marines in signaling, the use of torpedoes and mines, field telegraph and telephones, and searchlights. These Marines with a Naval Beachmaster landed with Fleet Marines from the battleships *Kearsarge, Alabama,* and *Massachusetts* on July 8, 1901, near Great Point, Nantucket, Massachusetts. The detachment established a defensive position on shore, developed trenches, minefields, and communications, and mounted and fired guns at an imaginary enemy. The Marines landed again at Nantucket ten days later, establishing Camp Long. Heywood and the CinC of the North Atlantic station were pleased, with Heywood recommending similar maneuvers the following year.[4]

In mid-November 1901 the General Board recommended, and the Navy Department directed, the establishment of a Naval Advanced Base on Culebra, a small, mountainous island east of Puerto Rico. The battleships *Alabama* and *Massachusetts* landed Marines on Culebra on January 1, 1902, to clear a camp aptly named Camp Roosevelt. With the fleet offshore, Marines stormed ashore and emplaced guns, telephone lines, and a signal station to defend against an enemy amphibious assault.[5]

Culebra became even more important as a training site for what the Marine Corps called an ABF when President Roosevelt directed the General Board and Navy to expand the winter fleet maneuvers of 1902–3 as a show of force in order to prevent Germany from forcefully collecting unpaid debts from Venezuela. The landings at Culebra were interrupted by another revolution in Panama, prompting the Marine ABF to embark as an expeditionary force to Panama. Meanwhile, Heywood had formed a larger Marine battalion commanded by Colonel Percival C. Pope that arrived on the Navy transport *Prairie* at Culebra on November 20, 1902. Pope's Marines—on a larger scale than the previous year—manually hauled four- and five-inch naval guns from the fleet to shore, erected defenses, dug a canal between Great Harbor and Target Bay, laid telephone and telegraph lines, and built better roads.[6] These exercises ended on January 3, 1903, and the battalion returned to the United States. Another Marine battalion returned to Culebra and joined a small fleet of four cruisers and a ship tender as part of a newly formed Caribbean Squadron created to support the ABF at Culebra or to serve as an expeditionary force wherever needed.

After 1903, however, the Marine Corps struggled to develop a permanent force that could acquire and defend overseas naval bases for the fleet. There were several reasons for this. First, the General Board expected the corps to not only develop the ABF, but also to act as an expeditionary force whenever problems arose in the Caribbean or the Far East. The many expeditionary operations mandated by the State Department and conducted by Marines during the first two decades of the twentieth century slowed the development of the force. Second, the Navy Department had limited interest in the ABF and consistently reduced funding for the acquisition of equipment at the Advanced Base School that the corps had established in Philadelphia in 1910. Third, Commandants Heywood and his successor, George Frank Elliott, were unable or unwilling to establish a permanent ABF for utilization in training and deployment.[7]

The turn of the twentieth century found Captain Lejeune ashore after completing his sea duty aboard the *Massachusetts,* and assigned on May 10, 1900, for temporary duty to the brigadier general commandant's office in Washington, DC. In June, he served under Major Lincoln Karmany at the Marine Barracks, Washington, on boards that reviewed applications for commissions in the corps. On July 3, 1900, Lejeune assumed charge of the Massachusetts-Maine recruiting district and opened new substations, traveling frequently to swear in recruits.[8] The patriotic sentiment of the time can perhaps be seen in the psychological inducements the corps used in their recruiting posters. One popular poster pictured a national hero, Admiral of the Navy George Dewey, over a caption that read: "He did his duty, will you? Join the active service land and sea, U.S. Marines!" Another poster appealed to the adventurous at heart: "Men wanted for the U.S. Marines, an opportunity to see the world, duty on shore, at sea, and in our island possessions!"[9]

The Lejeunes were living in a Boston boardinghouse when daughter Ellie suffered a dangerous bronchial attack that required an assignment change for Lejeune to a southern station. Accordingly, on November 10, 1900, the corps transferred Lejeune to command the Marine detachment at Pensacola, Florida, an old Navy yard reopened during the Spanish-American War.[10] Lejeune was commended at least twice during his tenure at Pensacola. The first was when his Marines put out a fire at the nearby Army post of Fort Barrancas, prompting a letter from the naval commandant at Pensacola, Captain W. W. Reisinger, to the commandant of the Marine Corps: "Most buildings were saved by the prompt action of the Marines. It gives me great pleasure again to testify to the promptness of the guard here in responding at times of emergency."[11] Second, Major C. M. Lauchheimer, the assistant adjutant and inspector of the Marine Corps, commended Lejeune for the condition of the post: "The report of my inspection of your command is extremely satisfactory, and I shall take the opportunity of inviting the General's attention to the excellent condition in which I found your command."[12]

While daughter Ellie rapidly regained her health in Florida and a second daughter, Laura Turpin, was born on June 9, 1902, Lejeune suffered ill health in Pensacola and was listed by the corps as "unfit for duty" due to gastrointestinal irritation.[13] Lejeune was placed on sick leave until diagnosed and operated on for appendicitis in Baltimore on November 13, 1902.[14]

Ironically, it was fortunate for the Marine Corps's future—and for Lejeune's career—that Lejeune was not available for duty when Commandant Heywood on December 26, 1902, attempted to attach Lejeune to a battalion of Marines embarking for the Philippines.[15] Recovering good health a few months later and promoted to the rank of major on March 3, 1903, Lejeune received orders for an independent command that eventually resulted in his landing Marines in Panama to secure the isthmus for the canal builders. One of Heywood's last orders as commandant on August 8, 1903, directed

Lejeune to command the "floating battalion" aboard the *USS Panther* for possible expeditionary duty in Cuba.[16] Lejeune's promotion made him eligible to command the battalion.[17]

Excited with his first major command, Lejeune faced yet another trial with the Navy as the captain of the *Panther* was none other than Commander J. C. Wilson, whom Lejeune knew well from his days as a midshipman aboard the *Vandalia* in 1889 during the crisis with Germany over Samoa. Wilson was one of many naval officers who disliked Marines and probably wanted them removed from naval vessels. When Lejeune reported to Wilson on August 16, 1903, he found that Wilson's view of Navy–Marine Corps command relationships was as authoritarian as ever, with the Navy in almost complete control of all activities. The situation was a Marine commander's nightmare. Aboard ship, Lejeune was given command only of battalion drills and instruction, was without independent tactical authority when landed ashore, and was subjected to naval harassment. Wilson and his naval officers habitually violated the Marine chain of command. Wilson worked any Marine as he saw fit. Personal relations between Marine and Navy officers were poor, easily marking this period as the darkest in Lejeune's professional career. Despite the strained relationships, Wilson rated Lejeune highly on his fitness report with marks of "very good" as to professional ability, manner of performing duties, and zeal, intelligence, and judgment, and with marks of "excellent" on attention to duty, general conduct, bearing, and military appearance.[18]

Fortunately, Lejeune had inherited a well-trained and disciplined battalion of Marines with good officers. The battalion had been thoroughly trained by Major H. C. Haines during the previous months ashore in camp on Culebra. Lejeune pressed his officers to maintain high morale among the men and to bear the present situation until the battalion was transferred, which it was on October 26, 1903, to the transport *Dixie.*[19]

Determined to avoid a repeat of the ordeal aboard the *Panther,* Lejeune labored assiduously to establish good relations with Captain Francis H. Delano and his naval officers aboard the *Dixie.* Thus, not only did he have to maintain a constantly alert fighting organization, but he also had to win the admiration and respect of the crew of the *Dixie.* To his credit, Captain Delano accepted fully the primary Marine roles of defending an Advanced Naval Base or restoring order during emergencies ashore as a Marine Expeditionary Force. Delano agreed to work only through Lejeune or his office in command and liaison matters. In turn, Lejeune ordered one Marine company to attend to ship duty each day, while the remaining three companies underwent a rigorous training program.[20] For his efforts, "Major Lejeune worked out a sensible relation with the ship which set a pattern followed to this day between embarked landing forces and the naval authorities."[21]

Lejeune's battalion on the *Dixie* was an integral part of Rear Admiral J. B. Coghlan's Caribbean (cruiser) Squadron, which stood ready to implement Theodore Roosevelt's "Big Stick" policy in the Caribbean. President Roosevelt was ready to build a canal across the Isthmus of Panama and was angered when Colombia rejected the Hay-Herrán Treaty of January 22, 1903. According to the terms of this treaty, the United States was prepared to give $40 million to the defunct French New Panama Canal Company for rights to build the canal and $10 million plus an annual subsidiary of $250,000 to Colombia for America's perpetual control of a five-kilometer-wide zone across the isthmus.

Not a patient man, Roosevelt was pleased when Philippe Jean Bunau-Varilla of the French Canal Company conspired with his New York attorney, William N. Cromwell, to arrange Panama's revolt against the Colombian government in the isthmus. The Panamanian revolt of revolutionary troops against Colombian troops had reached a dangerous point when the *Dixie* received orders in Kingston on November 2, 1903, to "maintain free and uninterrupted transit [of the isthmus] and prevent landing of any armed force with hostile intent, either government [Colombian] or insurgent [Panamanian] at any point within fifty miles of Panama."[22] The gunboat *Nashville* had arrived off Colón on the Caribbean side of Panama, but had not received the orders and allowed about five hundred Colombian troops under Colonel Eliseo Torres to land at Colón at daybreak on November 3, 1903. Commander John Hubbard soon after landed a small party of sailors to occupy the Colón station and placed the *Nashville* nearby to provide fire support. Torres, whose force outnumbered Hubbard's sailors ten-to-one, maneuvered his regiment into firing position and threatened to kill every Yankee in Colón. After bluffing attempts by both commanders failed, the situation grew critical.

The *Dixie* arrived at this juncture at 7:25 p.m. on November 5 and received a signal from the *Nashville* requesting that the Marine battalion be landed quickly. By 7:40 p.m., Lejeune had over two hundred Marines over the side in full combat paraphernalia. By 8:15, he had landed the Marines on the Colón wharf despite a driving rain. Torres had no stomach for a fight, however; he accepted money from the Panamanian revolutionists and departed on the royal mail steamer *Orinacco* for Colombia.[23]

Captain Delano was first to congratulate Lejeune on his firm but prudent conduct. "In this connection," he wrote in an official report to the Navy Department, "I wish to comment most favorably on the energetic and efficient handling of the Battalion at all times by Major Lejeune and the officers under his command, and to the alacrity with which the enlisted men responded to the call, and to their general good conduct."[24]

Under overall naval command that included the Pacific and Caribbean squadrons offshore, Lejeune had independent command of his battalion on the isthmus for most of the period from November 1903 to December 1904 and kept Colombian and Panamanian troops away from a five-mile stretch of land parallel to the rail line. This action allowed a free flow of traffic from the Caribbean side to the Pacific, winning for Lejeune numerous commendations from Navy, Marine, and civilian sources. When Coghlan failed to reach a peaceful settlement with Colombia, the United States entered into a treaty with the new Republic of Panama for the same terms formerly offered to Colombia, making Lejeune responsible for defending the isthmus against a possible overland invasion from Colombia.

The importance of Lejeune's mission was demonstrated when Major General Commandant George Elliott arrived in Panama with more Marines and formed a brigade to briefly support Lejeune's battalion. This was only the second time in history up to that point that a Marine commandant took to the field.[25]

Lejeune took measures to protect his battalion from the tropical heat and humidity and from the illnesses prevalent in those conditions—malaria, yellow fever, smallpox, and dysentery. Selecting a campsite 150 feet above sea level near Empire, he had the twenty-year-old French Canal Company's wooden houses cleaned and disinfected, and installed a clean water system.[26] As a result, the Marines suffered very little sickness. Civilian, Navy, and Marine officials were pleased with Lejeune's selection for the camp. One newspaper reporter saw the camp as "beautiful, well laid out, and allowing the maximum in comfort and health."[27] Despite his persistent drive for soldierly proficiency, Lejeune never forgot the welfare of his men. Although 70 percent of the native population had some form of malaria (and there were sporadic cases of yellow fever among the Marines at Panama during Lejeune's tenure), no case of yellow fever occurred at his camp. Chief sanitary officer of the Isthmian Canal Commission, Colonel W. C. Gorgas, told Lejeune: "Your command remained in excellent state of health during the time they were on the Isthmus. I attributed it to the care and attention which you personally gave to sanitary measures among them, and also to the excellent state of sanitary discipline in which the men were kept."[28]

To keep the Marines busy during off-duty hours and away from the foul liquor, gambling, and prostitutes at nearby towns, Lejeune developed competitive athletic programs, especially an excellent baseball league in which each company competed four afternoons a week. He also gave out hunting passes and assigned camp-improvement projects.[29]

When Coghlan warned Lejeune that an expedition of four hundred men had left Cartagena, Colombia, "with a determination of invading Panama,"[30] Lejeune, who had already personally reconnoitered the area and developed defensive plans, positioned his troops for defense and attack.[31] The attack never came. In late March, Colombia recalled its troops and announced it would not invade Panama.[32] For the Navy, Lejeune also selected the site for a wireless station. In November of 1904, Lejeune mobilized his entire battalion and prevented an insurrection by General Esteban Huertas's Panamanian Army against the civilian government of President Dr. Manuel Guerrero Amador.

Lejeune enjoyed good relations with the Navy until Rear Admiral Charles D. Sigbee replaced Coghlan as CO of the Caribbean Squadron and placed Lieutenant Commander Hilary P. Jones, junior in rank to Lejeune, aboard the *Scorpion* off Colón to direct Lejeune's battalion at Empire. Before the transfer, Coghlan had supervised Lejeune himself and given his subordinate discretion in the management of tactical events on the isthmus. Sigbee, however, had apparently returned to the command practice of the days of sail when naval officers commanded Marines on shore, placing a naval officer junior to Lejeune to supervise Lejeune's tactical authority on land. Lejeune thought he had settled the rank issue aboard the *Massachusetts* in 1900, but here there was a complication, for the secretary of the Navy had assigned "the duty of preserving the integrity of the transit across the Isthmus . . . to the senior naval officer present, either at Colón or Panama, without regard to squadron."[33]

Lejeune nonetheless believed Navy Department regulations superseded temporary arrangements of command and quickly worded his dissent to Sigbee's order. "Lieutenant Commander Jones is junior to me," he wrote to the admiral, "and I therefore respectfully protest against being placed under his command."[34] The point at issue was a debatable, highly technical one, and obviously Sigbee was miffed when a lowly Marine officer challenged his decision. Sigbee used the full force of his authority to quash the young Marine's protest. "I regret," he wrote Lejeune, "that you should see fit . . . to protest against my orders to Lieutenant Commander Hilary P. Jones." After a lengthy rebuttal to Lejeune's carefully worded argument, he proceeded to reprimand his subordinate: "Although bearing in mind your continuous zeal and ability while under my command, I regret that you should have seen fit to protest against orders without more fully acquainting yourself with regulations and precedents." "An officer," he concluded, "should not lightly protest against orders received or indeed use the word 'protest' when it can be avoided. It is better official form to submit an 'appeal,' or to ask for reconsideration."[35]

Although it was a repeat performance of Lejeune's discontent aboard the *Panther,* he nevertheless placed his opposition on record to an admiral of the Navy, a command problem that often plagued Navy–Marine Corps relationships. Within the corps, Lejeune's action strengthened his reputation for being an advocate for Marine rights, reinforced the belief among progressive Marines that the senior Marine should command ashore, and revealed that he valued principle even more than the maintenance of congenial (but unsatisfactory) intraservice command relationships. In fact, however, Lejeune continued to exercise tactical direction and supervision of his Marines in Panama.

Lejeune's last official duty as his assignment ended in Panama was to personally escort Secretary of War William Howard Taft during his inspection tour of the isthmus. Lejeune and the members of the battalion were eager to return home after their long assignment when Lieutenant Colonel Thomas N. Wood's battalion arrived to assume the defense of Panama. Governor-General E. W. Davis looked upon Major Lejeune's departure with regret, for civilian-military relations had been excellent, due largely to the diplomatic efforts of Lejeune. "It gives me great pleasure," wrote the governor, "to say that your work on the Isthmus since I came here has been of great assistance and of the utmost satisfaction to me."[36]

Appreciation of Lejeune's tenure at Panama next came from an unexpected quarter, the Navy. "The conduct, bearing, and efficiency of the Caribbean battalion while under your command, gave me the greatest satisfaction," wrote Rear Admiral Coghlan, "and its work under regular war conditions on the Isthmus of Panama, all last winter, reflected the greatest credit on yourself as its commander." Then, the admiral, not unmindful of Navy-Marine friction over command relationships, added: "Your own cheerful example in smoothing the way under the new conditions of service showed a lively appreciation of, and a determination to overcome all the perplexities of our work. . . . with such help a Commander-in-Chief always feels that the enemy alone is all he has to fight."[37]

Panama was a transitional step in Lejeune's career and for the future of amphibious operations. For the first time, with his initial important command, Lejeune was strategically placed during a major historical event on a national stage, securing the Isthmus of Panama for the canal builders and winning recognition from top military and civilian leaders.[38] Lejeune also acquired a favorable reputation among many Navy and Marine officers of intermediate command (one or two grades above Lejeune), men who would soon rise to positions of prominence in the military establishment. Their support was essential for Lejeune's further advancement. Such support, for example, came from Commander Lucien Young of the *USS Montgomery,* an officer who commanded the naval station off Colón. "I sincerely trust that you will continue with the same good results you made for yourself on the Isthmus. You certainly deserve a great deal of credit and I don't know but what the [Navy] Department will, in the course of time, give you full credit. . . . I would like to shake your hand before going away."[39]

Most important for Lejeune and the Marine Corps was that the acquisition of the Canal Zone by the United States was a joint Navy and Marine Corps venture, a sea-to-shore amphibious operation that provided momentum towards a new mission for the corps.

After leave spent with his family, and the birth of another daughter, Eugenia Dickson, Lejeune received assignment on January 16, 1905, as CO of the Marine Barracks at Washington, DC. In addition, Lejeune became advisor to the commandant from 1905 to 1907, where he was responsible for drafting regulations for the government of the corps. His recommendations—after review by various boards, Major General Elliott, and heads of the staff departments—would be submitted to the secretary of the Navy.[40] Most important, Elliott asked Lejeune to recommend personnel changes to a committee that was to appear before Congress. Thus Lejeune began his crusade for promotion by selection rather than seniority. Lejeune suggested that majors and company-grade officers—men who led Marines into battle and were often over fifty years of age—should be younger and that the relative proportion of senior-grade officers be increased to make room for exceptionally qualified junior officers. Further, all inefficient, unfit, or morally unqualified officers were a burden to the corps and should be placed immediately on the inactive list. Finally, since Congress would not allow promotion or retirement by selection (only by seniority), he recommended rigid examinations for promotions up to and including the senior grades by permanent boards. This would ensure superior leadership and allow retirement of officers passed over for promotion. While most of Lejeune's recommendations were too progressive for that era, they revealed his modern approach to old problems, and eventually all became law.[41]

One early characteristic of Lejeune that distinguished him from many military men of the day was his habit of rewarding keen intelligence whenever he discovered that trait in junior officers or officer candidates. One striking illustration occurred in the spring of 1905. At that time, Major Lejeune served as president of a board examining seventeen young men from civil life competing for eight vacancies for commissions as second lieutenants in the Marine Corps. Bennet Puryear Jr., a recent Texas A&M graduate, scored highest on the mental exam but failed the physical due to a minor physical defect. Although it was easily correctable by minor surgery, rules specified that he could not be commissioned until physically qualified. To Puryear's surprise, Lejeune recommended that Puryear be commissioned upon completion of the surgery ahead of the other successful candidates. While he was not sworn in until September, his commission dated back to June 19, allowing him to rank the others—a very important factor in those days of promotion by seniority. "Major Lejeune impressed me at that time," recalled Puryear, "as eminently fair, friendly, and helpful. Without any solicitation on my part he advised me, and was instrumental in getting me (still a civilian) admitted to the navy hospital where a navy surgeon operated." Puryear went on to say that Lejeune was not what is called a "'spit and polish' soldier, but in my humble opinion an eminently able, courageous, and honest one. His word was as good as his bond. Naturally, I started my career in the Marine Corps with great liking and affection for John A. Lejeune."[42]

Lejeune led another battalion to Panama in 1906 as part of the provisional regiment commanded by Lieutenant Colonel J. E. Mahoney to prevent violence during new elections at the city of Panama.[43] On this expedition Lejeune was unable to protect the health of his battalion because the governor of the Canal Zone, Charles E. Magoon, insisted that Lejeune's battalion camp near Panama rather than at the Marine camp at Bas Obispo. Magoon overruled Mahoney's and Lejeune's objections and stationed Lejeune's battalion at Corozal, which was low, swampy, and void of adequate mosquito protection. "The mosquito [menace] was much greater than at Camp Elliott," wrote the Navy surgeon-general, "and while all men were given mosquito nets for sleeping . . . it was impossible to avoid mosquito bites. . . . During the period July 13th–21st, 1906, when the strength of the battalion was 298 officers and men, 215 or 72% had acute malarial paroxysms. Probably the whole battalion was infected."[44] Due to the sickness, the transport *Columbia* departed Panama with Lejeune's battalion for Boston. On July 21, Lejeune, one of the many with violent chills, transferred to the Chelsea Naval Hospital. Fortunately, no fatal cases occurred and Lejeune recovered in about two months. The lesson learned, as summarized in a letter by Lejeune to Elliott, was: "In connection with the malarial infection of the battalion, [there is] danger involved in the interference with military dispositions by civilian officials. That the shoemaker should stick to his lot is a safe rule to follow, especially in dealing with the operations of military forces."[45]

In 1907 Lejeune was ordered to the Philippines by Elliott for service with the US Asiatic Fleet and the First Brigade of Marines stationed at Manila.[46] There Lejeune helped develop an ABF to fortify the entrance to Subic Bay on Grande Island during a "war scare" with Japan. Japan, with military victories over China in the Sino-Japanese War in 1895 and over Russia in 1904–5, had become a formidable naval power in the western Pacific. "Japan," wrote President Theodore Roosevelt, "was a power jealous, sensitive and warlike, which if irritated could at once take both the Philippines and Hawaii from us if she obtained the upper hand on the seas."[47] The "war scare" occurred when labor unions in California sought to exclude immigration of Japanese workmen who would work for less pay than American workers. Accordingly, the San Francisco school board segregated Asians from American children, designating on October 11, 1906, a special "Oriental Public School" for all Japanese, Chinese, and Korean students.[48] A further strain on Japanese-American relations occurred when the California Assembly passed a bill limiting Japanese and Chinese land ownership, prompting an angry barrage of Japanese protests.[49]

As tensions increased, the Marines in the Philippines received orders on July 1, 1907, to fortify the entrance to Subic Bay (fifty miles northwest of the Cavite Navy Yard, across Manila Bay and the Bataan Peninsula) with thirty-five naval guns of 3-, 4.7-, and 6-inch caliber located at the Cavite Navy Yard. Under the immediate command of Major Eli K. Cole, Lejeune's Marines at Cavite moved the guns from the ordnance park to Manila Bay, loaded them on barges, towed them to a supply ship, and hoisted the guns aboard. The Marines at Olongapo (near Subic Bay and Grande Island) unloaded the guns, hauled them up to gun positions on Grande Island and the mainland, dug gun pits, mounted and manned the guns. All this work was done during the typhoon season under heavy rain and storms.[50]

Lejeune and Cole were only partially successful in the establishment of an ABF, because the manual movement of thirty-five heavy cannon from the Cavite Navy Yard to Subic Bay was difficult and slow. The Marines also had to dig rifle pits, emplace the artillery, and work with worn-out and obsolete naval equipment and materials. Further, the cannon had no fire-control systems. Although the Marines worked diligently in this endeavor, it became obvious that the ABF as conceived by the Navy and Marine Corps needed considerable improvement to become functional.[51]

Fortunately for the United States, no Japanese amphibious attack came, for this crisis was resolved by President Roosevelt and the State Department. San Francisco opened its regular schools to Japanese children, and the president, with Japanese and congressional approval, limited the immigration of Japanese laborers to the United States.[52]

Lejeune became the temporary brigade commander in the Philippines and was promoted after Colonel William Phillips Biddle, the Marine brigade commander at Manila, returned to the United States in April of 1908, followed shortly after by the ill Lieutenant Colonel James E. Mahoney. Lejeune was promoted to lieutenant colonel by the Naval Appropriations Act of May 13, 1908, which made Marine Commandant Elliott a major general.[53]

At this time, Lejeune and all Marines were stunned when President Roosevelt suddenly ordered the Marine ship guards to be removed from Navy ships. This crisis for the corps was sparked when the Marine Corps's nemesis, William F. Fullam, now a commander in the Navy and still the leader of the "progressive" naval officers, tried once again to remove Marines from naval warships. Fullam still felt that Marine guards aboard ship were an insult to the efficiency and self-respect of sailors. Fullam and the progressives also wanted to remove other perceived threats to the power of naval line officers by abolishing the Navy Bureau System and adopting a general staff system similar to the one recently enacted by the Army. This time Fullam had the attention of Commander William S. Sims, naval aid to Roosevelt. At about the same time, on October 16, 1908, Rear Admiral John E. Pillsbury, chief of the Bureau of Navigation, convinced Secretary of the Navy Victor H. Metcalf to substitute sailors for Marines aboard ship. Seemingly the last to know of these actions, MGC Elliott met directly with Roosevelt on November 9 in an attempt to keep Marines aboard warships, but it was too late. Roosevelt was firmly committed to removing Marines from naval warships. To make matters worse for the corps, when Roosevelt asked Elliott if he felt that removing Marines aboard the ships would signal the end of the corps, Elliott answered that he, unlike many other Marine officers, did not see the abolition of the ships' guards as the "death knell" of the corps. Overly optimistic, Elliott then drafted an executive order redefining the corps's duties as manning Navy yards and stations, guarding the Isthmian Canal Zone, and furnishing expeditionary forces for service around the world.

Roosevelt incorporated Elliott's memorandum into Executive Order 969 (November 12, 1908), which removed Marines from ships. Many Marine officers, including Lejeune, perceived this order as abolishing the Marine Corps. Elliott, however, had obeyed his CinC and was determined to define a new mission for the corps, forbidding disgruntled Marine officers from lobbying Congress to reverse Roosevelt's decision. That Elliott was wrong in trusting Roosevelt's word that he wanted to see the corps develop a new mission was validated when Major General Leonard Wood of the Army, a confidant and friend of Roosevelt, but an enemy of the Marine Corps, proposed to incorporate the corps into the Army. Roosevelt supported Wood on this issue. When Marine officers began lobbying Congress to stop Roosevelt and the Army in this bid to eliminate the corps, an irritated Roosevelt expressed his true feelings about the corps to his military aid: "The Marines' influence which they have gained by pandering to every political influence, has given them such an abnormal position for the size of their corps that they have simply invited their own destruction. They should be absorbed into the

Army and no vestige of their organization should be allowed to remain."[54]

Justifiably feeling he had been betrayed by Roosevelt, Elliott now led the fight in Congress to rescind the president's order. Lejeune, still in the Philippines, was concerned over the entire affair: "We are still waiting news of the final outcome of the fight in Congress over the future of the Marine Corps. If Marines are not restored to the ships, there is no future ahead of us as a Corps, and a transfer to the Army will be the eventual outcome."[55] Fortunately for the corps, the House Naval Affairs Committee, led by Chairman Thomas S. Butler, father of Marine Captain Smedley Butler, recommended to the House the restoration of Marine guards to the ships. The Senate, by a vote of fifty-one to twelve, also voted to restore Marine guards to the ships. When the Navy Board recommended restoring the Marines to Navy battleships and cruisers to a new secretary of the Navy, George von Lengerke Meyer, and to the new president, William Howard Taft, Meyer issued an order on March 26, 1909, reinstating the old regulations.[56]

Lejeune, like a few other progressive Marine officers, was frustrated that Marine Headquarters and Elliott were also slow in developing a fully operational ABF, a promise made by Heywood, the preceding commandant, to the Navy and General Board. The General Board and Admiral Dewey were also disappointed in the corps's failure to form a fixed defense regiment.[57] While keeping an official silence, Lejeune in a letter to his sister revealed his feelings for Elliott. He called Elliott "weak" for not insisting that Lejeune's overdue replacement in the Philippines adhere to the official schedule.[58] Elliott's quick temper created another controversy, an incident that threatened the corps from within. When Elliott berated his adjutant and inspector, Colonel Charles H. Lauchheimer, the adjutant took what he perceived as insulting behavior to Secretary of the Navy Meyer. Concerned that this public feud and personality clash would provoke a scandal in the press, Meyer censured both Elliott and Lauchheimer. Later, this "disgraceful controversy" led Meyer on March 5, 1910, to order a board of inquiry. Although the board determined that Elliott had failed to maintain discipline at headquarters, the problem was deemed not grave enough to warrant a court-martial. Meyer detached Lauchheimer and Colonel Frank L. Denny, quartermaster, from headquarters, and Elliott retired because of age on November 30, 1910.[59]

A major step in the advancement of Lejeune's career was his performance at the fourteen-month course at the AWC,[60] September 1909 to October 1910. His success here strongly influenced his selection later by the Army to command a division in World War I. Lejeune's leadership as CO of the Second Division secured his reputation as the most prominent and popular Marine in the corps and ensured his selection as MGC of the Marine Corps in 1920.

The AWC utilized the applicatory method of instruction, a system developed by Helmuth von Moltke that enabled Lejeune to delve deeply into the art and science of military technique and the acquisition of sound military judgment. Lejeune had to earn his success at the college, however, for he had not received any formal military instruction since his brief orientation course as a second lieutenant in 1890. Lejeune studied late into the night, immersed in field manuals, charts, maps, and practical exercises. For all practical purposes, Lejeune became an Army officer, and he formed lasting friendships with officers destined for high command, such as Hunter Liggett, Fox Conner, and Marlin Craig. Lejeune developed simulated campaign studies based on the Franco-Prussian War of 1871 and the American Civil War. Later, when the AWC decided that Japan, not Germany, would be the next opponent in war,[61] Lejeune developed two case studies on the military geography of Guam and Alaska.[62] He wrote operational reports on how to defend California, Samoa, and Guam from an enemy attack and developed plans to attack Samoa and Guam.[63] Given the small contingent of Marines and the weak defense at Guam in the exercises (a similar condition that existed at Guam in early World War II), Lejeune recommended an orderly withdrawal of Marines to Hawaii. Unfortunately, in 1941, the United States did not withdraw the small force defending Guam. These Marines surrendered to the Japanese.

The thoroughness of the course and Lejeune's efforts paid off, giving him a vigorous sense of professional competency. "In looking back on my career . . . during the years that followed the completion of the course I have been conscious that I possessed greater mental power than I before realized, and have felt able to meet successfully any difficulty which might confront me, or to overcome an obstacle which I might find in my path."[64] Lejeune's achievements and reputation at the AWC became common knowledge within the Marine Corps. "Lejeune . . . not only posted the finest record ever made there," wrote General Gerald C. Thomas, USMC (Ret.), himself a distinguished Marine, but "impressed everyone who observed him there. Pershing *had* to give him a division in the war."[65] General Clifton B. Cates—a future commandant—was one of many young officers during this period who remembered Lejeune first and foremost as "a very brainy man who stood at the top of his class at the Army War course."[66]

Likely because of the confidence earned during his course at the AWC and his considerable ambition for himself and the corps, Lejeune, only a lieutenant colonel and forty-three years old, became a candidate for commandant during the spring and summer of 1910 when he heard that MGC Elliott was retiring. Lejeune was also concerned about the turmoil and lack of vision at Marine Headquarters and the absence of support from the new president. (Taft had returned Marine guards to the ships, but allowed the captain of the vessel to use Marines as he pleased in violation of the chain of command.) "Headquarters . . . has been badly upset by the recent action of President Taft," Lejeune wrote to his sister. "Fortunately the real Marine Corps is elsewhere and consists of the 10,000 officers and men who are scattered around the world attending to their duties: the politicians who are stationed at Headquarters are the least important part of the Marine Corps."[67]

Lejeune saw several reasons to be optimistic about his candidacy. First, President Taft in the past had often ignored seniority when selecting officers for high positions in the bureaus of the Navy, perhaps opening the door for less senior officers like Lejeune. While Lejeune and his supporters were not opposed to the secretary of the Navy selecting a senior colonel in the corps to be commandant, Lejeune wanted to be considered if the selection process included a review of younger officers. Lejeune, like many Marine officers of the line, was opposed to the selection of a staff officer at headquarters as commandant.[68] Also, Lejeune thought that the senior officers in the corps had records "not altogether good and the Secretary may pass them over."[69] However, Eli K. Cole, Lejeune's classmate and friend at the Naval Academy and junior in seniority to Lejeune, was an active candidate and campaigned hard for the job of commandant. Lejeune wrote that "Lt. Col. Cole . . . has many friends and backing and he is the man that I am most afraid of among my juniors."[70]

Lejeune had strong support for his candidacy for commandant. Senator George F. Chamberlain of Oregon, a cousin by marriage, was an avid supporter of Lejeune.[71] He introduced Lejeune to the senators from Louisiana, Samuel Douglas McEnery and Murphy J. Foster. These three senators visited several times with the secretary and the assistant secretary of the Navy as advocates of Lejeune.[72] While Lejeune's early quest for commandant was not successful, he had conducted a low-key and respectable campaign and was now on record as a candidate for the job at a later date. The senior colonels and their supporters in Congress, on the other hand, had waged bitter campaigns. After "a long and controversial period of political maneuvering," President Taft selected William F. Biddle, a senior colonel and member of a prominent and powerful Pennsylvania family. Biddle was supported by Senator Boies Penrose of Pennsylvania, who threatened to sabotage Taft's policies in Congress if Biddle was not chosen.[73]

5

EXPEDITIONS AND THE ADVANCED BASE FORCE, 1910–1917

On November 7, 1910, Lieutenant Colonel Lejeune assumed command of the Brooklyn Marine Barracks, the Marine Corps's largest post concentration of Marines, and embarked on the work that distinguished him as one of the corps's most successful administrators. The discipline of the Flushing Avenue Marines had been notoriously poor for years. The desertion and absent without leave (AWOL) rate ran nearly 10 percent a year—easily the highest in the corps. Almost immediately, Lejeune instituted a rigorous new program to minimize idleness, commonly known as "bunk fatigue." Much to the consternation of his officers, who believed that a sudden change would create ill will and a rebellious attitude among the men, Lejeune ordered all previously excused special and extra-duty personnel to attend reveille, drill, and classes of military instruction; revoked all special privileges such as liberty passes; promptly punished all men convicted of drunkenness and disorderly conduct on duty; improved meals and post entertainment; directed his officers to closely supervise chronic misbehavior; and established an active post athletic program. Most important, he treated his 325 permanent-post Marines (expeditionary) and 125 recruits (trainees) fairly and equally.[1]

Lejeune's actions bore fruit. Desertion decreased from a high of 8.5 percent in 1909 to 5.5 percent in 1911, 3 percent in 1912, and 2 percent in 1913.[2] Major Albert S. McLemore, assistant adjutant and inspector, noted the vast improvement in his annual report of October 30, 1913: "The general condition and efficiency of this post. . . . was most excellent, and especial credit should attach to the commanding officer, Lieutenant Colonel John A.

Lejeune. . . . I believe that this officer has manifestly and notably contributed, by his attention to duty, his ability, and energy, towards this condition of efficiency."[3] MGC William Biddle wrote to Lejeune that "these commendatory remarks by the Inspecting Officer are highly gratifying to me, and reflect much credit upon your administration of affairs at that post. I have directed that a copy of this letter be filed with your official record in the Adjutant and Inspector's Department."[4]

While Lejeune still had occasional problems with naval policy that hindered the development of the Marine Corps, he had learned through bitter experience how best to challenge what he considered naval partisanship at the expense of the corps. When Lejeune felt that a naval regulation discriminated against the Marine Corps, he respectfully asked the Navy for "reconsideration." In this case, on April 25, 1911, when the Navy Department and the commandant of the New York Navy Yard and Station, Rear Admiral E. H. C. Leutze, determined that only the offices of the naval commandant, not the CO of the Marine Barracks, could display the national ensign (the American flag), Lejeune requested reconsideration. Lejeune believed that the 400 to 500 enlisted Marines, chiefly recruits under instruction, needed to see the flag. Lejeune wrote, "I deem it of great importance that these recruits should be taught to respect and revere the colors from the very beginning of their careers in the service." Because of Lejeune's persistence, the naval order was suspended and the Marines were allowed to display the national ensign above the Marine Barracks.[5]

Lejeune wanted more field duty in addition to his administrative work. When President Taft and MGC Biddle mobilized officers and men from Lejeune's Marine Barracks for expeditions to revolutionary Mexico and Cuba, Lejeune voiced his displeasure at not being included in the expeditions. "I then and there went on record," Lejeune noted in his autobiography, "as an applicant for duty with every expeditionary force. I took this action because I wanted the field experience . . . and because I felt convinced that one's military reputation could only be enhanced through . . . active service in the field."[6]

Consequently, Lejeune commanded a battalion of four companies that joined senior Colonel Lincoln Karmany's First Provisional Brigade that landed and operated out of Fisherman's Point, Guantanamo, Cuba, in June of 1912. While Cuba was theoretically independent, it was a virtual American protectorate under an American-designed constitution and the Pratt

Amendment of 1901.[7] Lejeune's companies guarded American properties of copper and iron mines, railroads, and sugar mills in Oriente Province, allowing Cuban forces to defeat rebel bands led by Evaristo Estenoz's black "Army of Vindication."[8] Estenoz's army had revolted against the Havana government's Marau Law that prohibited a "colored party," and had destroyed American property in Oriente Province.[9]

The protection afforded by Lejeune's Marines around Santiago had been completely effective, so much so that D. B. Whitaker, vice president and general manager of the Juragua Iron Company, sent a letter of appreciation to the secretary of the Navy: "I cannot praise too highly the soldierly bearing, faithful performance of duty and high state of discipline of the officers and men, and I feel certain that their efficient and untiring efforts prevented the destruction of a large amount of property and more than likely the loss of a number of valuable lives." Then the manager gave his opinion of Lieutenant Colonel Lejeune: "I have lived in Cuba since 1898 and have had the pleasure of coming into close contact with many of the officers stationed here during two American interventions, and although the standards set by them have been very high, Colonel Lejeune seems to me to be conspicuous among them as an honor to his profession and a credit to the service."[10]

Lejeune returned to Cuba under Colonel George Barnett's First Regiment, part of the Atlantic Fleet, in response to the alleged murder of Francisco I. Madero by counterrevolutionary Victoriano Huerta during the "tragic ten days" in Mexico City, February 9–18, 1913.[11] Although Mexico entered into a bitter civil war that potentially endangered American lives and property, Washington retained the Marine brigade at Deer Point, Cuba, for two months, but decided against a Mexican intervention. One significant accomplishment from Lejeune's service in Cuba, however, was the establishment of the Marine Corps Association. Discussions by senior officers of the First Provisional Marine Brigade in Cuba—the largest force of Marines that had ever served together, including ninety-three officers, more than 25 percent of the commissioned strength of the corps—prompted the creation of the association. Most of these senior officers were still angry over Commandant George Elliott's acquiescence to Roosevelt's removal of Marines from capital ships in 1908 and continued efforts by President Taft and senior naval officers such as Robley D. Evans, Bradley A. Fiske, J. N. Hemphill, and especially William F. Fullam to undermine the existence and status of the Marine Corps. These Marine Corps officers—with Lejeune heading the standing committee—developed a written charter to oppose naval efforts to curb the traditional missions of the corps and to educate the officer corps on the Marine Corps's value to the Navy, primarily through the development of the ABF.[12] In addition, the association published its initial issue of the *Marine Corps Gazette* (*MCG*) in 1916, featuring Lejeune's article on the ABF as the first article.[13]

Lejeune also played a crucial role in the successful demonstration of a large-scale ABF in the Caribbean. The Culebra maneuvers took place because the General Board—dissatisfied with the reluctance of Commandants Heywood and Elliott to establish a permanent ABF—held hearings in September 1913 on the inability of the Marine Corps to form an operational ABF.[14] Thus, the General Board finally decided that the time had come to see if the Navy and Marine Corps could actually establish an ABF during the Atlantic Fleet's winter maneuvers of 1913–14. A few naval officers, especially Captain William Fullam, now in a position of influence, launched a campaign to convince Rear Admiral Bradley A. Fiske, aide for operations, that the Marines were incapable of staging successful maneuvers without a naval officer in charge. Despite considerable theoretical discussion, a few small demonstrations from 1901 to 1903, and writing within the Navy Department and the Marine Corps about the future of amphibious operations, little had been done since the Navy Board recommended the ABF concept and mission for the corps in 1900. Secretary of the Navy George von L. Meyer and his successor, Josephus Daniels, agreed with the board and ordered MGC Biddle to complete the assembly of force equipment at Philadelphia and organize an ABF brigade of about 1,600 men. The brigade would make an actual landing from the fleet, emplace guns, and repel a simulated enemy attack on the naval base.[15]

Accordingly, Biddle pledged his support and worked to provide a force of 1,797 officers and men for the exercise.[16] For this monumental effort by the corps, Biddle selected Colonel George Barnett, CO of the Philadelphia barracks and the ABF School, to command the corps's first operational brigade. The brigade was composed of the first regiment (fixed defense), commanded by Lieutenant Colonel Charles G. Long, and the second regiment (mobile defense), commanded by Lieutenant Colonel John Lejeune.[17] This brigade was directed to land in early January 1914, on Culebra Island, Puerto Rico.

The purpose of the ABF was for the brigade to land, establish, and defend a temporary naval base in order to support the fleet. The brigade would fortify the base and repel an assault from a small enemy fleet of cruisers, freeing up the American Fleet to pursue and destroy the main enemy fleet at sea. According to War Plan Black, the attacker would be Imperial Germany, considered at this time a greater threat than Japan. The war plan assumed that Germany would need a temporary naval base near the entrance to the Caribbean Sea to replenish its fleet before attacking the American Fleet and the US mainland.[18]

Thus, the corps was now on center stage, challenged to successfully carry out the planned amphibious operation. While Marine Headquarters and the ABF School worked to prepare the corps for the winter fleet maneuvers, Biddle spent an inordinate amount of time and energy defending the corps against its naval detractors. The corps's old nemesis, Fullam, now a captain and aide for inspections to the secretary of the Navy, chose this time to challenge the Marines' ability to perform the ABF mission. Fullam complained in several letters to the secretary of the Navy that the Marine Corps was unprepared to establish an advance naval base: "Considered from the viewpoint of real efficiency for war purposes, it may be said that practically nothing has been accomplished during the past thirteen years." Fullam again demanded that Marines be removed from battleships and cruisers and formed into permanent battalions for the ABF.[19]

Fortunately for the Marines, the General Board supported the corps and discounted Fullam's claims, blaming the Navy for not supplying the proper equipment to develop the ABF.[20] Further, "Daniels chose neither to support his aid nor to force either the General Board or the Corps to implement [Fullam's] reforms."[21]

A further challenge was another war scare with Japan, created when the California legislature passed a bill in April 1913 forbidding aliens "ineligible for citizenship" from owning land. The United States classed Japanese and other Asians as aliens ineligible for citizenship. The bill precipitated a large demonstration in Tokyo against California's insult to all Asians in general and the Japanese in particular. This threat of war placed additional pressure on the Navy and Marine Corps to establish a workable ABF. As William Braisted noted, "There were subsequent diplomatic efforts by the two governments to reach some sort of settlement, but the sting of discrimination remained to poison relations between the countries through the years to come."[22]

Lejeune faced a personal challenge to do well at the Culebra maneuvers when he applied once again for the job as MGC after Biddle suddenly announced in November 1913 his intention to retire after the maneuvers in January 1914.[23] From his post at the Brooklyn Navy Yard, Lejeune "took the train that afternoon for Washington, and remained there until last night. I found a big fight in progress and did all I could for myself. Cousin George is doing yeoman service, also Dr. Kennedy, and other friends. I have left no stone unturned that I thought would have weight."[24] Secretary Daniels interviewed Lejeune and told him it would be some time before the selection was made: "I have not yet concluded to go below the rank of colonel, and I will come to no decision until I have laid the whole matter before the President."[25] Lejeune was busy in Pensacola, Florida, preparing his regiment for the Culebra maneuvers, but kept in touch with Washington about the selection decision for commandant. By December, Lejeune wrote, "I have little hope that I will be the one and therefore will suffer no disappointment. . . . I only desire it because I am ambitious to reach the highest rung of the ladder and because I feel that I might be able to do good service for our country."[26]

Lejeune's mobile defense regiment on the transport *Prairie* and Long's fixed defense regiment aboard the transport *Hancock* landed at Culebra on January 9, 1914. While it took nine days for the fixed defense regiment to manually haul its heavy guns and equipment ashore, by January 18 the regiment had deployed with its five-inch and three-inch naval guns along the southwestern and southern coast of Culebra. The regiment positioned minefields to protect Great Harbor, a deeply recessed cove on the southern shore where the American Fleet placed its fleet train.[27] Lejeune's lighter mobile regiment disembarked more quickly, as Lejeune positioned one infantry battalion on the southeastern coast of Culebra to protect the left flank of Great Harbor. To maximize this protection, Lejeune stationed one company offshore at the islet of Culebrita and positioned his second battalion, supported by the automatic-rifle company, along the western and northwestern shoreline of Culebra to be able to sweep the likely landing beaches of the forthcoming enemy assault. In the rear of his infantry, Lejeune located his three-inch gun company on a hill to support the defense.

The enemy attack on Culebra began on the night of January 18, when ships of the Atlantic Fleet simulated an enemy bombardment on the Marine shore batteries and attempted to sweep the minefields. In turn, the Marine mining company ashore simulated the detonation of mines placed under enemy ships. On January 21, shortly before dawn, twelve hundred

Marines and sailors landed on the western coast, supported by naval gunfire. The Marine defenders responded immediately, pouring simulated rifle, machine gun, and artillery fire on the approaching boatloads of sailors and Marines. The chief umpire, naval Captain William S. Sims, noted that the landing boats were clearly visible because of the light from the moon, the searchlights from the bombarding "enemy" ships, and the bonfire lighted by the Marine defenders on the beach. Strangely enough, the sailors were dressed in white uniforms, an easy target for the defense. Sims decided that "it is improbable that the landing force could have affected a successful landing in sufficient numbers to have made any impression on the defense." Because of a prior arrangement with Colonel Barnett, Sims allowed the attackers to continue their assault from the beach. Soon after, however, at 7:00 a.m., he ordered a ceasefire and awarded a victory for the defense.[28]

For the Marine Corps, the successful Culebra defensive maneuver proved that the corps could, on short notice, put together an effective ABF to defeat an enemy assault from the fleet. In addition, the corps began to develop amphibious doctrine, such as the importance of combat loading of the transports, the need for proper landing craft, the necessity for ground transportation once ashore, and the usefulness of aircraft for reconnaissance. The most important result was that a Marine ABF finally was functional.[29] Despite their frequent use as expeditionary forces in Mexico, Hispaniola, and Cuba, the ABF became a fixture for the Marine Corps until almost the end of the decade.[30] As we shall see, however, the concept of the ABF—a defensive force operating near the United States—would be challenged by a few progressives in the corps, men such as Lejeune and Earl Hancock "Pete" Ellis. These Marines, familiar with the Navy's War Plan Orange[31] (war with Japan), realized that islands in the Pacific would be held and fortified by the enemy, necessitating an offensive operation to capture and establish a naval and air base for the fleet. This action would require a highly trained expeditionary assault force.

Lejeune's comments in his operational report on Culebra added to the accumulation of doctrine and techniques for Navy–Marine Corps amphibious operations. Lejeune recognized that the Navy needed larger and more modern transport ships. He wrote that "the *U.S.S. Prairie* is unfit for use as a transport for such a large number of men. . . . the messing and the berthing arrangements . . . are almost unendurable. . . . the bathing and washing facilities are wholly insufficient. . . . the ventilation of the lower decks is poor. . . .

more than 400 men should not be transported on board the *U.S.S. Prairie.*" The tools "for entrenching and clearing ground were very unsatisfactory" as well. This included machetes, picks, scythes, drills, wire cutters, axes, and spades.

The most important lesson learned was that land transportation was sorely needed. "It is absolutely necessary to provide means to carry equipment, rations, ammunition, water, and other supplies from the landing places to the defensive positions to be occupied by the troops." Lejeune's men had only a few packhorses available. Lejeune recommended that special service outfits should not be scattered about the brigade but placed under the command of the brigade commander in order to have a more flexible defense. In particular, he recommended that the brigade commander should have available to him the general service company, with teamsters, packers, and blacksmiths; the signal company; the engineer company; and the three-inch gun companies. For his mobile regiment, Lejeune needed more men: twelve infantry companies and one automatic machine-gun company of 125 men. Finally, Lejeune recommended that his men be encamped and exercised on shore as often as possible: "Nothing lowers more quickly the morale, efficiency, and physical condition of a military force than its long continuance on board of a transport."[32]

As far as the Navy was concerned, the Navy–Marine Corps team effort at Culebra went smoothly with only one major problem. While Admiral Charles J. Badger, the CinC of the Atlantic Fleet and the overall commander of the operation, was satisfied with the maneuver, he "regretted that the lost mines could not be recovered." The Navy and the Marine Corps offered different opinions as to the cause of the lost mines. Colonel George Barnett reported that the mining gear was broken and the mines became adrift or "hauled off into deep water by the [Navy] mine-dragging operations."[33] Admiral Badger, however, believed that the naval sweeping operations to recover the mines were not at fault. He thought that the laying of the mines (by Marines) was "unavoidably hurried and the maximum benefit could not be derived therefore." Moreover, Badger wrote that "the importance of this work to the Fleet has, perhaps naturally enough, not been fully appreciated by the officers of the [Marine] Brigade." Badger concluded his remarks by stating that the island of Culebra should not be developed as a permanent ABF in time of war because of the probability that enemy armored ships with great guns could destroy at long range the American Fleet train.[34] The overall result of this incident was a change in technique and further improvement in Navy–Marine Corps amphibious operations. In the future, the Navy would lay out mines in defensive operations.

At the conclusion of the Culebra maneuver, Secretary Daniels appointed George Barnett as MGC in early February 1914. Barnett turned over command of the brigade to Lejeune and left Pensacola on February 15 to assume his new duties in Washington. The decision was not an easy one for Daniels. The leading candidate was again senior Colonel Littleton W. T. Waller, but Daniels and President Woodrow Wilson were working for Philippine independence and Waller had been court-martialed for executing Filipinos during the insurrection. As Daniels recalled, "I became convinced that the best man in the Marine Corps was John A. Lejeune, but his rank was rather low for the position. . . . Senator Weeks, among others, brought my attention to the name of George Barnett. He was not as vigorous or able a man as Waller. He was not as able and learned a soldier as Lejeune, but he had a good record, and he was appointed."[35]

From Pensacola, Lejeune received orders on February 15 to proceed to Washington to take examinations for promotion to the rank of colonel. Consequently, he passed his examination on February 19 and was promoted to colonel that day by the Marine Examining Board.[36] Lejeune was concerned, however, about his next duty assignment, for no one at headquarters knew what the role of the Marine Corps would be in the growing crisis with Mexico. Lejeune wrote that "everyone in the Marine Corps is badly upset, and no one knows where we stand, but at the same time, I think that is the usual state of affairs with us." While Barnett wanted Lejeune to become assistant to the commandant, Lejeune was reluctant to accept the position while he still commanded the ABF Brigade in Pensacola. He accepted Barnett's offer provided the general would allow him to continue his command of the brigade until the crisis with Mexico was over.[37]

The reason for the Marine Corps's amphibious invasion of Mexico in 1914 was President Wilson's refusal to support a "government of butchers," led by General Victoriano Huerta, who had allegedly murdered the revolutionary leader Francisco Madera in early 1913.[38] Throughout the period of November 1913 to April 1914, Wilson used all measures short of war to force Huerta from power, supporting Venustiano Carranza, who had promised to carry out democratic reforms advocated by Madera. During the Mexican Civil War, Wilson sent Rear Admiral Henry T. Mayo with the Fifth Division of the Atlantic Fleet off the Mexican coast near Tampico and placed Rear Admiral Frank Friday Fletcher and his Fourth Division off the coast of Veracruz.

Lejeune's orders were to remain with his regiment aboard the *Hancock* while "the *Prairie* is to take one half of my old regiment down to Vera Cruz where they will wait for something to happen."[39] It was the "Tampico Incident" that gave Wilson his excuse to intervene in Mexico. This minor event occurred on April 9, 1914, when a small group of American sailors went behind Mexican troop lines at Tampico seeking fuel for the *Dolphin*. They were arrested at gunpoint by Mexican troops, but later released. In retaliation, Mayo lodged a strong protest, demanding a formal apology and a twenty-one-gun salute to the American flag. Huerta apologized but refused to provide a twenty-one-gun salute.[40]

Wilson went to Congress for authority to intervene and demand respect for the flag. On April 14 he ordered Vice Admiral Charles J. Badger's Atlantic Fleet to reinforce Mayo and Fletcher. From nearby New Orleans, Lejeune's Marines aboard the *Hancock* arrived at Tampico first, whereupon Mayo sent Lejeune ashore to study the terrain, and together they organized a brigade composed of the *Hancock*'s regiment of Marines, the *Minnesota*'s regiment of sailors, and a third regiment consisting of fleet Marines and sailors. When Mayo received orders from Secretary Daniels on April 20 to clear the Panico River of all American merchant vessels, he prepared to assault Tampico even though Badger's Atlantic Fleet was still one day away. Final plans called for Lejeune to land Marines from the gunboat *Dolphin* and seize the customshouse and fiscal wharf. In support, American cruisers in the river were to sink or capture Mexican gunboats while battleships outside the river would move in close to shore with sailors and Marines ready to land as reserves.

Suddenly, the situation changed drastically when Wilson learned that the steamer *Mexico* had arrived at Veracruz with 1,000 cases of ammunition and that the German steamer *Ypiranga* would arrive on April 21 with 200 machine guns and 15 million cartridges. Disappointed, Mayo called off his attack and dispatched Lejeune and the Marines aboard the *Hancock* along with the *Minnesota* and *Chester* to Veracruz. Fletcher at Veracruz was caught by surprise, but acted swiftly when Daniels ordered him to "seize the custom house . . . [and] not permit war supplies to be delivered to Huerta government or any other party."[41]

Fletcher did not wait for reinforcements that would arrive shortly with Lejeune's Marines on the *Hancock* from Tampico or for the imminent arrival of the entire Atlantic Fleet. Fletcher received Daniels's order of execution at 6:00 a.m. on April 21 and launched his amphibious landing of about 1,000 Marines and sailors under the command of Captain William Rees Rush, US Navy. This force included half of Lieutenant Colonel Wendell C. Neville's Second ABF Regiment of Marines.[42] Aboard the approaching *Hancock,* Lejeune was surprised to learn that Fletcher had not waited for reinforcements: "I don't see why they landed with such a small force when if they had waited until tomorrow 2,500 more men would have been there to assist them. As it is they didn't have enough men to take the town and only hold a small section of it."[43]

Lejeune's judgment was correct: four Americans died, and twenty more fell wounded that first day.[44] Upon his arrival at Veracruz, Lejeune noted that "we witnessed a scene which stirred us to the very depths of our souls."[45] The sailors revealed that their fighting qualities were best afloat. Marching across the open area of the Benito Juarez Park in close order at port arms, the massed formation drew intense rifle fire from the Mexican Naval Academy. Several bluejackets died on the spot. Most of the Marine casualties occurred in the ranks of Randolph Berkeley's and George C. Reid's battalions.[46] In all, about 200 Mexicans died and 300 were wounded; American casualties included 19 dead and 47 wounded.

According to Lejeune, "the night the first landing was made was something fierce, fighting having continued all night and only a small part of the city was held, but early the next morning (4:00 a.m., April 22nd), the Fleet having arrived during the night, about 2,000 more sailors and Marines were landed. . . . We arrived off Vera Cruz last Wednesday morning [April 22] at six o'clock and a most inspiring sight met our eyes. The Marines and sailors were swarming all over the city, firing and being fired at from the buildings, and the ships were firing their big guns at several of the buildings." Lejeune reported to Admiral Fletcher and immediately landed and took command of the Marines on shore, including the *Hancock*'s Marines. Since the city was divided into districts, Lejeune's companies of Marines searched every house and confiscated all arms, arresting every man in a house where arms were found. Further, "guards were posted at all street crossings and before nightfall the entire city was occupied and quiet was restored. This was the second day and night."[47]

Lejeune served as Marine provisional brigade commander from April 22 until senior colonels arrived. Colonel James E. Mahoney arrived on April 29 and took command until Littleton W. T. Waller, the senior line colonel in the corps, arrived on May 4 to command all Marines at Veracruz.[48] The Army's brigade arrived after the fighting was over, on April 29, even though Brigadier General Frederick Funston had awaited trouble in Mexico in Galveston, Texas, for nearly a year. The Army was reluctant to land because an Army invasion generally indicated a declaration of war, something Wilson wanted to avoid.[49] Although Funston was the senior ground commander at Veracruz, the Army's arrival touched off the perennial Army-Navy/Marine Corps debate: who should command all troops and lead an anticipated expedition into Mexico? Lejeune understood that the Marines and sailors who had secured the city were unprepared logistically to sustain a long drive into the Mexican interior. When the Army requested a unified command under Funston, Lejeune accepted the Army's rationale and recommended that all fleet Marines return to their ships while the Marine regiments remained to serve under Army command. Wilson and Daniels supported this position.[50]

The president was horrified by the bloodshed at Veracruz and "accepted an offer by the ABC Powers—Argentina, Brazil, and Chile—to mediate the differences between the two countries."[51] Wilson failed to change the course of the Mexican Civil War, and it continued despite the overthrow of Huerta on June 15, 1914. Carranza claimed to be provisional president, but Pancho Villa's forces occupied Mexico City. After seven months of "watchful waiting" by the Navy, Marine Corps, and Army, Wilson pulled the troops out of Veracruz in November of 1914. The American intervention accomplished little in Mexico, only propagating death and humiliation among the Mexican people, creating anti-American feelings that lingered for years.

One likely reason for President Wilson's disengagement from Veracruz was the start of the Great War in Europe in August 1914, an event that began to dominate American military and political thought.[52] Lejeune returned to Washington to serve as assistant to the commandant, putting in long hours learning the new job and acting for MGC Barnett when he left Washington for inspection trips.[53]

Despite President Wilson's political failure in Mexico, the Marine Corps, the Navy, and Congress learned many important military lessons at Veracruz. First, the corps had deployed units individually as they arrived in transports or with the Atlantic Fleet. The Marines did not develop "composite forces" or build combat power by committing the entire force in the attack. An overwhelming assault when all the Marines had arrived off Veracruz would have saved American and Mexican lives.

Second, the rapid transfer of command as Marine units attacked in a piecemeal manner caused confusion. In the first two weeks, the Marines ashore were commanded first by Lieutenant Colonel Wendell Neville, and, sequentially, by Colonels John Lejeune, James E. Mahoney, and Littleton W. T. Waller. This expedition highlighted the need for Marines to have officers with the rank of brigadier general. In fact, a brigadier general would have coordinated the assault of the corps.

Third, the Marine Corps had a problem with "strategic lift," meaning that the Marine units were scattered about on various Navy ships and could not arrive at Veracruz as one task force ready to attack. At that time, the Navy had only two transports available to carry the Marines and their artillery, equipment, and supplies. Thus, the Marines could not maintain unit integrity. Lejeune's ABF had to leave behind its heavy equipment and an aviation detachment that would have been useful at Veracruz. Most Marines arrived on nineteen battleships, cruisers, colliers, a target ship, and a chartered steamship. Veracruz demonstrated that the need for the Navy to build more transports to carry MEFs.

Fourth, the Marines did not have "sustainability," or the ability to deploy inland to Mexico City as originally planned. This would have required a logistical train of horses, carts, artillery, rations, ammunition, and supplies for an extended operation, which the Marines at Veracruz did not have.

Fifth, the Marines lacked training and the proper equipment for conducting urban warfare. The Mexicans defending buildings in Veracruz inflicted casualties on the Marines as they fought through the streets and buildings with only picks, shovels, and bayonets.[54]

Finally, the Navy and Marines had to learn how to cooperate with the Army in joint operations. Fortunately, Lejeune with his AWC experience appreciated and understood the different roles of the Army and the Marine Corps in amphibious operations. As one historian put it, "He may have been the first Marine to see life beyond the termination of the amphibious operation, a murky area in which we today still are experiencing sharp fights over command relationships."[55] Lejeune also understood that the Army was more prepared logistically to move inland to Mexico.

While the Navy was not yet aware of it, Veracruz was the last time that bluejackets provided the bulk of the men for amphibious landings. At this time, the Marine Corps had not yet developed the amphibious knowledge that would be exhibited during World War II. Consequently, most landing groups were primarily sailors. At Veracruz, however, Marines formed at least half of the men for the amphibious landing.[56] It was during the 1920s when MGC Lejeune developed the MEF and the basic doctrine of amphibious assault that the Navy accepted the fact that it would be the responsibility of the Marine Corps to project naval power ashore.

Lejeune assumed the post of assistant to the commandant on January 2, 1915, serving until September 15, 1917, the "busiest two years and eight months of my career up to that time."[57] Despite the rapid growth of the Navy and Marine Corps because of the war in Europe, the size of Corps Headquarters staff had not changed in three-quarters of a century. It was still composed of the commandant, a few clerks, and three staff positions: adjutant and inspector, quartermaster, and paymaster.[58] Lejeune recognized almost immediately that he needed to act as an executive officer or chief of staff for the commandant in order to fulfill rapidly increasing duties. With the permission of General Barnett, Lejeune utilized the commandant's three aides, Captains Thomas Holcomb, Earl Ellis, and Ralph Keyser. This action prepared headquarters for the future and allowed for war planning.[59]

While Barnett and Lejeune wanted to continue ABF exercises and maneuvers, that proved impossible. The Wilson administration used the Marines as expeditionary forces to occupy Haiti and the Dominican Republic in order to protect American and other interests in the event of violent revolutions. Lejeune was responsible for organizing and dispatching thousands of Marines to these two nations.[60] In addition, Lejeune often represented MGC Barnett on important occasions during Barnett's absence on inspection trips. Thus, Lejeune was a key figure in framing the Marine Corps Personnel Bill, part of the Naval Appropriations Act that became law in June of 1916. This congressional bill mandated the largest increase in ships, equipment, and personnel in naval history up to that date, supporting President Wilson's effort to build a naval fleet "second to none."

As a member of the Naval and Marine Personnel Board, Lejeune joined Assistant Secretary of the Navy Franklin D. Roosevelt; Rear Admirals David W. Taylor and Victor Blue; and Colonel Charles H. Lauchheimer, adjutant and inspector of the Marine Corps, to argue for an increase in corps personnel before the Senate Committee on Naval Affairs. Lejeune—with the approval of Barnett—pressed for an increase in Marine personnel proportionate to the increase in Navy enlisted men. The bill as passed authorized 75,000 sailors and 15,000 Marines with a proviso that President Wilson could further increase the Navy by 12,000 and the Marine Corps by 2,400. While the Navy won authority from Congress to enact promotion by selection and the right to eliminate officers not promoted in the line of the Navy, the Marine Corps was not included in this provision. According to Lejeune, "I have always regretted that the Marine Corps was not included in its scope, as I am profoundly convinced that such a system of promotion is the only sound system, and that promotion by seniority without elimination will ultimately result in a materially lower degree of efficiency, due to lack of incentive, too great age in grade, and the retention on the active list of inferior officers."[61] During his entire career, Lejeune would continually seek congressional approval for the right of the corps to institute promotion by selection/merit, a system not approved for the Marine Corps by Congress until the 1930s.

One much-needed provision of the Naval Appropriations Act was the creation of slots for eight brigadier generals for the Marine Corps, five from among colonels of the line and three for the staff. On November 29, 1916, President Wilson and Secretary Daniels promoted Lejeune to the rank of brigadier general.[62] The other line colonels promoted were Littleton W. T. Waller, Major General George Barnett (his permanent rank was colonel), Joseph H. Pendleton, and Eli K. Cole.

Barnett and Lejeune also worked for the creation of stations on the Atlantic and Pacific coasts for the organization of expeditionary forces, as part of the Marine Corps's war plans. Barnett's annual reports for 1915 and 1916 requested that the East Coast base be located on Chesapeake Bay or one of its tributaries. Also, the report recommended that the base should not be located within or near an active Navy yard, allowing the Marine Corps more terrain for rifle and artillery ranges and extended field exercises.[63]

Shortly after the United States entered World War I on the side of the Allies, members of an appointed board visited several sites and concluded that Quantico, Virginia, was the most favorable location.[64] At this point Lejeune revealed his political acumen by asking his protégé Smedley Butler to contact Butler's father, Representative Thomas S. Butler, to influence appropriations for the Marine Corps in the House of Representatives for a new East Coast base for the fleet and Marines for use in the war. Lejeune felt compelled to approach Representative Butler in this manner because both Butlers, son and father, disliked and were equally disdained by MGC Barnett.[65] Quantico became the primary base for the Marine Corps, where cadre trained thousands of Marines for service in the Great War. Later, the House Naval Affairs Committee selected San Diego as the site of the West Coast base, primarily because the city donated a large tract of land that added to the purchase of several other tracts by the government.[66]

This decade before 1920 was marked by the ideas and writings of several Marine Corps visionaries that laid the groundwork for improvement of the new amphibious mission for the Marine Corps. In the period after the Spanish-American War, from 1902 until 1920, a few progressive Marine officers wrote and lectured about amphibious operations as the new mission for the corps, focusing on the ABF. While most of these officers mentioned seizure operations, they concentrated on defense, assuming perhaps that islands in the western Pacific beyond Hawaii would be undefended. Only Earl Ellis and Lejeune anticipated seizure operations against defended islands, atolls, and archipelagos in the western, southwestern, and central Pacific, later known as amphibious assault. Ultimately, it was Lejeune in his lecture to the Advanced Base School in 1915 who firmly stated that the offensive amphibious mission was actually the true role of the ABF and the Marine Corps.[67]

There were other voices, however, among the officer corps. Many senior and less-educated officers still favored the role of the Marine Corps as colonial infantry in the Caribbean and Asia, a familiar and enjoyable mission that allowed Marines to act independently from the Navy. Also, after the Great War, some officers and senior enlisted men would see fighting alongside the Army as a reasonable mission. The visionary officers, however, understood that the Marine Corps needed a unique mission separate from the Army and one critical to the national interest. These few progressive officers actively promoted the mission of supporting the fleet by serving as an expeditionary force or an ABF, recognizing that the corps's future was necessarily tied to the Navy. These officers were graduates of the Naval Academy, were influenced by studies at the Navy War College and the Navy Board, and wrote and lectured frequently on the subject. The most active visionaries included Dion Williams, Robert H. Dunlap, Eli K. Cole, John H. Russell, and Lejeune. Earl Ellis, while not a Naval Academy graduate, was a strong advocate of developing the ability to conduct amphibious warfare, primarily to prepare for a war with Japan that he was convinced was coming. Each of these officers made a contribution, some in theory, to the development of amphibious capability. Most of these amphibious pioneers concentrated on the ABF, a defensive force, but a few anticipated offensive operations such as amphibious assault.[68]

Since the Marine Corps was a very small organization at this time, it is probable that these officers shared their ideas regarding amphibious operations with each other. Most of their thoughts had certain commonalities. These common ideas were carried out in the Culebra maneuver of 1914: Marines would land from transports on a site outside of but near the United States in order to defend the homeland. This ABF would establish a temporary defense against an enemy fleet with a landing party intent on establishing a base to support an invasion by the United States.[69] The ABF would consist of a fixed defense regiment with heavy cannon to repel an attack by enemy cruisers, and a mobile regiment composed mostly of infantry to stop an enemy infantry assault. The ABF would free the American Fleet to destroy the main enemy fleet in order to secure control of the sea. The ABF would also house the fleet train with its equipment and supplies and refuel the fleet.

The earliest and most prolific writer about amphibious operations was Dion Williams. Beginning in 1902, Williams advocated building defenses on the overseas naval stations won during the War with Spain in 1898.[70] Williams argued that these naval stations should be defended by the Marine Corps, part of the naval service instead of the Army—which would create command issues.[71] Williams is best remembered for advocating a specialized intelligence force to provide pre-assault reconnaissance on a predetermined site for an advance base.[72] Williams updated his 1906 article on this subject in 1917 to utilize new technology, such as the airplane and submarine, to secure an advance base. He also insisted on gathering hydrographic and topographic reconnaissance.[73] In 1912, Williams described better than all the visionaries the stages and actions of the ABF: accompanying and landing from the fleet, occupying and defending the base, replenishing the fleet, and thereby allowing the fleet to win sea supremacy over the enemy. He gave examples of its use in a projected war against Japan and Imperial Germany, in the event that they were to seek colonies in Latin America. Further, Williams described in detail the components of the fixed defense regiment, the mobile regiment, and the ideal transport ship needed for success. At best, Williams's articles served as a primer for the Culebra Maneuvers of 1914, but neglected to explain how an enemy-occupied base would be secured, focusing entirely on defending the base.[74]

Robert Henry Dunlap matriculated to Bowdoin College in 1897, but left to join the Marine Corps during the Spanish-American War. Teaching and lecturing at the Navy War College, he wrote two articles on the ABF in 1911 and 1912. Dunlap's greatest contributions to the study of the subject came from his focus as an artilleryman and on the criteria for the selection of a potential naval base. He used studies of British naval history and the Russo-Japanese War of 1904–5 to point out the advantage the Japanese had gained over the Russians by establishing an advance base for their fleet in the Elliott Islands. Like Williams, Dunlap relied heavily on the concept of strategic position, developing an advance base close to where the American Fleet was fighting the enemy fleet—as popularized by naval theorist and historian Alfred Thayer Mahan. Mahan taught at the NWC, writing in 1890 *The Influence of Sea Power upon History, 1660–1783*. Mahan's thesis tied sea power to national eminence, economic affluence, and control of the sea lanes of commerce.[75] Dunlap stressed the role of artillery in defending an acquired base. In a reference to an offensive operation, Dunlap noted that in the fleet bombardment of Port Arthur, the Japanese had used the wrong kind of shell against the Russian land defenses. The use of high-explosive shells (instead of armor-piercing shells) that exploded on impact did not destroy the underground Russian concrete bunkers and artillery, creating high casualties for the assaulting Japanese troops. This was an error the American Navy made during the early days of World War II, resulting in high Marine casualties in beach assaults. Also, like Williams during this period, Dunlap focused on how to defend rather than seize an advance base.[76]

Eli K. Cole became acquainted with the ABF in 1907 when he was charged to fortify Grande Island and install naval guns to defend Subic Bay in the Philippines during the war scare with Japan. Cole spent the rest of his career promoting the ABF and amphibious operations, beginning with an extensive critique of the Grande Island exercise while a student at the AWC from 1908 to 1909. Cole's report focused on the corps's unpreparedness and lack of training to develop the base: the large naval guns had to be manhandled into gun pits by the Marines; the length of time to emplace the guns was excessive; the base was vulnerable to attack from the rear; the materials available and the digging tools were inadequate; the guns had no fire control or range-finding systems; and no ammunition was provided. Fortunately the Japanese did not attack the Philippines, for the defenses were not in place.[77] Cole also wrote lengthy reports to the AWC and the Navy Board, recommending ways to improve the development of the ABF.[78]

In a lecture to the ABF School in Philadelphia on June 19, 1915, Cole traced the slow development of the concept from 1890 to 1915, commenting on the support of the Navy Board and Navy War College and the reluctance of the Navy to provide the latest guns, mounts, mines, torpedoes, supplies, communications equipment, and funds to the Marine Corps. He ended his presentation by emphasizing the need for the ABF in wartime—as important to the Navy as battleships—as an integral part of the fleet, stressing the need for the Navy and Marine Corps to work together as one body.[79] While Cole frequently used the word "seizure" of bases, he consistently referred to advance bases in terms of their importance to the Navy and the need for better organization and training, with the emphasis on defense.

John H. Russell, son of a Navy admiral, a graduate of the US Naval Academy, and MGC in the mid-1930s, also wrote at length about the ABF naval base prior to 1920, touching on the selection of bases, as well as the need for more personnel, better training, equipment, and supplies. Like Williams and Dunlap, Russell taught at the Navy War College, utilizing the institution's ideas as well as his own, developing theories for an ABF. First establishing the need for having fortified naval bases in "remote waters" to protect American interests abroad in wartime, Russell illustrated the use of temporary naval bases with examples—the Americans landing at Guantanamo Bay in the Spanish-American War and the British transporting heavy naval guns overland in Africa during the Boer War. Similar to studies by Williams, Dunlap, and Cole during this period, Russell's work emphasized the defense of naval bases.[80]

Russell's 1916 article "A Plea for a Mission and Doctrine" posited many ideas open to interpretation, leading some military historians to claim that he advocated specific amphibious operations such as the advance base mission. This is not the case, however, because Russell wrote in more general terms about principles and leadership. Russell supported a close relationship with the Navy. In speaking primarily about mission, efficiency, organization, policy, leadership, discipline, and doctrine, Russell made a case that the Marine Corps should have only one mission, rather than many minor missions, which created confusion. He implied that many officers of the corps had differing opinions as to the corps's real mission and suggested that under "leadership" the corps build more schools to provide for better theoretical and practical training. Also, he stated that the Marine Corps "has no doctrine and the lack of this important factor must necessarily reduce the efficiency of the Corps." Many Marine officers disagreed with Russell, believing that the corps already had a mission and doctrine.[81] Basically, Russell wanted the corps to develop "certain military principles" and "concise and clear doctrine," and felt that these principles and doctrines should relate to corps traditions in order to bind the organization together to develop a "cult of the Offensive."[82]

Earl Ellis lacked a college degree but was commissioned in the Marine Corps in 1901 after passing the comprehensive written examination.[83] Like Williams, Dunlap, and Russell, Ellis taught at the NWC and advocated the need for the ABF based on Mahan's concept that no nation could become a great power without controlling the sea lanes in peace and war. Visualizing Japan as America's great rival in the Pacific, with Germany as a menace in the Atlantic, Ellis developed elaborate scenarios for war with either of those powers. What distinguished Ellis's writings from the other Marine Corps progressives at this time was his equal concern for defensive and offensive operations. Ellis believed that the ABF would be hard-pressed to defend a base against Japanese assaults. Ellis was highly impressed by Japan's success at landing troops from the sea during wartime. As examples, Ellis provided detailed descriptions of Japan's landing operations and victories during the Sino-Japanese War (1894–95) and the Russo-Japanese War (1904–5). Most important, Ellis noted that the ABF would have to seize a temporary naval base before defending it. Ellis wrote: "It is probable that all points suitable for use as advanced bases by the United States Fleet will be denied in some strength. This will necessitate the A.[Advanced] B.[Base] Force being prepared for the execution of opposed landings."[84] Alone among the progressives, Ellis evaluated the characteristics of islands close to Japan that the United States would have to seize and defend in a war, details such as anchorages, size, location of reefs, tides, harbors, and depth of water.[85]

Lejeune knew these other visionaries of amphibious operations and supported the concept of the ABF. While there appears to have been no debate on the subject, it was probable that all were influenced by progressive thinkers in the Navy, the Navy Board, and the Navy War College; by the need for a more important Marine Corps mission with the Navy; and by the possibility of a future naval war with Japan or Imperial Germany. At the same time, Williams, Dunlap, Russell, and Ellis taught and studied at the Navy War College and were probably influenced by studies there, most likely influencing each other. Significantly, upon becoming MGC in 1920, Lejeune handpicked these same men to important positions in the Marine Corps.

It is probable that Lejeune was invited to speak to the Advanced Base School in Philadelphia in 1915 because of his reputation as a reform-minded Marine of integrity, honesty, competence, and experience. Lejeune's opinions on amphibious operations were important to the corps because he was considered an expert on the subject after commanding landing operations in the Spanish-American War, Panama, Culebra, and Veracruz. Lejeune was invited to speak to the ABF School in Philadelphia because he had practiced what other progressives wrote about in theory.

Lejeune had begun to see beyond the common focus on defensive amphibious operations. Lejeune prefaced his remarks in Philadelphia by stating that the ABF Brigade could also be used—in a more constructive manner—in offensive operations: "The most important factor then in this estimate of the situation is the determination of the true mission of the Marine Corps in the event of war." For Lejeune, when at war with another strong naval power, the United States had first to secure supremacy of the sea before the Army could move overseas to engage the enemy: "If . . . the Marine Corps be utilized as an Advance Base organization, it would have the opportunity to share with the Navy the glory always resting on those who strike the first blows at the enemy, and it also would have the satisfaction of feeling that it had an important, semi-independent duty to perform and that on the manner of its performance would largely depend the success or failure of the Fleet." Lejeune was thus implying an offensive mission with the fleet. "The Marine Corps would be the first to set foot on hostile soil in order to seize, fortify, and hold a port from which, as a base, the Army would prosecute its campaign. Here being again first on the scene, the corps could perform most valuable service, and would be ready to join the Army in its march against the armies of the enemy."[86] Lejeune's lecture would later be published as the first article in a newly created professional journal, the *Marine Corps Gazette* (*MCG*).[87]

The articles and lectures presented by progressives in the Marine Corps from 1902 to 1920 helped to establish the ABF as the amphibious mission of the corps before 1920. This new role was fundamentally a defensive mission that supported the Navy's effort to win control of a base outside the continental United States. Only Earl Ellis and John Lejeune discussed the need for an offensive mission for the ABF. Lejeune went one step further by advocating that the offensive mission was the true role of the force. Before Lejeune and the Marine Corps could turn their attention officially to further developing the offensive amphibious mission, the nation prepared for and fought a land war in France against the Central Powers in World War I.

6

LEJEUNE, THE MARINE CORPS, AND WORLD WAR I

Because the Royal Navy had already won control of the Atlantic Ocean during World War I except for the German submarine menace, the US Navy did not need the Marine ABFs for securing control of the sea. Consequently, MGC George Barnett; Brigadier General John A. Lejeune, assistant to the commandant; and Josephus Daniels, secretary of the Navy, appealed to President Woodrow Wilson and the War Department to allow Marines to serve under the Army's forces in France. As it turned out, the Army allowed only a brigade of Marines to participate in the Great War—about 8,000 Marines as contrasted to a projected Army of 2 million soldiers.

The United States gradually moved toward entry into World War I on the side of Great Britain, France, Italy, and Russia against Germany and the Austro-Hungarian Empire. On August 29, 1916, the largest Naval Appropriations Act to date became law, authorizing a Navy second to none and substantially increasing personnel in the Navy and Marine Corps. After almost three years of "absolute neutrality," the US Congress declared war on Germany on April 6, 1917.[1]

In order to prepare the corps for the fight in Europe, Barnett and Lejeune appeared before the House Naval Committee on April 24 to support a bill to increase the Marine Corps to 30,000 men.[2] It was well known, however, that General John J. Pershing, newly appointed head of the American Expeditionary Forces (AEF), as well as most senior Army officers, wanted an "all-Army show." Nevertheless, Barnett utilized his political connections in Congress, and with help from Secretary Daniels, who gained the support of President Wilson, a limited number of Marines fought in the war.

President Wilson directed Daniels to prepare a small number of Marines for service with the Army: "In pursuance of the authority vested in me by law, it is hereby directed that you issue the necessary orders detaching for service with the Army a force of Marines to be known as the 5th Regiment of Marines." Wilson added that "this force will serve with the first expedition which has been directed to proceed to France in the near future. . . . You will direct the Major General Commandant to report to the Secretary of War for this duty."[3] This Navy and Marine Corps initiative, however, was not well received by the secretary of war or the Army. Daniels recalled: "When war was declared, I tendered ready and equipped two regiments of Marines to be incorporated into the Army. Senior officers were not keen to accept them."[4] Actually Daniels offered only one regiment to the Army in early 1917—the Fifth Marines—later offering the Sixth Marine Regiment, which would make up a Marine brigade.

Despite the typical interservice squabble with the Army, Lejeune eagerly sought a combat command in Europe. In a letter to his sister, Lejeune noted, "I have made all arrangements to be relieved of my duties here [assistant to the commandant] about the middle of September [1917]. Colonel Long will be my successor, and I will go to Quantico in command of the big post there. It is my ambition to be assigned to command the Brigade of Marines which is to serve in France. I think I am the logical man for the job, on account of my French ancestry."[5] Lejeune was undoubtedly disappointed when Colonel Charles A. Doyen—a Naval Academy classmate of Barnett—was promoted to brigadier general and sent to France to command the Marines' Fourth Brigade during the winter of 1917–18. At that time the brigade was training with the Army's Second Division.

Lejeune's opportunity to go to France came when Doyen was invalided home by Pershing. Lejeune wrote to his sister: "I am writing you . . . to let you know that I expect to go over to France between May 20th and 31st. Brigadier Gen. Doyen has been ordered home on account of ill health and I go over as his relief."[6] Lejeune was taking a chance in going to France, however, for Pershing had already replaced Doyen as commander of the Marine brigade with Army officer Brigadier General James G. Harbord, Pershing's chief of staff. In addition, Pershing made it clear that he did not need any more Marine generals in France: "In the event that a Brigadier of the Marine Corps is sent from the United States to replace General Doyen it will be necessary to assign him to a unit not actively engaged in the line."[7]

Lejeune went to France anyway, arriving on June 8, 1918, and used his positive connections with those senior Army officers with whom he had studied at the AWC to arrange a meeting with Pershing at the AEF Headquarters at Chaumont. Lejeune wanted to relay Barnett's hope to raise a division of Marines for service in France under the Army and to look for his own combat command. Lejeune wasted no time and met with Pershing on or about June 19. At the beginning of their meeting, Pershing remarked that he was highly pleased with the dash and vigor and the first victory of the Marines over the Germans at Belleau Wood and expressed sorrow over the heavy casualties the Marines had suffered. Pershing was impressed that the Marines had engaged in open warfare and hand-to-hand fighting in dense woods with little artillery support. When a staff officer reminded Pershing that a regiment of the First Division which had captured Cantigny had also suffered heavy losses, Pershing was less impressed: "Yes, that is true, but the circumstances were different, it was trench warfare—a set piece attack, thoroughly prepared by artillery fire."[8]

Recent scholarship has criticized Pershing for his initial preference for a war of maneuver and his concept of open warfare with limited artillery support. Earlier in the war the British and French had attempted to establish a war of maneuver in order to break through the German lines, but the German Maxim machine gun changed all that. The Maxim machine gun, developed by American inventor Hiram Maxim, was a water-cooled, belt-fed 7.92 mm weapon that weighed less than sixty pounds and could fire five hundred rounds per minute. This awesome defensive weapon had an effective range of two thousand yards, but was still fairly accurate at four thousand yards. The British called it the "Devil's paintbrush," and the French named it "the lawnmower" or "coffee-grinder."[9] Even as late as 1918, Pershing insisted that "the rifle and the bayonet remained the supreme weapons of the infantry soldier . . . and the ultimate success of the army depends upon their proper use in open warfare."[10] Open warfare in World War I, however, without the support of artillery, produced unacceptable casualties. Brigadier General James Harbord, a loyal subordinate of Pershing, was in command of the Marines at Belleau Wood and lost hundreds of wounded and killed in minutes and more than nine thousand before taking Belleau Wood five days later. Harbord learned enough from his excessive losses that he came to agree with the Marine Corps Brigade commander there, Lejeune, who declared, "the reckless courage of the foot soldier with his rifle and bayonet could not overcome machine-guns, well protected in rocky nests."[11]

It was fortunate for the Allies that "Pershing had subordinate officers who quickly realized that their doctrine had to change. The adaptations, tactical and otherwise of men like Robert Bullard, John Lejeune, Charles Summerall . . . enabled the best of the American divisions to contribute so hugely to the Allied victory."[12]

Later in his meeting with Lejeune, Pershing said that he appreciated the "splendid service" of the Fourth Marine Brigade, but he could not approve the assignment of a Marine Division, reasoning that its presence there would "interfere with his plan for a homogeneous army and would add greatly to the many complications incident to providing replacements."[13] Later, Lejeune asked Pershing's chief of staff, Major General James McAndrew, for a command assignment, preferably to lead the Fourth Marine Brigade after Harbord's promotion to a higher position. McAndrew told Lejeune, "I will look out for you, and it now seems altogether probable that you will eventually receive the assignment you desire; but, in the meantime, you will be ordered to duty as an observer with the 35th Division for familiarization in training and experience in trench warfare."[14]

Lejeune was eager to learn all he could about German, French, and American strategy, tactics, and planning during the Great War. For example, he spent his time studying the plan of defense of one brigade of the Thirty-Fifth Division in the sector of the Vosges Mountains. The other brigade was training for attacking in open warfare, not trench warfare. Lejeune crossed the mountains, traveled to the Thann Valley in Alsace, and met his old friend Major General William Wright at Third Corps Headquarters. Lejeune also visited with General Renouard, CO of a French division, and made many trips to the front lines of the Thirty-Fifth Division. Lejeune studied the French system of supplying troops in that particular mountain sector. Lejeune's next stop was to travel to the headquarters of the Thirty-Second Division, joining Major General Wright, the corps commander; Major General William G. Hann, the division commander; and Colonel William D. Conner, chief of staff, to inspect the units of the Thirty-Second Division. Later, Lejeune received orders to command the Sixty-Fourth Brigade. Lejeune there revealed his philosophy of leadership as commander of the brigade: to earn the goodwill and the affection of the officers and men: "I wanted to know them and I wanted them to know me."[15]

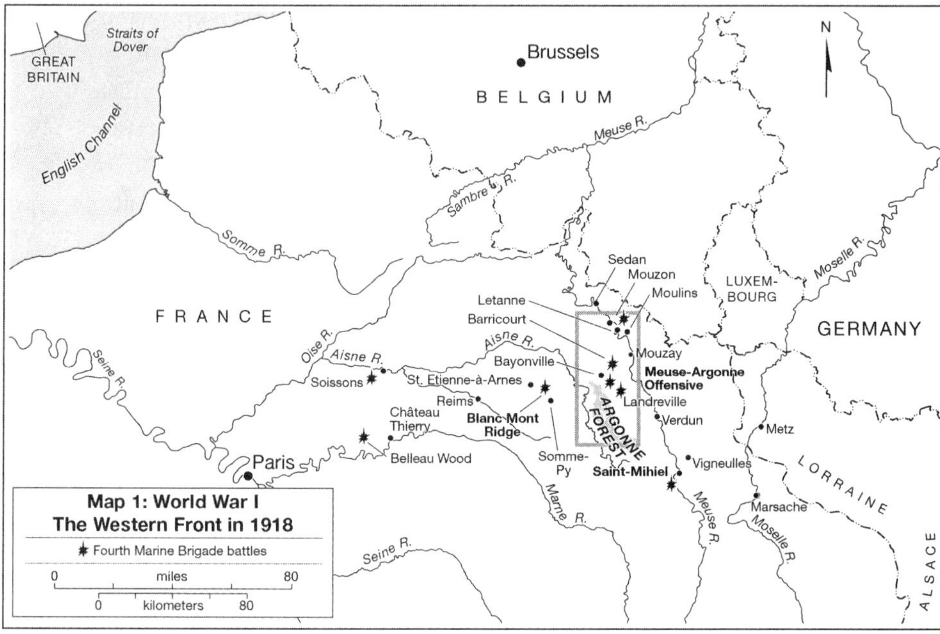

Map 1: World War I
The Western Front in 1918

He visited each regiment, battalion, and company, traveled to every front-line position, and walked miles through the trench system of the brigade. On one occasion, awakened by cannon fire, Lejeune learned that a German attack was in progress on a small combat unit of the French regiment on his extreme right. Lejeune gave orders for one regiment of his brigade to repel the German troops at the breakthrough point, but before the regiment could attack, Lejeune received orders that the Thirty-Second Division was being relieved by the American Twenty-Ninth Division.

Lejeune would soon realize his dream of gaining a Marine command, for on July 12, 1918, he suddenly received notification from Harbord that commanding the Fourth Marine Brigade of the Second Division was likely.[16] In an even more sudden turn of events, on the morning of July 28, Harbord notified Lejeune that Pershing had promoted Harbord to command the Service of Supply of the AEF and had appointed Lejeune, who was the senior brigadier general in the division, to command the Second Division. As Lejeune recalled, "To say that I was surprised is putting it far too mildly. I was stunned. To become suddenly the commander of a division after only a brief experience as the commander of a brigade in a quiet sector, especially of a division with such a remarkable combat record . . . brought to me the fullest realization of the responsibility which rested upon me."[17]

Lejeune's elevation to high command and his responsibility for the lives of thousands of young men apparently tempered and humbled his ambition. Writing to his oldest daughter, Ellie, Lejeune remarked, "I became the Division Commander temporarily" and "I don't know whether or not I will be promoted in the next few days. Personally, I don't care, but I think I could do more for the Marines as Division Commander. . . . I have lost all personal ambition and have only the burning desire to give all my strength and such ability . . . to help our country's cause." Lejeune realized "it is a big task ahead of us, but things look more hopeful now than ever before, as our troops have shown that they are a match for the Germans. The French are jubilant and most complimentary."[18] Lejeune received his promotion to major general from President Wilson on the recommendation of the War Department a few days later on July 28, and officially took command of the Second Division.[19]

From his recent experiences in France, Lejeune knew that AEF attacks could not proceed at bearable cost without preplanned but flexible artillery support. While Lejeune was pleased with the successful Marine attacks at Belleau Wood, he was aware that the assault had very little artillery support, was in the face of "withering" machine-gun fire, and resulted in very heavy casualties. In his autobiography Lejeune noted that "on July 2nd the 3rd Army Brigade attacked and captured the fortified town of Vaux. The attack was conducted in the most approved manner. Artillery preparation for the attack was thorough and complete. The infantry advanced behind a creeping artillery barrage. . . . the casualties on our side were not heavy."[20]

Before Lejeune took command, the Second Division had already earned a distinguished combat record in the Great War, commanded respectively by Army Major Generals Omar Bundy and James G. Harbord, and had won costly victories at major battles at Château Thierry, Belleau Wood, Vaux, and Soissons. Deployed across the Paris–Château Thierry road, the Fourth Brigade at Bouresches and Belleau Wood in early June 1918 stopped the German advance toward Paris, earning a reputation for great valor, but suffering heavy casualties. The Second Division's attack at the Soissons–Château Thierry highway beginning July 18 was equally high in casualties. The fights at Belleau Wood and Vaux depleted the Second Division of 170 officers and 8,793 men; the Fourth Brigade alone suffered the loss of 112 offi-

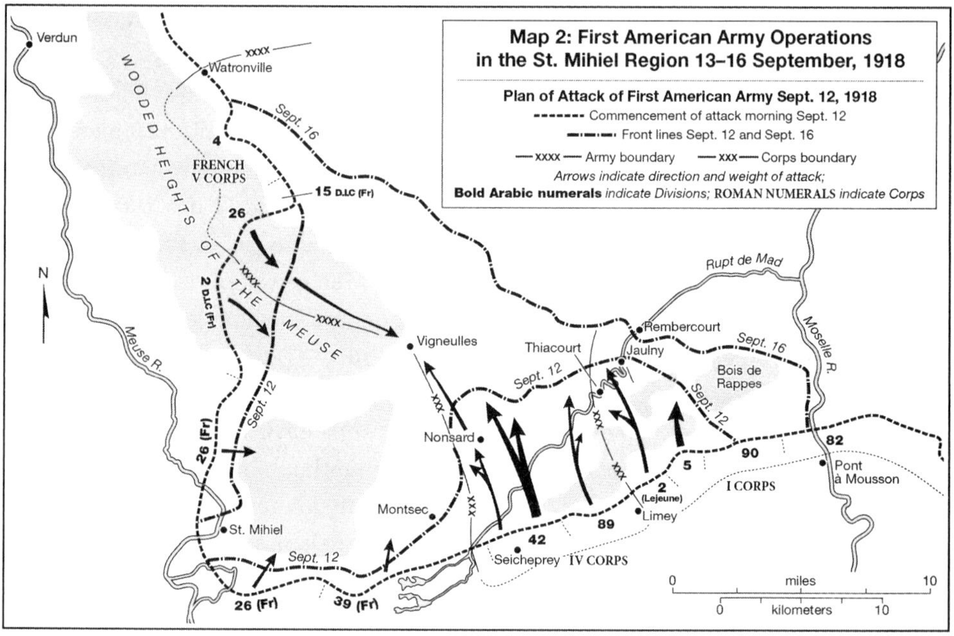

cers and 4,598 men. Probably more than 1,000 Marines had died. The action at Soissons was also costly: the Fourth Brigade suffered an additional 2,000 new casualties.[21]

Lejeune commanded the division from July 28, 1918, through the major battles of St. Mihiel, Blanc Mont, and the Meuse-Argonne, up to the Armistice on November 11, 1918, and as part of the Army of Occupation of Germany on the Rhine until returning to the United States in August 1919. It is worth noting that division commanders in World War I led many more men—nearly 30,000 soldiers—than division commanders of World War II, who led about 5,000 troops. Consequently, division commanders in World War I had far greater logistical demands and much more territory to cover than modern divisions.

The battle of St. Mihiel involved removing a large German penetration into the French lines on the Meuse River (about twenty-five miles south of Verdun) that had restricted French communications and logistics for almost four years. The Second Division was part of the First American Army that included four corps and an attacking force of thirteen divisions—more than 300,000 men—that went over the top on September 12, surprising the

Germans who were already withdrawing from the salient. Before the battle, Lejeune expressed his thoughts to his sister: "We are all busy day and night and it is a very solemn time for me, as I am about to take part in my first battle. . . . it makes my heart blue to think of the many sad hearts there will be at home; there is no other way of defeating the Hun except by shedding the blood of our splendid young men. I believe that God will accept the sacrifice and give us the victory for it is His cause as well as our own."[22]

After the battle Lejeune felt some comfort in the relatively small losses suffered by the division: "During the past ten days I have had a very strenuous time, first preparing for battle and the actual experience itself. The attack took place during the early morning hours of September 12." Lejeune ordered the artillery bombardment to begin at 1:00 a.m. "At 5 a.m. the infantry attack . . . was wonderfully successful and losses surprisingly small, about 1,000 all told, including almost 135 killed. We captured 50 German officers, 3200 men and over 90 cannon, also the city of Thiaucourt and the towns of Xammes and Jaulny."[23]

The next battle for the Second Division, the fight for the Blanc Mont Ridge, was probably the most difficult and bloodiest battle for the division during the war. Instead of joining the opening attacks of the great Meuse-Argonne offensive, Pershing was pressured by the French to use the Second Division to support the French Army of the Center, particularly the Fourth French Army, commanded by General Henri Gouraud, for the battle in the Champagne region. German control of this wide, elevated, and heavily fortified ridge dominated the area between the towns of Somme-Py and St. Etienne-à-Arnes, allowing the Germans to observe and rain down heavy artillery along the entire Fourth Army front.

Besides the ferocious German defense, Lejeune had to deal with two great problems. First, although Lejeune admired and respected General Gouraud, who supported Lejeune's tactical decisions, Lejeune discovered that the chief of staff of the Fourth Army in Gouraud's absence wanted to take the Third Army and Fourth Marine brigades from the Second Division and assign them separately to the much smaller French divisions. Second, the French divisions—exhausted from five years of war and assigned to advance alongside to protect the flanks of the Second Division—often lagged behind, allowing the Germans to flank the division and fire upon the Marines and soldiers from the flanks and rear.

Lejeune convinced Gouraud that he was confident the Second Divi-

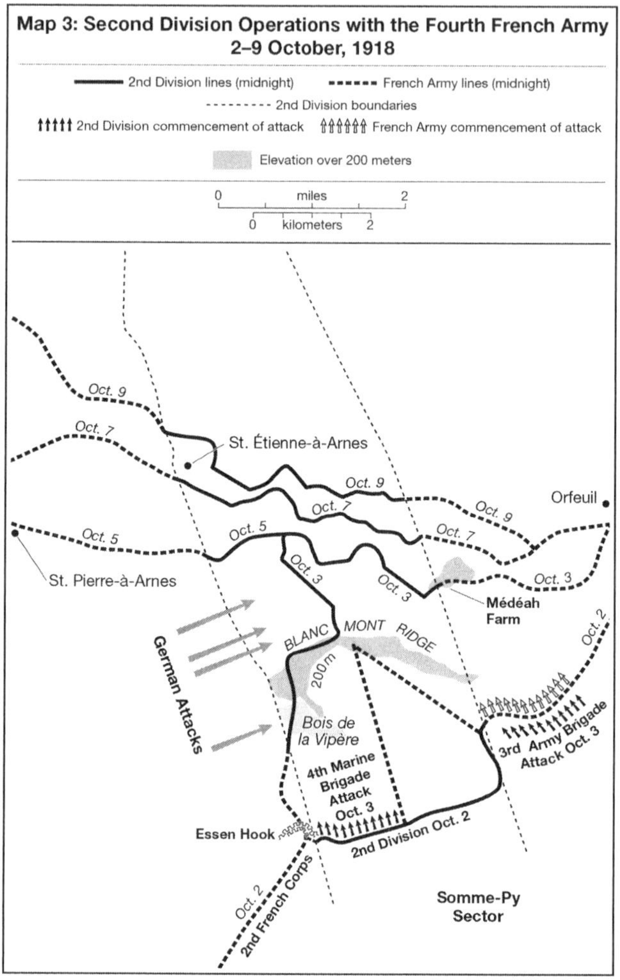

sion could take Blanc Mont Ridge, advancing beyond the ridge and holding the position.[24] Lejeune and his staff developed a daring plan of attack on a three-mile front. In order to best protect his flanks, Lejeune had the two brigades separate within the sector with one attacking forward from the left front and the other attacking forward from the right front with a mile of open terrain in the middle, with the brigades later converging on Blanc Mont Ridge.[25] The attacks began on October 3 and lasted until October 9 with the Americans and the Germans both suffering heavy casualties. On the left the French division protecting Lejeune's flank could not keep up, creating so many losses in the Fourth (Marine) Brigade that Lejeune had to pull back on October 6–7, but one battalion of the brigade remained with the replacement brigade from the US Thirty-Sixth Division to capture St. Etienne on October 8. The Third (Army) Brigade made an oblique attack from the right front sector of the Second Division area, penetrating the German line between Médéah Ferme (farm) and the town of Orfeuil. The Third Brigade also lacked support from a French division that was to advance simultaneously and protect its right flank, receiving flanking fire from the Germans. Eventually the two brigades converged beyond the objective to mop up the triangular space between them.

Gouraud was overjoyed with the results, for the Germans had to evacuate other points along the Fourth (French) Army's line, thereby freeing up Rheims and forcing the enemy back nearly thirty kilometers to the Aisne River. This was an accomplishment that the French had failed to achieve for over four years.[26] The Second Division paid a heavy price, however, for its victory. In a letter to his daughter, Lejeune wrote, "The mission assigned to my Division was the capture of Blanc Mont Ridge, the valley of the arch of the German position. It was a difficult task, but accomplished magnificently. . . . I was ordered to advance beyond in spite of my protest that my flanks were unguarded. And in doing so I lost over 5,000 men killed and wounded. The men fought like tigers and held their positions with the greatest tenacity."[27] In a letter to the assistant to the commandant asking for 3,500 additional replacements, Lejeune wrote, "The [Marine] Brigade lost over 2,000 men in the engagement. The 3rd [Army] Infantry Brigade lost practically the same number."[28]

In taking Blanc Mont, Lejeune's men had broken the center of the enemy's defensive center in the Champagne. Lieutenant Lemuel Shepherd had advanced with the Fifth Marines at dawn on October 3, having been at Belleau Wood and St. Mihiel, battles that to Shepherd seemed like "skirmishes" when compared to Blanc Mont. "As far as I'm concerned," Shepherd told an interviewer many years later, "October 3rd at Blanc Mont was the toughest day of the war. And I think most of the men agreed."[29]

The last battle for the Second Division—the Meuse-Argonne Offensive—was bittersweet for Lejeune. Despite the division's outstanding success in its powerful assault through the German lines and vast fortifications, Lejeune received a poor fitness report from his new Army CO. Organizationally, the Second Division was assigned to V Corps, commanded by Major

General Charles P. Summerall, part of the American First Army. Summerall wrote that "Lejeune's attitude towards higher authority is lacking in that absolute subordination and eager acceptance of difficult tasks imposed on his command is lacking. . . . when Lejeune commits himself to an undertaking, he pursues his objective with admirable vigor, resourcefulness, and self-sacrifice. A strong will as well as resolution on the part of superiors will obtain the finest results from this officer."[30]

Lejeune was undoubtedly hurt and angered by this fitness report, but never mentioned it in his public or private correspondence. That it bothered him for the rest of his life is evident, for he wrote to the MGC two years before his death requesting that it be removed from his officer qualification record.[31] In contrast to Shepherd's criticism, Lejeune received a more favorable and positive evaluation from the First Army Commander, Lieutenant General Hunter Liggett: "Qualified for staff or line duties: a very good disciplinarian; very good knowledge of supply; is aggressive; has excellent qualifications for leadership; and has shown himself to be an excellent division commander in the field."[32]

The criticism from Summerall was caused by the differing leadership styles of the two men. For example, before the Meuse-Argonne attack Summerall warned his subordinates, including Lejeune, that he had been compelled to relieve a number of officers from their commands because of their failure to carry out orders, adding that he would continue to do so in the future no matter who might suffer the consequences. Summerall utilized this threatening style of leadership as did Pershing and many of his subordinates. In Lejeune's opinion, "such officers were drivers of men, and they failed to gain the unquestioned loyalty of their subordinates."[33] In response to Summerall's threat, Lejeune told him that "the Second Division will carry out their orders because of their *esprit,* their pride in and love for their division, and their devotion to the cause for which they are fighting. In fact, we have come to feel that it matters but little what happens to us as individuals, and that the only things which really matter are the welfare of the great Division to which we belong and the speedy and decisive defeat of the enemy."[34]

Lejeune led the Second Division in the final phase of the Meuse-Argonne Offensive, the largest single battle in American history, involving more than 1.2 million soldiers in twenty-two divisions, in which 120,000 soldiers fell wounded and 26,277 died.[35] In this massive assault fought in the region bordered on the east by the Meuse River and on the west by the dense Argonne

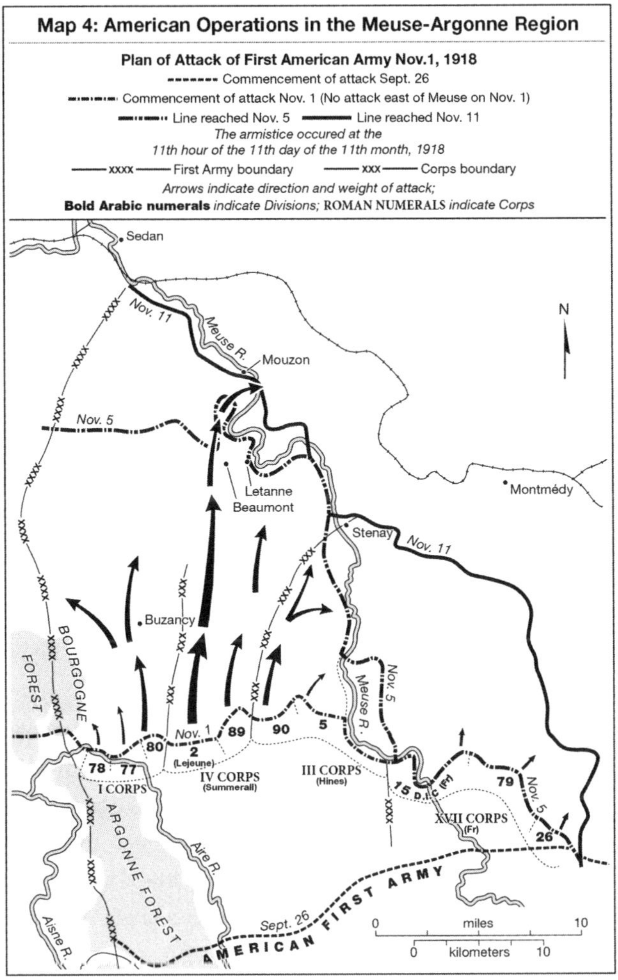

Map 4: American Operations in the Meuse-Argonne Region

Forest, November 1–11, 1918, Lejeune and the Second Division led the other divisions in the center of the line, advancing sixteen miles to the Meuse River.

Before commencing the assault, Lejeune anticipated the German tactic of placing machine-gun units two hundred yards in front of the German lines to avoid the preliminary artillery barrage in order to decimate the Americans going "over the top" at "H" hour. Instead, Lejeune moved his brigades back behind the front line and had three artillery brigades lay down a tremendous two-hour barrage beginning two hundred yards in front of the German lines, followed by a creeping barrage that preceded the Second

Division's brigades advancing northward on their four-kilometer front.[36]

On the first day of the assault, the Fourth Marine Brigade and Third Infantry Brigade of the Second Division smashed five miles into heavily fortified German defenses. Major General Summerall was ecstatic. In a letter of commendation to Lejeune, the corps commander wrote, "The Division's brilliant advance of more than nine kilometers, destroying the last stronghold on the Hindenburg line, capturing the Freya Stellung . . . may justly be regarded as one of the most remarkable achievements made by any troops in this war. . . . The Division has more than justified the distinguished confidence placed in it by the Commander-in-Chief when it was selected to take the lead in the advance from which such great results are expected."[37]

It was in this situation that Summerall began his practice of disregarding corps boundaries, ordering Lejeune to cross over into the sector of I Corps to the left (instead of moving north in the assigned sector for V Corps) and attack the city of Buzancy. In response, Lejeune realigned his brigades to move west. However, upon informing the I Corps of the new orders, Lejeune found out that the I Corps was also planning to assault Buzancy the next day. Summerall had to cancel the order and was miffed when Lejeune had to delay the attack northward the next day in order to again realign his brigades. Lejeune later noted that "the Corps, somehow, seemed unable to appreciate the difficulties we had in changing the direction of attack on November 2nd, and was rather impatient because of the delay on that day."[38]

Perhaps to make up for the delay, Lejeune, seizing upon the successful initial advance and the surprise and demoralization of the German troops, directed the Third Army Brigade to advance after dark in a series of night operations in which the soldiers silently moved through enemy lines in pouring rain and total darkness and captured many sleeping German troops. When the leading troops encountered German resistance, troops from the rear would flank and surround the enemy, sending them back to American lines as prisoners.[39] When the Third Brigade—which had advanced six kilometers behind German lines with the forward echelons existing on short rations and cabbages cultivated by the Germans—came under fire from the enemy on their left flank as well as German artillery on the east bank of the Meuse, Lejeune ordered the Fourth Marine Brigade forward to cover the flank.[40]

On November 6, 1918, Summerall again ordered Lejeune's Second Division to cross corps boundary lines into the I Corps area in order to accompany the First Division in a mad dash to be the first divisions to capture the important city of Sedan, thus angering the French, the American I Corps CO, and the CO of the American First Army.[41] The French Army passionately wanted to enter Sedan first because it was there that Prussia defeated France in 1870 in the Franco-Prussian War. "Sedan had great sentimental value to the French. . . . no Frenchman could forget the crowning defeat there in 1870."[42]

Fortunately for Lejeune and the Second Division, Summerall countermanded his earlier order and directed the Second Division to remain in place and hold the line on the west bank of the Meuse. The ensuing confusion that the First Division created forced Summerall to withdraw the First Division. First Army CO Hunter Liggett termed Summerall's action an "atrocity." Clarence R. Huebner, who was involved in the march, commented: "Someone was glory hunting. An army officer is dangerous when he begins to be a glory hunter."[43]

Two days later, with rumors of an armistice in the air, Lejeune faced a painful dilemma. Summerall had ordered the Second and Eighty-Ninth divisions to cross over to the east bank of the Meuse River on what was to be the last night of the war, defended on high ground by well-positioned German troops, machine guns, and artillery. As Lejeune wrote in his autobiography eleven years later, "The night of this last battle of the war was the most trying night I have ever experienced. The knowledge that in all probability the Armistice was about to be signed caused the mental anguish, which I always felt because of the loss of life in battle. . . . many a brave man made the supreme sacrifice for his country in the last hours of the war."[44] To save lives and achieve the same results, Lejeune recommended an alternative plan at a conference of the V Corps before the battle. Lejeune suggested that those American divisions to the south that had already crossed the Meuse River move north and clear out the German defenders on the east bank of the river, making it possible for the Second and Eighty-Ninth divisions to cross the river without opposition.[45] However, Lejeune's plan was not approved by Summerall. As an obedient member of the AEF, Lejeune sent two battalions of the Fifth Marines across the river near Letanne on makeshift bridges, but at a heavy loss of lives. At that time, Lejeune could see the necessity of the action should the Armistice fail to occur as planned on November 11. Because of this possibility, Marshal Ferdinand Foch, the supreme commander, felt that aggressive action up to the end was necessary to force the Germans to accept the terms of the Armistice.

Notwithstanding that the Army did not want the Marines in the war and resented the favorable publicity the corps received at home—out of proportion to its numbers in the war—the Second Division proved itself an outstanding division. The division advanced sixty kilometers against the enemy, more than any other division in the AEF; captured 12,026 prisoners as compared with the First Division (6,469) and Eighty-Ninth Division (5,061); and captured 343 cannon as compared with the Eighty-Ninth Division (133) and First Division (119). The aggressiveness of the Second Division came at heavy cost, however, suffering 23,218 casualties as compared with the First Division (15,520) and Third Division (15,401).[46]

Until his death, Lejeune considered his command of the Second Division in the Great War to be his greatest military achievement. Although Lejeune would later pioneer amphibious assault in the 1920s as MGC, he did not live to see its eventual execution in World War II. Lejeune helped develop the Second Division Association and attended and spoke at every yearly reunion as long as his health allowed. Even Lejeune's problems with AEF Headquarters (and there were many) and his poor efficiency report from Summerall in 1918 did not dim his enthusiasm for his beloved Second Division in the Great War.

Lejeune continued to have problems with AEF Headquarters after the Armistice. First, the Second Division was exhausted and sick, needing rest and recuperation, yet the AEF almost immediately sent the division with several others on a march to the Rhine River as the Army of Occupation.[47] To make matters worse, early the next morning a staff officer acting for the CO of III Corps ordered Lejeune to march his division forty kilometers south to cross the Meuse River and then march back up north twenty kilometers to begin the trek to Germany. When Lejeune suggested crossing the Meuse at a site closer to the division, the staff officer said he could not authorize the change. When Lejeune threatened to wake up Major General John L. Hines, CO of III Corps, the order was changed, but Lejeune's action did not endear him to Hines.[48]

Next, on the march to Germany, General Pershing passed the marching columns in his staff car and was incensed over the appearance of the Second Division, noting that it was an "eyesore," presenting a "slovenly appearance."[49] Lejeune fired back in a memorandum stating that these remarks were "intensely humiliating" to the men of the Second Division and should be withdrawn. Lejeune wrote that "the Division should have been rested and refitted with clothing and equipment [after the Armistice]." The men were still wearing their dirty and wet clothing worn in battle. In addition, Lejeune wrote that "the 2nd Division has fought, marched, moved by rail or camion, and bivouacked in the woods continually since March 15th, last. It has fought five pitched battles, always defeating the enemy . . . has rendered service of incalculable value to the Allied cause . . . [while] thousands of their comrades have made the supreme sacrifice for their country and thousands more have been maimed or crippled for life." Lejeune managed to continue the march, requested help from the corps commander for new clothing and shoes, and succeeded in having Pershing inspect his division at a later date in Germany.[50]

Probably more than any other Marine leader, Lejeune worked diligently to maintain good relations between the Army and the Marine Corps. When problems did occur, Lejeune approached each one in a professional, congenial manner. For example, when a detachment of soldiers led by a young second lieutenant from the Third Division publicly disrespected and ridiculed a Marine captain during the occupation of Germany, Lejeune wrote a confidential letter to the CO of the Third Division. In reply, Major General Robert M. Howze privately reprimanded the guilty parties. Howze also canceled newspaper articles that demeaned Marines in the Third Division's newspaper, *Watch on the Rhine.* Likewise, Lejeune forbade Marines from making uncomplimentary remarks about the Army. Defending the Marines in a letter to Howze, Lejeune remarked that "no units of this Division have claimed anything that did not belong to them, nor are they discontented with their legitimate honors, neither have they reached out for honors not due them to the detriment of their Comrades in Arms. Furthermore, they have not made attacks on any other Division, or engaged in any controversies whatever."[51]

In retrospect, it was understandable why many soldiers resented Marines, for the Marine Corps often received favorable publicity from newspapers and magazines back in the United States at the expense of the Army, publicity that was far out of proportion to their smaller numbers engaged in the Great War. This was largely due to an excellent public relations program in the Marine Corps as well as the Marine officers and men led by J. Walter Thompson, who worked so well with the press. Also, many senators and congressmen were supporters of the corps. It was Congress, for example, that several times stopped the Army's attempt to absorb the corps—efforts that have continued throughout the corps's history. Lejeune was aware of this press support and worked to correct misinformation that credited the Marine Corps for Army victories. When the press gave credit to the Second Division for the machine-gun battalion that stopped the German offensive at the bridge over the Marne River at Château Thierry on May 31, 1918, Lejeune "personally told the correct story to a number of misinformed persons, and . . . endeavored to have the credit of that action given to the 3rd Division."[52]

The final difficulty that Lejeune had with the Army's senior command occurred when the General Headquarters of the AEF (GHQ) minimized the Second Division's service to the war effort. For example, when Pershing issued General Order 201, GHQ, AEF, citing the First Division for its "magnificent work" from October 1 to November 1 in the battle of Meuse-Argonne, he did not cite the Second Division for equally distinguished service from November 1 until the Armistice.[53] In addition, the Second Division's major battle northwest of Château Thierry (Belleau Wood), from June 6 to July 5, 1918, was minimized. The division lost nearly 10,000 men when helping stem the German drive on Paris, but was not included on GHQ's list of major operations. This action by the Second Division was instead placed in the same class as trench raids, skirmishes, and patrol encounters. Similarly, the Second Division's participation in the Champagne Offensive from September 26 to October 13, 1918, including the major battle of Massif du Blanc Mont, in which the division lost 4,975 men, was not included in the list of major operations. This was probably the reason why GHQ dismissed almost 50 percent of Lejeune's recommendations for awarding the Distinguished Service Cross to deserving Marines and soldiers. Since the battles of Belleau Wood and Massif du Blanc Mont heavily involved the Fourth Marine Brigade, it is possible that the Army in its lack of recognition of these fights as major battles was expressing its enmity toward the Marine Corps.

In his nearly ten-month campaign to seek reconsideration from GHQ to acknowledge these honors for the Second Division, Lejeune was supported by Generals Summerall, Gouraud (Fourth French Army), Harbord, and Liggett, all to no avail. Lejeune's friend Harbord had to relay the news of a lost cause: "I am very sorry not to be able to do what I would so much like to do for the 2nd Division, but the CinC [Pershing] considers that to reopen the matter and change the rules at this late date would involve them in even greater injustices than to let it stand as it is."[54]

To his credit, Lejeune never criticized, publicly or privately, Summerall, Pershing, or any other Army officer. He remained on good professional terms with both men for the remainder of his career. Not all Marines responded as well as Lejeune, however, but actively expressed their dislike of Summerall. In response to a letter from Lejeune asking about his efficiency report, Summerall wrote a very complimentary letter back, but noted: "Considering the brilliancy with which your Division took part in the final battle of the war, I have been greatly surprised and pained to hear from very reliable sources that officers of the Marine Corps had made complaints with reference to the crossing of the Meuse on the night of November 10th. I am at a loss to understand how such complaints could have arisen among officers, whose part in the battle had been taken so worthily. . . . I wish, therefore, that you would ascertain who were responsible for these complaints and the reason for their existence."[55]

Years later, in his memoir, Summerall revealed his dislike for Marines: "I learned later that the brigade of marines in the Second Division resented the order to cross the Meuse River, as the Armistice came immediately afterward, and blamed me for their losses, which they said were unnecessary. Of course, I knew nothing of an armistice and was obeying the most urgent orders from the high command." Summerall was also critical of Lejeune, saying that, "no doubt, he [Lejeune] wanted to gain credit for the Marines [in crossing the Meuse]." Finally, Summerall revealed his true feelings. "From my experience with the Marines, they should never be employed with the army or under army officers. They fight no better than the army, and they complain, seek quick relief, and try to gain publicity."[56] Summerall's negative statements about Lejeune and the Second Division in the Meuse-Argonne have been criticized by recent historians. "Summerall shifted responsibility and said he was obeying orders. . . . his statement was unfair and did little to foster joint cooperation."[57]

Lejeune and the Marine Corps learned many lessons from the corps's participation in World War I. The Great War was a major catalyst in moving the corps from its old mission to a new mission, which would be fully developed by Lejeune in the 1920s. Lejeune and the Marines learned that modern combat against a great military power such as Germany was much different from the actions in which Marines had previously fought, serving as constabulary forces in the Caribbean, China, Korea, and the Philippines against poorly trained and armed rebels and natives. For the first time, Marines had to learn how to fight a modern war—utilizing greater firepower through the combined-arms tactics of infantry, machine guns, artillery, tanks, and aircraft in the attack against a powerful and determined enemy. As the world war developed into trench warfare with German artillery and machine guns dominating the field, the French, British, and Americans, including the Marines, learned how to attack, utilizing greater maneuverability and superior firepower than the enemy. The Army and the Marines succeeded in pushing back the Germans, but the cost in casualties was very high.[58]

The use and effectiveness of aircraft provided another hard lesson for Lejeune and the Marines. As Lejeune remembered, "Darkness and the lack of fires were the most pronounced characteristics of the World War. . . . The deadly airplane brought about almost a reversion to the primitive days when fire and artificial light were unknown. In previous wars, even the pickets in outposts built bonfires and derived much cheer from their warmth and brightness. In the World War, millions of men were deprived of these."[59] Most important, air superiority over the battlefield was vital in preventing enemy aircraft from bombing the infantry and directing enemy artillery fire on friendly troops.

The Marine Corps learned other lessons during their participation in the war: careful operational planning was crucial to obtain objectives and minimize Marine losses; combat units down to the battalion level needed effective operational staffs; success in battle depended upon continuous logistical support; battlefield communications had to be vastly improved; and night advances were effective against the enemy during inclement weather.[60]

The final lesson that Lejeune and the Marines learned was that the Army deeply resented the praise heaped on the Marines back home by the newspapers. The friction between the Army and Marine Corps over recognition of the Marine Fourth Brigade carried over from the AEF in Germany to the Departments of War and the Navy in Washington. Some of the Army's senior officers were convinced that the Marine Corps would do anything to "belittle the regular Army's reputation." In 1919, the press—probably encouraged by the War Department—asserted that the Marine Brigade had not saved Château-Thierry. This claim brought counterclaims from the Navy Department. The crisis in the press finally ended when the War Department admitted that Belleau Wood was part of the Château-Thierry operation. Although Lejeune and other leaders in the Marine Corps endeavored to honor the Army and its senior officers, the end result was that many Marine officers distrusted the War Department and the Army's general staff.

Lejeune's parents, Laura and Ovide Lejeune.

USMC History Division.

Old Hickory manor house, c. 1830s–1840s, in Lacour, Louisiana, the boyhood home of John Lejeune.
State Library of Louisiana.

Lejeune as a cadet at LSU, 1882.
USMC History Division.

Andrew David Lytle, *Cadets Marching in Front of the Pentagon Barracks,* downtown campus, LSU.
University Archives Photograph Collection,
Louisiana Digital Library, Baton Rouge, La.

Lejeune as a midshipman at the
US Naval Academy, Class of 1888.
USMC History Division.

View from the wrecked *USS Trenton* of the *USS Vandalia* sunk alongside, following the Samoan hurricane of 1889.
Courtesy of the Naval Historical Foundation. Collection of Admiral Richard H. Jackson, 1965.

Ellie Murdaugh Lejeune, 1897.

USMC History Division.

Lejeune with Marine Corps rifle marksmanship medal, 1913.

USMC History Division.

Major General George Barnett, Lieutenant General Lejeune, and Colonel Powers, 1913.
Library of Congress Prints and Photographs Division.

Marine Corps officers at Veracruz, Mexico, 1914.
Left to right: F. H. DeLario, John Henry Quick, Wendell C. Neville, Lejeune, and Smedley Butler.

Lejeune at the front in France.

USMC History Division.

Lejeune and staff planning the St. Mihiel offensive.

USMC History Division.

Lejeune receiving the Croix de Guerre with Palm.
USMC History Division.

Lejeune with his insignia of commander in the French Legion of Honor.
USMC History Division.

Postwar (c. 1919) portrait of Lejeune in the Marine officer wintergreen uniform of 1917, with the star-and-Indian-head insignia of the Second Infantry Division. The insignia was discontinued in 1920.
USMC History Division.

Smedley Butler, President Warren Harding, John J. Pershing, and Lejeune at the reenactment of Pickett's Charge, 1922.
Library of Congress Prints and Photographs Division.

Lejeune with a Gettysburg survivor, at the Pickett's Charge reenactment.
Library of Congress Prints and Photographs Division.

Lejeune with Secretary of the Navy Edwin Denby in July 1923.

Library of Congress Prints and Photographs Division.

Officials of the Marine Corps and other dignitaries looking at map of Battle of New Market, 1923. Lejeune is second from the left.
Library of Congress Prints and Photographs Division.

General Lejeune decorating Virginia Boy Scouts, 1925.

Library of Congress Prints and Photographs Division.

General Lejeune with his daughter Eugenia at the Navy-Princeton football game, 1925.
Library of Congress Prints and Photographs Division.

Lejeune and Wendell C. Neville. Neville took
over as commandant of the Marine Corps on March 5, 1929.
Library of Congress Prints and Photographs Division.

Lejeune at Second Division reunion.

Courtesy of H. B. Hull.

USS Lejeune troop transport on Whangpoo River, Shanghai, 1946.

Carol Reynolds Collection, Naval History and Heritage Command.

Statue of Lejeune in front of Lejeune Hall, US Naval Academy.

US Navy photo.

Lejeune Hall, LSU.

Photograph by Mandy McDonald Scallan.

7

WAR PLAN ORANGE

The Marine Corps at a Crossroads, 1919–1920

Lejeune emerged from World War I and the occupation of Germany with the permanent rank of major general and a distinguished war record, the most prominent Marine officer in the corps. Despite the Allied victory in Europe, the US military now faced an inferior position in the Pacific Ocean and Far East. The world war had focused on Europe, the Near East, and the Middle East, creating a vacuum in the Far East–western Pacific region, allowing Japan to increase its influence there. Japan had expanded its territorial ambitions and aggression in Manchuria and China, and took advantage of Allied involvement in the war by seizing Germany's colonies in Micronesia, the island chains above the equator in the central Pacific.

After the war, based on Japanese aggression in China and intelligence reports, senior officers in the US Navy were concerned that Japan might fortify these islands in Micronesia by developing naval bases and airfields that in a war could threaten the United States' Pacific way stations of Guam, Midway, and Wake, and block the main sea-lanes to China and the Philippines.[1] Consequently, the General Board of the Navy, the Navy War College, and the Navy's Office of Operations began in 1919 to review War Plan Orange, the basic plan for war against Japan.[2]

War Plan Orange was a secret plan developed by the United States over nearly four decades to defeat Japan in a war that many naval officers thought would eventually come. Outwardly, the two nations maintained friendly relations despite a trade rivalry in the western Pacific, especially in China, and an American concern for the self-determination of Asian nations. On the other hand, Japan lacked the vital natural resources necessary at home to achieve their plan for national greatness. Consequently, Japan looked to dominate and control China and Southeast Asia. Japan was also eager to exclude the US Navy from the region. In contrast, American foreign policy supported the "Open Door" in China, free international trade in the Orient, and the security of the Philippines and Guam.

The Orange Plan, developed primarily by the Navy, projected a naval war in order to avoid fighting the large Japanese army based in China. The plan predicted three phases of a potential war. First, Japan would initiate war by seizing weakly defended American naval and air bases in the Philippines and Guam so as to protect its flank, enabling the Japanese army and navy to secure the oil, rubber, and other raw materials in the French, British, and Dutch possessions west and south of the Philippines. Because of the vastness of the Pacific Ocean and the distance to the western Pacific, the United States recognized that it could not prevent these Japanese conquests. Instead, the United States would mobilize naval forces at home and in the eastern Pacific. Second, over a period of two to three years, the United States with superior naval and air forces would steam westward to capture Japanese islands and bases in the central Pacific and regain a base in the Philippines to blockade Japanese trade with Southeast Asia. In a location chosen by the Japanese, the Imperial Fleet would attempt to destroy the American Fleet and the blockade. Instead, the US Fleet would cripple or destroy the Japanese Fleet in a huge gunnery battle between battleships. In the third phase, the victorious American Navy would move northward toward the Japanese homeland with air power, impose a devastating economic blockade, and destroy Japanese industries by air bombardment until the enemy sued for peace.

Although the Navy was confident of an eventual victory over Japan, over the years there were many challenges to the Orange plan. The geography of the vast Pacific Ocean initially favored the Japanese over the Americans. The Japanese naval and air bases in the homeland and Formosa were much closer to the American possessions and bases in the western Pacific than was the US Navy. To illustrate, the American naval and air base in Manila in the Philippines was only 1,500 miles from Japan, but 7,000 miles from the West Coast of the United States and 5,000 miles from the nearest major American base in Hawaii. Further, Plan Orange incorrectly assumed over the years—up until December 7, 1941—that the Japanese could not attack and destroy the large American Fleet and air bases in Hawaii. Consequently, the remaining Pacific Fleet was hard pressed to initiate offensive action at the beginning of the war.

While early planners of War Plan Orange—including the Navy Board—hoped for congressional funding to develop a system of fixed overseas bases similar to that of Great Britain, Congress declined to fund and develop strong bases and navy yards outside of their constituencies in the United States.[3] Navy planners also felt that military budget cuts by Congress after World War I unwisely crippled the American Fleet. While Germany and Japan openly rebuilt and increased their military in the 1920s and during the Depression of the 1930s, the US Congress cut military spending and focused on disarmament and rebuilding the nation's economy.

Naval planners also created their own internal problems. For a period of over thirty years, naval personnel developed significantly different strategies and versions of Plan Orange that created conflict, confusion, and uncertainty for the naval establishment. The planners that recommended a gradual westward movement to develop naval and air bases throughout Micronesia were labeled "Cautionaries," while more impatient senior officers such as Admiral Robert E. Coontz and Army Generals Leonard Wood and Douglas MacArthur were "Thrusters," planners who demanded a rapid (and dangerous) large fleet movement directly to the Philippines or Guam. The debates between the planners clouded the Orange Plan for far too long.[4] The more rational central Pacific offensive proved to be the best plan and was basically followed by the Navy, Marine Corps, and Army during World War II. In addition, three consecutive chiefs of naval operations (CNOs), from 1924 to 1933—Edward W. Eberle, Charles F. Hughes, and William V. Pratt—were indifferent to war planning. Pratt was actually opposed to the process.

Another challenge to Plan Orange was the belief of many naval officers that an economic blockade would force Japan to surrender. Japan, however, would not surrender so easily. The fanatical Japanese military government utilized a huge national propaganda machine to recreate the Samurai ethic of self-sacrifice within the Japanese military machine. For the Japanese soldier, marine, or sailor, death in battle was an honorable fate and preferable to surrender. This culture produced suicidal kamikaze pilots and human bombers. The Japanese resistance to surrender would create the unwelcome prospect of a bloody and costly American invasion of the Japanese homeland.

The American government—through the Washington Conference on

Naval Disarmament in 1922—once again handicapped the Navy and Plan Orange by denying to them potential naval and air bases in the western Pacific.[5] While the Japanese agreed to a smaller fleet of capital ships than that of the United States and Great Britain, the United States agreed not to increase fortifications on bases west of Hawaii. Consequently, the United States lost the possibility of developing significant fixed naval and air bases in the Aleutians, Philippines, Guam, Wake, and Midway.

Plan Orange was abandoned by CNO Harold R. Stark on December 17, 1940, thirty-four years after its inception. Because of the rise of fascist powers in Europe, and at the urging of Great Britain, the United States in 1940 adopted a "Europe First" policy, believing that Germany and Italy were greater threats to the United States than Japan. The Rainbow Plans replaced Plan Orange after the German defeat of France in June 1940 and the fear that Great Britain would soon also fall. While the Orange Plan was based on a two-nation and one-ocean war with an all-out effort in the Pacific, the Rainbow Plans projected a two-ocean war fought with other Allied powers against Japan, Germany, and Italy. In 1941, the United States sent almost half of the Pacific Fleet to the Atlantic.

Returning to 1919, shortly after World War I, the Navy expected the Marine Corps to participate in War Plan Orange—in effect establishing a new mission of amphibious assault—but the corps was experiencing great internal stress due to budget cuts and rapid disarmament, the result of the American public's strong distaste for everything military after World War I. In just a three-year period, the corps went from a force of slightly over 10,000 men in 1916 to 75,000 in 1918, only to fall back to 17,000 men in 1920. This reduction greatly lowered the morale of those men who hoped to remain in the peacetime corps. In addition, the State Department directed the postwar corps to commit significant forces for occupation duty in the Caribbean, prompting MGC Barnett to request more men to provide expeditionary forces for War Plan Orange. Because of a budget-conscious Congress, Secretary of the Navy Daniels and the Joint Army-Navy Board had to accept Barnett's position that the amphibious mission did not supersede traditional Marine Corps missions.[6] Thus, by early 1920, the ABF—developed over the last twenty years—was in limbo, unable to support the Navy's challenge in the western Pacific. In effect, the Marine Corps had returned to its old mission of providing troops for expeditionary and occupation duty in Haiti and Santo Domingo, acting as colonial infantry. Visionary

Marines who supported the Navy's new mission in War Plan Orange did not want to return to the past, but did not have the power to establish amphibious assault as the corps's new wartime mission.

After his return from occupation duty in Germany in October 1919, Lejeune commanded all personnel at the Marine Corps Base at Quantico, Virginia. Since the Marines of the Fifth and Sixth regiments—formerly part of the Army's Second Division—had been discharged in August, Lejeune's task was to restore the morale of the officers and men remaining on duty. Lejeune resumed drills, inspections, and military formations and developed a Field Officers' School—the beginning of the Marine Corps Schools—and created under the immediate supervision of Colonel William C. Harllee a comprehensive educational system for enlisted Marines. Its most prominent component was the Marine Corps Institute, a worldwide system of free correspondence education for Marines and their dependents. The institute, approved by MGC Barnett on February 2, 1920, was heavily promoted by Smedley Butler and Harllee, but it survived and thrived under Lejeune.[7]

On March 2, 1920, Lejeune was summoned before the House of Representatives' Committee on Naval Affairs with MGC Barnett at the invitation of Chairman Thomas S. Butler, to discuss increasing the size of the corps despite the rapid downsizing after the world war. Lejeune utilized the opportunity to express his opinion that the wartime mission of the Marine Corps should be amphibious assault. At the time, Lejeune was still the CO of the Marine Corps base at Quantico, Virginia.[8] Butler asked Lejeune to "state to the committee your views as to the importance of maintaining organized expeditionary forces of marines, the size of these forces, and their location."[9] Lejeune began by stating that the mission of the corps had to be determined first before the proper size of the corps and its expeditionary forces and location could be ascertained.[10] Lejeune also noted that the Navy Board had formulated a wartime mission for the Marine Corps which had been approved by the Department of the Navy. Lejeune then stated that "the Marine Corps will supply expeditionary forces for service with the fleets in the event of war."[11]

Lejeune went on to make two important observations as to the real mission of the Marine Corps—notwithstanding the corps's participation in the world war. He first noted that "in the last war the Marine Corps did not carry out this mission . . . due to the fact that we entered the war after the enemy fleet, except submarines, had been swept from the seas. Consequently, there was no naval mission for the Marine Corps, and unless it had served with the Army in France, the Marine Corps could not have taken any part in the Great War."[12] Second, Lejeune stressed the need for the corps to be ready for a future war. He stated that "there is always the danger that the next war may burst upon us just as suddenly as did the last war on England and France, when the readiness of the British fleet for immediate service saved the nation from invasion."[13] In the event of a surprise attack on the United States, Lejeune felt that as part of the fleet the Marines had to be prepared. He said, "these expeditionary forces of Marines . . . must be kept in a similar state of readiness."[14]

Lejeune then boldly clarified the wartime mission of the Marine Corps: "The duty of the expeditionary force with the fleets would be the seizure, occupation, fortification, and defense of temporary naval bases. Fleets cannot operate without bases."[15] Lejeune noted that the corps also had to have its expeditionary forces in readiness for peacetime use, stating that over the past twenty years the corps had "an average of one expedition per annum with expeditions to Santo Domingo, Haiti, Mexico, Cuba, and Nicaragua."[16]

Although it was apparent to the committee that Barnett and Lejeune were in agreement as to the wartime and peacetime missions of the corps, the testimony also made it obvious that each man approached the wartime mission differently in obligation to matters of priority. Lejeune wanted to accept the wartime mission of providing an assault force for the Navy immediately, even if the corps lacked adequate manpower at the current time, with the hope that sufficient manpower would be allotted as the Marines proved their value to the Navy. On the other hand, Barnett apparently accepted the wartime mission contingent upon the committee's willingness to recommend funding the corps at the authorized enlisted strength of 27,400 men instead of the currently funded manpower of about 17,000 Marines. This difference was made apparent when Barnett corrected a statement made in Lejeune's previous testimony. Lejeune stated, "General Barnett said a few minutes ago that these plans for the Marine Corps provide for two expeditionary forces, one for service with the Pacific Fleet, to be stationed on the west coast, and the other for service with the Atlantic Fleet, to be stationed on the east coast. I think the size Gen. Barnett mentioned was 6,000 or 8,000 men for each force."[17] Barnett quickly replied, "That [statement] was not signed or approved by anybody, but was just a tentative plan drawn up; because, of course, the plans have changed materially since the Pacific Fleet went out."[18] Barnett was concerned that the postwar strength of the corps might continue to decline. The funded strength of the corps at that time was only 962 officers and 16,085 men. Before developing a significant expeditionary force for the fleet, Barnett wanted Congress to fund the corps to the authorized enlisted strength of 27,400 men.

Soon after this hearing, Barnett wrote a letter to clarify his vision and decision regarding the size and use of the MEF, a decision dependent on an increase in manpower for the corps. The MGC replied on March 8, 1920, to a letter previously received from the CNO regarding the function of the Marine Corps in war plans. In his letter to Barnett on January 28, 1920, Admiral Robert E. Coontz had described the Navy's tentative strategic plan of the Pacific "for the capture of certain bases in the Caroline and Marshall Islands as the fleet advances across the Pacific."[19] For the combined Atlantic and Pacific plans, Coontz suggested as policy that the corps "maintain on the West Coast an expeditionary force of from 6,000 to 8,000 men, fully equipped, ready for service in 48 hours."[20] Coontz suggested the same number of men for the East Coast. In addition, the CNO assumed that the corps would continue its traditional missions—to supply forces for the policing of Haiti, Santo Domingo, Cuba, "and such other detachments as may be necessary, to provide advance base detachments on Guam and other points until their permanent fortification is assured by the Army" as well as supply the usual Marine detachments for vessels of the fleet and guards at naval stations for the protection of property. Coontz recognized that the development of these numbers for the expeditionary forces would take "a considerable period of time to build up and equip such forces. . . . if such a policy is decided upon it will furnish a definite point of aim, which will permit . . . the logical development of the Marine Corps for the duties it will be called upon to perform under the War Plans."[21]

Coontz's recommendations were unacceptable to Barnett, with the corps facing budget cuts and declining manpower during the postwar era of military retrenchment. Barnett replied to Coontz that "the Marine Corps would supply expeditionary forces subject to the following conditions: 1. The organization given below includes only the forces which are to be held available at Quantico and San Diego for Expeditionary and Advanced Base duty; 2. It is believed that this organization will serve as a standard for the usual type of expedition which the Marine Corps may be called upon to perform; 3. When the Marine Corps has been recruited to its full strength

(27,400) there will be available for Expeditionary duty the following troops: Quantico (includes 300 for aviation) 5,852; San Diego (includes 200 for aviation) 1,900."[22]

Barnett also added a fourth point, that "the infantry regiment at San Diego and one regiment of infantry at Quantico included in the above tables will be trained and equipped not only as infantry but also as Advanced Base Force Technical Troops."[23] Barnett's response implied that no expeditionary troops would be available for the war mission unless the Marine Corps was funded to its authorized strength of 27,400 men. Given the downsizing of the military at this time, no increases were likely to happen. Even if this strength was funded, a smaller expeditionary force than what Coontz recommended would be provided, but primarily for traditional Marine Corps missions, such as expeditions to the Caribbean and ABF operations of a defensive nature. Therefore, Barnett was advocating that no expeditionary forces would be available to accompany the fleet in a westward movement in War Plan Orange unless Congress increased the size of the corps.[24]

As a result, the Marine Corps Headquarters of early 1920 was just as slow to respond to a new mission of amphibious operations as the corps of 1900 had been to accept the new concept of the ABF as promoted by the Navy's General Board. Consequently, Barnett would continue to stress traditional Marine Corps missions—providing ships' guards, security detachments for naval bases, and occupation duty in the Caribbean. Thus the Joint Board and Secretary of the Navy Daniels had to accept Barnett's decision that the corps could only undertake to provide its traditional missions. Consequently, by 1920 the ABF, acting to defend a base or to seize a base, was not available to assist the Navy in War Plan Orange.

This apparent loss of momentum for the Marine Corps toward the new amphibious mission seemed to justify Secretary Daniels's decision to relieve George Barnett as MGC on June 18, 1920, and appoint John A. Lejeune. This was not the case, however.

Daniels's dismissal of Barnett and appointment of Lejeune as MGC was not the result of a power struggle between Lejeune and Barnett or a means for Daniels to empower Lejeune to move forward to establish amphibious assault as the new wartime mission for the Marine Corps. Rather, it was Daniels's dislike of Barnett for actions Barnett had taken without informing him, as well as Daniels's established policy of limiting the Navy's bureau chiefs and the MGC to one four-year term of office. Daniels was influenced in 1913 by the advice of the outgoing secretary of the Navy, George von L. Meyer, to retain the power of directing the Navy in the office of the secretary. Daniels was a former editor of a small newspaper in Raleigh, North Carolina, a progressive egalitarian who protected the rights of the enlisted ranks and disliked officers from the privileged elitist class of inherited wealth. Daniels had been an avid Democratic national committeeman for years, supported Woodrow Wilson for president, and was determined to prevent the slack administration of important Navy and Marine Corps posts by key officers who remained too long in office.[25] Wilson approved Daniels's recommendation to limit the tenure of his senior subordinates to a four-year term.

Unfortunately for Daniels, Barnett's and the Navy's bureau chiefs' four-year terms of office had expired in 1918 during the world war. It was necessary, therefore, to keep the same leaders in office. According to Daniels, Barnett and the bureau chiefs "were reappointed with the full understanding that upon the termination of the struggle their resignations would be accepted. All chiefs of bureaus gave Daniels their letters of resignation to take effect at the pleasure of the President." Barnett, however, on February 25, 1918, preferred not to sign the resignation letter, saying, "I am a gentleman, and no gentleman would remain a day after his resignation was desired. I will tender it if you desire as soon as the war is over."[26] Barnett had a different recollection of the conversation. He refused to sign the letter of resignation because he believed that he served at the pleasure of the president, not the Navy secretary.[27]

Barnett angered Daniels further by going behind his back in obtaining senatorial support for his own promotion in 1918. In May 1918, Barnett, who had many Republican friends in Congress, tried to arrange his promotion to lieutenant general and his principal staff officers at Marine Headquarters to major general.[28] Congressman Thomas Butler, chairman of the House Naval Affairs Committee, father of controversial Marine Smedley Butler, rose up in the House of Representatives to denounce the bill, calling Barnett a "rocking chair warrior."[29] Undoubtedly, Thomas Butler's dislike of Barnett was influenced heavily by his son Smedley, who shamelessly utilized his father's position to advance his own career in the Marine Corps. Although Smedley was a natural and brave military leader who had received two Medals of Honor, his impulsive tendency to lash out at individuals who disagreed with him later destroyed his career in the corps. President Herbert Hoover tried to court-martial the younger Butler but was unsuccessful. Smedley was a member of the old corps who favored fighting rebels as colonial infantry in the Caribbean over the new amphibious mission, preferred officers promoted from the ranks, and disliked Navy and Marine officers who were graduates of the Naval Academy, especially those officers who emphasized the professional study of warfare. In addition, the younger Butler felt that Barnett had kept him from a combat role in the world war.

Daniels was eager to force Barnett's resignation and appoint Lejeune commandant at the end of the world war, which occurred on November 11, 1918. Lejeune, however, was not available, for he and the Second Division were part of the occupation force in Germany and did not return home until the late summer of 1919. Daniels summoned Lejeune to his office on or about September 20, 1919. After explaining his policy of only four-year appointments for bureau chiefs and the commandant, and the necessity of reappointing them only until the war ended, Daniels told Lejeune "what he had decided long ago, that he would recommend my appointment as Commandant to the President upon my return home from 'overseas,' and he, therefore, would request the President to appoint me as soon as the President returned to Washington from his speaking tour. He then closed the interview by charging me to keep what he had told me in the strictest confidence."[30]

Wilson was conducting a speaking tour across America to convince the people not to accept the reservations of Republican Senator Henry Cabot Lodge limiting the United States' acceptance of the Treaty of Versailles and entry into the League of Nations. As it turned out, Wilson collapsed on September 25 in Colorado and had to return to Washington, suffering a massive stroke that left him partially paralyzed. Daniels called Lejeune to his office on or about October 15, 1919, to tell him that "on account of the President's illness, he was unable to carry out his plan to recommend my appointment as Commandant then, but that he would do so as soon as the President recovered his health sufficiently." Daniels again charged Lejeune to regard his pending appointment as "strictly confidential."[31] Daniels did not keep his own advice, however, telling Congressman Butler of his plan to appoint Lejeune as commandant. Smedley Butler learned of this from his father and brought up the subject to Lejeune as both men drove to Quantico a few days later.[32]

Lejeune heard no more about Daniels's intentions during the winter of

1919–20. Finally, in May 1920, when Barnett was away inspecting Marine facilities on the West Coast, Daniels called Lejeune to his office to recommend outstanding Marines for promotion to the rank of general, an action that should have been taken by the commandant. Upon Barnett's return, Daniels intended to ask Barnett for his resignation.[33]

Daniels finally met with the ill Wilson on June 17, 1920, to gain the president's approval of his plan to remove Barnett and appoint Lejeune as commandant. Wilson backed Daniels, as attested to in a letter to Lejeune by Wilson's personal physician, Dr. Cary T. Grayson. Wilson told Grayson that "Lejeune's appointment shall be one of merit, and his leadership as Commandant of the Marine Corps shall be an inspiration to the other officers of that Corps, particularly to the younger members."[34] In the same letter to Lejeune, Grayson wrote, "In recommending you, Mr. Daniels did what he conscientiously thought was for the best for the Corps and the President backed him to the limit, and afterwards referred to your appointment and record with great pride."[35]

Barnett did not leave office willingly. In his unpublished memoir, Barnett remarked that Daniels's comments about his removal were untruthful and maintained that he was "an upstanding and competent officer who was humiliated by not being allowed to finish a second four-year term."[36] Many of Barnett's friends asked Dr. Grayson to "intercede with the President in his behalf, and Mrs. Barnett was particularly active and persistent in that direction—a number of letters sent to the President by Senators and Congressmen of both parties—no doubt inspired by her efforts."[37] Barnett's wife, the former Lelia Montague Gordon, a wealthy widow and Washington socialite, spent over twenty years—long after Barnett's death—in a continual effort to rehabilitate Barnett's reputation and publicly proclaim that her husband had been dismissed as the result of a political plot that implicated Daniels, the Butlers, and Lejeune.[38]

When Lejeune reported to Barnett on June 30, 1920, to assume the office of commandant, Barnett asked Lejeune why as a friend he had failed to tell him of the "plot." Lejeune could only say that "his hands were tied." Barnett then had Lejeune stand at attention while he chastised him for disloyalty, unprofessional conduct, and for being a false friend.[39] Much later, in 1932, Mrs. Barnett—who never forgave the people she believed had destroyed her husband's career and her social position in Washington—wrote to Lejeune, saying, "You took part in it [the plot] and finally gave in to General

Butler. . . . The thing that was done helped kill my husband. . . . He loved you as a friend. . . . [He] bore that pain to his death."[40]

In the final analysis, Daniels, responsible to the president for the Navy and Marine Corps, had the right and duty to select the man he deemed best qualified to be commandant. Barnett's anger and anguish over being removed as commandant was fanned and probably largely engineered by Mrs. Barnett, who made it her life's work to defend Barnett and herself. As late as 1947, long after the deaths of Barnett and Lejeune, Mrs. Barnett sued Daniels over an anecdote in his memoirs referring to her husband as "The-Man-Afraid-of-His-Wife."[41]

Lejeune became commandant on July 1, 1920. Although distressed over the unpleasant circumstances of his promotion, he was determined to modernize the Marine Corps and facilitate a more positive relationship with the Navy, Congress, and the public. Even though Lejeune supported the traditional missions of the corps, he eagerly sought to advance War Plan Orange and a new mission of amphibious assault.

Daniels and Barnett share blame for the unpleasant and agonizing nature of Barnett's dismissal. It would be an understatement to say that Barnett and Daniels communicated poorly with each other. While Daniels took far too long to gain the president's approval to dismiss Barnett, Barnett's reputation would not have suffered had he resigned gracefully. Undoubtedly, his continuing intransigence was encouraged by his wife, who spoke to almost everyone in Washington for years about the unsavory "cabal" and "plot" that destroyed her husband. Lejeune had been placed in an awkward situation, told by Daniels of his intention to dismiss Barnett and swearing him to secrecy. This "secret" plan placed Lejeune in an untenable position because he and Barnett were longtime friends. Lejeune was not responsible for Barnett's firing, a fact known by almost everyone, and he was wholeheartedly welcomed as commandant by the corps and the Congress.

8
REINVIGORATION OF THE MARINE CORPS

Major General John A. Lejeune served three terms as commandant of the US Marine Corps, from July 1, 1920, to March 5, 1929, and most likely would have been reappointed in 1929 had he wanted to continue his tenure. He was appointed as commandant by Secretary of the Navy Josephus Daniels and President Woodrow Wilson (Democrats) on June 20, 1920, by Secretary Edwin Denby and President Warren G. Harding (Republicans) in March of 1921, and by Secretary Curtis D. Wilbur and President Calvin Coolidge (Republicans) in 1925.

Lejeune revitalized and invigorated a lethargic corps, spurring its transformation into a modern and proactive Marine Corps. He changed the old corps's role of acting as colonial infantry to a new mission of amphibious assault, a unique role that gave the corps a major place in the American defense establishment. Ambitious for himself and the corps, Lejeune went on record at the very beginning of his tenure as commandant "to make the Marine Corps the most efficient military organization in the world."[1] To achieve this distinction, he understood he would have to undertake significant military reforms to modernize the corps. Consequently, Lejeune set out to obtain the enthusiastic and loyal support of the corps's officers and men, the American people, members of Congress, the White House, and the Department of the Navy.

Although he boldly presented to Congress the personnel and budgetary needs for the corps to accomplish a new mission, Lejeune followed the dictates of the American public and Congress to achieve efficiency with fewer resources. To achieve his goals for the corps, he improved on a good public relations program in order to "sell" the public on the value of the corps to the nation, indirectly influencing Congress and the Navy Department. Lejeune had already earned the respect of many members of Congress during his tenure as the assistant to the commandant, 1914 to 1918, as he made frequent visits to lobby for Marine Corps budgets and the development of Quantico as a major base. His reputation was enhanced during World War I as he became the only Marine to command a division in the war. He was the longest-serving CO of the Army's Second Division, arguably the most distinguished American division in the war. The fighting abilities of the Marine Brigade in this division had won acclaim from the American public.

After the war, Lejeune served as CO of the Marine base at Quantico in 1919–1920. Lejeune impressed the members of the House Committee on Naval Affairs when he and his staff started a school of vocational and basic academic education for enlisted Marines at Quantico. The school was modeled after the International Correspondence School of Scranton, Pennsylvania. While the Marines received advanced military training and education during the morning hours, they had the opportunity to learn a civilian trade through enrollment in vocational and academic programs in the afternoon or at night. Marines who had only a short time left in their enlistment or were not interested in this instruction served on guard duty or performed other military functions in the afternoon. Those interested in receiving career education had a wide choice in selection. Available courses included automobile repair, electrical engineering, stenography and typewriting, English, Spanish, mathematics, drafting, concrete, brick and stone masonry, carpentry, forestry, plumbing, and bookkeeping, to name just a few. This training not only prepared the men for work as civilians after leaving the corps, but also served as an added inducement for men to enlist in the Marine Corps. Lejeune stated that "the Marine Corps will be popularized with the American people, because they will feel we are trying our best for the young men who come from the homes of the people of the United States to serve the country in the military service." As commandant, Lejeune institutionalized this program as the Marine Corps Institute. Lejeune also developed additional training for company and field-grade officers at Quantico. This program later became the famous MCS. Key members of Lejeune's staff at Quantico included Brigadier General Smedley Butler, Colonel William C. Harllee, and First Lieutenant John H. Craige. As a means of showing their approval of this new program, the members of the House Committee on Naval Affairs applauded when Secretary of the Navy Daniels lauded their support of these programs and said, "Therefore we welcome them [representatives] here [at Quantico] as worthy to be enrolled in the Corps."[2]

One of Lejeune's first actions as MGC was to balance the selection process for junior officers seeking permanent commissions in the post-war corps. The first selection board as led by Colonel John H. Russell—appointed in January 1919 by MGC George Barnett—appeared to discriminate against those officers who had served with distinction in the Fourth Marine Brigade in France during the world war. The perception by some Marines, especially those who had fought in the war, was that the Russell board selected only officers and gentlemen with good education and family. The fact that no members of the Russell selection board had served with the brigade in France appeared to lend credence to this belief. There was a rumor afloat that Russell had advised the members of the selection board to remember that they were selecting the young officers that they would invite to their quarters and whom their daughters might marry.

In response to criticism of the first selection board, MGC Lejeune appointed Major General Wendell C. Neville, former CO of the Marine Brigade in France, to head a second selection board. The selections of the Neville board favored officers for permanent commissions who had demonstrated leadership in battle regardless of education and family connections. Probably influencing this approach was board member Smedley Butler. Another board member was Brigadier General Harry Lee, who had formerly commanded the Sixth Regiment after the first day of fighting at Belleau Wood. The new selections seemed to win favor for fairness with the public, Congress, and Secretary Daniels. The down side, however, would appear years later when many of these officers receiving permanent commissions from the enlisted ranks proved to be too old, undereducated, and unable to provide efficient leadership at higher levels of rank and responsibility. Some of these men would become the world war "hump" that Lejeune would try unsuccessfully to eliminate from the service in the late 1920s because of the policy of promotion and elimination by seniority.[3]

One of the greatest challenges Lejeune faced as he assumed office as MGC was the general public backlash against the military services. After American participation in the terrible, costly, and indecisive Great War, the new policy of the Republican presidents during the decade of the 1920s was to drastically reduce government expenditures—especially for the military services—and to balance the budget. For this purpose, Congress created the

Bureau of the Budget with General Charles G. Dawes as its first director.

On assuming office on July 1, 1920, Lejeune had only 16,100 Marines in the corps as a result of "war service only" Marines who had left the corps for civilian jobs. It was also a far cry from the wartime strength of 75,000 Marines in 1918. Appearing in January of 1921 before the House Subcommittee on Appropriations in reference to the Naval Appropriations Bill for fiscal year 1922, Lejeune stated that the corps had "an almost impossible task [of having on July 1, 1920] to comply with the expressed mandate of the naval committee and Congress to bring the Corps up to an average strength of 20,000 men."[4] Actually, this was a positive development, for this figure was well above the prewar strength of the corps. Undoubtedly, Lejeune had previously influenced the committee and Congress to set a goal of 20,000 men.[5]

Lejeune ordered an active recruiting campaign. In his first few months as MGC, he reorganized the recruiting service and set quotas for every man on recruiting duty. These Marines were held individually responsible for results. Failure resulted in being relieved from recruiting duty, reassigned, and replaced. Lejeune opened many new recruiting offices and assigned more men to recruiting duty. Colonel David D. Porter enthusiastically led this drive, bringing the corps up to authorized strength by Christmas of 1920. Because only a few Naval Academy graduates were interested in the corps that year, and in light of a considerable number of officer vacancies, Lejeune sent a letter to all COs seeking qualified noncommissioned officers who were likely to pass the examination for training as officers. Lejeune also considered some graduates of distinguished military colleges for commissions.[6] When the corps reached full strength, Lejeune cut the recruiting service by two-thirds, returned 500 men to line duty, closed 105 substations, and secured cost-free recruiting space in federal buildings.

For the purpose of reducing costs in the corps, Lejeune resumed the system of clothing allowances and the Navy ration that had lapsed during the war. Lejeune was particularly concerned about the excess of enlisted men of high rank at Marine Headquarters and gradually reduced that group, as well as the number of civil employees and clerks. When Lejeune observed that the "Washington Marine Barracks were . . . brilliantly lighted up at night," he ordered lights out. The corps significantly reduced printing services, limiting the duplication of general orders from the War Department, except for those involving expeditionary regiments and battalions liable to serve with the Army.[7]

Lejeune also noted that "spending for motor transportation was enormous, $595,000 a year with $176,000 going for gasoline." He recommended "using mule-drawn wagons for short, non-emergency hauls when time was not vital."[8] Motorcycles that had been used in recruiting went to storage units, because these costs were less expensive than fuel. Lejeune also closed Marine Corps commissaries when duplicated by Navy stores.[9] The greatest savings occurred when Lejeune decided to discontinue two-year enlistments. "We are not going to take any more men for two years, but only three-and-four year enlistments. . . . since training, clothing, and travel costs were substantial, longer enlistments saved money."[10] These cost-reduction measures earned favorable recognition from the House Subcommittee on Naval Appropriations.[11] Charles G. Dawes, director of the budget for the Harding administration, told Lejeune that "one of the things that he admired most about the Marine Corps was the way in which they took what they could get without grumbling and made the best of it."[12]

Despite these measures of economy led by Lejeune, it appeared that some members of the House Subcommittee on Naval Appropriations wanted further cuts to the 20,000 Marines authorized by budget. In his testimony before the committee, Lejeune led a spirited, articulate, and honest defense of the need for at least 20,000 Marines. Lejeune actually believed he needed the 27,400 men as authorized by Congress, but not funded, in order to build up an adequate expeditionary force. Congressman Patrick H. Kelley of Michigan questioned the need for 20,000 Marines. He suggested that the permanent detachment at Parris Island had too many Marines, that the training centers at Parris Island and Quantico could be combined, and that the Marine Corps probably needed fewer men because of the existence of a larger Army that could act as a reserve force. In retrospect, it is likely that Kelley played the role of devil's advocate in order to allow Lejeune the opportunity to defend the use of funds and manpower and to convince the other members of the committee of the Marine Corps's legitimate needs.

Lejeune was polite, respectful, and direct in answering Kelley's questions. He stated that Parris Island and Quantico could not be combined or compared as bases. Parris Island had the proper terrain for the initial training of recruits. After completing basic training, these new Marines graduated to Quantico for a higher form of military training—to function as an expeditionary force. Quantico was an essential base because it was close to the Navy base at Hampton Roads on Chesapeake Bay. Further, Lejeune related that the Marine Corps was different from the Army, with a different mission. The corps was part of the Navy Department, providing the amphibious assault force against an enemy: "The fleet is the great defensive outpost of our country. It must never sleep. It must be ready at all times. The world war burst on England and France without notice. The readiness of the British fleet and the French army saved the world from being engulfed by the Teutonic hordes."[13]

Later, Lejeune stated to his staff "that it had been very gratifying to find in the House of Representatives an exceedingly friendly feeling for the Marine Corps. No one seems to have anything but kind words for the Corps as an organization" and "we have been reduced in strength, not because Congress had fault to find with us, but simply because of the necessity for cutting down and economizing along all lines."[14] Years later in his autobiography, Lejeune wrote that "both Mr. Kelley and Mr. French, his successor as Chairman of the subcommittee, were among my warmest personal friends."[15]

Despite Lejeune's close working relationship with Congress, that body was determined to reduce government expenditures. Consequently, Lejeune struggled to maintain an adequate force to fulfill the corps's mission. Lejeune reported to his headquarters staff in 1922 that the House of Representatives had appropriated money for only 17,500 men for the following year. Lejeune told the House Committee for Naval Appropriations that such a reduction in force would result in either removing the Marine brigades in Haiti and Santo Domingo or abolishing the expeditionary force: "As a compromise, appropriations for 19,500 men were provided for, but with the understanding that should the Marines in Santo Domingo be withdrawn . . . our strength will be reduced to 17,500 men. . . . we endeavored to get 18,000, but without success."[16]

Lejeune understood that to succeed in his campaign for economy and efficiency, it was first necessary to obtain the earnest and sincere support of his Marines. "I adopted [as] the guiding principle of my administration the rule that the good of the Corps, combined with the just treatment of all officers and men, was paramount and took precedence over all other considerations." For Lejeune, "the practice of this principle precluded the exercise of favoritism and brought about among the officers and men a feeling of confidence in the administration of Marine Corps affairs."[17]

Lejeune implemented his ideas in several ways, the most important being frequent conferences with key leaders. Lejeune was determined to involve the officer corps as much as possible in decision-making for the improvement of the Marine Corps. Only sixteen days after assuming office on July 16, 1920, Lejeune established weekly, monthly, and quarterly conferences of key staff at Marine Corps Headquarters in Washington, DC. Lejeune stated, "the primary purpose of the conferences is not to come to a definite decision on certain questions, but rather to get an expression of opinion from the officers present, which will enable the Commandant to eventually decide the matter in the best way." Further, Lejeune sent copies of the minutes of the conferences to all Marine Corps COs to get a "consensus of opinion from practically all officers on matters affecting the good of the Corps . . . to create opportunities for a free exchange of views and mutual understanding of policies . . . inculcation of proper doctrines and cooperation of effort."[18]

This conference format opened the corps to diverse thought, soliciting responses from throughout the organization. In early December 1920, for example, Brigadier General Joseph H. Pendleton on the West Coast responded with the memorandum: "This office read with a great deal of interest copies of Conferences at HQMC. Well worth expense of copies, excellent investment." This gave Pendleton an opportunity to convey that "his officers much prefer to wear civilian clothes in unofficial circumstances." Pendleton was shocked by Lejeune's reestablishment of the full dress uniform and strongly recommended its abolition.[19]

Lejeune also opposed form letters in favor of personal correspondence. Brigadier General Rufus H. Lane, adjutant and inspector, instructed his men, "The Major General Commandant remarked that there is a very strong tendency on the part of all government organizations to become purely routine in their dealings and to overlook the element of human contact. . . . in the early part of the World War, Marine Corps Headquarters maintained a touch of individuality. . . . the letters were not simply ground out by the yard."[20]

As an accessible commandant, Lejeune put his personal stamp on the Marine Corps in many ways. Lejeune always worked to showcase the corps in the best light as an honorable institution, supportive of the government and the public. He was upset when a group of Marines from the Washington Barracks went to the aid of a fellow Marine arrested by the police for a "disturbance." (This disturbance was probably a Marine fighting a civilian when one or the other was intoxicated.) Lejeune stated: "On duty or liberty, it was their duty to assist police, not interfere with the police. . . .

non-commissioned officers on duty or not should use their authority to prevent such disturbances. . . . any NCO who aids disturbances is not worthy to be an NCO and will be tried by courts-martial."[21]

Lejeune was an effective leader because he believed in the importance of cultivating personal relationships with his officers, men, and the families of his Marines. In his recruiting strategies he stressed: "The primary requisite was to satisfy parents that their boys would benefit mentally, morally, and physically by being in the Corps. Parents could not be won over by appeals to patriotism, but by the certainty that the service would do their boy real good." Lejeune believed that "every officer is responsible for the physical, mental, and moral welfare of men under him. If any officer fails to do this in every case he fails his duty to the Marine Corps, to parents, and to the boy himself." Lejeune compared the corps to a large university, with officers and men like instructors and pupils. "Bring this fact home," he said to recruiters, "and we will have no difficulty in recruiting."[22]

Lejeune's positive relationship with his officers and men was long-lasting. When Lejeune toured the country with President Calvin Coolidge, he met in St. Louis, Missouri, a former soldier who had served under him in the Second Division during World War I. This man sought out Lejeune rather than the president because he had met Lejeune during the war. During a brief lull in battle after an exhausting forced march, this soldier and others stood to attention when their division commander arrived. The soldier remembered that Lejeune said: "Sit down, men. It is more important for tired men to rest than for the Division Commander to be saluted."[23]

Writing about effective leaders, one Marine officer cited this example of Lejeune's regard for his soldiers and Marines. "This soldier's account illustrates the relational intelligence of a great leader who understands the value of personal interaction with his subordinates. The soldier chose to speak with Lejeune rather than the President of the United States because he had a relationship with Lejeune. Although Lejeune's interaction with the man was brief, the impact was significant."[24]

To Lejeune, the Marine Corps was an elite organization. He mentioned at one meeting that he had received many complaints about former Army men who had later joined the Marines. "Even some of the former Army men with considerable service did not seem to grasp Marine Corps ideas. These former Army men entering the Corps should be sent to recruit depots for training, not for drill, but to imbue them with Marine Corps ideas."[25]

General Lejeune was quick to respond to what he perceived as injustice or insubordination. Unlike a few senior Marine officers of this period who disliked and denigrated the Navy, desiring independent commands on land in places such as Haiti and the Dominican Republic, Lejeune always supported the Navy and the Marines' role as assault troops for the fleet. That did not mean, however, that Lejeune would tolerate naval abuses of power. On one occasion, Lejeune officially protested to the assistant secretary of the Navy that the Marine Corps had not been invited to a conference of commandants and managers of Navy yards. At this conference the Navy officials changed command relationships, whereupon the Marine CO of the Marine Barracks would now report to the naval captain of the Navy yard instead of to the commandant of the Marine Corps. In response, Lejeune protested that this proposed change would interfere with the immediate jurisdiction of the commandant over the Marine CO of the Marine Barracks. Lejeune insisted that "this change was highly undesirable . . . and . . . belittles the prestige of the Marine Corps." Further, Lejeune noted that the Marine officer was usually senior in rank to the Navy officer and that this change would cause problems with the Marine courts-martial process, for all cases had to be approved by the MGC. As a result of Lejeune's straightforward approach, the secretary of the Navy restored the previous command relationship.[26]

In his quest for fairness and justice throughout the corps, Lejeune would not accept insubordination. He stopped the practice utilized in the old corps of some officers going over the head of the commandant to a senator or congressman in order to change orders for transfers or assignments to a new station. At one conference Lejeune explained his feelings about this issue: "Once in a while—not very often—an officer tries to get out of complying with orders for a change in station through political influence. I am not prone to yield to any such importunities, and I feel that such action on the part of any officer has a tendency to attempt to break down the authority of the Commandant." Lejeune saw this as insubordination: "When an order for change of station is issued, we do not object to the officer, if he has good reason, laying his case before us, but we do emphatically object to having him go to some third party and try to force the Commandant to do something he does not want to do."[27]

In a major move to modernize the Marine Corps, Lejeune, in an order on December 1, 1920, reorganized Corps Headquarters. While the old administrative departments of paymaster, quartermaster, and adjutant and inspector continued to perform their usual functions, Lejeune organized a Division of Operations and Training to provide for the study of distinctly military questions in the areas of training, operations, intelligence, materiel, and aviation. The division was tasked to conduct a thorough study of those areas in order to allow the MGC to make decisions on operational matters. The functions of the division were similar to those of the General Staff of the Army and the Office of the CNO for Naval Matters.[28] Whereas Marine aviation had previously been under the control of the Navy—the chief of naval aviation—Lejeune arranged to have supervision moved to Marine Corps Headquarters.[29]

Lejeune and other Marine officers recognized that the corps needed an agency for internal war planning in order to work with the Army and Navy in joint war plans. At that time, the Army and Navy worked with the Joint Army-Navy Board to coordinate war planning. To participate in joint military planning, the War Plans Committee, previously operating directly under the MGC, became on November 14, 1924, a War Plans Section as part of the Division of Operations and Training.[30]

Under this reorganization, Lejeune also created the personnel, recruiting, and educational sections to relieve himself and his aides from routine administration. This was separate from the Division of Operations and Training. For independent field commands of brigade size or larger, the Marine Corps in 1922 utilized the term "Executive Staff," similar in function to what the Army termed "General Staff with Troops." For the corps, the executive staff was the body of assistants that coordinated staff functions for the CG of a brigade or division. These functions were organized into four main groups: (1) personnel and routine administration; (2) information on the enemy (intelligence); (3) operations, plans, orders, and training; and (4) supply, maintenance, transportation, and evacuation. Lejeune as CO of the Second Army Division in the Great War utilized these designations that were already in use in the French Army. When planning the first Civil War reenactment at Wilderness Run in 1921, the corps's "East Coast Expeditionary Force" of 4,000 Marines from Quantico would utilize the new system of staff designations.[31]

At the beginning of his tenure as commandant, Lejeune stated unequivocally to certain members of Congress and the Navy that he intended to do everything in his power to make the Marine Corps the most efficient military organization in the world.[32] One way to achieve this objective was to focus on military education. Thus, one of Lejeune's greatest and most enduring contributions to the corps was the establishment of the MCS. As commandant, Lejeune saw a great need for more in-depth military training for officers in order to modernize the corps. The officers' training camp prior to Lejeune becoming commandant was a four-month course dealing primarily in minor tactics and administration.[33] Based on his own experience, Lejeune knew that the average Marine officer received minimal formal military training, while a favored few—often with political connections—received appointments to study at such institutions as the AWC and the Navy War College. As a newly commissioned second lieutenant in 1890, Lejeune had only a two-month course of instruction at the Marine Barracks, Navy Yard, Brooklyn, New York. "I had no opportunity to attend a military school until 1909, when I went to the Army War College."[34]

Lejeune's rationale for his military education policy for all Marine Corps officers was published on September 16, 1921: "The particular object of the policy . . . is to assure and hasten the military schooling of the commissioned personnel as a whole, as opposed to the more comprehensive schooling of a small minority, to assure to each officer the basic schooling according to his rank, in connection with the main requirement that Marines be excellent infantry men trained as well to serve at sea."[35] The MCS became part of the new Division of Operations and Training at US Marine Corps Headquarters under the authority of the CO, MCS, via the CG, Marine Barracks, Quantico, Virginia. It was basically the same system followed by the Marine Corps today. The schools conducted three regular courses for officers: the Basic Course, the Company Officers' Course, and the Field Officers' Course.

The Basic Course included 376 hours of military instruction and was offered twice a year for all incoming, newly appointed second lieutenants. Enrolling for the first term were officers commissioned in June—young men whom the Marine Corps had selected from graduates of distinguished military colleges as well as qualified noncommissioned officers in the corps. Graduates of the Naval Academy that entered the Marine Corps and commissioned later took the second class. The basic course covered tactics, topography, and military law. The tactical curriculum dealt primarily with the study and operation of machine guns, light mortars, one-pounders (small cannon), grenades, military orientation, scouting, patrolling, musketry, combat orders, security, and fighting with the bayonet. Military law focused on naval courts and boards. Courses in topography included military sketching, both theoretical and practical. General subjects consisted of landing operations from the sea, infantry drill, ordnance and gunnery, and signals. Enforced discipline for student officers in the basic course ranged between the extremes of highly structured military prep schools and the relative freedom enjoyed by more senior officer-students at the Company Officers' Course and the Field Officers' Course.[36]

All Marine officers with the rank of lieutenant were required to take the Company Officers' Course in order to be eligible for promotion to the grade of captain. In addition, all officers with the rank of captain or above who had not taken the course would now be required to do so. The course began in early October and lasted thirty-four weeks, with 652 hours of instruction. This more advanced course also stressed tactics, topography, law, and general subjects, with a greater emphasis on offensive and defensive combat using military information, terrain exercises, and field engineering. The section on law was more comprehensive, encompassing law of evidence, criminal law, preparation of charges and specifications, and the rules of land warfare. Topography studies were also more detailed, using panoramic sketching, military sketching, and map reading. General subjects focused on administration, the staff functions performed by the adjutant and inspector, quartermaster and paymaster, as well as the use of ordnance, gunnery, infantry drill, landing forces, rifle and pistol marksmanship, and the old manual signaling systems of wig-wag (back-and-forth signaling) and semaphore (flag signaling).

The successful completion of the Field Officers' Course was necessary for an officer's eligibility for promotion to the rank of major. Moreover, all lieutenant colonels and majors who had not taken this course would do so now. The course began in early October and lasted eight months and one week, also focusing on tactics, law, and topography. This was the most advanced Marine Corps course at the schools. Tactics included the techniques of separate arms, combat orders, solution of problems, military history, tactical functions of larger units, military intelligence, logistics, care of animals and transportation, troop leading, methods of training, care of troops, psychology and leadership, map maneuvers and problems, general terrain exercises, and the study of probable theaters of operations. The curriculum on law covered John J. McKelvey's *Handbook on the Law of Evidence,* Lewis Hochheimer's *Criminal Law,* George B. Davis's *International*

Law, preparation of charges and specifications, rules of land warfare, military government, and martial law.[37]

In order to be flexible and offer other opportunities to corps officers, Lejeune would accept equivalent schooling in Army and Navy schools. For example, "in lieu of taking the Company Officers' Course of the MCS, a limited number of captains and senior first lieutenants who are graduates of the Basic School or had equivalent schooling may be assigned to take the Company Officer's Course at the [Army] Infantry School, Camp Benning, Georgia."[38] Similarly, a limited number of more senior officers could attend the advanced course at the (Army) School of the Line, Fort Leavenworth, Kansas. Also, a limited number of Marine officers above the grade of captain who were graduates of the Field Officers' Course could be assigned to the NWC, Newport, Rhode Island.

In the early days of the development of the MCS, the Marine Corps did not yet have schools that specialized in all of the combat arms, with the exception of infantry. A limited number of officers who were graduates of the Company or Field Officers' course could take courses at Army schools such as the Field Artillery School, the Chemical Warfare School, and the Signal Corps School. Marine officers who desired to go to the Naval Aviation School first had to have the requisite schooling in infantry subjects for their respective ranks. In all requests for alternative schools, Lejeune and the staff of the MCS had to weigh the advantages to the Marine Corps before the request was granted. "Junior officers with comparatively short commissioned service could not be assigned to duty in the office of the Judge Advocate General of the Navy."[39]

Lejeune's policy on military schooling extended to the instructors assigned to the schools. The quality and regularity of instruction at the MCS was crucial to Lejeune. For Marine officers, the duty of instruction took precedence over their own personal desire and opportunity for more military education at advanced schools. "It was further adopted as a policy that details for duty as instructors at the Marine Corps Schools should take precedence over duty as students at Army and Navy Schools. . . . the Marine Corps Schools are the primary agency for the military schooling of our commissioned personnel." Duty at headquarters or with expeditionary forces actually on or under orders for foreign station was the only exception to this policy.[40]

Lejeune took care to provide qualified instructors for the MCS: "Instructors for the Field Officers' Course will be selected so far as practical from graduates of the General Service Schools (Army), the Field Officers' Course, and the Infantry School (Army)." This requirement was also followed for instructors at the company officers' school and the basic school.[41] Lejeune was not pleased when a number of instructors left the MCS on fall maneuvers just prior to the opening of the school, delaying the opening and causing "confusion and delay." Therefore, "Lejeune directed all instructors of the MCS to be present at Quantico a month ahead of the opening date to prepare, so courses can be properly mapped out well in advance and schedules prepared."[42]

Since many senior officers did not have military schooling that he considered adequate, he expected these officers to take the appropriate courses. Lejeune's staff prepared a graph showing the expected progress of Marine officers with the rank of lieutenant colonel and major completing the Field Officers' Course over the period from 1924 to 1930. Out of 44 lieutenant colonels in the Marine Corps, 29 would not have attended the Field Officers' Course by 1924. By 1930, however, only 3 would not have completed the course. For 124 officers of the rank of major, 63 would not have completed the course by 1924, but all would have finished the course by 1929. Lejeune even kept in touch with the educational progress of junior officers. In 1924, there were 198 junior captains who had not attended the Company Officers' Course; by 1930, that number was projected to 13.[43]

Lejeune worked also to reduce the antagonism and conflict that had long existed between officers of the line and staff. Lejeune wrote: "Infantry is the foundation on which the military structure is built. It is the first duty of every Marine officer to make himself a good infantryman. [However,] . . . it is essential that officers should familiarize themselves with the duties of the military and administrative staff. An efficient staff is of vital importance to the successful functioning of a military organization. . . . broadly speaking there is in the Marine Corps no separation of the line and staff. All are Marine officers and all duties are Marine Corps duties." To make this policy successful, Lejeune used the "detail system," in which all officers rotated back and forth between line and staff duties.[44]

In 1922 Lejeune expanded Marine Corps education beyond Quantico by establishing Post Schools for junior officers. He believed that Post Schools were especially important for overseas detachments. "Therefore when an officer reports to a post after commencement of a subject and before the examination therein, he will be required by the post commander to take the remaining portion of the course and examination. . . . he will have as much time as possible to make up the lessons lost, if any, while in route from his old to new station." For Lejeune and the MCS, no officer was too junior and no post so remote as to escape their attention. To the Marine CO in New Orleans, Lejeune directed: "You will hold the Post School examination in Naval Courts and Boards for the junior officers under your command as soon as practical, on a date fixed by yourself."[45]

Lejeune also established schools for enlisted personnel. He felt it was the duty of the corps to educate enlisted men in order to increase their efficiency while in the corps and for "better fitting them for the duties of citizenship when they leave the service. . . . this conviction caused the Commandant to create the correspondence school, which under the name of the Marine Corps Institute, has functioned successfully since its inception."[46] By 1924, the Marine Corps Institute had about 10,000 students enrolled—40 to 50 percent of the corps's personnel, including Marines in the United States, at every foreign post, and ships' detachments with study rooms. The institute also offered bookkeeping courses for younger officers, as well as courses in accounting for post-exchange work, company administration, recruiting duty, and the quartermaster and paymaster departments.[47] In 1921 the Marine Corps Institute was moved from Quantico to the Marine Barracks in Washington, DC.[48]

New enlisted men received basic training at the recruit depots at Parris Island, South Carolina, and San Diego, California, and various rifle-range detachments. After basic training, Lejeune established additional training for enlisted men. The corps established the Quartermaster's School for enlisted personnel at the depot of supplies in Philadelphia, "to commence on or about 1 October 1925, for approximately nine months."[49] Lejeune started the Sergeant's School on March 1, 1923, as part of the MCS in Quantico. "The members of this class will be drawn from the ranks of sergeant-major, first sergeants, gunnery sergeants, and sergeants. To be eligible to attend, these non-commissioned officers had to be under forty years of age, have at least three more years to serve in current enlistment, and be recommended by their commanding officer. Additionally, their commanding officer must consider them good material to serve as temporary or reserve commissioned officers in time of war."[50]

The cumulative effect of Lejeune's educational and military training program was the blending of individual instruction at the MCS with branch and unit training. There were three basic training agencies: basic individual training (MCS), branch individual training, and unit training. For branch individual training, officers attended Army specialty schools in areas such as engineering, artillery, tanks, signal, and chemical. Enlisted men attended branch training centers in infantry, artillery, engineers, communications, tanks, chemical warfare, aviation, motor transport, quartermaster, paymaster, and sea schools (in Norfolk, Virginia, and San Diego, California). In addition, enlisted men could go to Marine or Army branch schools for training as bakers, cooks, band and field musicians, and clerks. The ultimate goal was unit training, which brought together officers and enlisted with the East and West Coast expeditionary forces, detachments afloat, and all other tactical organizations of the Marine Corps.[51]

Continuing his efforts to promote the Marine Corps, Lejeune organized the Marine Corps League in 1924. Membership included all former Marines who left the corps in good standing, as well as all present and future Marines in good standing. "The main object is simply to keep up the association of men out of the service with those in it at present, keep up interest in the Marine Corps, and keep them in touch with the Corps' progress and development. . . . it is not political and does not try to influence legislation."[52] In practice, the members of the league avidly supported Marine Corps sports and kept in touch with corps activities and programs.

Two prominent future generals who attended the MCS in the mid-1920s—Holland M. Smith and A. A. Vandegrift—apparently did not understand Lejeune's early agenda for the schools. Since many of the officers and men of the corps in the early 1920s had not fought in World War I and were relative newcomers to the military, Lejeune sought to teach infantry tactics utilizing the combined-arms approach, using infantry with modern weapons such as machine guns, more accurate artillery, tanks, and aircraft in the attack. This aggressive approach to combat would prove essential to later amphibious-assault operations.

General Smith, who led the Fleet Marine Force in World War II, went through the Field Officers' Course in 1926 and remembered, "The staff was still excited over the outdated thought and doctrine of the World War."[53] General Vandegrift—later to lead the First Marine Division at Guadalcanal and become commandant during World War II—attended the Field Officers' Course in the autumn of 1925. "The course was taught by an earnest and well-balanced group of instructors who knew their jobs. The curriculum reflected the transitory air of the day—we were trying to project ourselves away from the trench warfare of World War I into a war of movement, but were not yet ready for amphibious studies. Instead, we concentrated on conventional land strategy, weapons, and tactics, the latter proved most valuable to me."[54] In reality, however, the MCS began to shift its emphasis to amphibious operations in 1926—using the resources of its staff and students to study and develop the corps's new mission.

Lejeune added two more vital functions to Marine Corps Headquarters: publicity in 1924 and the Reserve Section in 1925. All reserve affairs were concentrated under a director of reserve who reported as an advisor to the MGC. This single staff agency included procurement, instruction, training, discipline, budget, and distribution.[55] While the corps had learned the value of good publicity that "bolstered its image on the public imagination" during and after the Spanish-American War in 1898, the function of publicity remained under its Office of Recruiting.[56]

In his effort to modernize the Marine Corps, maintaining adequate funding was not Lejeune's only challenge. First, while the corps had earned public acclaim for its fighting ability in the Great War, the period of Lejeune's tenure as MGC in the 1920s was free of major wars and witnessed a time of public apathy toward the military services. Consequently, Lejeune worked to keep the Marine Corps before the American people and Congress as a vibrant and efficient military service. Lejeune needed public and congressional support in order to institute his reforms and develop a new and permanent mission. Second, the corps faced a major crisis at the very beginning of his tenure as commandant: media allegations that Marines had brutalized and killed innocent civilians in Haiti threatened to rock the Marine Corps to its very core. To Lejeune, Secretary of the Navy Daniels, and the Wilson administration, these revelations threatened to undermine the public goodwill that the Marine Corps had earned by its outstanding performance and sacrifice in the Great War.

The anti-imperialist *New York Evening Post* saw the American occupation of Haiti as "bullying, not helping." *The Nation,* a prominent liberal publication, identified the intervention as "unbridled imperialism."[57] The National Association for the Advancement of Colored People (NAACP) wrote stories of "American perfidy and atrocity" in Haiti.[58] Republican candidate for president Warren G. Harding, in the election of 1920 against Democrat

James M. Cox, seized the opportunity to criticize President Wilson's foreign policy and proclaimed that "thousands of native Haitians have been killed by American Marines."[59] Another source of public alarm was the discovery of former commandant George Barnett's letter to Colonel John H. Russell—in charge of the Marine Brigade in Haiti—that included the phrase "indiscriminate killing."[60]

Colonel Russell investigated these reports of killings and found them isolated acts, aberrations from the highly supervised standard of brigade and *gendarmerie* conduct.[61] Amid this sensationalism, in July 1920 Lejeune and Smedley Butler hastened to Haiti and traveled throughout the country without an armed guard. Lejeune confirmed Russell's report, acknowledging that the killings were a few isolated incidents and noting that the guilty had been punished. Although President Wilson and Secretary Daniels were greatly relieved, Daniels established a naval court of inquiry in Haiti that cleared the corps of wrongdoing. A senatorial investigation in Haiti came to the same conclusion.

While these investigations probably calmed the public's anger, a later in-depth investigation found that these reports were a cover-up for a few Marines who had indeed killed innocent civilians. For example, Major Clarke Wells, commanding a district of the *gendarmerie,* sanctioned the killing of civilians who refused to build roads. Brigadier General Albertus Catlin relieved Wells of his command, labeling him a murderer, liar, and unfit to wear a Marine Corps uniform. Without enough evidence to court-martial Wells, Catlin sent Wells and his officers back to the United States "for the good of the Corps." A Captain Becker was accused of shooting pack trains filled with women. Becker was found "loony as a bug" and sent to an asylum. The corps did have evidence against Sergeant Louis Brokaw and Privates Walter Johnson and John McQuilkin for killing a voodoo priest and another prisoner. At their two courts-martial trials, both Johnson and McQuilkin were convicted and sent to prison for long sentences at hard labor. Brokaw was declared insane by a naval surgeon and sent to St. Elizabeth's Hospital in Washington, DC.[62]

Perhaps the greatest injustices to the Haitians were perpetrated by Louis Cukela, a former enlisted man who had received the Medal of Honor for bravery in the Great War. Now a lieutenant, Cukela executed a group of prisoners in a Marine camp in front of a superior officer. Cukela was transferred and not court-martialed.[63]

Many militant Haitians were also killed by Marines. A peasant uprising before 1920 in the hills of eastern and northeastern Haiti against Marines resulted in bloody guerrilla fighting, where Marines killed at least fifteen hundred Haitians (*cacos*).[64] The Marines also suffered casualties. The *cacos* were mostly poor, illiterate, former African slaves who spoke Creole. The *élite* (considered the upper class and ruling force in Haiti) paid the *cacos* over many years to support revolutions in Haiti against political opponents in order to maintain themselves in power. Forming about 10 percent of the population, the *élite* were Franco-blacks, many of whom were educated in France, spoke French, and prospered through government jobs, contracts, and enormous graft.

Not only were many Haitians killed, but it is clear that the American State Department, the Department of the Navy, and the Marines continually violated the Haitians' civil rights. Basically, the killings came as a result of American foreign policy to establish a guardianship of total control over Haiti from 1915 to 1934. With the building of the Panama Canal and for reasons of national security, the United States wanted naval control over the Caribbean and Latin America—the Roosevelt corollary to the Monroe Doctrine. The United States became alarmed over foreign interest in Haiti. Haiti's ports bordered on the Windward Passage and naval routes where several European powers coveted coaling stations and control over Haiti's customs ports in an effort to force repayment of Haitian debts.

In hindsight, it is clear that military intervention was the wrong way to secure American interests in the Caribbean. Most Haitians wanted the Americans out; many progressive Marines were not excited about the mission in Haiti and were anxious to leave. The occupation begun by President Wilson continued under Presidents Harding and Coolidge. Finally, President Herbert Hoover, a Quaker humanitarian, found the occupation distasteful and ended it before the treaty expired.

On his visit to Santo Domingo and Haiti in July of 1920, Lejeune discovered that Marines stationed there had inadequate naval transportation from the United States to Haiti and Santo Domingo. Concerned, Lejeune "informed the Navy of the absolute need of the Corps for transport for expeditionary purposes alone which should at all times be available in case of an emergency." Lejeune strongly recommended one additional transport from the Shipping Board.[65]

Lejeune handled the media crisis as well as could be expected and later wrote in his autobiography about the "outrageous attack on the conduct of the Marines in Haiti."[66] He blamed the press, which was "prone to be sensational" during the conduct of a national political campaign.[67]

Aware of the need for a positive public awareness of the Marine Corps, Lejeune assigned a public relations officer directly to his staff.[68] Lejeune was resourceful and enthusiastic about the value of good public relations. While previously the corps had combined the function of publicity with the Office of Recruiting, Lejeune established the first Publicity Office at headquarters in 1925 in order to personally monitor its operation. Lejeune understood that the very life of the corps depended upon the favor of the American people. Members of Congress recognized this public approval and acted to keep the corps alive and well, often in the face of the Army's resentment of the corps as well as the lack of interest of many senior officers in the Navy during the 1920s.

The good public relations enjoyed by the corps came primarily from the efforts of Major Joseph C. Fegan, whom Lejeune appointed in 1925 to promote all corps activities. Fegan was a skilled public relations manager who secured the interest of the newspaper, radio, magazine, and movie industries for Marine Corps maneuvers, sports, marksmanship contests, drill teams, and participation in the world war.

As an example of the news coverage, the *Nashville Banner* ran "When Uncle Sam's Marines Play at 'War,'" a series of photographs of the corps during a maneuver. With photographs from *International Newsreel Photo* and the Marine Corps, the newspaper featured the Christie Amphibious Tank, Whippet Tanks, the landing of a three-inch field piece, a landing party of Marines during a war game, the Marine transport *USS Henderson* loaded with Marines, and Generals Lejeune and Cole passing in review before Admiral Coontz, CNO.[69]

Lejeune's talent for public relations, coupled with the experience of Fegan, fashioned a dynamic public relations program for the Marine Corps in the mid- to late 1920s. Lejeune had recognized Fegan's abilities and his success in recruiting in the Los Angeles area after the war, transferring him from Santo Domingo to Corps Headquarters on September 3, 1924, to take charge of all publicity dealing with recruiting.[70] On September 21, 1925, Lejeune named Fegan as the Marine Corps publicity officer at headquarters.

Even with a small staff, Lejeune and Fegan fine-tuned the public relations program to such a degree that it regularly placed Marine Corps achievements and news before the people to the envy of the Army and Navy. The public relations officer had a central office at headquarters and worked directly with the MGC. Fegan supervised a staff of writers, typists, and photographers. Every action or news story contemplated by the central office was weighed and evaluated by Fegan and Lejeune as to the probable public reaction to the release. Fegan and his staff were in constant contact with the magazine and newspaper executives in the Washington area; Fegan and his staff prepared all statements made by the MGC and other senior officers. Fegan also supervised and maintained corps publicity organizations at all posts and stations in the United States and abroad, frequently traveling all over the Marine Corps to gather news and monitor local organizations.

The public relations team were important staff members of the post CO. The PR office sent out articles and stories designed to reflect credit on the post and the corps, placing before the public such activities as the achievements of athletic and rifle teams, promotions, and social activities. The public relations officer at each post kept in close touch with editors of local newspapers and advised the post CO about what the public reaction might be on all releases. Each PR section had a noncommissioned officer qualified as a photographer with equipment such as movie and still-picture cameras and a darkroom.

Likewise, public relations officers and staff were included in Marine Corps expeditions and Caribbean occupations. These officers worked to develop friendly relations with American correspondents accompanying the force. The experienced PR officer would give the CG of the expeditionary force expert advice as to the probable public reaction to his actions and press releases. The publicity section contained news writers, cameramen, and clerical help—with typesetting machine capability—that would provide film, photograph, and written information to the central office in Washington.[71]

In a memorandum, Lejeune stated that the success of the Marine Corps depended first on all officers and men efficiently performing their duty, and second, on the necessity of the publicity office bringing news of this efficient performance of duty to the notice of the public. Lejeune wanted "good" publicity and carefully monitored the release of information to spotlight Marines achieving good works. Such stories included protecting the US Mail against bandits in 1921 and 1926, assaulting an imaginary enemy utilizing the latest weapons and technology in Civil War reenactments, winning sporting events or national rifle matches, and tales of Marine heroics in the Great War. He directed that headquarters remove all photographs that were unflattering, unmilitary, or "staged," because "publicity for publicity's sake was undesirable."[72]

Lejeune continued to stress to his headquarters staff the importance of congressional support. "I have also heard from a number of Congressmen that the Corps stands exceedingly high in the estimation of the public, and it remains up to the officers and men to keep it so. It is entirely a matter of the manner in which the officers and men conduct themselves, and the degree of efficiency with which they perform the duties assigned them. So long as the Corps is efficient and well-behaved, we will have the goodwill of the American people."[73]

When the motion-picture industry revealed an interest in the Marine Corps, Lejeune was quick to approve a Motion Picture Section as an adjunct to the Recruiting Bureau in Philadelphia.[74] He announced in January 1926 that he had signed a contract with Metro-Goldwyn-Meyer to produce Marine Corps films. Herman J. Mankiewicz, an ex-Marine, wrote the script for the film *The Fighting Marine,* starring another former Marine, Gene Tunney. Lejeune held a private showing of the next film produced (*Tell It to the Marines,* with actor Lon Chaney) for the president and Mrs. Coolidge, cabinet members, senators, representatives, and the National Press Club. Lejeune mentioned, "We are going to get two complete films of the picture one of which will be sent to the West Coast where it will be shown at the various posts there and in the Orient." He also planned to send the movie to the recruit depots at San Diego and Parris Island to be viewed by recruits. Similarly, Marines at Quantico and larger posts on the East Coast and in the West Indies viewed the film. Lejeune wrote, "It is a splendid picture, and should afford good propaganda for the Corps."[75]

One of Lejeune's and Fegan's greatest achievements in public relations to boost recruiting and inform and interest the public was the development of athletics and sports teams in the corps. Lejeune had used sports successfully before to prevent boredom and boost morale during his commands of Marines in Panama and the Brooklyn Marine Barracks. Fegan had witnessed the excitement of athletic games for the Marines and soldiers in the American Expeditionary Forces (AEF) in Europe after the Great War in such places as Pershing Stadium. He also monitored the booming interest in college athletics in the 1920s. He was convinced that, if young men could not afford to go to college to participate in sports, they could find it in the Marine Corps.[76]

Lejeune and Fegan understood the American passion for competitive sports, athletics, and physical fitness, and took every opportunity to inform the public and potential Marine recruits that the Marine Corps was a physically fit, first-class military service. They used sports as a morale builder to counter the inevitable letdown experienced after the world war by making peacetime life in the corps invigorating, challenging, and interesting. Lejeune informed his staff, "We cannot have an efficient organization unless the physical, mental, and morale sides of the men are looked out for. A better word for what we mean by morale is '*esprit.*' The three go hand-in-hand to make up military efficiency."[77]

With Lejeune's encouragement, the Marine Corps developed organized teams in football and baseball, patterned after the system used by most of the nation's universities and colleges. The football and baseball teams had an athletic officer (a field-grade officer) and two assistants (junior officers). The corps later hired professional coaches for the baseball and football teams and developed the sports of boxing, track, and crew. Fegan encouraged general athletics throughout the Marine Corps in such activities as the hundred-yard dash and the high jump at posts around the world. For special athletics, the corps established all-Marine football and baseball teams at Quantico and started building a stadium that would seat about twenty-four thousand.[78]

In order to be competitive as the smallest of the military services against Army and Navy teams, the corps developed a system comparable to today's major- and minor-league baseball programs. All Marine Corps posts organized teams. Some posts such as Parris Island, Norfolk, and San Diego developed exceptional teams that frequently defeated rival Army teams in their areas. The best athletes at the post teams were sent to the all-Marine teams at Quantico, and were eligible for three years of competition. These athletes then returned to their post team as coaches or players, creating better post teams. This allowed the all-Marine football and baseball teams to play and defeat most college teams. Yearly, the all-Marine football team played the best Army or Navy team in Washington, DC, for the President's Cup. This game became so popular that it had to be scheduled at a different time to encourage attendance at the West Point–Annapolis college game. In memory of all deceased Marines, the corps planned to place bronze tablets naming each Marine around the wall of the stadium.

For Lejeune, "It was a source of great satisfaction to note that our All-Marine Football team is considered as one of the local teams here in Washington, and its games receive the same publicity as do the games of Georgetown, George Washington, Catholic University, and the University of Maryland." In fact, the all-Marine football team received nationwide publicity, with newspapers throughout the country generally carrying accounts of the games.

Fegan was quick to point out: "The sports program seems to interest the type of young men that we want in the Corps. They won't listen to promises of seeing the world, etc., but football [and baseball] as we play it does interest them. . . . we must use the proper appeal in order to get the right sort of men in the service. . . . the ex-Marines all over the country showed the greatest interest in the team, and usually formed a cheering section for us at our games away from home." Fegan also mentioned that several enlisted men were willing to extend their enlistments in order to make the all-Marine football team with the hope of earning an athletic scholarship at a college at the end of their tour of duty. Colonel Harold C. Snyder stated that "he had found that young people wanted to join the Marine Corps in time of peace because it offers more activity than other branches of the service." Lejeune agreed: "These competitions are not intended to take the place of military training, but are only an adjunct to it."[79]

A future commandant, Alexander A. Vandegrift, served as athletic and morale officer at Quantico in the early 1920s during "an impressive record of Marine football victories. . . . the Corps football team primarily played away from Quantico, competing against Georgetown, Vanderbilt, and Michigan State and filling their stadiums. . . . this was excellent publicity and increased Quantico and Marine Corps morale. . . . the All-Marine Baseball Team played exhibition games for spring practice with northern teams going south—Holy Cross, the University of Vermont, Brown, and Lafayette in April and May. The All-Marine Baseball Team also played southern teams moving north, such as the Virginia Military Institute and the University of Virginia. . . . it was cheap entertainment. . . . the men loved it."[80]

Funding to maintain all-Marine football and baseball teams was not insignificant, however, and had to come from self-generated monies, not public funds. Occasionally, the football team would generate enough revenue to cover its costs. Usually, though, to cover costs, the football team would have to play prominent college and university teams away from Quantico and attract crowds of at least twenty thousand spectators. Consequently, profits from the post exchanges throughout the corps supported the football and baseball teams, primarily from the post exchanges at the Washington barracks and Quantico.

The sports program in the Marine Corps thrived during Lejeune's tenure as commandant, increasing morale within the corps and receiving excellent publicity throughout the nation. The program continued until the 1930s but was discontinued during the Great Depression.

In 1921 the Marine Corps scored another public relations coup with the media and public by successfully guarding the US Mail against a series of violent armed robberies seeking valuables in registered mail carried in trains and trucks throughout the United States. At the request of Acting Postmaster General Hubert Work on November 8, 1921, and with the support of Edwin Denby, secretary of the Navy, and MGC Lejeune, the Marine Corps provided over 53 officers and 2,200 heavily armed Marines as guards to accompany mail trucks and trains, as well as outlying points in post offices and distribution stations.

Previously, for the twelve months ending April 9, 1921, there were thirty-six mail robberies involving over $6,300,000 worth of stolen goods. Even though all outside postal employees were armed by the War Department, many were killed or wounded and unable to defend against these violent thieves. The Marines halted the robberies, earning public acclaim for this dangerous work. Secretary Denby, a former Marine who fought in World War I, wrote a letter to the Marines that was read to them by Lejeune: "You must be constantly alert . . . keep your weapons in hand, and, if attacked, shoot, and shoot to kill. There is no compromise in this battle with bandits." Further, Denby warned: "If two Marines guarding a mail car are suddenly covered by a robber, neither man must hold up his hands, but both must begin shooting at once. One may be killed, but the other will get the robber and save the mail. That is the spirit of the Corps."[81] Lejeune, as well as Denby and Hubert Work, felt that the conduct and work of the mail guards was outstanding. Work praised the Marines for the "splendidly effective manner" in which they protected the mail against robbers.[82] In his annual report, Lejeune did not mention any Marine casualties. According to Lejeune, "It was an unprecedented condition, but the men rose splendidly to the occasion and proved themselves worthy of the great trust reposed in them."[83]

Beginning on October 20, 1926, the corps once again began furnishing guards for the US Mail against renewed thefts at gunpoint. Lejeune dispatched 2,520 Marines into two zones, one for the eastern mail-guard zone and another for the western zone. The East Coast Expeditionary Force at Quantico guarded the eastern zone, while the West Coast Expeditionary Force at San Diego protected mail in the western zone. The banditry ceased almost at once, although the Marines remained until February 19, 1927. As in 1921, the guard duty for the mail service was "very trying."[84] Lejeune, however, was "much gratified by the reports of the splendid conduct of the men on the mail guard duty."[85] Lejeune complimented Brigadier General Smedley Butler, who led the Marines in the West Coast sector: "I am sure that this is due to the enthusiasm and high state of *esprit* which you instilled in the officers and men. . . . I received a very commendatory letter about you from a Post Office Inspector on the West Coast."[86]

Keen on informing the American public that the bandits were no match for the Marines, Lejeune noted that "our men traveling around the country have given the general public a fine impression of the Marine Corps. Every indication points to the fact that the Corps still retains its great popularity among the people of our country and among members of Congress."[87]

Another activity to keep the Marine Corps in the news in a time of relative world peace was the reenactment of certain Civil War battles on the original ground during autumn maneuvers from 1921 to 1924. The opportunity arose when the Navy's plan for sea-to-shore maneuvers with the corps in 1921 never materialized. While Lejeune was disappointed by not being able to conduct amphibious maneuvers, he and Butler, CO of the base at Quantico, decided to stage a reenactment of the Battle of the Wilderness using modern weapons and equipment during September and October of 1921. Utilizing the entire expeditionary force at Quantico, with the Field Officers' School planning each step of the maneuver, the attack was conducted as a sea-to-shore assault to capture an imaginary island. For Lejeune, the exercise had several objectives: "One is to get the men out of Quantico for a short while and into the country, and help both officers and men keep up their interest in their military training; another is to test out the military equipment and see whether it is in good order, and whether they can actually use it under service conditions. Of course, the military training feature of it will be of great value."[88] Equally important, this reenactment and the three that followed each year from 1921 to 1924 trained the expeditionary force in combined-arms operations—the use of infantry, machine guns, artillery, tanks, and aircraft in the attack as Lejeune had experienced in the world war—and prepared the Marines for the amphibious assault maneuvers with the Navy that would soon follow.

Another goal of the reenactments, according to Lejeune, was to "develop the expeditionary strength of the Marine Corps to the fullest extent within the limitations fixed by Congress."[89] Butler, who commanded the Marines during the first three reenactments, called the force the "East Coast Expeditionary Force of the Navy." Complete with infantry, heavy and light artillery, engineers, signal troops, a mixed battalion of searchlight and antiaircraft guns, and an aircraft detachment, the force marched across country, crossing the Rappahannock and Rapidan rivers, following the route of General Joseph Hooker's Union Army to the Battle of Chancellorsville. As a result of their great weight, the battery of 155-mm guns pulled by ten-ton tractors could not use the Richmond Turnpike or the bridges, instead fording rivers and avoiding bridges. This was a significant improvement over the use of artillery in the world war, where cannon were often hauled by horses or mules.

To replicate an amphibious operation for the Marine Corps, Butler related that "Wilderness Run was considered the shore line, and all the terrain to the westward was considered to be the sea. The problem was entirely a naval one, and the columns that advanced from the imaginary transports and battleships moved in formation and with the number of men that could be carried in motor sailors and other boats, determined by Commander Keller, representing the Navy at Quantico."[90]

The initial landing occurred one hour before daylight, and "the remainder of the Fourth Brigade landed . . . one hour later, at daylight . . . through smoke screens put up by smoke bombs, and the first defenses—the beach defenses of the enemy were taken." The second phase involved capturing the remaining enemy positions on the island and consolidating the Marine position. In the third phase, Marines fortified the island, prepared the defense, and resisted a counterattack by a hostile fleet. Butler and Lejeune felt that the Aviation Section of the Marine Corps "did phenomenal work," bombing a diagram of a battleship laid out on the ground. On the deck of this imaginary battleship, the Marines mounted antiaircraft guns and searchlights based on the same positions as on the battleship *New Mexico*. In addition, Marines designated a landing field that was equal in size to the landing deck of an aircraft carrier being built for the Navy. Butler remarked that "we made them do all their landing on that space, and not one plane overlapped, although the wind blew from various directions."[91]

The success of this maneuver buoyed the corps's reputation, showcasing the power of modern weapons and building momentum toward the amphibious mission. Lejeune invited President Warren G. Harding, an avid Civil War buff, along with Secretary of the Navy Edwin Denby and other officials, including the governor of Virginia, to witness the assault phase of the maneuver. The attendance and later positive remarks of these officials added a semiofficial recognition of the Marine Corps's preparedness. Many thousands of visitors were excited and impressed by the reenactment, further enhancing the corps's reputation. In addition, even though the Marine Corps had no tanks at this time to participate in the assault, the Marines at Quantico showed their resourcefulness by building a tank from a five-ton tractor. Also, when Lejeune discovered that the little cemetery that contained the arm that General Stonewall Jackson had lost at Chancellorsville was in poor condition, he had the engineers build a special fence and repair the plot. This greatly pleased the governor and citizens of Virginia.

Significantly, this maneuver was one of the first modern expeditions that used motor trucks instead of mule wagons to carry materiel. A particular problem that emerged was the overheating of trucks that had to use low gear to keep pace with the marching infantry. The twenty trucks used were much more efficient, however, at hauling trailers and more equipage. Butler stated that it would have required a hundred mule wagons and a column fifteen miles long to carry the same amount of supplies and equipment as the trucks. Finally, the Marines adopted for the first time in the field the new division staff system that had been developed by the French Army—the staff components of G-1, G-2, G-3, and G-4 that supported the fighting force with specialist experts in matters of personnel, intelligence, operations, and supply and logistics. This staff system is still used by the Marine Corps and Army and is a testament to Lejeune's enduring legacy.[92]

The reenactment at Gettysburg in 1922 was more a field exercise than an amphibious maneuver, attracting interest all over the nation. Fifty-six years after this battle, which turned the tide of the Civil War and preserved the Union, the event still resonated with the public and heightened the admiration for the Marine Corps that had remained since the world war.

The event was attended by many elderly survivors of the conflict. The most important military result of this exercise was the demonstration of modern combined-arms operations since using combined arms would be a necessity in an amphibious assault.[93] Lejeune stated that "the march to Gettysburg and encampment there of our Expeditionary Force had done the Marine Corps a tremendous amount of good in the minds of the public. . . . the crowds which witnessed exercises at Gettysburg came from all over the country."[94] When the Marines changed the scheduled date of the reenactment of Pickett's charge from July 3 to July 1 for viewing by the president, the governors of three states, and a host of other distinguished guests, "telegrams came in from all over the country protesting the change." For this reason the Marine Corps repeated the reenactment on July 3, 1922, for the public.[95] More than 4,000 Marines participated in the exercise. Lejeune suggested that, had this attack over the same ground utilized all the modern implements of war, the result might have been different from the one in 1863.[96]

The field exercise of 1923 reproduced the Battle of New Market, Virginia, and was probably the most popular reenactment. A detachment of cadets from the Virginia Military Academy—of the same number as the cadets that marched off to join the Confederate troops during the Civil War—joined the Marine Corps in its annual fall maneuver from August 27 to October 7, 1923. Lejeune remarked: "It was estimated that about 100,000 people witnessed the demonstration, and that there were 25,000 automobiles parked in New Market and vicinity."[97] Because of the heavy rain and mud during the reenactment, Lejeune believed that the "training and experience gained in operating under field conditions were invaluable. . . . the weather . . . was extremely bad . . . and the force had severe conditions of weather and roads to contend with. These difficulties were met and overcome with splendid determination and served to demonstrate the high morale possessed by the members of the force. . . . the aviation detachments played an important part during the maneuvers and rendered distinguished service."[98]

The last Civil War reenactment was the Battle of Antietam near Sharpsburg, Maryland, conducted between August 24 and September 18 of 1924. Dion Williams, who commanded the expeditionary force, convinced Lejeune that this exercise should be conducted as a real military problem without attempting "a reproduction in pageantry form of the Civil War battle at that place, as little would be gained by either officers or men as regards lessons of a military nature." Consequently, Williams managed the attack as it would have been conducted in 1924, using modern strategy, tactics, weapons, technology, reconnaissance, motor trucks, and more aircraft than were used in previous reenactments. The maneuver attracted some 40,000 visitors and concluded with a review by the president, Lejeune, the CNO, and the assistant secretary of the Navy at the south portico of the White House.[99]

The Civil War reenactments had also included an unspoken agenda for Lejeune and the Marine Corps. The expeditionary force fought a simulated war utilizing the concept of combined arms, similar to the fighting in World War I. This was very different from the way Marines had fought before the war, as colonial infantry. Lejeune would show that this was an outdated mission in a changing world and that the new mission of amphibious assault demanded greater firepower, aggressiveness, and a combined-arms approach.

Public interest and recognition of the corps increased when Marine aviation under Lejeune pioneered the modern use of air power in the Caribbean occupations—the Marine Air-Ground Task Force. For the first time, Marine aircraft provided direct air support to small infantry units on the ground fighting rebels in Haiti, the Dominican Republic, and Nicaragua.[100] A young Marine officer, Major Alexander A. Vandegrift, stationed in Haiti, witnessed two of Roy Geiger's pilots loading a small bomb in one of the old Jennys.[101] Later the aviator dropped the bomb on a *caco* stronghold while the infantry attacked. Geiger also used planes to deliver mail and supplies to patrols and even rigged a transport plane with stretchers to evacuate wounded.[102]

Lejeune was an enthusiast on the subject of aviation. "I am convinced that it will be of vital importance, both by land and sea, when war is again precipitated."[103] He especially commended Major Ross E. Rowell, Major Louis M. Bourne, Lieutenant Colonel Thomas C. Turner, and Major Edwin R. Brainard for their groundbreaking service in aviation.[104] Because the Marine Corps included combat correspondents in every overseas operation, including Haiti, the Dominican Republic, Nicaragua, China, and Siberia, the press avidly covered every action to inform the American public. The most popular newspapers of the time covering the Marine Corps interventions throughout the Caribbean were the *Washington Post,* the

New York Times, and the *New York Herald.* In a time of relative peace for the Army and Navy, the interventions by the corps and the resulting combat operations made exciting reading for the American public, allowing the Marines to stand out from the other services.[105]

Combat air patrols using the De Havilland DH-4B[106] aircraft in Haiti in 1920, working in cooperation with ground troops, fired machine guns against bandits and were also used in reconnoitering and photographic expeditions.[107] Marine aviators also helped pioneer dive bombing. In 1919, Lieutenant L. H. Sanderson, using a makeshift bomb rack, discovered that he was able to more accurately bomb a target by diving down at an angle of forty-five degrees to 250 feet above ground to hit the enemy. This tactic was known as glide bombing in World War II. Famous German air ace Ernst Udet from World War I attended dive-bombing demonstrations in the United States by Marine flyers returning from Nicaragua. He later developed the infamous Stuka dive bomber that terrorized most of Europe early in World War II.[108]

Although Lejeune would have preferred continuing amphibious assault maneuvers with the Navy in the late 1920s, the State Department and President Coolidge did not hesitate to utilize Marines as an instrument of American foreign policy.[109] This was because a few influential Americans had business interests in the five republics of Central America. The State Department wanted stable governments in the Caribbean and used Marines to prevent civil wars within these republics as well as to prevent conflicts between the republics. Officially, the United States encouraged democratic governments based on popular elections, assigning Marines to prevent political violence, intervention by European powers, and agitation from revolutionary Mexico.

While the American occupation of the Dominican Republic ended on July 1, 1925, when the Dominican Congress selected President Horacio Vásquez, the Marines remained in Haiti until the early 1930s. In addition, by 1927, the Marine Corps had eight thousand Marines in Nicaragua and China; in 1929, two-thirds of the corps's total manpower was either at sea with the Navy or abroad in these military interventions. No Marines were available for amphibious operations.

Marine aviation came of age in Nicaragua in the late 1920s and early 1930s. Because of the rugged terrain, jungles, an absence of roads, and almost impossible overland travel, Marine aircraft was critically important in supporting troop movement, communications, and supply. Nicaragua—a country run by two parties, the liberals and conservatives, and dominated by alliances of families and regional *caudillos*—had the greatest potential for violence in Latin America.[110] Civil war broke out in Nicaragua after attempts by moderate conservatives and liberals failed to forge a coalition government. The liberals and the conservatives welcomed the American intervention, for neither side was strong enough to win a decisive victory. Eventually both sides agreed to disarm. One liberal leader, Augusto César Sandino, however, refused to disarm, denounced *Yanqui* imperialism, and continued to fight the coalition government and the Marines.[111]

Brigadier General Logan Feland ordered the Fifth Regiment of Marines north into the mountains near the border of Honduras to disarm all bands and find the rebel leader Sandino. Sandino and about 400 to 600 of his men in the early morning hours of July 16, 1927, attacked the Marines of Captain Gilbert Hatfield's garrison force in Ocotal. Hatfield had only 48 *Guardia Nacional* men (native troops led by a Marine) and 48 Marines. Against overwhelming odds, the Marines refused to surrender and held off Sandino's men until daylight. With daylight, Major Ross E. Rowell and a flight of five biplanes of VO-1M (De Havilland bombers) dive-bombed and strafed the Sandinistas. This was one of history's first dive-bombing attacks, which killed probably over 100 guerrillas and repulsed the attack. Sandino's force scattered. Only one Marine was killed in the engagement.[112]

Air patrols also saved the day for the Marine infantry in an early failed ground attempt to take Sandino's fortress at El Chipote. Sandino's forces ambushed one of two combat patrols that had about 100 Marines and *Guardias,* incapacitating 32 Marines and *Guardias* before the Marines could get air support. The Marine survivors rallied and fell back on Quilali, low on supplies and ammunition. At this point, about 400 Sandinistas besieged the Marines. In this desperate situation, Lieutenant Christian F. Schilt, flying a Vought 02U-1 Corsair biplane,[113] landed and took off ten times on the main street of Quilali, flying out 9 wounded and returning with supplies. For this remarkable feat, Schilt received a Medal of Honor.[114]

Early in 1928, coordinated air and ground attacks destroyed Sandino's mountaintop base at El Chipote. The strongly fortified base was bombed from the air on January 14. The mountain was full of rebels well entrenched behind strongly fortified trenches. From these trenches and forty or fifty shelters, the rebels had created machine-gun positions and cleared fields of fire that made an infantry approach from below almost impossible. "These positions and preparations were easily visible from our planes flying over the mountain. On January 14, four planes swept down from a great altitude at high speed, dropped bombs on the shacks on top of the mountain and, as the outlaws ran out, they bombed the groups of men and strafed them with machine guns . . . continuing down the slope of the mountain against the different groups and entrenched positions. The attack of the planes was carried out through a hail of bullets, and the planes were struck many times, but without injury to them or to their occupants." The air attacks cleared the area of the enemy and made the Marine ground assault successful.[115]

Despite many air and ground successes in Nicaragua, Lejeune's Marines were never able to capture the elusive and highly mobile Sandino. The Marine Corps simply did not have enough troops to successfully monitor the election of 1928 and destroy Sandino's forces, the two missions assigned by the State Department and the Navy. In addition to the brigade in Nicaragua, the corps had to maintain brigades in Haiti and China. Also, the corps had to guard the US Mail in early 1927 and provide Marines for the Navy's new aircraft carriers, the *Lexington* and the *Saratoga*.[116] Lejeune was disappointed that the expeditionary duty severely limited training for the amphibious assault mission. Until he retired in March of 1929, he continued to speak and write that amphibious operations were the true war mission for the Marine Corps.[117]

The end to American intervention in Nicaragua came with a new president of the United States. Herbert Hoover, in order to prevent a revolt in Congress, decided the United States could no longer protect foreign property in Nicaragua and ended the occupation. The Marine brigade returned home in 1933. Meanwhile, Sandino began extended negotiations with President Dr. Juan B. Sacasa of the Liberal Party, elected in the Marine-supervised election of 1932. Sandino agreed to disband and disarm in return for amnesty and land grants along the Coco River. General Anastasio Somoza, who controlled the native *Guardia Nacional,* deposed Sacasa, assassinated Sandino and his key officers in 1934, and established a dictatorship—backed by the *Guardia*—that lasted for over four decades.[118]

The supportive relationship Lejeune established with Congress set a Marine Corps standard that still exists for the corps. Lejeune made sure that the exploits and successes of the Marine Corps came to the attention of the American public and Congress. Lejeune demonstrated throughout his tenure as MGC that he was a master of creating a positive image of the Marine Corps. Lejeune probably appeared before Congress more than any other commandant and considered many congressmen and senators to be his personal friends. These relationships helped him cultivate support within Congress for the Marine Corps.

General Lemuel Cornick Shepherd Jr., who became commandant during and after the Korean War, 1952–55, served as Lejeune's aide in the early 1920s. Shepherd stated, "General Lejeune was highly thought of by Congress and usually obtained the appropriations he asked for in behalf of the Marine Corps. He was honest, forthright, and conservative in his requests to Congress where funds were difficult to obtain in the postwar period."[119]

Edwin Denby, secretary of the Navy from March 4, 1921, to March 10, 1924, supported Lejeune's efforts to lobby Congress in order to build an elite organization. In aviation, for example, Lejeune was committed to ground-air support. The Marine Corps "defined a pilot as a Marine employing a different weapon."[120] Since World War I had introduced great strides in aviation tactics and technology, Brigadier General Billy Mitchell of the Army Air Service was committed to strategic bombing and "aviation unity," or merger. By the time the Harding administration took office, eight congressional bills had called for the merger of aviation for all the services in various forms. Thanks to the work of Secretary Denby, the Harding administration opposed this merger, for Army, Navy, and Marine aviation operated in significantly different environments. Denby helped draft an institutional home for naval aviation and testified before Congress to advocate for a Bureau of Aeronautics. Denby and Lejeune earned congressional approval and secured appropriations for land purchases and an airfield conversion at Quantico. This airfield would provide tactical training between aviators and Marine infantry. Lejeune later reported to Denby that a coordinated aviation unit was operational.

Although most officers in the Navy and Marine Corps opposed the Harding administration's Washington Conference on Naval Disarmament, 1921–22, Denby convinced Congress that a conversion of the battle cruisers *USS Lexington* and *Saratoga* into aircraft carriers was a good investment and important for the future of the Navy.

Denby often helped Lejeune secure congressional funding. At this time, Congress was determined to liquidate the cost of World War I. To facilitate this, the Bureau of the Budget recommended a $50 million slash in naval appropriations. Denby informed the president and probably Congress that this action threatened the existence of Lejeune's prized MEF.

Always aware that the Marine Corps, as the smallest of the services, could be eliminated through legislative action or by being absorbed into the Army or eliminated by the Navy, Lejeune convinced Denby to allow separate Marine recruiting stations. Lejeune cleared the action with Charles Dawes, budget head, and received permission to locate recruiting stations in government buildings, saving rental expenses. This pleased Dawes, who rewarded Lejeune with a cigar.[121] With adequate funding, Lejeune was then able to establish a small Expeditionary Force on the East and West coasts. To support Lejeune in his determination to establish fleet–Marine Corps amphibious operations, Denby established the concept of a "Control Force" that helped Lejeune plan the first maneuver in the Caribbean.[122]

Firmly believing that the history of the corps had to be preserved as an inspiration to new Marines, Lejeune established the first historical section in the corps. In 1921, Lejeune began the tradition of annually celebrating the birth of the Marine Corps. Although the Marine Corps was actually signed into law by President John Adams on July 11, 1798, Lejeune and the corps decided to celebrate its birthday as November 10, 1775, when the Second Continental Congress established two battalions of Marines to serve aboard armed vessels of the Navy to fight the British Empire during the War of Independence.[123] Without fail, Lejeune—who was an inspirational, extemporaneous speaker—spoke at the annual birthday celebration in Washington, reviewing the proud history of the corps from the American Revolution to World War I and commemorating the exploits, valor, sacrifice, and fidelity of the Marines.[124] Lejeune directed that this annual message be read at each corps command worldwide on the birthday of the corps. His inspirational message was later placed in the *Marine Corps Manual.* This tradition continues today.[125]

Part of the program at the annual birthday ball in Washington, DC, is the tradition of honoring the youngest and oldest Marine living in the area. Shortly before his death on March 22, 2008, James B. Glennon, colonel, USMC (Ret.), the only grandson of General Lejeune, was honored as the oldest living Marine in Washington, DC.

Lejeune was always quick to respond to negative news about the corps. This became evident when the media criticized the corps during its occupation of Haiti. Lejeune, as well as other high-ranking officers of the US

Navy and Marine Corps, disapproved of the depiction of Marines in *What Price Glory?* This play by Maxwell Anderson and Laurence Stallings premiered in 1924 with 435 performances. It "depicted war as brutal, bloody, senseless, meaningless, and mundane" at a time when postwar cynicism was at its height. In the play, Marines "abandoned any sense of morality and virtue, used profanity, drank to excess and womanized without any consideration of feminine virtue." The play conveyed the message that "the most important aspect of war was not the carnage and the destruction itself but the senseless reaction that human beings have to the brutality of war."[126]

Lejeune probably expressed his displeasure with the play to coauthor Laurence Stallings, who was a Marine combat officer with the Second Division in World War I and was seriously wounded in the final charge that captured Belleau Wood.[127] Lejeune did write Stallings expressing his appreciation of the silent film *The Big Parade,* a more laudatory depiction of soldiers and war. Released in 1925, it was a highly successful silent film. Stallings wrote back to Lejeune, expressing his "keenest regret that I had involuntarily transgressed against the sensibilities of many officers whom I respect and admire, by some of the dramatic devices of *What Price Glory?*" Stallings also expressed his love of the corps, its traditions, its officers and men, camaraderie, and spirit.[128]

A final major reform that Lejeune sought in order to bring the Marine Corps into the modern era was to change the outdated policy of promotion by seniority for officers. Probably more than any other Marine, Lejeune labored throughout his career to change this flawed policy. Lejeune understood that the corps could not become the most efficient military service in the world without the most capable and assertive officers. Although he was unsuccessful in convincing Congress to allow promotion by selection and merit, it was most likely his untiring efforts to secure this change that finally prompted its approval by the Senate five years after his retirement. The continued lobbying efforts of MGC John Russell helped this to occur. Certainly, Lejeune's consistent efforts to convince Congress—especially the Senate—to institute promotion by merit gradually weakened congressional opposition.[129]

It did not take long for the young Lejeune to recognize that promotion by seniority discouraged individual ambition and efficiency. Soon after being commissioned as a second lieutenant in 1890, Lejeune became aware of the long wait for promotion because of the seniority policy. Several of his fellow naval cadets who joined the corps became discouraged at an early age and resigned from the service.[130] As a young major in 1906, serving at Washington, DC, Lejeune was asked to draft a policy on promotions to a committee appearing before Congress. Well-versed in the promotion systems of the Navy and Army, Lejeune recommended promotion by selection.[131] He wrote to Commandant George Frank Elliott "that in order to have an efficient military organization, it is necessary that the Majors and Company Officers should be young men; it is also necessary for the junior officers to feel that there is good opportunity for advancement ahead of them, otherwise they will unquestionably lose ambition and interest in the service." Lejeune also stated his belief that "the promotion of Second Lieutenants after three years' service would be only an act of simple justice to them, as they would be put on the same footing in that respect as their brother officers in the Navy. Nothing takes the heart out of a young officer quicker than to be left behind so early in his career."[132] Lejeune's proposal was apparently too radical at this time. Nothing came of his five-page proposal.

Shortly after becoming MGC, Lejeune requested that the Navy Department change its policy of requiring promotion by seniority in the Marine Corps in order to coincide with the new modified system of promotion by selection recently enacted in the Army through the Congressional Act of June 4, 1920. The Navy Department refused Lejeune's request and appeal, referring to the Congressional Act of August 19, 1916, by which the Navy Department still required promotion by seniority in the Marine Corps. Why Congress allowed different systems of promotion for the Army, Navy, and Marine Corps was not explained. In reality, however, many of the older and inefficient officers in the corps who would not be promoted in a system of merit had the attention of a handful of senators who protected them from involuntary retirement.[133]

Lejeune understood that promotion by merit was necessary to improve the overall efficiency of the Marine Corps. Supported by Congress, promotion by seniority encumbered the corps with many mediocre officers and slowed the advancement of assertive and talented younger officers. Lejeune spent a great deal of time discussing this problem in House and Senate committees considering new personnel bills. Lejeune noted that, "At the close of the Civil War, we undoubtedly had the most efficient Army and Navy in the world. After twenty-five years, owing to the lack of incentive (promotion being entirely by seniority) and to the old age of the officers, all branches of the service were in pretty bad shape." Lejeune added: "We had then seventy-five officers. We have now over a thousand, so the situation would be just fourteen times worse. . . . I base this on the fact, that, leaving out anything other than physical condition, our officers in the lower grades will be so old that they will be unable physically to conduct such an arduous and difficult [Nicaragua] campaign."[134]

In 1927, Lejeune characterized promotion by seniority as being "like a labor union system, where a poor workman sets the pace for all. There is no reward for efficiency, energy, and ambition, and the man who just barely makes the grade gets the same promotion and advancement that the most highly efficient officer does. Presently there are 100 captains and sixty-six first lieutenants who are older than the youngest major."[135] Lejeune also noted that, "Under the present law, if fifty officers were appointed a year, about twenty of them would reach the grade of colonel. However, they would not reach that grade until they were just about ready to retire for age."[136]

Lejeune's last effort to obtain from Congress a law that allowed at least some selection by merit was the Navy Board's proposal of November 1927, a mixture of promotion by seniority and merit. "This bill related to the general and field officers, while leaving the present laws relating to the promotion of company officers practically unchanged."[137] The essence of the bill "forced retirement for some field grade officers twice passed over for promotion. . . . this would result in the forced retirement of a maximum of approximately sixteen field officers each year, which is five-and-one-half percent of the field ranks, or one-and-one-half percent of the total commissioned strength of the Corps." There would be "no selection and elimination for the company officers. The latter will be handled as at present, that is, any company grade officer who fails twice on his promotion examination will be no longer eligible for promotion, but will remain on the active list until he reaches the age of forty-five years, when he will be retired with two-and-one-half percent of his pay for each year of service."[138]

Even this bill was doomed to defeat in Congress. Perhaps as an appeasement to Lejeune, Congressman Ralph Updike introduced a bill on April 28, 1928, to promote Lejeune to the rank of lieutenant general. Lejeune asked that this bill be withdrawn, stating that congressional enactment of promotion by merit was more important, for it would increase the efficiency of the corps.[139]

On January 4, 1929, Lejeune announced to his staff that the personnel bill for which he had lobbied had not moved out of committee. On December 11, 1928, the House Committee on Naval Appropriations had amended the personnel bill eight or ten times. "The discussions did not last very long—probably about an hour. Several members spoke in opposition to it, most of them in regard to the selection feature. There was only one vote counted, and that was when one of the five members moved to strike out the enacting clause. The vote was five or six to one against the motion." Clearly disappointed, Lejeune noted: "I propose, during the remainder of my term in office which expires on March 4th, [1929,] to devote myself enthusiastically and earnestly, with all the power that I possess, to securing the enactment of this bill. I do not believe that I could leave behind a legacy of greater value to our Corps than this proposed bill."[140] At his last conference, on March 1, 1929, Lejeune ended his tenure on a positive note, perhaps hoping for a better day ahead for the Marine Corps, a time when Congress would enact selection by merit. Temporarily, he had to admit defeat. "It doesn't look very hopeful for our Personnel Bill. It is opposed by two or three senators who won't allow it to come up."[141]

Despite Lejeune's inability to persuade Congress to enact promotion by selection, his continuous and reasonable crusade during his entire career laid the groundwork for MGC Russell's success five years after Lejeune's retirement. It would be Lejeune's testimony from retirement to the Senate in 1935 that helped preserve the new law of promotion by merit.

9

THE DEVELOPMENT OF AMPHIBIOUS ASSAULT, 1920–1929

In developing the mission of amphibious assault, Lejeune reshaped the Advanced Base Force into the Marine Expeditionary Force. This force became the Fleet Marine Force in 1934, which had essentially the same mission as the Expeditionary Force. By promoting, planning, and conducting amphibious assault maneuvers with the fleet and utilizing input from the MCS, Lejeune altered the face of the Marine Corps. Moving beyond providing a temporary base for the fleet and acting as a small constabulary force to protect American business and political interests in the Caribbean, the corps was being prepared to assume a major role in the American military establishment. Lejeune's foresight envisioned the strong possibility of a major war in the Pacific, in which the Navy would need a thoroughly trained amphibious assault force to secure naval and air bases. These bases across the vast Pacific would be vital in approaching and defeating an enemy in the Far East. This new wartime mission—a highly specialized and difficult military operation—greatly strengthened the prospects for the permanent survival of the Marine Corps, a small force in the American military that had been threatened with extinction for almost 150 years through abandonment by the Navy or by absorption into the Army.

The ABF was developed by the Marine Corps in the first two decades of the twentieth century due to pressure from the Navy Board, the Navy, and the secretary of the Navy. At that time, the threat of a naval attack against the United States from Imperial Germany (War Plan Black), was considered a greater possibility than an attack from Japan (War Plan Orange). War Plan Black assumed that a large German fleet would steam across the Atlantic and attack the American homeland. First, however, Germany needed a temporary naval base near the entrance to the Caribbean Sea in the Greater Antilles to replenish its fleet before attacking the American Fleet and the United States. To defend against such an attack, a Marine brigade making up an ABF would fortify a base with naval guns (such as the island of Culebra, located east of Puerto Rico) to defend and repel an assault from a small enemy fleet of cruisers, freeing up the American Fleet to pursue and destroy the main German fleet at sea. This threat ended when Germany was defeated in World War I, causing the Navy to consider Japan as a possible enemy in the Pacific.[1]

Alone among Marine Corps progressives, Lejeune and Earl Hancock "Pete" Ellis saw as early as 1915 the need for an ABF to prepare also for offensive operations.[2] Ellis had noted that the ABF would have to seize a temporary naval base before defending it. Lecturing before the Advance Base Schools, Lejeune mentioned that "the Marine Corps would be the first to set foot on hostile soil in order to seize, fortify, and hold a port from which, as a base, the Army would prosecute its campaign."[3] In a meeting before the House Committee on Naval Affairs on March 2, 1920, before becoming commandant, Lejeune testified that the wartime mission of the Marine Corps was to seize, occupy, fortify, and defend temporary bases for the fleet.[4]

When he assumed office as MGC on July 1, 1920, Lejeune brought to headquarters and other important positions those visionaries who had supported the amphibious mission in the first two decades of the twentieth century. Dion Williams commanded the Fourth Marine Brigade as part of the East Coast expeditionary force, led this force in the 1924 winter maneuvers, and participated in the 1925 exercises in Hawaii. Later Williams became the assistant to the commandant, 1926–28. Robert H. Dunlap helped revise War Plan Orange in the early 1920s, challenged the notion that amphibious operations were impossible after the Allied disaster at Gallipoli in 1915, umpired the 1925 fleet exercises, and later commanded the MCS. Eli K. Cole commanded the Marine Barracks at Quantico that supervised the MCS, headed the recruit depot at Parris Island, and led an expeditionary brigade at the fleet maneuvers at Panama and Culebra in 1924. Earl Ellis became intelligence and war plans officer in the newly created Division of Operations and Training, writing the prophetic war plan for "advanced base operations in Micronesia." John H. Russell, who was MGC from 1934 to 1936, did not come to headquarters, but served as proconsul in Haiti during

Lejeune's tenure as MGC. Despite news reports of past Marine brutality toward Haitians, Russell and Lejeune had the vision to rebuild Haiti's infrastructure. Lejeune also selected strong leaders to serve in his inner circle, men such as Logan Feland, Wendell Neville, Ben Fuller, E. B. Miller, Robert Dunlap, Dion Williams, and Earl Ellis. Neville and Fuller strongly supported amphibious operations as the wartime mission of the corps and served as commandants in 1929–30 and 1930–34, respectively.[5]

Only seventeen days after becoming MGC, Lejeune officially accepted the Navy's War Plan Orange, Part VII, War Portfolio, and the new wartime mission of amphibious assault for the Marine Corps. Lejeune informed the CNO that the corps, as of July 10, 1920, would make available a limited number of men: one reinforced brigade of 4,117 enlisted men for the Atlantic war plan, and 818 enlisted, one regiment for the Pacific war plan.[6] The troops for the Atlantic war plan would embark from Philadelphia, while the troops for the Pacific war plan would depart from San Diego.

Lejeune was also eager to have the Joint Army and Navy Board approve the new mission of the Marine Corps. Previously the board had passed over item number 96—"Determination of functions of the U.S. Marine Corps in peace and war"—for several meetings, including their meeting on May 22, 1920. The reason for passing over this item, as presented by the report of the Joint Planning Committee, is unknown but can be speculated upon. The presiding officer of the meeting was General P. C. March, Army chief of staff. It is likely that the Army was not interested in formalizing the mission of the Marine Corps. Also, George Barnett was still commandant and was probably not ready to commit the corps to a new mission. At the next meeting, on July 15, Admiral R. E. Coontz, CNO, became the presiding officer of the board, and Lejeune was the new commandant. To unify the Navy–Marine Corps team, both men wanted the board to endorse the new mission of the Marine Corps. Consequently, the joint board adopted the recommendation of the report of the Joint Planning Committee and accepted the "determination of functions of U.S. Marine Corps in peace and war."[7] In addition, items 101, 90, and 89—"strength of Marine detachment at Pearl Harbor," "extent and development of Pacific bases required for campaign in the Pacific," and "joint Army and Navy actions in coast defense"—all of which had been passed over at the May 22 meeting, were adopted at the meeting of July 15.[8] The "determination of functions of U.S. Marine Corps" was approved by the secretary of war on July 22 and by the secretary of the Navy on July 23.[9]

The Joint Army and Navy Board was established by President Theodore Roosevelt in 1903 to help coordinate the actions of the Army and Navy in war and peace. That a coordinating body was badly needed was evidenced by the lack of cooperation between the Army and Navy during the Spanish-American War in 1898. The joint board was an advisory group staffed by representatives from the Navy's General Board and the Army's general staff. In effect, however, it exhibited the friction that often occurred between the leaders of the Navy and Army. For example, the two services could not agree on how to defend the Philippine Islands from attack. Lejeune supported the Navy's role in the defense of Cavite and took issue with one decision made by the Joint Army and Navy Board meeting in June 1921: "The Army Air Service apparently is [was] not to participate in any definite manner in the defense of Cavite from air attack." Lejeune felt certain from his experience in the world war that an "adequate defense of a locality from air attack is secured only by superior aircraft, and that ground defense was of little or no avail against air attack." Lejeune knew that antiaircraft guns, searchlights, and protective balloons were entirely inadequate to defend Cavite against enemy air attacks. Lejeune advised the Navy to bring this information to the attention of the War Department.[10] The Army, Marine Corps, and Navy would disagree over the roles of the Army and the Marine Corps in the revision of the *Joint Army and Navy Action in Coast Defense* pamphlet of 1920 during discussions in 1925 and 1926. More important, during joint board discussions in 1926, 1927, and 1928, the Army and Navy could not agree on unity of command issues in the execution of War Plan Orange.

To prepare for the corps's wartime mission, Lejeune acted quickly in late 1920 to reorganize the ABF, relocating it from Philadelphia to Quantico, which became the home station and headquarters for the ABF and the MCS. Lejeune believed the ABF and the MCS needed to work closely together. Consequently, Lejeune designated Quantico, which had a much larger land area than the base in Philadelphia, as the training and preparation site for the expeditionary troops on the East Coast. To make the force more effective, Lejeune secured sixteen 6-inch Filloux guns with complete equipment from the War Department to replace the corps's 8-inch howitzers, which he felt were "unsuitable for advanced base work."[11] To further improve the corps's artillery, Lejeune secured fifty 3-inch, 75-mm motorized guns with complete equipment "to be used to accompany more closely the infantry in the attack."[12] Despite this, Lejeune and the corps planned to obtain a lighter gun than the 3-inch 75-mm, which was too heavy for the amphibious mission.[13] While the Fifth and Sixth regiments of Marines that fought in the world war had been disbanded during the rapid downsizing of the corps after the war, Lejeune had already refilled and activated the Fifth Regiment, which "was in readiness for an emergency."[14] In addition, Lejeune's staff at Quantico had begun activating and training the Sixth Regiment, as well as the Sixth Machine Gun Battalion, the First Regiment (composed of a battalion of engineers, a battalion of signal troops, and a mixed battalion of searchlights and antiaircraft guns), and the Tenth (artillery) Regiment.[15] Lejeune instructed Butler, commanding Quantico, "to fill up these organizations as rapidly as possible, even in advance of the 6th Regiment."[16]

At about this same time, Lejeune appointed several Marine officers to key posts within the naval establishment to learn what the Navy was planning with regard to amphibious operations. Unable to appoint a Marine officer to the Joint Army and Navy Board and aware that some senior naval officers did not take the Marines seriously, Lejeune appointed Colonel Ben H. Fuller to the planning staff of the NWC and Major Holland Smith to the Navy office of the director of the War Plans Division with the permission of the CNO. Fuller kept Lejeune up-to-date on the NWC's war plans to control the western Pacific in the event of a war with Japan.[17] Smith, an outspoken officer who hated the Army, also kept Lejeune apprised of Navy plans that would involve the Marine Corps.[18] Smith, whom Lejeune had previously appointed to the war-planning staff of the NWC in December 1920, experienced difficulties trying to convince old-line naval officers that Marines should command amphibious operations ashore.[19]

Despite these other responsibilities, the corps continued to reorganize the expeditionary forces for the Atlantic coast at Quantico by including the Fourth and Third brigades, "ready for any emergency which may arise."[20] To train these brigades more efficiently, Lejeune utilized the growing expertise of the MCS, which he had started to develop in January 1920 when he commanded the base at Quantico.[21] Lejeune was encouraged when Logan Feland, director of the Operations and Training Division, part of Lejeune's newly developed headquarters reorganization in December 1920, announced that "Naval Operations was working out a plan for joint maneuvers in about a year . . . the seizure of some point by the Navy, followed by

Marines taking over the point." Feland expressed his opinion that the "Marine Corps has a difficult job, requiring great preparation, and must train early in the coming year to build a competent force."[22]

That same year, President Harding and Secretary of State Charles Evans Hughes delivered a far more damaging blow to the Navy and Marine Corps by scheduling with other world naval powers the Washington Conference on Naval Disarmament, whch occurred in 1921–22. This would prove to be a direct challenge to the Navy's War Plan Orange, basically eliminating the development of heavily fortified American naval and air bases in the western Pacific, thus handicapping the Navy in a possible war with Japan. While the intent of the conference was to limit the naval arms race between the United States, Great Britain, and Japan, and to reduce the threat of war in the Pacific, the net effect was to deny to the US Navy the construction of permanent fortifications in the western Pacific beyond Hawaii.

One outcome of the conference was the Five Power Treaty, which restricted Great Britain and the United States to a capital ship tonnage of 500,000 tons each, with Japan limited to 300,000 tons. France and Italy were each allowed a tonnage ceiling of 175,000. Japan, which in reality already had a smaller fleet, received the greatest advantage; the terms of the treaty prevented the United States from developing stronger fortifications to naval and air bases in the Philippines, Guam, Wake, Midway, and the Aleutians. Without strong bases in the western Pacific and Southeast Asia, the US Navy would have to travel great distances to protect and defend American possessions in Asia. Japan would have the clear advantage of being much closer to American bases and possessions in the western Pacific should war break out between the two nations. Although Japan agreed not to fortify Formosa and the islands of Micronesia, Japanese military buildups were usually conducted in secrecy, making it difficult to monitor compliance. A future ally of the United States in World War II, Great Britain was also handicapped, agreeing not to fortify Hong Kong, Borneo, and the Solomon and Gilbert islands. A further consequence of this treaty that angered American officers in the Navy and Marine Corps was that the Navy had to retire some capital ships and stop construction on new capital ships already in process of construction.[23]

Another product of the conference was the Four Power Pact, which pledged that Japan, the United States, France, and Great Britain would not interfere with each other's Pacific possessions. Finally, the Nine Power Pact bound all the nations that had some claim to "spheres of influence" in China to maintain the political and territorial integrity of China.

While Lejeune and most officers in the corps were disturbed by these naval treaties in 1922, Lejeune learned that the treaties exempted the Marine Corps from personnel cutbacks. Always alert to any opportunity to increase the manpower of the expeditionary force, Lejeune pointed out to the Navy Department and the Navy's General Board that the savings forced on the Navy by the treaties could be made up by the Marine Corps. Lejeune used this opportunity on January 23, 1922, to remind the Navy that the amphibious mission of the corps was alive and well: "The primary war mission of the Marine Corps is to supply a mobile force to accompany the Fleet for operations on shore in support of the Fleet: this force should be of such size, organization, armament and equipment as may be required by the plan of naval operations." In addition, to ensure that the Marine Corps could continue combat operations once the shoreline had been secured, Lejeune noted, "Also, it should be further utilized in conjunction with Army operations on shore, when the active naval operations reach a stage as to permit its temporary detachment from the Navy."[24]

Lejeune stated that there was no need for additional Marine manpower for operations guarding naval property in the United States or maintaining strength in Haiti and Santo Domingo.[25] There was an urgent need, however, for adequate personnel and materiel to "maintain in readiness in the United States on the Pacific Coast and on the Atlantic Coast, the nuclei of such Marine Corps organizations as may be necessary to guarantee success in war to any naval expedition requiring a mobile land force." Moreover, Lejeune said, "War would necessitate a large increase in the number of Marines required for duty as a mobile force with the Fleet. About 25,000 Marines are considered necessary with the advance elements of the Fleet for the purpose of seizing naval bases." Concluding his memorandum, Lejeune recommended maintaining a sufficient strength of Marines at Pearl Harbor for defense against "a foreign uprising," and "discontinuance of the use of the term 'Advanced Base Force' as now applied to organizations of the Marine Corps."[26] Lejeune preferred the name "Expeditionary Force" over the term "Advanced Base Force," even though he and others in the corps and Navy still used both names on occasion. For Lejeune the mission of the ABF—a defensive force to allow the Navy to protect the coastline of the United States—was a thing of the past; for the future, the mission of the Marine

Corps was amphibious assault, to assist the fleet in securing western islands in the Pacific and control of the sea.

Although Lejeune was unable to secure an increase in the personnel of the mobile force because of the continuing downsizing of the military services, he was able to formalize the new wartime mission for the Marine Corps and convey its importance to the Navy. Lejeune's declarations did not go unnoticed. Writing about the aftermath of the Washington Conference on Naval Disarmament, Philip Rosen noted, "Eventually, the American Navy would benefit from several other tactical and technological developments that began during the 1920s. Thanks largely to the work and inspiration of General John Lejeune, the US Marine Corps began developing appropriate strategies and tactics for conducting offensive amphibious warfare in the Western Pacific."[27]

Lejeune may have been the first commandant who believed that the United States would go to war with Japan sometime in the future.[28] Lejeune was a student of history and aware of Japan's rapid rise to world-power status. Japan was a latecomer to world power and superior naval operations. The isolated nation had been ruled for centuries by a decentralized feudal oligarchy of territorial lords and an aristocratic caste of warriors called samurai. Opened to the West by the forcible intervention of American Commodore Matthew Perry in 1853, the Emperor Meiji, 1867–1912, led Japan to modernize to avoid being colonized and dominated by the West. The Japanese looked to the Prussian-German model for its army and to Britain's Royal Navy for a modern fleet.[29]

As an island nation, Japan began developing amphibious operations in the late nineteenth century and successfully landed armies against a weak China in 1894 and a disorganized Russia in 1904–5. With the beginning of World War I, Japan sent expeditionary forces by sea in 1914 to take German colonies in the Shantung Peninsula and the islands of Micronesia in the central Pacific. Of all the major naval powers, Japan had the longest tradition of modern amphibious warfare. By1921, the Japanese Army had the world's most formidable amphibious force.[30]

Lejeune had been a Marine since 1890 and was aware of the growing competition with Japan in the Pacific over trade with China as well as Japan's increasing aggression, which probably began with the diplomatic crisis and near conflict with the United States over its annexation of Hawaii in 1898. Lejeune was also aware of the war scares with Japan in 1907 and

1913 over Japanese migration to California. As a student in 1909–10 at the AWC, he participated in the shift of war planning from Europe to Japan.[31] During the war scare in 1907, Lejeune's battalion helped prepare a defense to counter a possible Japanese attack against the Philippines.

Despite having inadequate manpower to develop offensive amphibious operations in a way he deemed necessary, Lejeune nevertheless worked with what he had to accept for the Marine Corps, the Navy's War Plan Orange. To prepare the Marine Corps for a possible confrontation with Japan, in the fall of 1920 Lejeune brought back Brigadier General Logan Feland and Major Earl Ellis from the Dominican Republic to serve in the greatly expanded headquarters organization. Feland became director of the new Division of Operations and Training, with Ellis heading up the intelligence section within the division. Convinced that the United States would fight a war with Japan, Ellis had already requested from Lejeune "orders to organize a reconnaissance of both South America and the Pacific." Ellis offered "to adopt any personnel measures (submit undated resignation and travel as a civilian) which the Major General Commandant may deem necessary to ensure that the United States shall not become embarrassed through my operation."[32]

Using Marine and naval intelligence, Lejeune learned of Japanese actions in East Asia and the western Pacific that conflicted with American objectives, as well as Japan's capability for war with the United States. Lejeune heard from the CinC of the Asiatic Fleet based in China that "relations between the United States and Japan cannot be said to be satisfactory. Incidents are daily created which cause irritation and animosities, and unless the situation is cleared up, the two countries will probably drift into war."[33] Admiral Albert Gleaves believed that Japan's one great ambition was to dominate East Asia, to be in the East what the United States was in the West, and England in Europe: "Japan's overwhelming successes in the wars with China and Russia gave her a place in the sun, and started her on the road to Empire. She has been rattling the saber ever since."[34] The admiral felt that Japan was in actuality a military nation, modeled along German lines. "She has a large and well equipped army, a powerful navy, and a secret service which is credited with phenomenal efficiency. . . . I cannot close my eyes to the fact that they mean to dominate the East, and that we shall have to accept that domination or we shall have to [have] recourse to arms."[35] Finally, Gleaves was concerned that the military was in control of the Japanese government and was going to embark on a path of war. "It seems to me that the greatest danger of war lies in the conceit and cocksureness of the Japanese military party. . . . a prominent Japanese has recently stated that Japan could easily take the Philippines in forty-eight hours. We must be prepared."[36]

Another intelligence report concerning the increase of Japanese influence in the Territory of Hawaii reached Lejeune in late 1922. This report by Colonel George C. Thorpe, commanding the Marine detachment at Pearl Harbor, surmised that the high birth rate of the Japanese in Hawaii, plus new Japanese school registrations, would give the Japanese political control of the island by 1940. About 60 percent of the labor in Hawaii was Japanese, and they controlled the mechanical trades and contracting businesses.

More importantly, Thorpe was concerned about the Japanese economic and military penetration of Asia, especially strategic points in Manchuria and East Inner Mongolia. After Germany's defeat in World War I, the Japanese had seized Germany's commercial rights in Shantung, China, closing the open door policy at Kiaochow. As Thorpe put it, "They [the Japanese] forced the Chinese to 'sell' their properties to them, under threats of martial law, and they obtained mining rights in the same way. Jap immigrants were hurried into Shantung—30,000 by the end of 1918, as compared to 2,000 Germans there in 1914."[37]

Thorpe was also worried about the defense of Hawaii, because the commanders of the Army and Navy units in Hawaii refused to work together. "There is no cordiality between Gen. [Charles Pelot] Summerall and Admiral [Edward] Simpson . . . inasmuch as there is no attempt at cooperative planning. . . . the Navy here has no idea of what the Army would do in time of war, nor has the Army any idea of what the Navy would do." After Admiral Simpson had apparently been conceded seniority as the senior military officer in Hawaii, "Gen. Summerall opened the question and claimed priority. . . . Gen. Summerall would remain absent from functions rather than sit on the left. There were rows with the newspapers over printing the General's name before the Admiral's and vice versa." According to Thorpe, "each service conducted separate war games and no . . . cooperative estimate of the situation [is] made by the representatives of the Infantry, Field Artillery, Air, Gas, and Navy and Marine Corps."[38]

There were other challenges to American security in Hawaii as well, arising particularly from Japan's manipulation of business and commercial interests. Thorpe sent another secret message to Lejeune in November of 1922. "Japan seems to be the most enthusiastic backer of the Union [Pan-Pacific Union], probably as part of the Japanese program to make the U.S. a pacifist nation."[39] The Pan-Pacific Union was a coordinated alliance of business interests in the central and western Pacific that the Japanese were trying to control. While the "organizer of the Pan-Pacific Union was Alexander Hume Ford—around for twenty years with socialistic and antimilitary sentiment—he had to work hard to keep the delegates pacified. . . . there was bitter jealousy and suspicions between the Japanese and Koreans and Japanese and Chinese."[40]

Most likely alarmed by the rapid Japanese population growth in Hawaii and the lack of cooperation between the Army and Navy, Secretary of the Navy Edwin Denby made it clear that Hawaii was the cornerstone of the United States' naval defense in the Pacific. "The development of Pearl Harbor is an immediate and vital necessity for adequate naval preparation for national defense. This project is first in priority in carrying out the general base project."[41] Secretary Denby sent a copy of the War Portfolio, Book I, to Lejeune and others on the war distribution list. "The current plans for the temporary submarines and aviation bases already approved and underway are to be regarded as preliminary measures of this Development Plan."[42]

While Lejeune was committed to the war plans portfolio and the Marine Corps's role in it, congressional budget and personnel reductions prompted him to write to the CNO that the Marine Corps had to limit the expeditionary force to only one coast. The corps would continue to maintain forces to carry out the strategic war plans for Orange and Red, Orange, and Green.[43] "Thus the Marine Corps has only one Advanced Base Force."[44] "In view of the shortage in the enlisted personnel of the Marine Corps, it may be impossible to maintain nuclei of this force on both coasts."[45]

Despite the lack of personnel to conduct amphibious assault on a large scale, Lejeune accepted and approved the Navy's War Plan Orange for the Marine Corps on July 23, 1921. Lejeune sent three sections of the Marine Corps's war plan to the Department of the Navy: its war portfolio; a worksheet to accompany the war portfolio; and a study of "Advanced Base Force Operations in Micronesia," prepared by Earl Ellis as revised by the Division of Operations and Training. The latter included a chart showing water transportation required by the Marine Corps to carry out War Plan Orange.

The war plan was prepared jointly by the Division of Operations and Training and the Quartermaster's Department.[46]

The war portfolio contained war plans that could be put into effect immediately in a war against Japan based upon the current congressional funding for 20,000 men. This plan assumed that D-Day—the beginning of war—would be in 1921. Lejeune also included a war plan for 27,000 men—the authorized strength that could be approved only by the president in time of peace. Lejeune provided charts that outlined development plans to further increase manpower to prepare the corps in the event of war. The war portfolio revealed the various phases in the war plans: first, "Mobilize the 1st, 2nd, 3rd, and 4th Brigades in Hawaii [and] conduct intensive training." The second phase stated that the Marine Corps must "be prepared to accompany the Fleet and reduce enemy resistance in Marshall Islands; to hold there a temporary base for our Fleet and to deny the use of the remaining available islands or atolls suitable for bases to the enemy." Another phase alerted the corps to "be prepared to reduce Caroline and Mariana Islands in like manner and to recapture Guam if it has fallen to the enemy." Finally, Marines had to "be prepared to capture and hold suitable base or bases from which our Fleet can exert decisive pressure upon Japan and can take advantage of every opportunity to bring the enemy's naval forces to action."[47]

The worksheet that accompanied the war portfolio provided plans in the form of charts, progression curves, and graphics produced by the staff to cover the mobilization plan. These functions included the mobilization of the Marine Corps Reserve, plans to bring back recently retired Marines, and increased recruiting efforts. The worksheet specified the planning needed based on the requirements for weapons, supplies and equipment, transportation, organization, and training.[48]

The third part of Lejeune's war plan was a study and revision of Earl Ellis's prophetic manuscript titled "Advanced Base Force Operations in Micronesia."[49] Lejeune, the first Marine to write about the true mission of the Marine Corps in 1915—offensive amphibious operations—had given his protégé Ellis the task of providing a narrative with operational details for the corps's plan within the Navy's War Plan Orange. Lejeune trusted and respected the troubled but brilliant planner, knowing that Ellis agreed with him about the necessity of conducting amphibious assault operations across the Pacific. Lejeune also knew that Ellis was obsessed with the idea that Japan was fortifying the islands in Micronesia and planning for war with the United States. In response, Ellis had secluded himself at headquarters and written several war plans for the Marine Corps, including several versions of his operation plan 712.[50]

Ellis's plan essentially concluded that the Navy could not count on having any bases west of Hawaii. The Navy with attached Marines would have to steam west and reduce and occupy the Marshall and Palau islands across twenty-three hundred miles of the central Pacific. These plans outlined the early amphibious assault doctrines of surprise and rapid ship-to-shore movement by waves of assault craft protected by intense naval gunfire and aerial attacks. The plan asserted that the assault would succeed or fail at the beach. The fleet's guns would have to provide a "walking barrage" similar to the "box barrage" used in World War I to protect Allied advances.[51] Additional units such as light tanks and artillery, machine-gun detachments, and engineers known as "pioneers" would have to accompany the assault regiments. The pioneers used explosives and wire cutters to remove underwater and above-water barbed wire and obstacles in front of and on the beach. While the transports with assault troops would arrive under the cover of darkness, releasing special landing craft, the assault would occur early in the morning, utilizing smoke screens to mask the transport area, but not the enemy defensive positions.[52]

The major significance of the war plan was that it codified for the first time the basic requirements for a modern amphibious assault. Doctrines as defined by historians Jeter Isley and Philip Crowl were the working principles of war, as distinct from military techniques, the manner and means of implementing these principles.[53] While techniques can change with new technology, concepts or doctrine as an overriding philosophy endure over time. Marine Corps doctrine in the early 1920s stressed achieving surprise as to the site of the attack, while at the same time the waves of assault craft had to move rapidly from ship to shore and be protected by intense naval gunfire and aerial attacks. This early doctrine established in 1921 continued but was refined with better techniques acquired through advancing technology in the 1930s and 1940s.

Lejeune's foresight, knowledge, and intuition anticipated a future war with Japan that would involve amphibious assault operations for the Marine Corps. During his tenure as commandant, Lejeune adopted a "Cautionary Strategy" of amphibious operations, a plan to move westward and secure bases through the central Pacific.[54] Lejeune was mindful that the United States did not have strongly fortified naval and air bases west of Hawaii. The Washington Conference on Naval Disarmament in 1921–22 had provided that the United States could not build permanent fortifications in the western Pacific beyond Hawaii, limiting the defense of naval and air bases in the Philippines, Guam, Wake, Midway, and the Aleutians.

Lejeune was one step ahead of the Navy. While many senior naval officers (and War Plan Orange) still expected a major fleet action of battleships to win a war with Japan, Lejeune understood that victory across the broad Pacific Ocean would require the acquisition of naval and air bases in a step-by-step western movement to Japan. Lejeune knew that heavily defended enemy islands and bases west of Hawaii would need to be captured. Most importantly, these potential bases for the Navy would have to be captured by assaults from the sea. Finally, Lejeune was single-minded in desiring this mission for the Marine Corps. As early as 1922, he understood the need for close cooperation between the Navy and Marine Corps and acted to convince the Navy when he wrote to the CNO: "If the United States should undertake to cross an ocean in waging unlimited war, bases would be essential to the operation." Lejeune knew that "the crossing through necessity would be made by stepping from base to base, for the reason that a reasonable avenue of supply and communication must be maintained with the home country. Each step could be taken safely only after the security of the path in the rear was assured. . . . the Marine forces with the Fleet would have the task of capturing each base essential to the United States advance."[55]

It was the US Marine Corps led by Lejeune that—by establishing amphibious assault as the corps's new mission in 1920—dispelled the ghost of Gallipoli, negating conclusions held by most military analysts that future amphibious operations were doomed to failure.[56] Intensive review of that amphibious debacle became the primer for the Marines of the 1920s and 1930s, studies that would turn amphibious defeat at Gallipoli to later Allied amphibious triumphs in the Pacific, North Africa, Sicily, and Europe for the Marine Corps and Army during World War II.

While the failed Allied assault at Gallipoli during the Great War convinced Europeans, the US Army, and many military historians that assaulting a well-defended shoreline was no longer possible, Lejeune and the Marine Corps began an extensive study of Gallipoli to determine the causes of its failure.[57] The amphibious assault of Gallipoli by British, French, and

Anzac troops against the Turks under German leadership was a British war plan to force a naval passage through the Narrows of the Dardanelles, bombard Constantinople, push the Ottoman Empire from the war, and open the Black Sea to Allied naval power. The operation would keep Russia in the war against the Central Powers and provide Ukrainian grain for France and Britain.

Marine Corps historian Kenneth Clifford was certain that the corps's development of amphibious assault that began late in the decade of the 1920s and continued through World War II would include an exhaustive study of Gallipoli in the curriculum of the MCS to determine exactly why the assault failed.[58] In fact, the Marines began studying Gallipoli much earlier, for Lejeune had requested in 1921 that the CNO send Commander L. W. Townsend of the Strategy Department of the NWC to lecture on Gallipoli to the field officers' class at the MCS.[59] Under Lejeune, Marine Colonel Robert H. Dunlap analyzed the Gallipoli operation in 1921, becoming convinced that properly trained and equipped Marines could succeed against strong opposition on open beaches. Specifically, Dunlap noted that troops and equipment in Great Britain had been improperly loaded, causing the troop ships to land in Egypt for redistribution, creating a three-week delay and alerting the Turks and Germans of the impending invasion. Also, the Allies had an inadequate knowledge of the terrain at Gallipoli, relying on old, inaccurate maps, superficial aircraft reconnaissance, and observations from warships located too far from shore.[60]

Dunlap's article on Gallipoli relied heavily on a book written during World War I by Major General C. E. Callwell, who concluded that Britain and her allies failed to adequately study the conditions and feasibility of a Dardanelles operation before deciding on the venture. In addition, wrote Callwell, the Allies did not develop a comprehensive campaign plan or coordinate well the military and naval operations; did not first establish an advanced base for troops and supplies, operating from too great a distance from Gallipoli; failed to take out the well-fortified Turkish artillery and trenches because of the flat trajectory of the naval guns; and did not resupply the decimated Allied divisions quickly enough with reserve troops. Finally, the Royal Navy was not able to land water and supplies to the beach areas, and the Army was unable to distribute water to the troops ashore, to the detriment of the advancing soldiers.[61]

The failure of the amphibious operation at Gallipoli in 1915 was due to many factors. Among them, as noted by Callwell, were the lack of support from military and political factions in Britain that felt the Dardanelles fight was a "strategical fantasy" that utilized troops needed on the western front; the poor reconnaissance of the terrain of Gallipoli that hindered landings and advances; the grave underestimation of the resolve and quality of the Turkish soldiers and the "demonic energy" of officers such as Mustapha Kemal; the failure of the British naval fleet's guns to support the army ashore; the absence of drive or "forceful direction" of British Army commander Ian Hamilton and his subordinates; and the tactical failures at Sari Bair near Suvla Bay.[62]

More recently, T. A. Gibson focused on the third phase of the attacks on the Gallipoli peninsula, the August landings at Suvla Bay, months after the first landing. Gibson maintained that the first two phases of the campaign—the naval attack alone and the earlier amphibious assaults with close naval support—lacked enough troops and munitions to capture the peninsula. In contrast, the Suvla-Anzac plan was sound with sufficient forces for victory. He wrote that the British plan failed because of governmental, navy, and army inertia and inept leadership: "It was at Suvla where the full main thrust should have been delivered instead of launching forlorn assaults against impregnable semi-mountain positions from Anzac positions." The principal fault which lost this "priceless chance of open warfare across the Suvla Plain and up the Anafarta Heights was the shameful indecision of the 9th Army Commander . . . and certain other equally dilatory and incompetent officers."[63]

Because the study of Gallipoli coincided with the war mission of the Marine Corps, as early as 1923 Lejeune pressed for a thorough investigation of the Gallipoli campaign and questioned the early absence of an amphibious force. At one of his conferences, Lejeune mentioned that "the War Mission of the Marine Corps . . . is one of the greatest importance. Many instances are of record in history where the presence of such a force has resulted in the success of the operations of the Fleet and where its absence has resulted in failure."[64] Then Lejeune brought up the example of Gallipoli. "The most recent instance of this is the Gallipoli Campaign. In 1915 the British Fleet attempted to force the entrance to the Dardanelles by bombarding its defenses without the support of an expeditionary force for shore operations." Lejeune knew that this error would result in heavy losses. "Several months later," he noted, "the error was realized and a large expeditionary force was sent to operate in conjunction with the combined French and British warships, but by this time the Turks had had ample time to strengthen their defenses to guard against a combined land and sea attack, so this attempt resulted in failure, with a very heavy loss of life and material." Lejeune felt that this twin disaster could have been prevented: "Had the Fleet on its first attempt been accompanied by an expeditionary force, it could unquestionably have captured the forts, entered the Dardanelles, opened up the Straits of Bosphorus, and gained control of the Black Sea and the city of Constantinople. Such a success would not only have undoubtedly shortened the war by a considerable period, but it might have resulted in saving Russia from the disaster which overtook her later."[65]

Lessons learned from the study of Gallipoli became part of the Marine Corps–Navy maneuvers of 1924 and 1925. In the early 1930s, Brigadier General James C. Breckinridge, head of the MCS, significantly increased the study of the failed Dardanelles operations. The Gallipoli amphibious disaster became a key part in the study of landing operations and helped develop the landmark *Tentative Landing Manual* of 1934.

Lejeune hoped to have a large Navy–Marine Corps amphibious maneuver in the winter and spring of 1922 but was dependent upon the Navy's plans for the fleet. Colonel Ben H. Fuller, whom Lejeune had appointed to the NWC, informed Lejeune on August 1, 1921, that the college was planning "a very comprehensive problem covering all of the operations connected with a campaign for the control of the Western Pacific, including . . . the occupation and defense of an advanced base somewhere in the Marshalls or Carolines."[66]

Lejeune's original plan for maneuvers in 1922 was to "send everything we had, both on the East and the West Coast, to the Isthmus of Panama for maneuvers on a large scale. However, the Navy cancelled the Fleet maneuvers because of the lack of fuel appropriations . . . so the joint maneuvers were called off and the maneuvers on a small scale by the control force substituted therefore."[67] In December of 1921, the Navy suggested maneuvers using a much smaller naval force—called a "control force"—to accompany an MEF of from 2,000 to 2,800 men for maneuvers on Culebra or Guantanamo. At the same time, however, Lejeune learned he had to provide over 2,000 Marines to guard the US Mail against theft and could not provide 2,000 Marines for a maneuver, recommending against a small exercise.[68]

Sometime later, the planning section of naval operations advised Lejeune to send a small expeditionary force for maneuvers in the West Indies.[69] These small maneuvers involved only two companies of Marines that included one 155 mm gun with a ten-ton tractor and two 75 mm guns with three five-ton tractors. Other weapons included one 37 mm gun, two Lewis machine guns, and six automatic rifles. The troops involved were Marines from the Ninth Company, Tenth Regiment, that included three officers and 135 men; and the Thirty-Fifth Company, with three officers and 100 men. Commanded by Lieutenant Colonel Richard M. Cutts, this force embarked on the control force ships the *USS Florida* and the *USS Shawmut* in order to assault and defend the island of Culebra, near Puerto Rico, and Guantanamo Bay, Cuba.

According to Cutts, the Navy's ships' boats were too light and had to utilize attached platforms to land the heavy artillery. The Navy's boats failed to support the infantry, meaning that the landings were too slow, exposing the Marines to imaginary enemy fire from the beach for too long. In conclusion, Cutts wrote, "the above objections can be readily overcome by the design of a lighter for the transportation of this gun which will do away with practically all shore construction."[70] Lejeune was obviously not happy with the results of this maneuver and barely mentioned the exercise in his Report of the Commandant for 1922.[71]

There was a positive aspect to the exercise, however. Although it was similar to the Culebra maneuver of 1914, there were significant differences. Instead of Marines having to manually haul heavy cannon and carriages up the beach by hand as in 1914, these Marines in 1922 had utilized the five-ton and ten-ton tractors to pull the heavy artillery ashore. The Marines had first used this new technology during the Civil War reenactment at Wilderness Run in 1921. Above all, this exercise identified without question the need for new landing boats specially designed for amphibious operations.

At his weekly conference on September 28, 1923, Lejeune announced that he had scheduled winter maneuvers. The maneuvers of 1924 would be the largest amphibious maneuvers to date conducted by the corps. They would unfortunately demonstrate that the Navy was ill prepared to rapidly ferry the Marines from ship to shore, that the Marines needed more training, and that the ships' boats were inadequate.

Lejeune emphasized to his staff the importance of the new mission: "We are going to organize an expeditionary force consisting roughly of one regiment of infantry, one regiment of artillery with aviation, signal, engineers, hospital, and other units. . . . these maneuvers ought to be of great benefit to the officers and men taking part . . . and especially will they be beneficial in giving a practical demonstration of what the war mission of the Marine Corps is—viz, the supplying of a complete expeditionary force for shore operations in connection with the Fleet."[72] Lejeune stressed once again that the corps's success and future lay with the Navy. "The Marine Corps, of course, is eminently fitted for this duty on account of its constant service with the Navy, and these winter maneuvers are intended to still further train the officers and men for their mission and indoctrinate them with the feeling that they are intended for service with the Fleet."[73]

The maneuvers utilized the entire Navy Fleet except for those ships urgently required for duty at foreign stations and the entire expeditionary forces of the Marine Corps. One MEF (Force Blue) composed of 1,750 infantry, commanded by Brigadier General Eli K. Cole, was tasked to support a scouting fleet in the Caribbean to prevent transit of the Panama Canal by the Pacific Fleet (the enemy) into the Caribbean. After that, Cole's force would assault to capture the island of Culebra, defended by another MEF (Force Black), 1,550 officers and men commanded by Colonel Dion Williams.[74]

The MEF commanded by Cole consisted of a force headquarters and headquarters company, one regiment of infantry (the Fifth Regiment less radio men), one radio service company from the signal battalion, and one platoon from the gas company. Williams's MEF at Culebra consisted of one detachment from the headquarters and headquarters company, one service company, one engineer company, one gas company (less one platoon), one artillery regiment (Tenth Regiment less one battery), one signal battalion (less one radio service company), one aviation division with six DH-4B-1 seaplanes, one balloon section, one antiaircraft company, and one light-tank platoon. The Tenth Regiment of Artillery had six 155 mm guns with a range of 18,000 yards, twelve 75 mm guns with a range of 12,000 yards, and eighteen machine guns. The antiaircraft company had four 3-inch antiaircraft guns, and the light-tank platoon had three tanks with 37 mm guns. These light tanks weighed six and one-half tons.

From January 16 to 18, 1924, Cole's Marines departed the transport *Henderson* in ships' boats at night to achieve a surprise assault before dawn to occupy and (constructively) damage the operating machinery of the Gatun Locks or spillway at the eastern end of the Panama Canal, disabling the guns of the canal defense so that the Navy's Scouting Fleet could move in close enough to bring (constructive) fire to further damage the locks and dam. The eastern side of the Panama Canal Zone was defended by approximately 7,632 Army troops and heavy naval cannon at Fort Randolph, Fort de Lesseps (Colón), and Fort Sherman.

Cole's Marines had to travel too far in the inadequate ships' boats—seventeen miles in the dark—to reach the objective. While it was the Navy's job to shepherd the three waves of boats to the objective in heavy seas, the Navy's beachmaster's boat lost power and the assistant beachmasters proved to be untrained. Consequently, the Navy was unable to keep the waves together and bring the Marines to the proper harbor. When dawn broke, the defender's airplanes (constructively) attacked the boats that were still out in the open and unprotected, causing heavy imaginary damage to the Marine force.

Although Cole thought he had accomplished his mission, capturing Fort Randolph and the Coco Solo Base, he felt that the mission almost failed because of the lack of training in the Navy and the Marine Corps. While Cole wanted a permanent and well-trained MEF, he understood that the corps was too small for that capability. To improve the force, Cole recommended that Quantico be provided with landing boats and a transport for training. Finally, Cole remarked that "if war comes we will have to deal with many untrained men, both Navy and Marine Corps."[75]

Regarding the second problem, the assault of Culebra, Williams's defensive Force Black received some unanticipated support. In addition to the seven submarines assigned that scouted for the approach of the offensive Force Blue, the *USS Wright* arrived unexpectedly at Culebra on January 29, the day before the assault, with twenty-seven seaplanes, giving the defense aerial superiority. The terrain of Culebra, naturally hilly and heavily forested, aided the defense during the maneuver. Colonel Williams utilized Culebra's terrain to great advantage, locating his artillery on reverse slopes to negate the flat trajectory fire of the Force Blue battleships. This maneuver was not to test the defense, however, for the force that Williams was commanding was similar to the ABF of old and had already demonstrated its defensive ability in past operations, such as at Culebra in 1914. This operation was designed to test the new mission of Force Blue, an MEF, and its ability to conduct a successful amphibious assault.[76]

Cole's amphibious assault on Culebra began in the early morning hours of January 31, 1924, and revealed errors in planning and execution from the very beginning. At this stage, it was uncertain why Cole chose to assault at night during a complicated maneuver. Lejeune's approved War Plan of 1921 that included Earl Ellis's "Advanced Base Operations in Micronesia" specified an assault at dawn.[77] Ellis believed that an amphibious assault should be conducted after dawn for better visibility: "Night landings in force are hazardous unless the coast conditions and enemy defenses are well known."[78] This fact was noted later by Rear Admiral M. M. Taylor: "Problems should be first carried out by daylight to show up errors made by attacking forces."[79] At this point, it seemed likely that Cole and his MEF were trying to achieve surprise and copied the Japanese technique of night landings.[80]

After the exercise, Cole blamed the Navy for the poorly conducted landing operation. Even at this early stage of amphibious assault operations, developing doctrine established that the Navy was responsible for gaining sea and air supremacy of the area of attack and for transporting the Marines from ship to shore.[81] Admiral Taylor admitted that the Navy was unprepared: "This is the first time the Navy has undertaken a problem on this scale. . . . the Navy should develop a doctrine on the seizure, defense and attack of naval advanced bases."[82] At this time, most senior naval officers were still preoccupied with the theories of Alfred Thayer Mahan and the importance in war of the large battleship fleet, not amphibious operations with the Marine Corps. As a result, the Navy boat officers—unfamiliar with the designated landing beaches—did not maintain order, causing some boats to become lost or to land Marines on the wrong beaches. Cole noted that, "while landing the Blue Force from the *Henderson* was in progress, chaos reigned."[83]

An official observer of the maneuver noted that the Navy was also guilty of poor planning. The (constructive) bombardment of Culebra's defensive artillery by four Force Blue battleships three miles from shore was ineffective because of the flat trajectory of the ships' guns. This fire did not destroy Culebra's artillery, which was located on the reverse slopes of the hills and well concealed. Moreover, the attacking force should have used the airplanes on the aircraft carrier *Langley* to attack Culebra's artillery after the naval bombardment failed and during the Marines' movement to shore. For whatever reason, as noted by Captain S. H. R. Doyle, commanding the aircraft carrier *Langley,* the carrier was allotted only six aircraft, although it was supposed to have fifty-nine planes. In contrast, the defenders of Culebra had twenty-nine planes.[84]

Cole told the CinC of the fleet that the attacking force violated corps doctrine by not having a three-to-one manpower advantage over the defenders. This doctrine anticipated heavy losses assaulting a well-defended enemy.[85] (This doctrine would be practiced by the Marine Corps in World War II where the corps suffered heavy losses when assaulting heavily defended islands loaded with concrete bunkers and underground tunnels in campaigns against Japan.) Further, Cole insisted that the Navy's motor launches were not dependable or seaworthy, did not mount machine guns, and offered no protection from enemy fire.[86]

The observer reported that because of these many errors, the assault of Cole's Force Blue at Culebra against Williams's defensive force was not successful. The observer wrote that during the Blue landings the Marines were exposed to accurate and effective shrapnel fire at long and mid ranges by the Force Black artillery. Consequently, many of the Blue small boats were either hit or damaged by the Black artillery fire. Force Blue was so seriously crippled on their approach to Culebra that they would have been prevented from carrying on a successful operation on shore. While later landings of Blue Marines allowed them to move into the interior of the island and actually capture a Force Black battery and most of its gun crews near the beach, the surviving Blue Marine Force was stopped by Black tanks, machine-gun fire, and artillery fire. Finally, the observer decided that the Blue landing force was too small and suffered so many losses that not enough Blue forces were available to penetrate Black's main line of resistance and could not have captured Culebra.[87]

Despite these problems, the winter exercises were significant. They were the first attempt to carry out a large-scale combined Navy–Marine Corps amphibious assault—a very difficult operation—with all the necessary players in place and actively participating. The most positive aspect of the maneuver was that it brought to light numerous mistakes by the Marine Corps and the Navy. These mistakes challenged the organizers for many years to come. Even with the many problems and failures, Lejeune was not displeased with the maneuver. He wrote that "an invaluable amount of experience was gained in the many features of the work which is the mission of an expeditionary force to perform. . . . during these maneuvers the expeditionary force exhibited a satisfactory degree of training and discipline. A high degree of morale existed throughout the force."[88]

In contrast to the 1924 exercises, the Navy–Army–Marine Corps maneuver of 1925 at Oahu in the Hawaiian Islands—drawn up by the joint board—was successful for the corps. Lejeune was determined to provide better planning and organization, more detailed intelligence gathering, and the input of the MCS. Rather than accept the recommendations of the joint board to quickly select a commander and staff for the MEF, Lejeune made the maneuver a "Marine Corps Affair," which allowed the staffs of the MCS and Marine Headquarters to participate.[89] On Friday, February 13, 1925, the field officers' class was temporarily discontinued and assigned to help plan for the exercise.[90] Lejeune was also eager to prove to the Army—which believed the Marine Corps could only handle small-scale operations—that the Marines could effectively manage a large force.[91] Lejeune procured from the CinC of the US Fleet very detailed information on the terrain and beaches of Oahu, including an early survey by Wendell C. Neville, dated September 4, 1911. This information mapped shorelines, interior lines of movement, trade winds, fog patterns, anchorages, tidal currents, possible landing sites, and bays surrounding the islands.[92]

The maneuver of spring 1925 was a Marine Corps–Fleet attack on the island of Oahu "with the idea of testing out the Army's defenses."[93] The MEF would only have a "skeletonized" force of 1,500 Marines, however, because of further personnel cuts. The "constructive" force represented a much larger Marine force of two divisions of 42,000 men. In order for 1,500 Marines to represent a force of 42,000, small groups of Marines represented larger organizations and carried unit flags of the international signal code that could be recognized by friendly and enemy forces and the umpires judging the maneuver. For purposes of identification, the fleet and the MEF were considered as "Blue," while the defending Army and Navy units in the Hawaiian Islands were the "Black" force.

The Marine Fleet and the MEF of the 1925 maneuvers successfully assaulted and landed units against Army and Navy defenders of Oahu from April 25 to May 1, 1925. The attack was to secure Pearl Harbor and Honolulu as a naval and air operating base for the Blue fleet. Admiral Samuel S. Robinson was the CinC of the Blue force that included the fleet of eleven battleships, six light cruisers, fifty-six destroyers, submarines, minelayers, the aircraft carrier *Langley* with aircraft, two aircraft tenders, and the MEF. Fourteen imaginary transports carried the "constructive" force of 2,384 officers and 42,677 enlisted Marines. In terms of weapons, this constructive force included two regiments of 155 mm howitzers of forty-eight guns, one regiment of antiaircraft artillery, one regiment of pioneers (engineers) to clear the beach area, and an air service of 135 officers and 1,000 enlisted Marines. The *Henderson* would actually land a 75 mm and 155 mm howitzer, a machine-gun company, two three-inch mortars, two 37 mm guns, forty-four Browning automatic rifles, and forty rifles with grenade dischargers, eight machine guns, two three-inch mortars, and four whippet tanks. The officers were armed with the 1912 model 45-caliber Colt semiautomatic pistol, while the men carried the model 1903 Springfield rifle. The *Langley* carried a pursuit squadron of twenty-four planes, commanded by Lieutenant Colonel T. C. Turner, Air Service.[94]

Lejeune selected Major General Wendell Neville to command the Marines, with Brigadier General Logan Feland commanding the First Marine Division and Brigadier General Dion Williams commanding the Second Division. Colonel R. H. Dunlap, CO of the MCS, was designated as chief of staff.[95] The Force Black defenders of Oahu had 20,000 actual Army troops. (The regular army garrison of Oahu had 15,000 troops; the remaining 5,000 troops were from the National Guard and Army Reserve.) The Army was assisted by ships of the Fourteenth Naval District at Oahu, a limited force, including a submarine group (less Submarine Divisions Nine and Fourteen), a scouting fleet, a small control force, a fleet base force of minelayer ships (less Mine Squadron Two), and a naval reserve force. Both Army and Navy units at Oahu had active air forces.[96]

The actual force of 1,500 Marines left San Francisco on the *USS Henderson* on April 15, 1925, under simulated war conditions. The ships were arrayed in a formation designed to protect the actual battleships and the fourteen "constructive" transports and fleet train from submarine attack in the eastern Pacific. The *Henderson* carried ten fifty-foot Navy motor sailors, three beetle barges, and two fifty-foot Navy motor lighters for the actual landings.

When attacking Oahu, Force Blue had to prepare for probable early defensive actions of Force Black. These actions could include the following: Black naval and air forces sent seaward to determine the approach of Blue; Black submarine attacks on Blue ships, especially the transports; Black fire from coastal defensive batteries against Blue ships; Black reserve forces gathered in central Oahu to repel Blue infantry attack; powerful searchlights from Black observation posts to identify the Blue fleet miles out from Oahu; movement of highly mobile Black troops to prevent Blue landings;

poisonous gas attacks to delay the Blue advance ashore, limiting mobility and speed of advance; placement of beach obstructions and mines at landing zones; and the use of Black motor transportation, allowing a rapid movement of reserves to front lines.

The attack plan of Force Blue included the capture of advance bases east of the target island of Oahu. Without replenishment, Force Blue could not simply attack Oahu after a two-thousand-mile voyage from Blue's home base. Also, since Black's Army and Navy force had a combined air force larger than Blue's, Admiral Robinson planned to launch a preemptive air attack on the defenders' air force before the main landings in order to win control of the air over Oahu. To accomplish this, a Blue scouting fleet that included Marines captured advance bases and landing fields on the islands of Molokai and Lanai (east of Oahu).[97] Force Black anticipated that Blue would first attack the outlying islands east of Oahu. Consequently, Black located seven DH4B airplanes on the island of Lanai. Admiral Robinson kept the aircraft carrier *Langley* at a safe distance from Black submarines, sending airplanes to occupy the landing fields at Lanai and Molokai. He used the *Langley*'s actual aircraft and the MEF's "constructive" air force for the strike. While Black's aircraft at Lanai constructively sank a Blue tender and inflicted some damage against the Blue landing force, they could not stop the Blue attack.[98] When the umpires ruled that the "constructive" air force of the MEF could not be used, Black had air superiority over Oahu for the entire maneuver.

In an attempt to achieve surprise, on the morning of April 27, the Blue fleet sent a small naval force to assemble off the east coast of Oahu to deceive the Army as to the actual landing site, then sent two battleship divisions, one cruiser division, one destroyer squadron, and fourteen constructive transports to land Marines for the primary attack on the northwest coast. A smaller Blue force of one battleship division, one destroyer squadron, and two construction transports landed Marines on the southwest coast as a diversion. These landings avoided the high mountain ranges behind the beaches on the east and west coasts and utilized the broad beach areas that led to fairly open terrain for access to Pearl Harbor and Honolulu. Landings scheduled by Blue to begin before daylight at 1:30 a.m., April 27, were changed by orders to begin at daylight "to obviate the inevitable hazards to life and material involved in making landings at night."[99]

These diversions by Blue drew the Force Black Army away from the main northwest-coast landing, temporarily deceiving the Army commander as to which one of the landings was the main effort.[100] The Army commander of Force Black was criticized by the umpires for placing most of his force too far south than they believed to be justified. He assumed that a Blue landing on the northwest coast in the vicinity of Haleiwa would be too far away from Blue's main goal of capturing Pearl Harbor. Conversely, a Blue main landing in the vicinity of Barbers Point on the southwest coast seemed likely, for it was twenty-five miles closer to Pearl Harbor. Unfortunately for the Force Black infantry, Black did not have a mobile reserve of sufficient size to shift quickly and stop the northwest-coast main landing.[101] After the landings, the fleet discarded amphibious doctrine and brought in battleships close to the landing zones to (constructively) shell the Army defenders. Thus, the fleet's battleships were vulnerable to possible Force Black air and submarine attacks and coastal artillery. It is probable that the fleet felt it was necessary to disregard doctrine in order to protect the Marines as much as possible, especially since the defenders had air superiority. The fleet's aircraft launched from the *Langley* were too few in number to counter the defenders' air superiority. The MEF landing at the northwest site suffered heavy losses but pressed the assault with Marines "constructively" landing wave after wave. The southwest landing, a diversion, involved fewer Marines, met heavy seas, and was stopped by a greater number of Army defenders.

By noon, successive waves of Marines had moved several miles inland and had achieved numerical superiority (constructively) over Army defenders, supported by the heavy bombardment from the battleships that fired just ahead of the advancing Marines in premarked zones. At this point the umpires declared the exercise ended, for the amphibious assault phase was completed.

The exercise of 1925 confirmed that the Marine Corps had changed the prescribed time of assault from dawn to before dawn. This was a significant change from Lejeune's war plan of July 23, 1921. Earl Ellis's prophetic paper "Advanced Base Operations in Micronesia" clearly specified that, while the transports with assault troops would arrive at the destination under the cover of darkness, releasing special landing craft, the assault would occur during daylight, early in the morning. Two major commanders in the exercises of 1924 and 1925, Eli K. Cole and Dion Williams, agreed that amphibious assaults should be at night in time of war.[102] Since Cole and Williams were close confidants of Lejeune, one must assume that doctrine for the time of assaults had been changed from dawn to under the cover of darkness. This change proved to be unfortunate and unworkable for these exercises of the mid-1920s. The Marines of the 1930s changed the time for assault back to dawn. During World War II, major landings were at dawn, exactly as Ellis had predicted in 1921, as the best time for the amphibious assault.

A critique of the exercise by officials of the Navy, Army, Marine Corps, and umpires determined that ordinary ships' boats were inadequate as landing craft, that the transports carrying the landing boats had to move faster hoisting the small boats in and out of the water, that more and larger aircraft carriers were needed to achieve air superiority over the landing area, that the Navy and Marines needed more frequent training in order to disembark faster from transports to boats and to the beach, and that—since radio, field telegraph, and telephones were crucial in an amphibious assault—they should be waterproofed and reduced in size and weight to facilitate portability and dependability.[103]

Major General John L. Hines, the Army chief of staff, complimented the Navy and Marine Corps for excellent planning for Force Blue, especially for the close cooperation between the Marines and the Navy, and for the attention to detail during the landings. Hines also recognized the need for better and faster landing boats. "There is no doubt that highly trained, well led infantry can establish a beachhead once the troops are ashore—but getting ashore, there's the rub."[104] Most important, Hines recognized the need for "a more comprehensive doctrine for Joint Army and Navy action than is contained in the 1920 pamphlet *Joint Army and Navy Action in Coast Defense.*"[105] Hines also noted that a command problem occurred in Force Black's Army and Navy air arms on Oahu. While the Army air commander wanted all aircraft to attack and demolish the landing fields on the Force Blue Molokai and Lanai air bases, the Navy air commander advised waiting until the location of the aircraft carrier *Langley* with her airplanes was determined. Consequently, no aircraft from Oahu moved forward. Hines recommended one commander for all Force Black aircraft.[106]

Lejeune was pleased with the Hawaiian war game "to support the fleet, or any part thereof, in the accomplishment of its mission . . . the exercises, which took place at Oahu, were completely successful from the standpoint of the Marines. The plans worked to perfection and the landing was accomplished. In this connection it should be said that the cooperation on the part of the Navy was the determining factor which insured our success."[107]

Lejeune recommended better hats and leggings for the men in future amphibious operations and the replacement of the Marine Corps's 75 mm gun by the new Army 75 mm howitzer. Lejeune also wanted to experiment with a new light tractor to transport these guns on their own wheels for faster unloading on the beach.[108] Reflecting on the Oahu exercise at a later date, Lejeune stressed that increasing firepower was necessary in the amphibious assault. He discussed the "Cutts Compensator" invented by Colonel Richard M. Cutts. This mechanical device reduced the shock of recoil for infantry-held automatic weapons, allowing the gun to be steadier, more accurate, and increasing the volume of fire for the Browning Automatic Rifle (BAR) and the Thompson submachine gun. "It gave the BAR the firepower for which the weapon was originally designed and which it never had."[109] Lejeune felt these weapons were absolutely necessary during an amphibious assault, especially when the enemy had control of the air, as was the case at Oahu. While Lejeune planned for and needed air superiority in the assault, he understood that enemy aircraft could break through air cover by friendly aircraft and attack his Marines: "In strafing such a small object as a boat, the plane must come down the line of its trajectory, thus swapping trajectories with the [ground-based] automatics. The planes can also be kept far enough away to largely destroy the accuracy of their bomb work. . . . the boats are small targets when the planes are forced up in the air." Further, Lejeune knew that rapid movement toward the shore was essential to the success of an amphibious assault. "There is no stopping and digging in, you either succeed or fail," and "if you fail to get ashore and secure the beach head, the whole operation fails, conclusively. . . . with expected losses, the units that do get ashore must have maximum firepower, even with limited numbers . . . to secure a penetration sufficient to relieve the subsequent landings."[110]

The Army was impressed with the planning and execution by the Marine Corps and the Navy during the amphibious maneuver. Consequently, Dwight F. Davis, secretary of war, requested of the secretary of the Navy that one Army infantry officer be allowed to attend the MCS each year, "in order that the War Department may keep in close touch with the Marine Corps with a view to becoming acquainted with the development of landing and allied operations, and on account of the possibility of combined operations between the Infantry and the Marine Corps."[111]

The end of the Hawaiian maneuver marked the beginning of a major change in the curriculum of the MCS. While Lejeune had involved the students and staff of the schools in the Civil War reenactments and the fleet exercises, his original intent in developing the MCS in the early 1920s was to utilize his experiences in the world war to teach new officers and recruits infantry tactics and how to fight a modern war using a combined-arms approach. This approach stressed greater firepower by combining infantry, artillery, tanks, and aircraft in the attack against a powerful enemy. Although this focus remained until the mid-1920s, it later became clear that Lejeune wanted to use the combined-arms approach for amphibious operations.[112]

It was Colonel Robert Dunlap, selected by Lejeune to run the MCS—one of the visionaries who supported amphibious assault and a participant in the Hawaiian exercises—who wrote a critique recommending that the schools incorporate more on amphibious operations into the curriculum. Dunlap suggested maintaining at least one amphibious battalion at the schools to regularly demonstrate landing operations to the students, shortening the curriculum by one month to allow the students to participate in an actual amphibious maneuver, dropping the study of courts and boards and administration in order to devote more study to amphibious operations, developing a board of Marine and Navy officers to recommend a suitable boat for amphibious assault, preparing a manual for overseas operations, and expanding the study of ship-to-shore and overseas landings in the schools.[113]

Not surprisingly, Lejeune agreed in March 1926 to expand the study of overseas operations and ship-to-shore landings in the MCS.[114] Lejeune, however, did not agree with the recommendation of Dunlap—who was supported by John Beaumont, director of operations and training, and by Eli Cole, CG, Marine Barracks, Quantico—to completely drop the study of courts and boards and administration. Lejeune knew by experience that the knowledge of general courts-martial and administration was important. For example, during the occupation of Germany by the Army's Second Division after World War I, Lejeune had to correct the tendency of officers to disregard improper conduct by their fellow officers. In a memorandum to the division's officers, Lejeune wrote: "I have observed with regret a tendency on the part of general courts-martial to show too great a leniency towards officers undergoing trial. I attribute this tendency to the fact that our Courts Martial are composed chiefly of officers who have but little experience in the administration of Military Justice." Lejeune noted that officers often shielded their friends from the ramifications of improper conduct—"a noble impulse, but there are higher things with which it cannot be allowed to interfere. These are honor, and the duty which we owe to our country and to the service to which we belong. . . . the honor, the reputation, and the good name of the Second Division is in our hands." Therefore, "let us set our standards of conduct high, let us see to it that those who bring discredit on the Division are made to suffer the just consequences of their acts."[115]

On March 3, 1926, Lejeune agreed to increase the length of the school term to allow greater time for amphibious study and to eliminate in the Field Officers' Course the study of naval courts and boards and international law while continuing the law course dealing with relations with civil authorities in domestic disturbances and military government. For the company officers' course, Lejeune compromised by keeping in the curriculum courses in law and administration, but reducing the study to fifty hours. As to the recommendation to detail a small expeditionary force to the MCS—to demonstrate amphibious assault to the students—as well as preparing an overseas manual, Lejeune decided to "hold [this] in abeyance for the present."[116]

For the major decision, Lejeune ordered "that the subjects of overseas expeditions and ship-to-shore operations be developed and made an important feature of the tactical course in both the field and company officers' schools. The preliminary research and study of these subjects will be begun as soon as possible."[117] Soon after, Lejeune asked the CNO to detail a naval officer to the MCS: "It is requested that a Naval Officer, preferably one of War College experience and of the rank of lieutenant commander, be detailed on the staff of the Marine Corps Schools to assist particularly in the conduct of the course in overseas expeditions and the operation of the Marine Expeditionary Force with the U.S. Fleet."[118]

New courses on amphibious operations emerged in the MCS for the year 1926–27, a total of forty-nine hours as compared to five hours in 1925. The new courses included the strategy of the Pacific Ocean, naval considerations for an overseas expedition, and the tactical principles of securing a beachhead. For the school year 1927–28, the MCS tripled the curriculum that dealt with landing operations. In addition, outstanding Army and Navy officers became instructors or visiting lecturers, men such as Dudley W. Knox, Raymond A. Spruance, and Frank H. Schofield. Even in Lejeune's last year before retirement, 1928–29, when most instructors were sent to

Nicaragua and China, the emphasis on landing operations at the MCS did not decrease.[119]

In summary, Lejeune's decision to place the MEF and the MCS together at Quantico paid off, providing intellectual input for better amphibious maneuvers and practical experience for the students. Taken together, both groups clearly enhanced and improved the developing doctrine for amphibious operations.

Although Lejeune wanted the corps to continue practicing its war mission during the late 1920s, circumstances prevented additional large exercises with the fleet. State Department demands for Marine expeditions increased rapidly after 1926, effectively preventing Lejeune from conducting large amphibious exercises. In June 1927 Lejeune wrote to the CNO that no Marines were available for the Pacific war plan: "Attention is invited to the fact that there is no force available on the Pacific coast, due to the fact that a Marine brigade of 4,266 enlisted has been sent from there on expeditionary duty to China. Also, the entire force for the Atlantic war plan . . . is at present on duty in Nicaragua."[120]

One of Lejeune's greatest challenges during his tenure as MGC was to improve the relationship between the Navy and the Marine Corps. Lejeune understood that the future of the Marine Corps lay with the Navy and worked diligently to bring the Navy and Marine Corps closer together. Because many senior naval officers in the 1920s did not take the Marine Corps seriously, Lejeune worked to convince the Navy that the Marine Corps and the mission of amphibious assault were important to the Navy. Lejeune's vision was hard to sell in the 1920s, however, for several reasons—it was a decade without a foreign threat to the United States, there lingered a negative reaction of most Americans against all things military after the bloody world war, and the government was committed to economy and the growth of big business. While Lejeune had only limited success in converting the Navy to his viewpoint, he succeeded in inspiring younger progressive leaders in the Marine Corps and Navy as to the importance of the new mission, a challenge that motivated these men to adopt and refine the mission of amphibious assault in the 1930s and 1940s.

Lejeune recommended to the Navy that the MEF become an integral part of the fleet, convinced the special board of policy of the Navy's General Board that the MEF was essential to the fleet for conducting ship-to-shore operations, updated the pamphlet *Joint Action of the Army and Navy* (1927) to officially establish the corps's role as the first to seize advanced bases in amphibious operations, and reinforced these ideas by continually writing and lecturing on the Marine Corps's importance to the Navy.

In a memorandum to the Navy Department prior to the maneuver of 1925, Lejeune wrote that "the Major General Commandant believes (a) First, that a Marine Expeditionary Force should be an actual component of the U.S. Fleet in any landing operations either in peacetime exercises or in war."[121] In addition, Lejeune felt that landing operations were the role of the Marine Corps, not the Army: "(b) Second, that the Marine Expeditionary Force of the Fleet presumably would be adequate to accomplish its mission of seizing a base for the Fleet." At the same time, should "unforeseen contingencies" make Army reinforcements necessary, these Army troops would be considered as reserves under the Navy CinC and serve under the immediate command of the MEF commander. "This is in conformity with a principle of war—that of cooperation, which demands unity of command. With a Marine general in command of Fleet landing operations, the chain of command would be unbroken from the Admiral to the lowest rank in either the Marine force or the Army reinforcing troops." Lejeune went on to discuss the importance of the Navy's close relationship to the Marine Corps, both as part of the Navy Department and separate from the Army. "The Marine officer is essentially an expert in landing operations. He is constantly brought in contact with phases and features of landing operations. For years he has been indoctrinated along these lines. It is part of his life. No Army officer has the opportunity to prepare himself in such a way. He is a stranger to this class of military operations and entirely out of his element."[122]

Again in 1926, Lejeune recommended that the MEF become a part of the fleet. He wrote to the CNO that "in order to clarify terminology, it is recommended that the Marine Expeditionary Force or Advanced Base Force,"[123] which would serve with the fleet in "a war calling for maximum effort, (such as an ORANGE war), be designated, 'Marine Corps Force, U.S. Fleet.'"[124] Unfortunately at this time the Navy was not prepared to recognize the MEF as part of the fleet. In response to Lejeune's memorandum, Admiral E. W. Eberle, the CNO, wrote that "the terminology recommended for Marine Expeditionary Force or Advanced Base Force, in reference, is not considered advisable."[125]

Lejeune was not deterred by such occasional setbacks and continued advocating the value of the Marine Corps to the Navy. He used the conclusions of the report of the Navy Board's special board of policy to remind the Navy Department that "the board is of the opinion that the Marine Corps should be organized, equipped and trained in such manner as to best meet the requirements of its mission as stated in paragraph 1—to support the Fleet, or any part thereof, in the accomplishment of its mission."[126] Lejeune used this report to remind the Navy that the mission of the corps came from naval policy dated December 1, 1922, that compelled the Marine Corps to support the Navy by providing detachments to vessels of the fleet, guarding shore stations, garrisoning outlying positions, and maintaining an expeditionary force.

In his summary, Lejeune focused on the wartime mission of the Marine Corps, stressing such points as the unity of command: "A naval officer cannot command Army forces or vice versa, but this restriction does not apply to the Marine Expeditionary Force which would constitute an integral part of the Fleet." In addition, Lejeune stressed the historical commonality of the Navy and Marine Corps: "Throughout its history the Marine Corps has been indoctrinated with the naval sea idea by having certain of its personnel serve as part of the crews of the ships of the Fleet, and by expeditionary service in naval transports, and also by keeping alive a traditional interest in all naval affairs." Thus, Marines were trained in duties aboard ship, "the habits of the sea," imbued with the "ideas, customs, and traditions of the Navy."[127]

Lejeune also continued to impress upon the Navy that "the primary mission of the Marine Corps requires that its Marine Expeditionary Force shall act as an integral part of the Fleet." Finally, Lejeune reminded the Navy that in time of war the corps was involved in the "first phase of the naval operation to gain command of the sea . . . to furnish the Expeditionary Forces required by the Fleet to seize and defend naval advanced bases, or to wrest such bases from the enemy, or to deny suitable sites for such bases to the enemy."[128]

When the joint board decided to update the publication on joint coastal operations that caused confusion between the Army and Navy, Lejeune seized the opportunity to promote the special role of the Marine Corps. The outdated pamphlet *Joint Army and Navy Action in Coast Defense* (1920) was revised in 1927 and retitled *Joint Action of the Army and Navy*.[129] In response to the secretary of the Navy's memorandum to naval units including the MGC,[130] Lejeune stated that "it would be a logical and proper step to change the name of the pamphlet to *Joint Army and Navy Action,* and to increase its scope accordingly."[131] Then Lejeune added his recommendations for enclosure in the new pamphlet: "The Marine Corps will support the Fleet or any part of the Fleet in the accomplishment of its mission: . . . As an Expeditionary Force to seize and hold advanced bases in cooperation with the Fleet and to defend such bases until relieved by the Army." Such cooperation of the Army and Marine Corps "is important as it will preserve the mobile character of the Marine Corps and facilitate the relief of Marine advanced base detachments by permanent Army garrisons when the line of communication has been made secure," and "such part of the Marine Corps as may not be required by the Fleet after it has gained control of the sea may be detached for service with the Army."[132]

While the new pamphlet did not include Lejeune's actual words, his intent was communicated: "General Functions of the Marine Corps are, as an adjunct of the Navy, to provide and maintain forces for land operations in support of the fleet for the initial seizure and defense of advanced bases and for such limited auxiliary land operations as are essential to the prosecution of the naval campaign."[133] The phrase "initial seizure" was important, for it gave the Marine Corps a mission separate from the Army and implied that the corps was an elite organization, the first to land. In addition, Lejeune secured recognition that Marines could continue to fight by serving under the Army in extended land operations. The new publication stated that "as an adjunct of the Army, its general functions require the Marine Corps to perform such duties on land as the President may direct." While it was Lejeune's intention that the new publication would recognize that only the Marine Corps could initiate landing operations, the document also gave the Army the right to conduct landing operations against shore objectives. At the same time, the publication gave special recognition to the expertise of the Marine Corps in landing operations: "Marines organized as landing forces perform the same functions as above stated for the Army, and because of the constant association with naval units will be given special training in the conduct of landing operations."[134] Consequently, the new publication legitimized the Marine Corps's role in amphibious assault within the military establishment and paved the way for the corps to conduct numerous landing maneuvers with the fleet in the 1930s.

During his years as commandant, Lejeune seized every opportunity to speak and write about the new war mission of the corps—amphibious assault to secure naval and air bases to allow the fleet to establish sea supremacy—and the necessity of the corps having a close and trusting relationship with the Navy. In a talk to students and staff at the Navy War College in 1923, Lejeune stressed that "the Marine Expeditionary Force is as much an integral part of the Fleet as any other fighting unit and that all impedimenta, supplies, etc., must be transported by the Navy."[135] In a similar speech in 1924 which was obviously intended to woo the Navy, Lejeune wrote: "I deem it pertinent to add that there is the closest kind of liaison and cooperation between Corps Headquarters and the bureaus and offices of the Navy Department. There is no friction and the machine functions in high gear without any serious jolts or jars. We are working, so far as our abilities permit, for the welfare and upbuilding of the entire naval establishment and not in the interests of any clique or faction."[136]

In a second address to the students at the NWC in 1925, Lejeune outlined the difficulties confronting the Marine Corps in preparing for its naval war mission—crucial for victory against a major naval power—and appealed to the Navy for regular annual maneuvers in order for both members of the naval service to hone their skills: "Throughout my first term as Major General Commandant, I strove unceasingly first, to assemble, organize, and train an expeditionary force; and second, to have it join the Fleet during its annual maneuvers. The first task was accomplished with much difficulty, and although the size of the force assembled is heartbreakingly small, yet the best that could be done has been done with the small number of enlisted men for which appropriation is made."[137] Lejeune went on to say that the second task was begun in the 1924 fleet maneuvers at the Isthmus of Panama and the island of Culebra and that he anticipated support from the fleet in the exercises at Hawaii later that month. With enthusiasm and fervor, Lejeune spoke to the importance of the joint war mission: "I am confident that the greatest benefit to all branches of the National Defense will be the realization of the enormous difficulties involved in landing a large force on a hostile coast, and of the necessity of providing in advance the facilities which are essential to the success of such an enterprise." Indeed, gaining victory in war against a great power "requires the most painstaking preparation in peace. Nothing can be left to chance. . . . towards the attainment of that objective all our efforts are being directed, and I ask the good will and support of the Navy in the accomplishment of this task."[138]

In articles he wrote for the *United States Naval Institute Proceedings* (*USNIP*), Lejeune appealed to naval officers "for a more complete and thorough coordination and cooperation between the Fleet and the Marine Expeditionary Force . . . by frequent exercises of these forces on overseas maneuvers with the Fleet."[139] To achieve the necessary unified-team approach, Lejeune considered it "necessary that every Marine from the general to the private must feel that he is of the Navy and in the Navy, and likewise that everyone in the Navy from the fourstar admiral to the man before the mast must feel that the Marine is part of the personnel of the Fleet with a definite and clearcut line of duties to perform in the general scheme of naval operations in peace and war." In addition, Lejeune reminded the Navy that before the world war, the Marine ABF frequently practiced maneuvers and exercises "in West Indian waters and in the Philippines, but for the three years following the close of the war [1919–21] it was not practical to have such overseas exercises of the Marines with the Fleet." While Lejeune scheduled Civil War reenactments during the latter part of this period to 1924, "to keep [the corps] trained in readiness," he clearly thought that frequent fleet maneuvers needed to begin again. "It is hoped that all plans for future naval exercises and maneuvers will include the participation of a Marine Expeditionary Force, for in no other way can this force be prepared for the final test of naval warfare of major magnitude."[140]

Lejeune stressed the value of the Marine Corps to the Navy in his 1926 article in the *Proceedings,* this time recognizing the common heritage of the corps and the Navy: "The mission of the Marine Corps is not new, but has remained, to all intents and purposes, the same in the century and a half of its existence." Lejeune knew "the real justification for the continued existence of the Marine Corps. Duty aboard the vessels of the U.S. Navy is the oldest duty the Marine Corps performs. In fact, it is the service which originally brought about a Marine Corps. Since the United States has had a Navy, Marines have served aboard naval vessels composing it."[141]

Even as the Marine Corps had to provide brigades abroad in 1927 for secondary missions for the protection of American lives and property during political revolutions in Nicaragua and China, Lejeune still saw amphibious assault as the primary mission of the Marine Corps with the Navy. "The Corps, being a component part of the naval service, is assigned a mission, which in general terms, is to furnish an expeditionary force to the fleet, to enable it to seize and hold the necessary overseas territory for fleet bases and bases for overseas land operations, with secondary missions in peace and war of furnishing ships' detachments, navy yard guards and overseas expeditionary forces for minor shore operations, such as those now being conducted in Nicaragua and China."[142] It was "with great reluctance" that Lejeune had to temporarily withdraw Marine detachments from nearly all ships of the fleet, ending all opportunities for Navy-Marine amphibious maneuvers in the foreseeable future. Still, in this article, Lejeune let it be known that "the future of the Corps is dependent upon its ability to accomplish this primary mission successfully. Its efforts in peace time are directed toward fitting itself for the efficient accomplishment of the mission in all its phases."[143]

It is fair to say that Lejeune was only partially successful in his efforts to solidify the Marine Corps–Navy partnership. Many old-line senior naval officers never agreed to embed the MEF as part of the fleet, rather giving lip service to the importance of amphibious operations while dreaming of big battleships and decisive fleet engagements to win a war in the Pacific. Even the General Board, a longtime supporter of the Marine Corps, still advocated the primacy of the battleship at sea: "Nothing that occurred during the world war has served to change the opinion of the General Board as to the vital importance in war of the battleship; the ship that can at once give and take heavy blows."[144] As late as January 4, 1929, shortly before Lejeune's retirement, the Senate Naval Committee would not conduct hearings on the Marine Corps's personnel bill until Senator Frederick Hale's cruiser bill was approved.[145] After Lejeune's retirement—with the exception of those leaders whom Lejeune directly influenced—it was primarily in the MCS that the mission of amphibious assault was still alive and well. Not until the mid-to-late 1930s and early 1940s—when war with Japan became a probability—did the Navy begin to take amphibious assault and the Marine Corps seriously. Even then, an all-out effort by the Navy to prepare for an amphibious assault mission with the Marine Corps did not occur until the Japanese attack on Pearl Harbor on December 7, 1941.

Lejeune was more successful in convincing progressives in the Navy of the need for proper landing craft—an essential element in the development of amphibious assault operations. Lejeune and other visionaries in the Marine Corps of the 1920s actually planned and worked with naval officers to build, test, and utilize three different types of landing craft. At the same time, however, senior naval officers saw the amphibious mission as secondary to the development of the "big fleet" of capital ships such as the battleship and cruiser, necessary to fight a projected climactic fleet action in order to win control of the seas against another naval power such as Japan. Consequently, the Navy considered landing craft for Marines as "experimental craft," which had a limited budget. As a result, the Navy built only three landing craft in the 1920s as prototypes. Still, this was the official beginning of the search for adequate landing craft and the three boats built allowed the Marines at Quantico to prepare for the amphibious mission. Lejeune and other progressives in the corps had long recognized that naval boats were inadequate as landing vessels.[146] This was the most important obstacle to overcome in refining amphibious assault. Aware that the Navy would not initiate the development of specialized landing craft, Lejeune—after the first amphibious maneuver in 1922 again revealed the shortcomings of ships' boats—determined to establish standards for and facilitate the building of new landing craft.

Lejeune's involvement in the development of new landing boats came as a result of the small maneuvers at Guantanamo and Culebra in January–April 1922. In his report to Lejeune, Lieutenant Colonel Richard Cutts, commanding this first maneuver, noted that the Navy's ships' boats were inadequate to land the 155 mm gun and ten-ton tractor.[147]

Lejeune responded by contacting the CNO, requesting development of a lighter to move men and equipment quickly from transport to shore, drastically reducing exposure to enemy artillery and machine-gun fire. Lejeune went into great detail listing the ideal characteristics of a suitable lighter: speed, self-propulsion, unsinkability, overhead and frontal cover, shallow draft, arrangements, and capacity. Sufficient speed was necessary to "reduce the time under fire and to present a target difficult to hit." Self-propulsion was crucial to allow the boat to "zigzag," to avoid being hit and to remove the possibility of a towing boat being destroyed, causing the landing boat to "wallow around" without power. "Unsinkability" meant "interior division into wells that would prevent a single shell from sinking the lighter." Overhead and frontal cover would protect the Marines from shrapnel from artillery shells exploding overhead and machine-gun and rifle fire from the front. The shallow draft would permit "a close approach to the beach."[148] "Arrangements" would allow the boat to mount and fire machine guns or 37 mm cannon at the enemy on the landing beach. For "capacity," Lejeune allowed some latitude, suggesting that the Navy develop boats to carry 65, 125, or 250 men.[149]

Lejeune's next memorandum to the CNO about new landing craft clearly reveals the early techniques and doctrine he planned to use in amphibious assault. Lejeune specified that the lighter "is intended for the use of the first landing force composed of infantry with its infantry weapons and of artillery equipped with seventy-fives [75 mm cannon] and their tractors. . . . after the first landing force had obtained a foothold on shore, another or base landing force with the additional equipment of 155s [155 mm cannon] would land."[150] This was a second landing wave carrying the heavier artillery and the ten-ton tractors. Lejeune's wording indicates that a second type of landing boat could be used to land the heavy artillery: "It is not believed that this heavy artillery would require speedy or self-propelled lighters as these guns probably could not be landed under heavy fire. However, it is desirable, if practical, to make one type lighter suitable for all Marine needs."[151]

The CNO supported the request, asking the director of war plans to proceed with the development of a lighter. The director agreed with Lejeune and suggested that the Bureau of Construction and Repair maintain a close liaison with the command-officer control force and the MGC in the design of these lighters.[152]

The Bureau of Construction and Repair requested that Lejeune furnish plans and weights of the 37 mm gun and the 75 mm gun and their tractors.[153] Lejeune recommended that a board be appointed to determine the best type or types of lighters and all phases of their use. Lejeune also recommended that Lieutenant Colonel C. C. Campbell, commanding the artillery regiment at Quantico, be appointed a member of the board.[154] While the secretary of the Navy approved the design and construction, he only approved the building of one lighter, "in view of the shortage of funds and the experimental nature of this lighter." The secretary noted that "it is particularly desirable that this lighter be completed in time for the winter [the 1924 Panama Canal Zone and Culebra] maneuvers."[155]

Eli K. Cole, commanding the assault force for the 1924 maneuvers, felt that the performance of the first lighter constructed, the so-called "beetle boat," was unexceptional. Cole also reported that a new boat to replace the beetle boat should be seaworthy enough to go twenty miles under its own power, and mount machine guns.[156]

Lejeune, too, was not pleased with the performance of the beetle boat or a special boat designed by a private company. Lejeune noted that "two special types of boats for landing operations were used experimentally with interesting, although not decisive, results."[157] The Marine Corps also worked with American engineer and inventor J. Walter Christie (who mostly developed vehicles) before the 1924 maneuvers.[158] Christie developed an early version of an amphibious tank that performed well on tests on the Hudson and Potomac rivers but was unseaworthy.[159]

This first landing boat especially designed for Marine Corps amphibious assault was "a derivation of the British beetle boats first used by them at Suvla Bay, Gallipoli, in August 1915." It was an awkward, top-heavy boat that featured a frontal dropdown ramp for unloading the 75 mm gun.[160] Lieutenant General Victor H. Krulak remembered that the "Troop Barge A," "Beetle Boat," or "Kelly Cole"—named after Cole, who led the campaign to persuade the Navy to build it—was a death trap because of the heavy steel canopy intended to protect the passengers from small arms fire.[161] Krulak felt that, should the boat capsize, the heavy steel canopy would prevent the Marines aboard from escaping the boat.[162] The board investigated the adaptability of the boat and recommended constructing a new boat to land either troops or artillery, but not both at the same time.[163]

Lejeune concurred with the recommendation. Accordingly, the Bureau of Construction and Repair began design of a new barge for landing troops only and made plans to build a second lighter, a non-self-propelled artillery lighter C for landing heavy artillery, either the 155 mm gun without tractor or a 75 mm gun with a tractor.[164] The new motorized troop landing lighter designated "A" was a sleek lighter that proved to be much superior to the beetle boat of 1923.[165] On June 23, 1925, Lejeune approved the bureau's new design plans for both the troop and artillery lighters.[166]

Shortly thereafter, the director of the Navy's War Plans Division recommended the construction of a third new lighter. In addition to the new motorized troop lighter A, which carried 120 Marines, the director suggested building a second motorized troop lighter B that would be smaller, unarmored, and slower, to be used to land the main body of troops after the assault wave had secured the beach. This second motorized troop lighter was cheaper to build, would take up less space on the transport, and carry from 60 to 70 men. It would be used to tow the artillery lighter C.[167]

Several groups of Marines and one Navy group witnessed a number of successful tests of the fifty-foot motor troop lighter A and the first, but unsuccessful, test of the non-self-propelled fifty-foot artillery barge C. When the 155 mm gun and tractor were lowered on the artillery barge C at 1:30

p.m. on July 9, 1926, the barge settled and the deck became awash. The barge subsequently capsized at 3:55 p.m., dumping the gun, tractor, and equipment overboard. The artillery barge C was then towed bottom-up to the pier about 4:00 p.m., sinking alongside the pier at 6:00 the next morning.

The motor troop lighter A performed well during testing, carrying on various sea trials with Marines numbering 106, 128, 134, and 149 at an average speed of 8.2 knots per hour. The major problem was the slow unloading of Marines, taking about one minute and twenty seconds to two minutes to unload 100 Marines on the beach.[168]

Lejeune had serious doubts about the future of the artillery lighter C but was pleased with the performance of the motor troop lighter A, especially its ability to retract from the beach under its own power. He did, however, want to increase the lighter's firepower by adding two 37 mm cannon to the two machine guns located in the forward top canopy.[169]

Work to improve the landing boats came to a temporary halt in 1927 when most Marines were on expeditionary duty abroad in China, Haiti, and Nicaragua.[170] In 1928, the Marine Corps and Navy resumed work to improve the fifty-foot motor troop lighter A, and to test the motor troop lighter B, reduced in length to forty feet. The fifty-foot artillery lighter C had been scrapped, but the Navy planned to build a forty-five-foot artillery lighter. In September, Rear Admiral Watson T. Cluverius, commandant of the Norfolk Navy Yard, recommended to Lejeune that the three prototype boats being built at Norfolk be sent to the Marine base at Quantico upon completion.[171] Lejeune, however, was reluctant to accept boats with unresolved performance and unloading problems.

Lejeune's reluctance was confirmed when Louis McCarty Little, director of the corps's Division of Operations and Training, cautioned Lejeune against acceptance of these boats until they fully met corps specifications. Little feared that, if the Marine Corps accepted the boats and later found them unsatisfactory, the corps would probably experience great difficulty in having the required changes made.[172] Lejeune agreed and refused to accept the lighters until they were fully tested by Marine officers.[173]

The status of the new landing boats for the MEF as of May 3, 1929—two months after Lejeune retired—was as follows. The type A, armored, fifty-foot motor troop landing lighter, capacity 150 men, was built, had passed tests exceedingly well, had a speed with full load of 8.5 knots, was able to land and retract through four-foot waves, and could override beach obstacles in weather prohibitive for other types of boat. Marine Corps headquarters planned to order twenty-seven type A boats.

The type B, non-armored, forty-foot troop landing barge, designed for the landing of the second and subsequent waves of Marines, had a speed of 7.5 to 8 knots, carried 70 Marines, and could tow the type C artillery lighter. One type B barge had been completed and given a preliminary test. The speed of this barge with the artillery lighter in tow was unsatisfactory to the Marine Corps. If corrected, the Marine Corps planned to order ninety type B boats.

The type C artillery barge—45 feet long, not powered, designed for being towed—could carry two tanks, or two tractors (ten-ton), or two 75 mm guns and two caissons, or one 155 mm gun and caisson. One barge of this type was built and tested but found deficient in plating. It was being rebuilt with heavier, welded plating. The Marine Corps planned to procure twenty-seven type C boats.[174]

Despite the work of Lejeune, the Marine Corps, and the Navy, these specially designed landing craft never went beyond the stage of prototypes. Because of the Navy's limited budget that permitted the building of only one of each of the experimental type A, B, and C boats, there is no evidence that any additional boats were ever built, and yet the "A" boat was used during troop landing maneuvers at Quantico, at least in June and July of 1931. Marines used the artillery lighter C to practice loading and unloading five-ton artillery tractors on the beach at Quantico in 1935 in conjunction with the type A troop motor lighter.[175]

The major significance of Lejeune's and the corps's work in developing new landing boats is that it provides compelling evidence of their commitment to further develop the new amphibious mission. While Lejeune and his Marines of the 1920s were not the first to recognize that the Navy's ships' boats were inadequate to land Marines against a strongly entrenched enemy, they were the first to propose and participate in the development of landing boats specifically designed for amphibious assault. The prototypes gave the corps its own assault boats on which to practice amphibious landings at Quantico in the late 1920s and the early 1930s when most Marines were overseas on expeditionary duty and when there were no major maneuvers with the Navy.

Although a number of historians and Marine leaders have maintained that Marines of the 1930s developed the mission of amphibious assault, claiming that Lejeune's work in the 1920s was embryonic, the archival evidence shows that Lejeune did indeed develop and demonstrate the new mission and establish new doctrine. Although the Marine Corps of the 1930s greatly refined and improved the execution of the mission, Lejeune originated and practiced the concept. He gave the corps a new and major mission that distinguished it from the Army, anticipated a future war with Japan, and laid the groundwork for the corps's achievements in World War II.

10

LEJEUNE'S LEGACY

The Marine Corps of the 1930s

Lejeune's greatest legacy to the Marine Corps of the 1930s—and even to the corps of today—was his capability as a strategic leader in providing direction, purpose, and identity. Lejeune could envision the near future and communicate its components to the Marine Corps, the Navy, the Army, the US government, and the American public. He had the political and social competencies to convince the Navy Department and the Joint Army and Navy Board that his vision for the Marine Corps was realistic.[1] Lejeune established for the Marines "their own separate and very distinct culture and identity."[2]

Perhaps Lejeune's greatest strength was his ability to anticipate future conflicts and prepare the corps to successfully deal with them—specifically, a likely war in the Pacific. Lejeune made the visionary decisions that changed the culture of the Marine Corps and laid the foundation for the development of amphibious warfare that established the standards realized during World War II and after.

Lejeune believed that the corps had to be useful to the Navy, meaning that the Marine Corps had to be efficient. "If they [officers] allow the Corps to deteriorate, its mission as the Navy's expeditionary force in peace and war will pass into stronger and more capable hands and the Corps will be marked for extinction."[3] The corps also had to be useful to the government and the citizens of the United States in war and peace,[4] and become the finest fighting organization in the world.[5]

As a gifted communicator, Lejeune expressed his ideas convincingly throughout the Department of the Navy. He was an eloquent speaker and used every opportunity to articulate his vision for the Marine Corps—through speeches, writings, and countless correspondence. He founded and wrote regularly in the *MCG* and the *Leatherneck Magazine,* as well as for the *USNIP.* He spoke often to groups at the NWC, the Navy Board, the Joint Army and Navy Board, Congress, and to government leaders.

Lejeune was also a master practitioner of political and social interaction. As he stated in his autobiography, he "kept in close touch with Members of Congress, especially the members of the Committees having jurisdiction over Marine Corps' legislation and appropriations, and established and maintained friendly relations with the officials of the White House, the State, War, and Navy Departments."[6]

Lejeune's farsightedness and clarity of vision led to significant accomplishments for the Marines of the 1930s. They followed his direction and wrote the *Tentative Manual on Landing Operations* in 1934, a how-to manual for the conduct of amphibious assault; they won Congressional approval to institute promotion by merit rather than seniority; they secured the Navy's permission to embed the FMF as part of the fleet, as important to the fleet as battleships, cruisers, aircraft carriers, destroyers, submarines, and other vessels; and they conducted important maneuvers—Fleet Landing Exercises (FLEXs), from 1935 to 1939.

To understand and appreciate what the Marine Corps of the 1930s accomplished in the further development of amphibious warfare, it is appropriate to analyze Lejeune's unofficial support from retirement as well as the events and the context of the decade. The corps of the 1930s faced grave difficulties, such as severe budget cuts imposed during the Great Depression; an attempt by the Army to absorb the corps; President Herbert Hoover's antipathy toward the corps, as fueled by key Army officers; and a final attempt by some Marines to reverse Lejeune's direction for the corps. During this same decade, however, the fortunes of the corps improved with the election of Franklin Roosevelt as president in 1932 (a former ally of the corps as assistant secretary of the Navy under Woodrow Wilson); the return of Marines from expeditionary duty, making them available for new maneuvers; and a growing respect within the Navy for the corps and for the further development of amphibious assault—in response to the growth of militant dictatorships in Japan, Germany, and Italy that suggested the possibility of another world war.

Lejeune took several actions in retirement, and precedents that he had previously established assisted the Marines of the 1930s in continuing his work to develop the new mission and modernize the corps. These actions included Lejeune's choice of Wendell C. Neville to succeed him as commandant; his return to Congress to help the corps survive severe budget cuts; his previous work that led to the development of the *Tentative Manual for Landing Operations*; inclusion of the MEF within the fleet; achievement of promotion by selection; and his support of the decisions followed by succeeding commandants Ben H. Fuller, John H. Russell, and Thomas Holcomb.

Although Lejeune embarked on a new career after his retirement from the corps—as superintendent of the VMI in Lexington, Virginia, from 1929 to 1937—his heart remained with the Marine Corps, and he did all he could to support the corps when called upon by Marine Headquarters. Senior officers of the corps saw Lejeune "as its 'Elder Statesman' and a great tower of strength and wisdom to be held in reserve for a crisis."[7]

In anticipation of his retirement in March 1929, Lejeune strongly recommended Major General Wendell C. Neville be appointed as his successor. Lejeune's choice was approved by President Calvin Coolidge, Secretary of the Navy Curtis Wilbur, the Senate, and, later, by newly elected President Herbert Hoover on March 4, 1929.[8] Neville was a close friend who shared Lejeune's vision for the corps. Neville had led the Marine brigade under Lejeune's command of the Second Division during the Great War, had commanded the MEF in the successful Hawaiian amphibious maneuvers in 1925, and was Lejeune's choice as assistant to the commandant from 1920 to 1923. Unfortunately for Lejeune and the Marine Corps, Neville died after only sixteen months in office. Neville's death was tragic news for Lejeune. Not only had he lost his best friend in the corps, but he felt that he had lost his hope for the continuation of his vision for the Marine Corps. Despite his brief tenure, however, Neville began the study for the development of the *Tentative Manual for Landing Operations.*

Lejeune counted as well on other well-placed "intimate friends" and protégés to carry on his vision. These notables included Harry Lee, Rufus H. Lane, Robert D. Dunlap, James C. Breckinridge, Cyrus Radford, Hugh Matthews, Thomas Holcomb, R. S. Keyser, Charles Barrett, Joseph C. Fegan, and dozens of other younger officers.[9]

Neville was a very capable officer and according to one writer was expected to maintain focus on further refining the mission of amphibious assault, supporting the fleet, and convincing Congress to establish promotion by merit.[10] As was the case with Lejeune, however, Neville had to contend with a small corps whose Marines were still mostly in Haiti and Nicaragua on expeditionary duty, making large-scale ship-to-shore maneuvers with the Navy impossible. Having fewer Marines at home also reduced enrollment in the MCS.

Neville and his successor as commandant had to contend with several challenges in the early 1930s. These included the election of Hoover as president (March 4, 1929–March 4, 1933), the stock market crash of 1929, the Great Depression, which continued to worsen after 1932, and the isolationism of Congress in the realm of foreign affairs. Hoover had three basic ideas influencing his thoughts and actions toward the military. First, he despised war and would do almost anything to prevent it. Second, he promoted government austerity and economy, especially for the military. Third, he believed that a small but prepared military establishment would be a deterrent to American involvement in a war.[11] His hatred for warfare came from his experiences during World War I when he served as chairman of the Belgian Relief Commission and witnessed the horror of war from both sides. Hoover believed that he had to balance the budget even during the country's economic collapse and defined military preparedness in a narrow sense—the ability of the military to defend North and South America from an enemy invasion.

Hoover distrusted the military establishment and secretly planned to save money by cutting the defense budget. He was a shrewd politician, however, and wisely chose loyal Navy and Army advisers who would support his policy of military retrenchment. He selected Charles Francis Adams, a descendant of two presidents, as his secretary of the Navy and Admiral William Veazie Pratt as CNO. Patrick J. Hurley became his secretary of war, with General Douglas MacArthur as Army chief of staff.

Diplomatically, Hoover was determined at all costs to avoid war. He also did not want a costly naval and military arms race with Great Britain and Japan. Consequently, he promoted arms limitations through recognition of the Kellogg-Briand Pact—in which nearly fifty nations renounced war and pledged to peacefully settle international disputes.[12] When the Japanese Army invaded Manchuria in 1931 and Shanghai in 1932, Hoover and the League of Nations invoked the pact in nonrecognition of this territorial gain by Japan. While the league and the United States took no action against Japan, Hoover counted on world opinion to persuade Japan to withdraw from Manchuria. In fact, Hoover was not particularly concerned about this action by Japan. He saw Japan as a bulwark against the spread of Soviet communism into Asia. It was Hoover who instigated the London Naval Conference in 1930 to limit construction of naval warships and the World Disarmament Conference of 1932 to limit the size of armies.[13]

In his retirement from the corps, Lejeune maintained contact with old friends such as Neville. He did not like the actions of Hoover and his administration. In mid- and late 1930 he wrote to Colonel J. C. Breckinridge: "I still take the same intense interest in everything pertaining to the Marine Corps that I did when I was Commandant. . . . the Navy is very much perturbed about the London Treaty. With the exception of a very small number of officers, the treaty seems to meet with vigorous opposition from the Navy. Personally I cannot see any reason for a treaty. We can get along pretty well on our own and I think it is better to be independent than to be prohibited from doing what we want to do by other nations."[14] Later he wrote again to Breckinridge: "Everything over here is quiet, but, there is a constant pressure to reduce the armed forces. I do not like the London Treaty and I like even less the attitude which seems to be prevalent that it is not necessary to build up to the naval strength allowed by that treaty. In addition to further reductions, the Navy and the Marine Corps have had to stand a reduction in their present appropriations which could only be accomplished by cutting down enlisted personnel."[15]

At the same time, Lejeune, who served as a divisional CO in the Great War and witnessed the horrors of combat, did not like war: "It is inconceivable that sensible, civilized human beings should be so foolish as to engage again in warfare, owing to its terrible destructive nature."[16] Yet he was a realist and noted in a letter to Brigadier General Harry Lee in December 1930 that "Russia, China, and India are in a grave state of unrest, as well as the peoples of other parts of the Orient. In Europe, too, each country seems to be carefully watching the other."[17] Lejeune had spent years preparing the Marine Corps to implement War Plan Orange—war against Japan—and believed that war would come, even predicting when it might take place. "I don't believe any outbreak will come while you are on the active list, but it might affect your boys and my grandson."[18] This was a prophetic statement. At that time, Lejeune's grandson, James Blair Glennon Jr., was twelve years old. Ironically, Glennon was twenty-three years old and a young Marine officer serving with the fleet at Pearl Harbor on December 7, 1941, when the Japanese attacked the installation and brought the United States into World War II.[19]

The death of Neville after only sixteen months in office was a great blow to the retired commandant. Neville was a strong and conscientious leader for the Marine Corps, but the unyielding pressure from the Hoover administration and Congress to reduce manpower affected his health. In a letter to Lejeune, Neville remarked: "Yesterday was an all-day session with the appropriations committee, answering questions of Mr. French and others. I was as nervous as a cat, but got by all right. I think a great deal of my [high] blood pressure is due to worry as to whether I will be doing the right thing, especially before this committee. . . . the Personnel Bill is a constant worry."[20] Neville suffered from chronic hypertension and suffered a major stroke on March 26, 1930. Lejeune was very concerned about Neville and contacted Smedley Butler about Neville's health: "I was very uneasy about him from reports that I had heard, but his assurance that his sickness was much exaggerated has relieved my mind greatly."[21] In another letter to Breckinridge, Lejeune said: "The doctor told me he had a thrombosis which resulted in partial paralysis. He is much better but has not regained the use of his leg. It has been now about three months since his stroke and I am rather worried about him as his recovery has been so slow."[22] Unfortunately, Neville did not recover and died of coronary sclerosis on July 8, 1930.[23] Gone, then, was Lejeune's ally and fellow advocate for continuing to develop the corps's new mission.

In his brief tenure, Neville had begun the development of the *Tentative Manual for Landing Operations.* The impetus for this was a request in early 1930 from the Army's chief of infantry for written doctrine from the MCS relative to the attack and defense of coastlines. Probably embarrassed because the Marine Corps was known by the Army and Navy as the specialists on amphibious operations, Neville had to inform the chief of infantry that the schools could not provide him with any written information on the topic.[24] While the corps had significant information in reports scattered about as learned from amphibious maneuvers, planning documents, and many articles on the subject, the information had not been consolidated in a cohesive instructional manual. At about the same time, staff at the AWC and the Navy War College also requested information on doctrine governing landing operations. The Army's interest in landing operations became more apparent in 1931 when the Army sought the temporary attachment of a naval officer to deliver lectures on landing operations to the general service schools at Fort Leavenworth.[25] In response, Neville, on February 5, 1930, directed James C. Breckinridge, commandant of the MCS, to develop a course in landing operations. From this course, Neville wanted Breckinridge to compile in a document the tactics, techniques, and doctrine utilized in a landing operation. This information would then be compiled and printed and become available to service schools. The document would not provide any information on secret war plans but would consist of a "series of abstract studies including an ample number of illustrative problems."[26]

During this period, the Marine Corps was beginning to suffer from budget cuts. When Lejeune was contacted by Marine Corps headquarters on January 18, 1930, concerning severe budget cuts and a misunderstanding by Congress about appropriations to personnel that occurred during his tenure, Lejeune traveled to Washington, DC, to talk to members of Congress. He renewed his friendship with key members of Congress and established better communications between Congress and the Marine Corps. He also helped alleviate personnel problems by recommending a temporary action of selection and elimination by merit.[27]

To understand Lejeune's involvement in the corps's budget crisis, it is first necessary to understand the events leading up to the budget problems. Brigadier General Ben H. Fuller, who had been appointed MGC by President Hoover on July 9, 1930, after Neville's death, suffered as much as his predecessor under Hoover's budget ax. Fuller had formerly served under Lejeune as commandant of the MCS, from July 17, 1922, to January 1, 1924, and later as Lejeune's assistant to the commandant beginning on July 2, 1928. He managed that office effectively after Lejeune's retirement and during Neville's long illness.

Fuller was actually a contemporary of Lejeune, graduating from the Naval Academy one year after him. Lejeune considered the Fullers and the Lejeunes "close friends"[28] and supported Fuller in his new position. In a letter to Breckinridge, Lejeune wrote: "I saw Fuller a month or two ago when I was in Washington. He seemed to be well and measuring up to the responsibilities of his position. I do not know a finer character than Ben Fuller. Surely all Marines can be confident that he will give to the corps the very best that is in him. No man can do more."[29]

Like Lejeune and Neville, however, Fuller found it difficult to muster enough manpower and funding to conduct large amphibious maneuvers. Lejeune was sympathetic to Fuller's dilemma and wrote to Harry Lee, "I hear from Fuller occasionally. He has a big problem on his hands in cutting the expenditures for the Corps this year and probably next year. It is easy to expand but hard to contract. I am glad to learn from your letter that he has the loyal support of the command at Parris Island. The success and growth of the Corps depend on its being united as one man behind the Commandant."[30]

The financial pressure on the MGC intensified throughout Hoover's term of office. Hoover and his secretary of the Navy, Francis Adams, did all they could to downgrade the corps, proposing that personnel be cut from 19,380 in 1929 to 13,600 in fiscal year 1933. Adams closed half of the Navy's and Marine Corps's recruiting stations, abolished the Marine Corps band, and tried to close the training facility at Parris Island. Even Lejeune's prized all-Marine football and baseball programs, which contributed to high morale in the corps, were eliminated. When Congress funded the corps's manpower to 17,500 men, Adams reduced it back to 16,000. The Marine Corps suffered much more than the Army and Navy during Hoover's one term of office. While the Army lost no personnel from the manpower cuts during the fiscal years of 1931–34, the Navy lost 5.6 percent and the Marine Corps (a small service to begin with) lost 24.4 percent. In addition, Hoover approved no new naval ship construction during his time in office.[31]

In frustration, Fuller wrote to Lejeune, "This is some job now with the Secretary telling me not to spend $700,000 of our appropriations for this year."[32] These cuts threatened further work on the amphibious mission. Fuller had to explain to the House Naval Affairs Committee that the personnel cuts "have made it impossible to carry out its primary mission of supporting the United States Fleet by maintaining a force in readiness to operate with the fleet."[33]

From retirement Lejeune did what he could to help the corps, beginning when he received a letter from Major E. A. Ostermann of Marine Corps headquarters about the concern in Congress over the minority report by the House Committee on Naval Affairs over the Marine Corps personnel bill.[34] This budget had been submitted by Lejeune before he retired and was misinterpreted by the House committee, which incorrectly reduced officer personnel. Later, he received a letter of concern from his old friend Refus H. Lane, adjutant and inspector, concerning congressional hearings on the Marine Corps personnel bill.[35] According to Lane, "Congress has the bit in its teeth and must show the country that it is doing something to affect economies."[36]

For the first time in three years, Lejeune left Lexington and VMI to visit Capitol Hill. He talked with Senator Frederick D. Hale and Representatives William Ayres and Frank A. Oliver, but missed Representative Burton G. French. In a letter to French, Lejeune wrote: "I had a copy of the bill sent to me and studied it personally just after it passed the House. I also read Mr. Ayres's report on the bill. After doing so I was convinced that the bill so far as it related to Marine Corps officer personnel was based on [an] erroneous assumption and that the reduction in the appropriation was much greater than it should have been." Lejeune noted that his "action in going down to Congress is caused by an entirely personal interest in the old corps with which I served for so many years and which I love so greatly."[37] Lejeune wrote to Lane at headquarters advising him of his visit to Congress and suggested that Lane and Fuller propose a plan to the Senate committee to correct the situation.[38]

Since Senator Hale had told Lejeune that there was no hope of increasing the amount appropriated for personnel, Lejeune suggested that headquarters come up with a temporary officer promotion and retirement plan to retire all captains and first lieutenants over forty-five years of age who had been denied promotion, and promote younger first and second lieutenants to fill the vacancies. "This would leave all vacancies in the grade of second lieutenant, and be helpful rather than harmful. . . . it would eliminate a large portion of the World War 'hump,' . . . give promotion to 76 first lieutenants . . . and to 85 second lieutenants . . . and with the provision for the appointment of 30 new second lieutenants, would leave the door open for an increase of officers later on."[39] Lejeune's plan was a temporary means to invigorate the officer corps and achieve a more efficient use of limited officer slots, an adaptation of his long fight to achieve congressional approval of promotion by selection.

Lejeune's visit to Washington helped the corps with the personnel problem. Lane wrote: "I think that you did some very effective work with Senator Hale and with members of the House, as there has [*sic*] been indications of a more sympathetic attitude. . . . a meeting of the Sub-committee of the House Appropriations will be held tomorrow . . . to hear the troubles of the Marine Corps and consider relief measures, if any." Lane added that he was hopeful "that there will be some good come of it, and in any event we have to thank you for the favorable state of mind created. Our trouble has been in our inability to interest Senators and Representatives more than perfunctorily."[40] Lane thought it was a good plan, solving many problems. Unfortunately, there were still objections from the House and Senate over eliminating officers who were former noncommissioned officers rewarded with commissions for their service in the world war. Also, according to Lane, Lejeune's plan "would not provide the benefit of a housecleaning in the higher grades, which is badly needed." Fortunately for Fuller, the retirements of disgruntled aspirants for commandant, Major Generals Smedley Butler in 1931 and Logan Feland in 1933, opened the door for Fuller to bring in his own "team," fellow Naval Academy graduates and supporters of the amphibious mission: Dion Williams, Robert H. Dunlap, Charles H. Lyman, and John Russell.[41] Finally, headquarters had already placed a concrete plan before Congress for the elimination of overage officers denied promotion in all grades except for second lieutenants.[42]

At the very least, Lejeune's foray into the personnel problems of the Marine Corps eased access between the corps and Congress. Lejeune helped to restore the good relationship between Congress and the corps that he had established during his tenure as commandant. Senator Hale remarked to Lejeune: "I have had a talk with General Fuller about the plan to correct the officer situation in the Marine Corps and he will present some sort of plan to the Committee when we hold hearings. I think the present plan is to retire certain of the higher officers as well as those that you suggested. I am hoping that we can straighten out the matter."[43] Later, Representative French of the Committee on Appropriations confirmed that the "House Appropriations sub-committee handling the Navy appropriations has had a further hearing with General Fuller and his assistants and we have gone over the problems to which you directed attention. Of course, the Senate must act before the matter will come to the House again and our thought was to try to be in position to be advised of the greatest needs of the Marine Corps and what could be done under the present circumstances. I am very glad that you were helpful in arranging for the conference."[44]

While the policy of promotion by selection (merit instead of seniority) and elimination by retirement of overage officers denied promotion was not approved by Congress until 1935, Lejeune's influence helped Fuller and the Marine Corps in 1932 to eliminate overage officers, promote younger officers, and survive the unyielding pressure for cuts to personnel from the

Hoover administration. In a letter to Fuller, Lejeune congratulated him for his actions to preserve personnel for the corps: "I have learned from the *Army-Navy Register* and from a letter written me by General Lane that the Senate has saved the day so far as Marine Corps personnel were concerned. I am writing to express my congratulations to you and to your assistants."[45]

During another stressful period when President Hoover's Army chief of staff, General Douglas MacArthur, urged Hoover to allow the Army to absorb the corps, Lejeune was unfortunately not available to help.[46] While on an inspection trip of new construction at VMI on September 19, 1932, Lejeune suffered a serious fall that fractured his skull and broke his left arm. He nearly died. Lejeune was unconscious for two weeks and unable to resume his duties as superintendent of VMI for one year. Doctors removed four to five inches of bone from his skull, severing a number of nerves in the process. He had to relearn the ability to speak and his speech was slower, forcing him to use prepared notes. His mind remained clear and insightful, however, and he returned to work at VMI until retiring in 1937 at the age of seventy.[47]

The year 1933 brought better news for Fuller and the Marine Corps. Pressure from the State Department, Congress, and the public forced President Hoover to begin withdrawing Marines from Nicaragua, making them available for amphibious maneuvers.[48] The election of Franklin D. Roosevelt as president in 1932 also encouraged the corps. Roosevelt was a friend of the Marines, dating back to his days as assistant secretary of the Navy under Secretary Josephus Daniels, 1913–21. In his inaugural address in 1933, Roosevelt announced his "Good Neighbor Policy" in international relations, a policy of nonintervention in local affairs, applying specifically to Latin America.[49]

Only one month after Neville's death in August 1930, Fuller took up the former commandant's work of developing a manual for landing operations. Fuller appointed Brigadier General Randolph C. Berkeley to command the MCS, the first general officer to direct the schools.[50] Fuller directed Berkeley in January of 1931 to convene a board to make recommendations regarding the MCS curriculum. The board would consist of Louis McLittle, James J. Meade, Bennett Puryear Jr., Samuel M. Harrington, and Robert H. Pepper.[51] In response to Fuller's verbal request, Brigadier General Robert H. Dunlap, CO of the MCS from September 28, 1924, to January 6, 1928, offered his opinion in January of 1931 that the schools' curriculum did not include sufficient education and training for overseas expeditions to capture and retain bases for the fleet in a major war. This was the first priority. Dunlap noted that the corps had vast experience in ship-to-shore operations and small wars, but that this "experience which is possessed solely by the Corps has never been placed, to any extent in usable form. It is buried in the minds of participants in the campaigns, and in the records of those campaigns. . . . the Corps should collate all this matter in the form of text books, manuals, letters of instructions, etc., to be used in our schools for officers and in the organization and training of the Corps."[52]

Berkeley formed a special committee in March 1931 under the direction of Charles Price to start work on a tentative text for Marine Corps landing operations. Other members of the committee from the Field Officers' School were Charles D. Barrett and Lyle H. Miller.[53] Later, Price asked Berkeley to assign Barrett and Miller to work full-time on the preliminary work of preparing the tentative text.[54] In May of 1931 Fuller approved Berkeley's and the board's report and recommendation to increase manpower at the MCS to include a battalion assigned to demonstrate amphibious maneuvers.[55]

In response to Fuller's direction and support, Berkeley on June 22, 1931, appointed a committee of Majors Charles D. Barrett, L. H. Miller, and Pedro del Valle "to develop and write the text for *Landing Operations and Small Wars.* They are hereby relieved of such assignments as they now have and will devote themselves entirely to the work outlined above. . . . the committee will complete its work on or before 1 June 1932."[56] The committee—now named the Landing Operations Board—studied many historical accounts of amphibious operations, such as the successful German amphibious assault against Russian islands in the Baltic Sea during the world war. The board requested detailed information from the ONI on this German assault, including the composition of the German Forty-Second Division, training of the covering force, details of the landing boats, information on naval gun-fire support, location of firing ships, types of shells used, the use of oblique or overhead fire, and method of coordinating naval gunfire with movement of leading boat waves.[57]

At this point in preparing a text for landing operations, Berkeley felt it was necessary to ask a fundamental question on jurisdiction: who would publish the text, the Marine Corps or the Navy? Berkeley wrote Fuller: "It appears necessary . . . that naval and Marine Corps doctrines and techniques . . . be developed simultaneously and incorporated in one publication applicable alike to Navy and Marine Corps personnel. . . . the method of publication should be decided before proceeding further with the work, and a decision in regard thereto is requested."[58]

It is to Fuller's credit that he recognized at that time—the early 1930s—that the Marine Corps had a much greater interest than the Navy in developing doctrine and practicing amphibious assault. Fuller's decision was that the "board preparing a text on landing operations at the MCS should proceed with its work, including the preparation of such Navy doctrines as involves covering naval gunfire, aviation support, and the providing, manning, equipping and operating the small craft required for landing operations as may seem desirable without immediate decision as to the method in which the text will finally be published."[59] Fuller felt that the naval officer assigned to the board, Lieutenant Walter C. Ansel, was in a "position to obtain informally naval thought on questions of naval doctrine that may arise. . . . if any questions should arise that could not be settled by the board, the board should contact the Major General Commandant for a decision."[60]

In a seemingly quick decision by Fuller, Brigadier General Berkeley was reassigned on November 7, 1931, to command the Second Marine Brigade in Nicaragua.[61] Since no reason was given for this transfer, either a man of Berkeley's experience was needed to command this unit in combat or Fuller needed a more assertive CO for the MCS. While there is no reason to account for the delay, recently promoted Brigadier General James C. Breckinridge, protégé of Lejeune, was appointed commandant of the MCS on April 25, 1932, and served until January 6, 1935.[62]

Breckinridge had new ideas for military education at the MCS, based on information from the experimental college at the University of Wisconsin. Breckinridge believed that research and development at the schools should be based upon a study of situations rather than a study of subjects. This approach led the schools to assign fundamental or arbitrary military subjects such as the mechanics of gunnery, field engineering, or ordnance to young lieutenants in the basic course. For the Company Officers' Course, Breckinridge used these ideas to extend the horizon of its students to think beyond the arbitrary limits of mechanical things and actions. This new philosophy saved the best for last in the most advanced course. The Field Officers' Course removed from its students the limitations and restrictions to originality, encouraging students to utilize their own innate abilities in every situation in order to analyze the situation and come up with their own decision.[63]

Like Lejeune, Breckinridge was a student of military history and incorporated it into the MCS curriculum. For a fresh start in developing a tentative manual for landing operations, Breckinridge considered the British official history of Gallipoli, the most critically and thoroughly analyzed history in print; he used it as the starting point to suggest the continued development of modern amphibious operations. Breckinridge stressed initiative and original thinking in his student officers and would not tolerate tunnel vision that focused on past precedent or established solutions. He questioned traditional doctrine and current thinking on amphibious operations and encouraged new and transformative solutions to old problems. Memorization was a taboo mind-set for Quantico officers. Breckinridge worked to develop the minds of the students, encouraging new information, innovative answers, and solutions to challenges. Breckinridge brought to fruition Lejeune's desire to make the schools the intellectual center of the Marine Corps. Lejeune's early focus on tactics, techniques, combined operations, and the start of amphibious training had been long established at Quantico. Now was the time to develop and encapsulate modern amphibious doctrine.[64]

Breckinridge kept many of the same men Berkeley had appointed for researching and preparing the groundwork for the *Tentative Landing Manual,* including Marine Majors Charles D. Barrett, Pedro del Valle, and Lieutenant Walter C. Ansel of the Navy. In order to stimulate the thought and interest of Marines outside the MCS, del Valle prepared abstract studies of Marines assaulting enemy-held islands defended by a well-prepared enemy.[65] Del Valle also came up with new conclusions based upon close study of previous amphibious operations, including General Burnside's army crossing the Rappahannock River at Fredericksburg, Virginia, during the Civil War; the Spanish amphibious assault at Al-Hoceima and Cebadia Beach against Morocco in 1925; the British landings at Zeebrugge on the Belgian coast in 1917; and the German attack upon the Baltic islands of Oesel, Moon, and Dago in 1917 against the Russians. In his study of landing boats, del Valle concluded that small, squad-sized, even unarmored boats, widely dispersed, were superior to large, armored assault ships carrying 300, 500, or even 2,000 men. He also believed that the landing boats should be self-propelled and fast to facilitate rapid access to the shore. Finally, the element of surprise was vital as it led to success in most of the operations studied.[66]

Ansel, the naval officer on the committee, studied—with the help of other naval officers—how naval gunfire could be used more effectively to support Marine landings. Ansel understood the early limitations of naval gunfire to support a Marine landing. For example, troops could not approach as closely behind naval gunfire as compared to their own artillery in land warfare. Ansel thought, however, that better communications between ship and shore could help. Even at Gallipoli in 1915, when a telephone cable was extended from ship to shore, British warships were able to fire on objectives only five hundred yards from their troops. Also, while naval gunfire had a straight trajectory and could not fire on reverse slopes, the higher mobility of newer ships could provide fire support from the flank. Naval guns had a much greater range than land artillery, a much higher velocity, and could be fired at a faster rate. Finally, the great improvement in aircraft since 1915 would enable more precise observation and shelling.[67]

Ansel was overly optimistic about the effectiveness of naval gunfire to support Marine assaults in amphibious landings. With the exception of Ansel and a few other naval officers, the Navy was not especially interested in developing effective naval gunfire support in the 1930s or early 1940s. While most naval studies focused on transferring World War I land artillery concepts to naval fire support ashore, the Navy could not provide the same high-angle fire to provide what the Marine Corps needed most—methodical, consistent, pinpoint fire to destroy heavily fortified enemy bunkers and below-ground emplacements. Naval gunfire traditionally functioned to sink enemy ships at a distance by penetrating their armor with flat-trajectory, high-speed shells. The Navy's idea for fire support was for its ships to steam along the shore at high speed—laying down intense area fire or neutralizing barrages—thus avoiding enemy artillery ashore. This approach did not destroy an enemy that was buried underground protected by concrete bunkers. Consequently, there was little real progress during this period in effective ship-to-shore fire support for Marine landings.

At about this same time, Major Barrett headed a new board called the Landing Operations Test Board. Along with Majors Lyle Miller and del Valle and Lieutenant Ansel, Barrett analyzed historical research in order to write a treatise titled "Landing Operations," intended as a model for extended research. Their ideas were put to the test in a small Army and Navy maneuver in Hawaii in 1932 that featured a battalion of infantry and an artillery battery in an amphibious landing assault. The operation was uncoordinated, however, because the leaders providing naval gunfire, air support, and the assault troops did not follow the same tenets. While disappointing, the maneuver highlighted a need for a comprehensive doctrine.[68]

A major change in the direction of the MCS occurred when Breckinridge appointed Lieutenant Colonel Ellis Bell Miller as his assistant in July 1932. With the support of Breckinridge, Miller discarded all courses based on the Army schools at Leavenworth and Fort Benning, replacing the Army tables of organization with the Marine Corps tables of organization and equipment. From that time forward, the corps utilized its own system of units, equipment, textbooks, and organization to advance their training in amphibious operations.[69]

A major problem that Miller and the Marine Corps faced in the 1930s was the lackadaisical attitude of many senior naval officers toward the Navy's key role in supporting the corps in amphibious operations. Like many senior Marines, Miller knew the Navy had to embrace the amphibious mission of the corps in order for it to be successful. His obsession with this problem and his often abrasive style of communications offended many naval and Marine officers. In his writings and correspondence, Miller simply urged the Navy to "get moving." In a 1932 article, he was publicly critical of the Navy, saying that the Navy did not appreciate the corps's ability to attack and secure naval and air bases in the Pacific. The naval officers that did appreciate the corps thought only in terms of inconveniences—tons of equipment and cargo handled, or the number of Marines housed aboard ship. Miller emphasized that the fleet could not destroy an enemy fleet and achieve control of the sea without the corps.[70]

Miller wrote a second article in 1933, clearly addressed to the Navy, outlining the emerging doctrine of ship-to-shore operations. In this complex, technical article detailing the many steps in a landing operation and focusing on getting Marines ashore, Miller referred to the Navy as "you" and often referred to landings and fire-support responsibilities as "a Navy problem."[71]

In a third essay, Miller challenged the Navy to provide better gunfire support for Marine assault forces and to improve gunnery communications with all units. Miller stated that if the Navy could make gunnery changes to defend against air attacks, it could make changes to support the Marines assaulting the enemy. Miller attacked sacrosanct beliefs held by many senior naval officers, such as the concept articulated by Alfred Thayer Mahan that victory at sea could only be won by a climactic fleet action between battleships. Miller also questioned an ingrained belief that the Navy could not afford to risk capital ships of the fleet to enemy gunfire and submarines while supporting the minor role of Marines assaulting an island. Miller demanded that the Navy update its thinking, declaring that "it is now past time that we should realize that naval guns must be able to fire at land targets . . . that the Navy already had rifles such as the five-inch antiaircraft gun which had a dual-purpose modern indirect fire control system . . . with a high angle of fire with high explosive and shrapnel shells." Finally, according to Miller, the Navy had to work more frequently with the Marine Corps in combined training and amphibious maneuvers.[72]

Miller used these articles as the basis of his essay "The Marine Corps in Support of the Fleet" in June 1933, also incorporating new material written by staff and students at the MCS. Obsessed with these ideas, he spent the remainder of his time at the schools trying to incorporate his thoughts into the *Tentative Landing Manual,* first published in 1934. While many of Miller's ideas went into the 1934 publication, they were omitted in revisions and later publications, especially the Army and Navy manual adopted as the *Fleet Training Publication—167* in 1938.[73]

One powerful incentive pushing the MCS to finally write the *Tentative Landing Manual* was the Navy's acceptance in 1933 of the concept of embedding the Marine amphibious force within the fleet, making the Marine force a part of the fleet. Obviously, an organized Marine landing force needed a textbook of doctrine and tactics to guide it in an amphibious assault or defense. Indirectly, Miller had a role in promoting the idea of including the Marine force as part of the fleet. Miller had good professional credentials—he was a graduate and former instructor at the NWC and a graduate of the MCS and the AWC—and encouraged cooperation between the MCS and the NWC. One correspondent of Miller was Colonel Richard M. Cutts, the Marine Corps representative to the NWC. Cutts wrote to Miller and Brigadier General John T. Myers, assistant to the commandant in 1932 and 1933, suggesting that the Marine base force be located in the operating forces of the fleet.[74] When Brigadier General John H. Russell replaced Myers as assistant to the commandant in February 1933, he clarified the ideas of Miller, Cutts, and Myers and recommended to the MGC that the Marine Corps discontinue the term "expeditionary force," rename it the "fleet base defense force" or the "fleet Marine force," and include the force as an integral part of the fleet under the employment of the CinC, US Fleet. General Fuller approved this recommendation. The Navy was supportive at this time, and Secretary of the Navy Claude A. Swanson approved the concept on December 7, 1933.[75]

Dozens of Marine, Navy, and Army officers contributed to the *Tentative Manual for Landing Operations,* and it was completed by June 13, 1934, using a series of committees to develop the final text. On May 15, 1935, Lieutenant Colonel Charles Barrett headed a board to revise the 1935 edition of the manual. Later, General Alfred H. Noble wrote that Barrett was "an outstanding original thinker who almost single-handedly wrote two thirds of the *Tentative Manual* based on the mass of uncoordinated material assembled at the time."[76] Over time, the manual was updated, with improvements in 1936, 1937, 1938, 1941, and 1943. The 1941 version, entitled the *Landing Operations Doctrine, U.S. Navy,* was based on innovations and experiences gained from the FLEXs conducted by the Navy and Marine Corps every year after 1935 until 1941. The 1941 edition guided the Guadalcanal landings in August 1942 during World War II. The last edition—issued in August 1943 and based on further experiences and landings in the Solomon Islands and in North Africa—was utilized during the remainder of the war.[77]

Lejeune indirectly influenced the writing and publication of the *Tentative Manual for Landing Operations.* During his tenure as commandant, Lejeune had demonstrated the new mission through several maneuvers, such as those in 1924 and 1925, creating a need for a document to explain how the new mission would be accomplished.[78] Lejeune established the organizational structure that allowed him to oversee and control the development of amphibious assault—the MEF, MCS, and an expanded headquarters organization, especially the division of operations and training.[79] The schools provided excellent military training for all officers, not just a few officers with political connections. This schooling and training increased the overall intellectual ability of most Marine Corps officers, enabling the most efficient and brightest of them to write the manual.

In addition, while updating the 1920 pamphlet *Joint Army and Navy Action in Coast Defense*—which had created confusion as to the responsibilities of the Army, Navy, and Marine Corps—Lejeune suggested clarification by helping create the new *Joint Action of the Army and Navy* publication of 1927. Approved by the Joint Army and Navy Board,[80] Lejeune's revisions officially reaffirmed the role of the Marine Corps: "The general functions of the Marine Corps are, as an adjunct of the Navy, to provide and maintain forces for land operations in support of the Fleet for the initial seizure and defense of advanced bases and for such limited auxiliary land operations as are essential to the prosecution of the naval campaign."[81] In effect, the publication recognized that the Marine Corps had the unique capability as a naval service to conduct the initial seizure and assault in the new mission. This document also gave the corps of the 1930s both the authority and the groundwork to continue developing and refining the new mission, leading to the next step in the evolution of the mission—an instructional manual.

The Tentative Manual for Landing Operations of 1934 and the improved *Landing Operations Doctrine, United States Navy, 1938* were remarkably comprehensive illustrated documents that covered every aspect of joint Marine Corps–Navy landing operations in wartime.[82] The 1938 document had 239 pages in nine chapters that covered in great detail the subjects of landing operations: task organizations, landing boats, ship-to-shore movement, naval gunfire, aviation, communications, field artillery, tanks, chemicals, smoke, and logistics. The 1938 manual was an optimistic and confident document, stating, for example, "The use of standard ships' boats is not contemplated for expeditionary forces."[83] At that time, the Marine Corps did not have newer and better boats and was still using the inadequate ships' boats, but was hopeful that better craft would soon be adopted by the Navy. The document also offered new techniques for landing operations. For better coordination, the *Landing Operations Doctrine* had the officers of a particular landing force embarked on the same transport with the officers of the boat-landing group that landed them on shore.[84]

Lejeune had no direct input in the writing of the document, for he had been retired for six years and was still recovering from his serious accident in 1932. He did, however, pave the way for the document. As commandant, Lejeune had cleared away many years of uncertainty about the mission of the Marine Corps, definitively establishing the new mission of accompanying the fleet with an expeditionary force in order to assault and capture enemy defenses, providing for naval and air bases, and allowing the Navy to secure control of the sea.

Lejeune's creation of the MCS directly influenced the creation of the *Tentative Manual for Landing Operations* of 1934. Lejeune's new policy was unlike the earlier system of military education in the Marine Corps, which in some cases favored officers with political connections who received appointments to the Army or Navy War Colleges, while most Marine officers received little military education. Lejeune's policy mandated that all Marine officers attend all levels of the schools to be eligible for promotion. In effect, the MCS intellectually prepared Marine officers to operate more efficiently and to contribute to the corps. Some of these officers helped to refine the amphibious mission and develop the *Tentative Manual for Landing Operations.*

Lejeune inspired and mentored those key Marines who later wrote the bulk of the document—Charles Barrett, Keller E. Rockey, and Alfred H. Noble. Lejeune's friend Colonel R. S. Keyser—a former aide who also served on the staff of the Second Division in the Great War—was now on the Corps Headquarters staff. Keyser gave a great deal of credit to his former mentor: "Their labor is about completed and it is going to be the Marine Corps' contribution to military science and one in which we can all take pride. When it has been reproduced I plan to send you a copy as I am sure you will be interested as it is the product of the advanced educational system that is one of your great contributions to the Corps."[85]

Fundamentally, it was Lejeune's legacy that necessitated the creation of the *Tentative Manual for Landing Operations*. Lejeune had reformed and changed the face of the Marine Corps in the 1920s, developing a new mission that addressed the Navy's need for amphibious troops to secure a pathway across the Pacific in an anticipated war with Japan. Lejeune and the Marine Corps of the 1920s and the Navy had bequeathed to the writers of the new manual early amphibious doctrine, such as the need to surprise the enemy as to the time and place of the assault, to minimize friendly casualties by landing Marines from transports as quickly as possible, to reduce enemy resistance by gaining control of the sea and air, to inflict heavy casualties on the enemy and protect Marines by utilizing bombardment from ships' guns and aircraft, and to gather detailed advanced reconnaissance on the enemy's positions.

This doctrine provided basic elements in the *Tentative Manual for Landing Operations.* Some parts of the document seem to have been taken directly from techniques developed during Lejeune's maneuvers in the 1920s. For example, the manual included almost exactly the same approach that Lejeune recommended in 1927 when he stressed using automatic weapons fire in the landing boats against attacking aircraft.[86] Furthermore, the *Landing Operations Doctrine, United States Navy, 1938,* stressed landing heavy artillery in separate lighters only when "the landing beach is reasonably secure from the direct fire of enemy weapons." Lejeune had said basically the same thing in 1922 when he commented, "It is not believed that this heavy artillery would require speedy or self-propelled lighters as these guns probably could not be landed under heavy fire."[87] The 1938 document improved on this, however, as it called for self-propelled artillery lighters. Also, the landing techniques specified in the document of 1938 were clearly superior to the techniques utilized in the 1920s: "The smallest and fastest boats should be assigned to assault platoons."[88] By contrast, Lejeune had recommended landing the first wave of troops in the large fifty-foot Motor Troop Lighter A, capable of carrying 120 Marines. This large lighter developed in the 1920s—landing under heavy enemy fire—put at risk too many Marines in a single boat.[89]

The *Tentative Manual of Landing Operations* of 1934 and the improved *Landing Operations Doctrine, United States Navy, 1938* were giant steps forward as compared to the documentation Lejeune left while pioneering amphibious operations in the 1920s. While Lejeune and his Marines had developed detailed plans for the landing maneuvers of 1924 and 1925, they did not compile a written guide or plan as a model for future landing operations. Lejeune could not have anticipated the rapid technological advances in tanks and aircraft, nor the vast improvements in communications and logistics that became key features of the documents of 1934 and 1938. The *Landing Operations Doctrine, United States Navy, 1938* directed that tanks land with or ahead of the leading troops. Tanks facilitated the passage of infantry through the immediate beach defenses by destroying enemy wire and machine-gun emplacements and covering the flanks of the first landing force.[90]

While Lejeune set the stage in the 1920s to embed the MEF within the fleet, it was in 1933 that John H. Russell, assistant to the commandant, convinced the Navy that the Marine Corps's expeditionary force should be an integral part of the fleet. This meant that in the future, Marines in transports were just as important to the fleet as battleships, aircraft carriers, cruisers, destroyers, and submarines. After receiving MGC Ben Fuller's approval, Russell recommended this policy on to the CNO on August 17, 1933. At this time, the Navy was receptive to embedding Marine forces within the fleet. On December 7, 1933, the Navy Department issued General Order 241 designating the force as the Fleet Marine Force.[91] This acceptance by the Navy was another important step toward the amphibious mission. Commandant Lejeune had recommended this same action several times to the Navy in the 1920s, but the Navy Department and the CNO were not ready to make the MEF part of the fleet.[92]

Colonel Thomas Holcomb, Lejeune's former protégé, now at Marine Corps headquarters, wrote to Lejeune about this accomplishment: "You will probably remember that you sought to bring our expeditionary forces closer to the fleet, back in 1926 or '27, by asking the CNO to list the force in the fleet organization, etc. You will also recall that the proposal was rejected, apparently under the suspicion that we were trying to put something over. Recently the proposal was revived, and has been enthusiastically received by the CNO and the CinC. Our expeditionary force is to be called the Fleet Marine Force."[93] Lejeune responded: "I am glad to know that the Marine Corps expeditionary force at Quantico has been listed in the fleet organization. I remember distinctly recommending that action but somebody in naval operations objected to it. . . . I think the depression has driven the Marine Corps and Navy closer together than they have been in many years. We cannot prosper without the friendship of the Navy and I am glad to hear that the Marine detachments afloat have been increased. The more of our officers who serve at sea, the better."[94]

There are several probable reasons why Lejeune was unable to secure the Navy's permission to embed the MEF as part of the fleet in the 1920s—and why Russell was successful in 1933. First, as Lejeune mentioned to Holcomb, the Great Depression probably brought the Navy and Marine Corps closer together. Second, Franklin D. Roosevelt—now president—felt a kinship with the Marine Corps due to his long association with them beginning when he was assistant secretary of the Navy under President Wilson. Third, Russell had been a personal friend of Roosevelt since 1915 and cultivated this close relationship. This friendship bore fruit for the corps when Russell arranged for the president's son James to be commissioned—without prior service—as a lieutenant colonel in the Marine Corps Reserve.[95] Colonel Roosevelt became the spokesman for Marine Corps policies at the White House. One of his assignments was to promote the FMF.[96] Fourth, the Army and Navy in the 1920s both wanted to command the joint forces participating in War Plan Orange. This disagreement led to conflict, animosity, and arguments during Joint Army and Navy Board meetings in 1928 about which organization should have overall command in a war against Japan. Because of this problem, the Navy most likely turned to the Marine Corps in the 1930s—a component of the Navy Department—to become part of the fleet and be commanded by the senior naval officer.[97]

Lejeune had also worked tirelessly as commandant to convince Congress to allow the corps to promote officers by merit. Using the same arguments that Lejeune had presented during his tenure, Commandant John Russell finally persuaded Congress to approve selection by merit instead of seniority. More than any other commandant, Lejeune had paved the way for this achievement. Lejeune knew that the corps needed its best officers to fight another war, a war in the Pacific that would require mastery of the complex operation of amphibious assault. Upon his selection as MGC in 1920, Lejeune stated his most important goal for the corps: "I intend to do everything in my power to make the Marine Corps the most efficient military organization in the world."[98]

At the same time, full credit must be given to John Russell, who had the tenacity to pursue a necessary, but unpopular, promotion policy. Russell was highly regarded by the State Department and the Navy, and had been appointed commandant in February 1934. Russell was a graduate of the Naval Academy, instructed at the NWC, worked for the ONI, and served as high commissioner of Haiti. He supported Lejeune's vision of amphibious operations as the wartime mission of the Marine Corps,[99] and made the amphibious mission his own goal for the corps in the 1930s.[100] Russell also supported MGC Ben Fuller's (1930–34) plan to detail in writing all aspects of an amphibious assault in the *Tentative Manual on Landing Operations*.

The Marine Corps Personnel Act became law on May 29, 1934, confirming promotion based on merit and by a selection board. This law eliminated promotion by seniority and vacancy, allowing for the promotion, distribution, discharge, and retirement of officers.[101] Russell had testified before a subcommittee of the Senate Naval Affairs Committee on April 20, 1934, in support of this much-needed reform. When Russell and members of the House and Senate committees heard that some Marine Corps officers would contest the proposed new law, Russell called on President Roosevelt on April 25, 1934, to ask for his support. The president's Marine Corps aide, Major Joseph Fegan, also wrote to Roosevelt's secretary asking for Roosevelt's help.[102]

The results of the new promotion system were gratifying. A future commandant spoke for many progressive young Marine officers in the 1930s: "He [Russell] also achieved a long overdue reform by instituting promotion by selection. Many indignant screams accompanied the passage of this law which finally cleared away a cord or two of deadwood, permitting in turn long-delayed promotions, particularly of juniors. In 1934 after fourteen years a major I became a lieutenant colonel."[103] Many highly qualified Marine Corps officers who were stuck in the lower grades for years because of the system of promotion by seniority almost immediately received promotion. These officers would play key roles in World War II, men such as Roy S. Geiger, Harry Schmidt, Pedro del Valle, Julian C. Smith, Charles Barrett, John Marston, Graves B. Erskine, and Alexander A. Vandegrift.[104] In addition to Vandegrift, three more Marines would receive promotion and later become commandants: Thomas Holcomb, Clifton B. Cates, and Lemuel C. Shepherd.[105]

The only major flaw in the new selection process established by the Marine Corps Personnel Act of 1934 was the omission of several ranks of officers who could not be retired if deemed unworthy of promotion by selection boards. While first lieutenants, captains, and colonels passed over for promotion could be retired after a specified period of service, officers of the rank of major and lieutenant colonel not promoted could continue to serve until the mandatory retirement age of sixty-four. Russell recognized this anomaly in the law of 1934, prompting him to return to Congress to propose a new law to include all ranks of officers in the selection process. Disgruntled officers who would not be promoted under the selection by merit process found support in the Senate to oppose the proposed new law, and there were numerous personal and professional attacks against Russell.[106]

Major General John A. Lejeune, USMC (Ret.), still superintendent of the VMI, was called upon once again by Marine Corps headquarters to assist the corps under duress. Headquarters asked Lejeune to support Commandant Russell in order to preserve the new law of promotion by merit. In 1935, Russell came under attack by Senator Hugo Black, who supported those officers that would be compulsorily retired under the new system of promotion by merit. Black viewed promotion as a reward for past service, whereas progressives such as Russell and Lejeune sought promotion for younger, better educated, and more capable officers with potential to increase efficiency and further develop the new mission.

The officers destined for removal under the new law were also championed by retired Major General Smedley Butler.[107] Butler, a highly decorated Marine officer with little formal education beyond high school, had won two Medals of Honor and believed in the "egalitarian warrior ideal."[108] Butler supported the corps's old mission, was ambivalent about the amphibious mission, and believed that the Marine Corps performed better when separated from the Navy.[109] Butler believed in supporting men such as Captain Louis Cukela, a Medal of Honor winner and hero in the Great War, who rose from the ranks to become an officer, an immigrant who spoke broken English.[110] Butler conveniently forgot that Cukela had committed war crimes murdering natives during the Marine occupation of Haiti and the Dominican Republic in the 1920s. One highly respected Marine officer wrote that many of these former enlisted men up for promotion in the middle grades "were either too old or without the formal education needed to be effective career officers. . . . some drifted into alcoholism during the long years of slow promotion that followed."[111]

Black and Butler's strategy was three-pronged. First, Black wanted the Marine Corps to return to a policy of promotion by seniority, or delay as long as possible the policy of selection by merit in order to allow officers who would be immediately retired an opportunity to retire at the age of sixty-four. Second, Butler and Black hoped to deny promotion of Russell to the permanent rank of major general. Although Russell held the title and rank of MGC, his permanent rank was brigadier general. If denied promotion by the Senate, Russell would have to retire because of age (sixty-four) in 1936 with the permanent rank of brigadier general. Third, Black and Butler wanted to prevent the passage of new legislation that would close the anomaly in the law of 1934 that had not included majors and lieutenant colonels in the new law of promotion and elimination by merit. There were officers in these ranks that Russell and headquarters considered inefficient and hoped for their immediate retirement. Without the new law in 1935, these officers, even if not promoted, could continue to serve in the Marine Corps until the mandatory retirement age of sixty-four.

Black and Butler attempted to discredit Russell by labeling him as incompetent and unworthy of promotion. Among other issues, Butler claimed that Russell failed in his performance of duty at Veracruz in 1914 and was responsible as CO of the brigade in Haiti for the indiscriminate killings of innocent civilians in 1920. To validate these charges, Butler asked an old friend, former MGC John A. Lejeune, to testify before the Senate. Lejeune, however, supported Russell, for all progressives in the corps understood that selection by merit was the key to an efficient Marine Corps.

According to Butler's biographer, the retired Butler was probably asked by many Marines to lead the campaign for Russell's removal. As evidence of this, a month before the hearings Butler received a note from retired Colonel "Fritz" Wise, who asked: "Are you willing to help me chew John Henry Russell whose permanent Maj. Gen. is being held up. I want the Water Works, Vera Cruz brought out. Senators King [Utah] and Black [Alabama] are after him."[112] It is likely that these same senators and others who believed in promotion for past service were those who had stymied Lejeune's attempt to achieve promotion by merit in the 1920s.

Before the Senate Naval Committee, in his own submission, Butler testified that Russell had failed in his duties in Veracruz in 1914 and in Haiti in 1920. In a telegram to Lejeune, Butler suggested that his testimony was an opportunity to "bring [the] Marine Corps back [to the] leadership approaching you and Neville."[113] Butler testified that Russell had panicked while in command of three Marine companies guarding the waterworks at El Tejar, Mexico, during the American occupation of Veracruz in 1914. One of Russell's outposts had received a captured letter detailing an upcoming attack against the waterworks by an approaching thousand-man Mexican army. Russell had telegraphed this message to headquarters asking for support, just in case the report was true. As a result, Colonel Lejeune, who commanded the Second Regiment of Marines at Veracruz, moved to El Tejar for support. The attack never occurred. Butler testified that Lejeune had criticized Russell and removed him from command.[114]

At this juncture, with Russell's leadership of the corps and the future of promotion by merit an issue, Senator Park Trammell, chairman of the Senate Naval Committee, called on Lejeune to appear before the committee to validate or deny Butler's accusations against Russell, accusations that Russell denied.[115] Lejeune's response was immediate: while he could not appear before the committee because of the serious head injury he had suffered in 1932, he wrote, "I might say here that I can write much better than I can talk, as a hesitancy, or difficulty in enunciation is one of the after effects of my badly fractured skull."[116]

In a letter to Senator Black, Lejeune defended Russell's actions as CO of Marines protecting the waterworks at El Tejar. No one knew whether the note threatening the waterworks with a thousand Mexican troops was legitimate or not. As regimental commander, Lejeune moved to El Tejar and actually conducted a reconnaissance with Russell, finding no Mexican troops. Nevertheless, both officers selected defensive positions and outposts in case of a Mexican attack. None ever came. Lejeune testified: "According to my recollections of the El Tejar incident, we considered it a joke, and we were fond of 'joshing' the officers who were there at the time about the famous battle of El Tejar!" Further, Lejeune asserted that he did not criticize Russell or relieve him of command. Russell's relief from his battalion occurred during the normal course of change of command.[117]

Butler also submitted that Lejeune as the new MGC in 1920, in a secret visit with Butler to Haiti, had criticized Russell to Secretary of the Navy Daniels for his involvement in the indiscriminate killing of Haitian civilians during the American occupation of Haiti. In a letter to Senator Trammell, Lejeune wrote that several thorough investigations had confirmed Russell's conclusions that the killings in Haiti were a few isolated incidents, had cleared the Marine Corps of wrongdoing, and noted that the guilty had been punished. These investigations were conducted by Lejeune, a naval court of inquiry, and a comprehensive senatorial study.[118] Lejeune also defended Russell's eleven years of work in Haiti as the senior officer present, as high commissioner, and as diplomatic representative of the United States. Lejeune wrote: "I consider that he did magnificent work there. . . . he required the Haitian officials to administer their offices in an honest manner. . . . he took and executed measures that worked a revolution in the health of the people, and that fostered the education, welfare, and prosperity of the people." In addition, "he was a great builder, leaving behind a magnificent network of highways, bridges, docks, and buildings."[119] Lejeune concluded with a statement in support of the new law enacting promotion by merit. "I rejoice that the present law was enacted, as I believe, if perfected in accordance with General Russell's recommendations, it will work a beneficent revolution in the officer personnel of the Marine Corps, making it in fact, as well as in song and story, the most efficient military organization in the world." Commenting on the old system of promotion by seniority, Lejeune was emphatic: "The system of promotion by seniority, I believe has been far worse. The meritorious, the energetic, and the able have been smothered very often by the worthless, the lazy, and the stupid."[120]

Members of Corps Headquarters, including Russell, Ralph Keyser, and Thomas Holcomb, were grateful for Lejeune's "splendid letter" to Trammell.[121] As a result of Lejeune's support, Keyser wrote that the "ten members present at the hearings on Monday voted General Russell's name out of the committee unanimously. Senator Black has, however, succeeded in objecting to its consideration on the floor and so far has refused to agree on the date for discussion. When this takes place undoubtedly the Marine Corps is going to be in for some very unfavorable publicity. . . . All of the charges made against General Russell were trivial and came from those who have had their personal interests suffer as a result of the Selective System."[122]

Apparently Senator Black was not about to let go of his belief that Russell was leading the Marine Corps in the wrong direction and was unfit to lead the corps. Black wrote Lejeune several times, implying that Holcomb and Keyser had traveled from Washington to Lexington to influence Lejeune's letter to Senator Trammell.[123] Senator Black believed that these Marines had actually written the letter for Lejeune. It became obvious that some disgruntled Marines had told Black that, since Lejeune's injury, Lejeune was no longer mentally fit. In return, Lejeune wrote Black three times, affirming that he had written the letter to Trammell himself. He also responded to Black's comments about Russell's lack of leadership at Veracruz and Haiti.[124]

Finally, Lejeune had had enough of Black's insinuations. In his last letter to Black, he wrote: "Before considering my answers to the questions contained in your most recent letter, I think I should inform you that the tone of your letters, especially the first, was such that my natural pride and my feelings were wounded because your questions indicated that you believed that I was incapable of the task of preparing my letter to Senator Trammell and was not able, unassisted, to arrive at a decision as to what to write." Then Lejeune stated what was becoming obvious to many senators and Marines: "My natural inference is that some interested unfriendly person so informed you, because I have not had the pleasure of meeting you since my retirement from active service." Lejeune concluded his point with the comment that "I am glad to state before commencing to answer your questions that my mind is as clear and active as it has ever been and the only effects of my injury are entirely confined to minor physical defects."[125]

Lejeune began by answering a related charge against Russell regarding the selection board in the Marine Corps. Many malcontents in the corps had criticized Russell because he served on selection boards, while Lejeune, as commandant, had not.[126] Lejeune had not served on selection boards in the 1920s because promotion was by seniority, where his presence and influence would have been limited. Lejeune defended Russell's practice of serving on the selection board under the new system of promotion by merit.[127] Lejeune felt that, under the new board practicing selection by merit, it was necessary for Russell to serve. "At the present time, the Commandant would have no voice in the selection of his subordinates to exercise high command in the line or . . . as Heads of the Staff Departments who serve directly under him."[128]

Officers at headquarters were still concerned that a Senate inquiry would damage the Marine Corps and might even reverse its course in training for amphibious warfare. In writing to Lejeune, Holcomb thought that Lejeune's second letter to Black "would settle the matter. But we were not reckoning on the vindictiveness of Senator Black. . . . He [Black] told me that he hoped to get money to have a complete investigation of the Marine Corps, down to the smallest detail; and you doubtless know of the speech he made on the floor right after I left." Furthermore, Holcomb observed, "A group of discontented officers are doing their best to wreck the Corps, and they apparently do not leave a stone unturned. You would be astounded at the things Black claims officers have told him, or written to him. Apparently they have no vestige of loyalty." Holcomb ended his letter to Lejeune saying, "I am greatly worried. At best we are faced with a nasty row on the floor of the Senate; at worst, Heaven knows what."[129]

Keyser was also deeply perturbed. In another letter to Lejeune he remarked: "It is all very annoying and rather disgusting and I am particularly disturbed that you should be further harassed by this matter. The whole case is very indicative of the need for a house cleaning that has existed in the Marine Corps for a long time. We have accumulated during the course of thirty-five years some few bad eggs and now we are smelling them."[130]

In his final letter to Senator Black, Lejeune appealed to his sense of justice and asked him not to conduct a senatorial investigation: "I want to ask you as a friend to consider most carefully and prayerfully the effect on the efficiency and welfare of the Marine Corps before deciding on a course of action which some disgruntled individuals may advise you to take." Lejeune added: "My love for the Marine Corps comes next to my family and it would distress me beyond measure if through a mistaken sense of justice on your part the Corps should be torn to pieces by a senatorial investigation."[131]

Senator Black continued his personal attack on Russell but articulated his real concern on March 5, 1935, that he viewed promotion as an essential reward for previous service: "For non-selected officers, the new system will cut off their military careers and send them out of the service, even though they wear the decorations of American service in the form of bullets and the ravages of disease."[132] In effect, Black and Butler were defending those over-age officers who rose from the ranks, fought well in World War I, chased rebels on Caribbean islands, and were content with the old mission of the corps. They were not amenable to, perhaps did not understand, the new, more important mission.

Fortunately, Lejeune's letters and reputation helped to isolate Black from his Senate colleagues. One former Marine noted that Lejeune was a legendary and highly respected former commandant who had the well-deserved reputation of always placing first his devotion to the best interests of the Marine Corps, a loyalty second only to his family. When caught between the conflicting interests of his friends Butler and Russell, he chose what was best for the corps. Thus his correspondence with the Senate supporting Russell had great influence.[133]

Lejeune's support of Russell did not stop Black's attack, but his letters most likely inspired other senators to support Russell and discredit Black. Senator Park Trammell of Virginia, together with Senators Millard Tydings of Maryland and Peter Gerry of Rhode Island, led the effort to support Russell. Gerry remarked that, while a young Marine could be a man of great bravery and earn a distinguished record as second lieutenant, it did not guarantee that he would continue to develop later as an outstanding high-ranking officer in the Marine Corps. This same officer would need to mature and develop other qualities such as judgment and intelligence in order to promote efficiency in the corps.[134] On March 5, 1935, the Senate rejected Black's motion to send Russell's nomination for promotion back to the Naval Affairs Committee, and on a voice vote confirmed Russell's promotion to permanent major general.[135]

In effect, Black and Butler impugned the reputation of Russell and all progressives in the Marine Corps in order to protect and retain those former enlisted men who were commissioned for valiant service in World War I and those older men who had served well nearly two decades before but were not qualified to lead the corps in an approaching war. Later, Black would ingenuously claim that he attacked Russell only to protect those valiant men who fought so well in World War I. Thus, he only opposed "the bill now in the House sponsored by General Russell, requiring removal from the service of any Marine officer who has two times failed of selection by the board."[136] In reality, Black "had little doubt Russell would be confirmed. . . . I did want to lay the ground work to defeat the legislation which is intended to automatically kick a lot of good Marine officers out of the service. I hope I accomplished that purpose."[137] For all his machinations and deception, Black could only prevent for several years the forced retirement of those Marines who had not been selected for promotions, mostly captains and majors.

As a consequence, the political power of malcontented officers, the old corps, and their supporters in Congress was broken for good. Lejeune had struggled against these officers and their supporters in Congress throughout the 1920s. In preparation for a possible war with Japan, Russell was confirmed as commandant and effectively moved the corps toward updating amphibious doctrine. In 1936, he was followed as commandant by Thomas Holcomb, who further refined his predecessors' work of preparing and leading the corps into World War II.

General Holcomb was Lejeune's most famous protégé, the first commandant of the Marine Corps during World War II. As commandant in the 1920s, Lejeune had inspired a generation of Marines—including those leaders who became commandants in the 1930s—to strive to make the corps more efficient and further develop the amphibious mission and prepare for a probable war with Japan. While Lejeune's motivation and support for Commandants Wendell Neville, Ben Fuller, and John Russell—as well as their achievements—have been demonstrated, it was Holcomb, commandant from 1936 to 1943, who was perhaps Lejeune's most dedicated advocate. Probably Holcomb's greatest accomplishment in the war was to reinforce Lejeune's insistence on a command structure that gave Marines authority to direct the land portion of an amphibious operation.

Holcomb first worked under Lejeune when Colonel Lejeune served as assistant to MGC George Barnett from 1915 to 1918. Lejeune understood the necessity of war planning and acted as Barnett's de facto chief of staff, utilizing Barnett's three aides—Captains Ralph S. Keyser, Earl Ellis, and Thomas Holcomb—as his planning staff to prepare for future conflicts. Years later, Holcomb "enthusiastically" recalled what it was like working for Lejeune. "Those were exciting days. Ellis and I felt as though we were in the thick of things, with officers dropping in to discuss both official and personal matters with us or to pay their respects to the Commandant or the Assistant Commandant. . . . I performed a wide variety of tasks for Gen. Lejeune, but my work principally involved procuring officers for the war we all saw was inevitable."[138]

As a young officer, Holcomb learned from Lejeune and Ellis the value and necessity of detailed planning, including the development of alternate plans should events change in ongoing operations. This diligence undoubtedly helped Holcomb become an effective leader during the Great War. The influence and actions of Lejeune and Ellis had a lasting effect on Holcomb as he became a senior officer dedicated to securing for the corps a crucial role in the nation's defense, and as commandant during World War II, supporting, encouraging, and training his staff and subordinates.[139]

Holcomb greatly admired Lejeune and understood the value of Lejeune's reforms for the corps during the 1920s.[140] Holcomb served under MGC Lejeune and recalled that "Lejeune's postwar plans were clear: he would rebuild the Marine Corps with the framework of his three 'Es': economy, efficiency, and education. . . . I can add some 'Es' that applied to Gen. Lejeune's Marine Corps. Enthusiasm and excitement and energy come to mind. And the adjectives most often applied to him by his admirers in Congress were ethical and earnest. They believed him and trusted him implicitly."[141] Holcomb's success in the corps was surely partly due to Lejeune's influence as his role model and mentor.[142]

While Lejeune undoubtedly provided a foundation for Holcomb's success as commandant, Holcomb earned his own way, winning a highly distinguished combat record as a battalion commander during World War I. Although highly intelligent, Holcomb never obtained a baccalaureate degree, but he took advantage of every opportunity to gain more education. He mastered the Chinese language while serving as attaché to the American minister in Beijing. He excelled in his courses at the MCS, the Army's Command and General Staff School at Fort Leavenworth, and the war colleges of the Army and Navy. He achieved distinction as an outstanding marksman and became CO of the Marine Corps rifle team and won the individual world championship for long-range marksmanship at Ottawa in 1902, stressing proficiency with the rifle as a high priority for the Marine Corps throughout his career. While Holcomb was not the motivational speaker Lejeune was, he was able to adapt to changing conditions, was determined to succeed, and always displayed an even temperament even under stressful conditions.

Holcomb proved to be an innovative leader with a capability to institute needed reforms in the corps.[143] It was under Holcomb in the late 1930s and early 1940s that civilians finally provided the corps with proper landing boats. Andrew Higgins and Donald Roebling—private contractors—developed and built effective landing boats for the Navy. Higgins built the "Eureka" or Landing Craft Vehicle Personnel (LCVP) boat for landing troops and the Landing Craft Mechanized (LCM) boat to land tanks, wheeled artillery, and vehicles. Roebling built the "Alligator," forerunner to the amphibious tractor or Landing Vehicle Tracked that later landed thousands of Marines and soldiers in the central Pacific, North Africa, Sicily, Italy, and France.

Aware of the necessity of determining the proper roles of the Navy and Marine Corps in ship-to-shore assaults, Holcomb left Washington and traveled to Guadalcanal, where he vigorously intervened in October and November of 1942 to clarify command relationships between the Navy and Marine Corps. The battle for Guadalcanal was the first major land engagement between Japanese and American forces, a bitterly fought campaign that hung in the balance until the Americans finally secured the island in early 1943. The naval assault-force commander, Rear Admiral Richmond Kelly Turner, consistently interfered with Major General Alexander A. Vandegrift's troop dispositions of the First Marine Division on Guadalcanal. During the intense struggle with the Japanese for control of Henderson Field, Vandegrift had to concentrate his forces to retain possession of the important airfield. Seemingly insensitive to the Marines' plight and having little knowledge of ground combat, Turner nevertheless tried to turn Vandegrift's reinforcements, the Second Marine Division, from Marine rifle battalions into raider or parachute battalions without Vandegrift's knowledge and prepared to send Vandegrift's reserves aboard ship on to the next objective before Henderson Field was secured.[144] Fortunately, Admiral William F. Halsey, CinC of the South Pacific Area, supported the position of Holcomb and Vandegrift.

With Halsey's support, Holcomb convinced Admiral Chester Nimitz, CinC of the Pacific Fleet/Pacific Ocean Areas, and later Admiral Earnest J. King, CNO, to modify *Landing Operations Doctrine, U.S. Navy, 1938, FTP-167,* the latest manual establishing doctrine for amphibious operations. Holcomb helped draft doctrine that gave the land-force CO (Marine or Army) and the Navy assault-force CO equal authority in planning for amphibious operations. The landing-force commander would be subordinate to the naval amphibious task-force commander aboard ship traveling to the assault area and during the initial landing. As to the land campaign, the Marine and Navy commanders had equal authority. Should there be disagreement, both commanders would submit their positions to their common superior.[145]

In his determination to settle this command issue, Holcomb was following the policy of Lejeune, who often had to deal with naval officers who considered themselves superior to Marines. In fact, it was not until the late nineteenth century that Marine officers, not Navy officers, commanded Marines and sailors ashore. Lejeune thought he had settled this command issue once and for all in the 1920s. In a memorandum to the Navy Department on July 23, 1924, Lejeune had made it clear that a Marine general would command all troops ashore: "Whereas under the Navy Commander in Chief, the senior Marine general would have immediate command of the Marine Expeditionary Force, he also should have command of any reinforcements from Army troops accompanying the Fleet, in any landing operation in connection with seizing and holding an advanced base for the Fleet."[146] Later, Lejeune added similar remarks when the Joint Army and Navy Board decided to remove confusion by updating the old pamphlet *Joint Army and Navy Action in Coast Defense* of 1920 to the new *Joint Action of the Army and Navy* pamphlet of 1927.[147] This pamphlet stated that the Marine Corps or Army would manage the land portion of an amphibious operation and that the Navy's role was "to escort and support Army forces engaged in overseas operations."[148]

The officers of the Marine Corps in the 1930s also assumed that command issues with the Navy had been settled. Admiral King's decision to stop naval interference in ground operations was based on the revised 1935 edition of the *Joint Action of the Army and Navy.* This document instructed a unifying commander to refrain from telling a subordinate how to conduct the tactical details of his assigned mission.[149] It is likely that Holcomb drew King's attention to this publication.

The Marine Corps was fortunate to have the veteran Holcomb at the helm from 1936 to 1943. He ably prepared and led the corps through the early stages of the war. At the same time, a great deal of credit must be attributed to Lejeune, Holcomb's mentor. Lejeune had been Holcomb's teacher and inspiration for many years, instilling in him all the important ingredients for success in modern amphibious operations and the proper role of the Navy and Marine Corps in joint operations.

It was during the heavy fighting at Guadalcanal that Lejeune died at the age of seventy-five on November 20, 1942, in Norfolk, from complications of prostate cancer. It is unfortunate that Lejeune did not live to witness the achievements of his beloved Marine Corps and the crucial importance of amphibious assault during World War II.

Lejeune was the primary force behind the development of amphibious assault as the distinctive mission for the Marine Corps, as well as the creator of the modern corps. Personally, Lejeune was always a gentleman. His legacy remains vibrantly alive in today's Marine Corps. His sense of honor, exemplary good character, visionary thinking, loyalty, tenacity, high ideals, pervasive goodwill, and love of country and the corps contributed to the modernization of a vital branch of the US Armed Forces. For Lejeune, "the greatest of all leathernecks" is a title much deserved.

NOTES

PREFACE

1. Merrill L. Bartlett's *Lejeune: A Marine's Life, 1867–1942* (Annapolis, MD: NIP, 1996), does not adequately cover Lejeune's years as commandant and underplays the importance of his hard work, vision, and perseverance that demonstrate his key influence in the development of amphibious doctrine.

2. Joe A. Simon to Misses Eugenia D. and Laura T. Lejeune, September 10, 1965; March 7, May 3, 1966. Lejeune sisters to Simon, October 12, 1965; January 13, May 14, 1966. Copies in author's possession.

3. See, for example, Allan R. Millett and Jack Shulimson, eds., *Commandants of the Marine Corps* (Annapolis, MD: NIP, 2004), 4. Later cited as *Commandants.*

4. Lance Corporal Adam Johnson, "United States Postal Service Unveils Distinguished Marines Commemorative Stamps," *Camp Lejeune News,* Camp Lejeune, NC, November 10, 2005. "We are very excited," said Mark Saunders, a USPS spokesman. "This is the first time the U.S. Postal Service has released a stamp depicting individual Marines." While these four Marines were selected by the Citizen Stamp Advisory Committee, John E. Potter, the postmaster general, had to make final approval. "The committee decided that these four individuals best represented the spirit and tradition of the Marine Corps," said Saunders. In addition, Saunders noted, "Lejeune, the 13th Commandant of the Marine Corps, served for more than 40 years and is often referred to as 'the greatest of all leathernecks.'"

5. For example: "The truth is that although halting steps were taken in the direction of building in the Marine Corps a truly efficient amphibious force, the goal was still far distant in 1929," Jeter A. Isley and Philip A. Crowl, *The U.S. Marines and Amphibious War: Its Theory, and Its Practice in the Pacific* (Princeton, NJ: Princeton University Press, 1951), 29; Merrill L. Bartlett in his biography of Lejeune wrote, "While the genesis of modern amphibious doctrine is rightly attributed to the visionaries of the 1930s, Lejeune's stewardship during the lean years of the Harding-Coolidge retrenchment of the 1920s set the stage" (*Assault from the Sea, Essays on the History of Amphibious Warfare* [Annapolis: NIP, 1983], 6).

6. The dissertation is located at the graduate offices of the Universities of Cumbria and Lancaster in Great Britain, cumbria.ac.uk, and at ETHOS at the British Library's thesis service, email@email.bl.uk.

INTRODUCTION

1. Lt. Col. J. D. Hittle, "Jomini and Amphibious Thought," *MCG,* May 1946, 37.

2. *Commandants,* 17–163.

3. Based on the example of the British Royal Marines, the word "marines" as utilized during the Revolution is not capitalized until its creation as the Marine Corps by Congress of the new nation of the United States of America. See James C. Bradford, "Samuel Nicholas, Senior Officer, Continental Marines," in *Commandants.*

4. Bradford, "Samuel Nicholas, Senior Officer, Continental Marines." While the Marine Corps includes Nicholas as its first commandant, officially he was the senior officer of the marines.

5. Brendan P. Ryan, "William Ward Burrows, 1798–1805," in *Commandants,* 27–35.

6. Gerald C. Thomas Jr., "Franklin Wharton, 1804–1818," in *Commandants,* 36–44.

7. Joseph H. Alexander, "Archibald Henderson, 1820–1859," in *Commandants,* 54–73.

8. Alexander, "John Harris, 1859–1864," in *Commandants,* 74–84.

9. Ibid., 85–96.

10. Ibid.

11. Allan R. Millett, Peter Maslowski, and William B. Feis, *For the Common Defense: A Military History of the United States from 1607–2012,* 3rd ed. (New York: Free Press, 2012), 241–48.

12. John B. Hattendorf, "Alfred Thayer Mahan and American Naval Theory," in Keith Neilson and Elizabeth Jane Errington, eds., *Navies and Global Defense: Theories and Strategy* (Westport, CT: Praeger, 1995), 51–67. Hereafter cited as *Navies and Global Defense.*

13. William R. Braisted, *The United States Navy in the Pacific, 1897–1909* (Annapolis, MD: NIP, 2008); Braisted, *The United States Navy in the Pacific, 1909–1922* (Annapolis, MD: NIP, 2008).

14. Jack Shulimson, "Charles G. McCawley, 1876–1891," and "Charles Heywood, 1891–1903"; Robert Cressman, "George Frank Elliott, 1903–1910," in *Commandants,* 97–162.

15. Jack Shulimson, *The Marine Corps' Search for a Mission, 1880–1898* (Lawrence: University Press of Kansas, 1993), 58–62.

16. Ibid., 81–85.

17. Ibid., 168–201.

18. Graham A. Cosmas and Jack Shulimson, "The Culebra Maneuver and the Formation of the U.S. Marine Corps' Advance Base Force, 1913–1914," in Bartlett, ed., *Assault from the Sea,* 107–20.

19. James H. Alexander, "Roots of Deployment—Vera Cruz, 1914," in Bartlett, ed., *Assault from the Sea,* 133–42.

20. Kenneth J. Hagan, "The Apotheosis of Mahan: American Naval Strategy, 1889–1922," in *Navies and Global Defense,* 93–115. War Plan Black was the war plan against a possible attack from Imperial Germany.

21. Leo J. Daugherty III, "Lieutenant General John A. Lejeune," 158–193, and "Major General John H. Russell," 243–71, in *Pioneers of Amphibious Warfare, 1898–1945* (Jefferson, NC: McFarland and Co., 2009).

22. Edward S. Miller, *War Plan Orange: The U.S. Strategy to Defeat Japan, 1897–1945* (Annapolis, MD: NIP, 1991).

23. Nathan Miller, "The American Navy, 1922–1945," in *Navies and Global Defense,* 139–60.

24. Stephen E. Ambrose, *D-Day: June 6, 1944: The Climactic Battle of World War II* (New York: Simon & Schuster, 1994), 45.

25. William L. Rogers, "Marathon, 490 B.C." in Bartlett, ed., *Assault from the Sea.*

26. Ibid.

27. C. N. Barelay, "Hastings, 1066"; Arthur J. Marder, "Mongol Attempts to Invade Japan, 1274, 1281"; and Alfred Vagts, "Spain as an Amphibious Power, 1538–1594," all in Bartlett, ed., *Assault from the Sea.*

28. Antoine-Henri Jomini, *The Art of War,* restored ed. (Kingston, Ontario, Canada: Legacy Books, 2008), xii, 196–99, 290–312.

29. Hittle, "Jomini and Amphibious Thought," 35–38.

30. Allan R. Millett, "Assault from the Sea," in Williamson Murray and Allan R. Millett, *Military Innovations in the Interwar Period* (London: Cambridge University Press, 1996), 50–54.

31. Jeremy Black, *Rethinking Military History* (London: Routledge, 2004), 138–39.

32. Kenneth Clifford, *Progress and Purpose: A Developmental History of the U.S. Marine Corps, 1900–1970* (Washington, DC: History and Museums Division, Headquarters, USMC, 1973), 27; Lejeune to CNO: Lectures, December 16, 1921, file 1975–70, RG 127, NARACP.

33. Allan R. Millett, *Semper Fidelis: The History of the United States Marine Corps,* rev. and expanded ed. (New York: Free Press, 1991), 319–29.

34. David J. Ulbrich, *Preparing for Victory: Thomas Holcomb and the Making of the Modern Marine Corps, 1936–1943* (Annapolis, MD: NIP, 2011), 94.

1. EARLY YEARS IN LOUISIANA

1. John Archer Lejeune, *The Reminiscences of a Marine* (Philadelphia: Dorrance & Co., 1930), 15, 16. Lejeune's father, Ovide, remembered his great-grandfather, Jean Baptiste Lejeune, and related this information to young Lejeune.

2. John Lejeune, "Louisiana's Fighting Marine Tells His Life Story," New Orleans *Times-Picayune,* March 5, 1939, Times-Picayune Historical Archives (online).

3. Ibid.

4. Ibid.

5. A seigneur was a Frenchman in French Canada who had been granted a fief by the king of France, with all the associated rights over people and property on his large estate. These estates were called seigneuries.

6. Diocese of Baton Rouge, Catholic Church Records, vol. 4, 1820–29, Department of Archives, Baton Rouge, LA.

7. *Times-Picayune,* March 5, 1939.

8. Tutorship of Ovide Lejeune, Suite 390, Old Probate Court Records, 1823–46, Clerk of Court, Civil Department, New Roads, Louisiana.

9. Raccourci Island and Old River, where the small towns of Batchelor, Lacour, and Morganza are today. *Raccourci* is French for "shortcut."

10. *Times-Picayune,* March 5, 1939.

11. Marriage Records, Jefferson County, Mississippi.

12. The Edict of Nantes was promulgated at Nantes in Brittany in France on April 13, 1598, by Henry IV of France, temporarily ending the ferocious religious war between Roman Catholics and Protestants, establishing civil equality between Catholics and Protestants. Louis XIV, however, revoked the Edict of Nantes in 1685, which led to the suppression of the Reformed Church in France and forced Protestants into exile or hiding.

13. "Brigadier General John A. Lejeune Commands Marines Fighting in France," *Baltimore Sun,* 1918, scrapbook (Lejeune Papers, reel 15).

14. J. Alexis Shriver, "John Archer: First Medical Graduate of the New World," Olney Farm, Jappa, Harford County, MD, *www.ncbi.nlm.nih.gov/pubmed/2266819*. Archer was the first medical doctor in the colonies because his name was first alphabetically in his class.

15. Lejeune, *Reminiscences,* 22; *Times-Picayune,* March 5, 1939.

16. Ted Tunnell, *Crucible of Reconstruction: War, Radicalism, and Race in Louisiana, 1862–1877* (Baton Rouge: Louisiana State University Press, 1984), 174.

17. Mark H. Bonner, "See Rural Louisiana First," *Rural Louisiana,* August 1954, 6–7.

18. Census data from 1860 given in Joseph Karl Menn, *The Large Slaveholders of Louisiana, 1860* (New Orleans: Pelican Publishing Co., 1964), 519.

19. Ibid.

20. Eric Foner, *Give Me Liberty! An American History,* 3rd ed. (New York: W. W. Norton and Co., 2012), vol. 1: 399.

21. Menn, *The Large Slaveholders of Louisiana, 1860,* 318.

22. Ibid., 519.

23. Capt. O. Lejeune to Honorable G. W. Randolph, Secretary of War, Frankford, KY, October 3, 1862. From records M320, roll no. 4, RG 109, NARAW.

24. John D. Winters, *The Civil War in Louisiana* (Baton Rouge: Louisiana State University Press, 1963), 85–102.

25. Joe Gray Taylor, *Louisiana: A History* (New York: W. W. Norton & Co., 1984), 57–114.

26. Ibid., 94; Joe Gray Taylor, *Louisiana Reconstructed, 1863–1877* (Baton Rouge: Louisiana State University Press, 1974); Judy Riffel, ed., *A History of Pointe Coupee Parish and Its Families* (Baton Rouge: Le Comité des Archives de la Louisiane, 1983).

27. "John Lejeune Recalls Carpetbag Reign of Terror," New Orleans *Times-Picayune,* March 12, 1939; Ovide Lejeune to Laura Lejeune, August 2, 1862 (Lejeune Papers, reel 1); Lejeune, *Reminiscences,* 22.

28. *Times-Picayune,* March 12, 1939.

29. Interview with Ovide B. LaCour III, April 1965. (All interviews are by the author unless otherwise noted.) At that time, LaCour managed seven thousand acres left to him by the original LaCour. The last "one-fourth-hand" system disappeared in 1965.

30. The LaCour general store was still doing business in the early 1960s in LaCour, Louisiana, located about five miles north of Morganza. Built of virgin cyprus around 1865, the large two-story building claimed the oldest hand-pulled elevator in the parish. As late as 1901 the store sold furniture, burial caskets, and mule teams. In the 1960s the store sold only general goods. Information from Mrs. Ovide B. LaCour II, interviewed by author, April 1965.

31. "They Talk of Johnny at Pointe Coupee," n.d., newspaper article, clippings (Lejeune Papers, reel 15).

32. Interview with Mrs. LaCour II, April 1965.

33. Eric Foner, *Forever Free: The Story of Emancipation and Reconstruction* (New York: Alfred A. Knopf, 2005), 190.

34. Lejeune, *Reminiscences,* 23; *Times-Picayune,* March 12, 1939.

35. Tunnell, *Crucible of Reconstruction,* 211.

36. Foner, *Forever Free,* 166.

37. Tunnell, *Crucible of Reconstruction,* 211.

38. Lejeune, *Reminiscences,* 25–26.

39. Ibid.

40. Gillis Vandal, *Rethinking Southern Violence: Homicides in Post–Civil War Louisiana, 1866–1884* (Columbus: Ohio State University Press, 2000), 108.

41. Ibid., 106.

42. Foner, *Forever Free,* 227.

43. James Roark, Michael Johnson, Patricia Cohen, Sarah Stage, Alan Lawson, and Susan Hartmann, *The American Promise* (Boston: Bedford/St. Martin's, 2005), 576.

44. *Times-Picayune,* March 12, 1939.

45. Teeney was nicknamed as a child (Ovide to Laura Lejeune, August 1, 1882, Lejeune Papers, reel 1); T. Heard Campbell, Walter Campbell, and Helen Campbell of Morganza, LA, knew her well, as she often visited Pointe Coupee in her later years (author's interview with Campbells, April 1965).

46. *Times-Picayune,* March 12, 1939.

47. Interview with Mrs. LaCour II, April 1965. This information was passed down to Mrs. LaCour from her mother; note sent to the older sister of Mrs. LaCour.

48. The Archers lived at Longwood Plantation, one mile north of Old Hickory. Longwood was located near the LaCour store, but was destroyed around 1890. When Dr. Archer died, Mrs. Archer left Pointe Coupee to live with her son in Bel Air, Maryland. Interview with Mrs. LaCour II and Miss Helen Campbell, April 1965.

49. "Episcopalians Will Assemble at Historic St. Stephens at Innis," Baton Rouge *State-Times,* April 27, 1936; *Times-Picayune,* March 12, 1939.

50. *Times-Picayune,* March 12, 1939; Lejeune to his mother, October 8, 1882, Lejeune Papers, LSU Archives.

51. Lejeune's copybook, July–August 1878, in LSU Archives. The copybook contained such sentences as: "An honest endeavor is worth ten promises; Better face a danger than be ever in fear; Form plans with care to execute with vigor; He who conquers self is the greatest victor; Never speak to deceive nor listen to betray; On their own merits sensible men are silent; Silence sometimes speaks more than words; Yield always to reason, but never to passion."

52. "Major General John A. Lejeune Tells How a Boat and Some Books Influenced His Choice of a Career," New Orleans *Times-Picayune,* March 19, 1939. Quote from Lejeune's address to Louisiana State University alumni, May 1, 1926, in LSU Archives.

53. D. Phillip Locklin, *Economics of Transportation* (Homewood, IL: Richard B. Irwin, 1960), 70.

54. Lejeune's address to Louisiana State University alumni, May 1, 1926.

55. Interview with Mrs. Ovide LaCour II, April 1965. She remembered these sights and sounds.

56. Lejeune, "Major General John A. Lejeune Tells How a Boat and Some Books Influenced His Choice of a Career."

57. Ibid.

58. William Atherton Du Puy, "They're Human," newspaper article, n.d. (Lejeune Papers, reel 10).

59. Address by MGC Lejeune to Louisiana State University alumni, May 1, 1926 (Lejeune Papers, reel 10).

60. MGC Lejeune, address to Philadelphia physicians, December 7, 1927; Lejeune address to the graduating class of 1934 of the VMI, May 1, 1935. Both in Lejeune Papers, reel 10.

61. Information from a marble plaque dedicated to his memory inside St. Stephen's Church.

62. *Times-Picayune,* March 19, 1939; "They Built the South," *Times-Picayune,* November 19, 1944.

63. Lejeune, *Reminiscences,* 28.

64. Lejeune's undelivered lecture to the first class at VMI, n.d. (Lejeune Papers, reel 10); *Times-Picayune,* March 19, 1939; "Civilized American Aborigines," a lecture by John Lejeune, n.d. (Lejeune Papers, reel 10).

65. Quote from *Times-Picayune,* March 19, 1939. George F. Elliott, who was from Alabama and attended West Point for two years, served as the tenth commandant, 1903–10.

66. Lejeune, *Reminiscences,* 32. Lejeune, "Rigorous Training at L.S.U. Recalled by Lejeune," New Orleans *Times-Picayune,* March 5, 1939.

67. Lejeune address to Louisiana State University alumni, March 1, 1926 (Lejeune Papers, reel 10).

68. *LSU Catalog* (Baton Rouge, LA, July 4, 1881), 24–25, in LSU Archives; *Times-Picayune,* March 26, 1939.

69. Register of Cadets, President's Office, LSU Archives.

70. Henry Kahn, Royal Consul, Columbian Woodmen, Charleston, MS, to Major General John A. Lejeune, June 21, 1920 (Lejeune Papers, reel 12).

71. Lejeune, "Rigorous Training at L.S.U. Recalled."

72. Walter L. Fleming, *Louisiana State University, 1860–1896* (Baton Rouge: Louisiana State University Press, 1936), 446–51.

73. *Cadet Regulations of the Louisiana State University and Agricultural and Mechanical College, 1881–1882* (Baton Rouge, 1881), 1–20.

74. John A. Lejeune's report card for the term ending July 1883, in LSU Archives; *Times-Picayune,* March 26, 1939.

75. Maj. Gen. Commandant Lejeune address to LSU alumni, May 1, 1925, LSU Archives. Interview with Mrs. Annie Boyd Grayson, daughter of Colonel Boyd, May 1966.

76. *Times-Picayune,* March 26, 1939.

77. *LSU Catalog,* 1882, Lejeune Papers, LSU Archives.

78. Lejeune to his mother, October 8, 1882 (Lejeune Papers, reel 1).

79. Ibid.

80. Lejeune Papers, LSU Archives.

81. Upton, a protégé of CG of the Army William T. Sherman, wrote *The Armies of Asia and*

Europe and the *Military Policy of the United States* after the Civil War, which included military ideas and reforms that dominated Army thought far into the twentieth century.

82. A. H. Ulm, "Lejeune, Composite of All Devil Dogs," *New York Times*, February 15, 1925.

83. Lejeune's report card for July 1883, in LSU Archives.

84. Lejeune, *Reminiscences*, 33.

85. "Memorial Held for Lejeune," in Baton Rouge *State-Times*, November 23, 1942. The student was Frank H. Waddill, a student in engineering who entered LSU a year after Lejeune resigned.

2. A NAVAL CADET

1. J. A. Turpin of L'Argent Landing, Tensas Parish, Louisiana, to William Turpin of Maryland, April 23, 1884 (Lejeune Papers, reel 1).

2. Lejeune, *Reminiscences*, 30; Report of the Superintendent of the Naval Academy, 1884, in the *Annual Report of the Secretary of the Navy* (Washington, DC: GPO, 1884), 78–82. All government reports such as the Report of the Marine Corps Commandant, Navy Bureaus, are printed by the GPO. Hereafter the Secretary's Report will be cited as Navy Report.

3. There were 164 applicants for the plebe class of 1884–85. One was overage, one withdrew, one was refused the exam, fifty-two failed the exam, and twenty-one were physically unfit (Navy Report, November 1, 1884).

4. This was the customary manner of informing the accepted candidates, as related in Major General George Barnett's "Soldier and Sailor Too," an autobiographical manuscript (Marine Corps University, Archives Branch, Alfred M. Gray Research Center [GRC]). Barnett, an 1881 academy graduate, became the Marine Corps's twelfth commandant, 1914–20.

5. Navy Report (1884), 69.

6. Captain John H. Craige, USMC, "A Fighting Man Who Led the Corps," *New York Times*, February 24, 1929.

7. Barnett, "Soldier and Sailor Too," 2; Lejeune, *Reminiscences*, 39–40.

8. A veteran of five wars, the frigate *Constellation* was launched on September 7, 1797, to fight French privateers in the Caribbean during the "Quasi-War" with France (Report of the cruise of the *Constellation*, August 31, 1884). Navy Report, 1884, vol. 1.

9. Conditions aboard the *Constellation* related in Barnett, "Soldier and Sailor Too," 3–5, and John A. Lejeune's address to new cadets at VMI, September 1936 (Lejeune Papers, reel 10).

10. Lejeune's address to cadets at VMI, n.d., 1937 (Lejeune Papers, reel 10); Report of the *Constellation*, August 31, 1888.

11. The USN had rescued the missing Adolphus Greely scientific mission in the Arctic (Navy Report of 1884, 8); Lejeune, *Reminiscences*, 43.

12. Report of the Board of Visitors, US Naval Academy, Navy Reports, 1885, 1886. The "new" building, built in 1866, was in bad condition and poorly ventilated. Report of the Superintendent of the US Naval Academy (USNA), Navy Report, October 1, 1888.

13. J. F. Kimball, Assistant Registrar, (USNA), to Joe A. Simon, April 20, 1966; Navy Report (1884), 72.

14. Reports of the Superintendent of the Naval Academy, 1884–88.

15. Lejeune address to cadets of VMI, September 1936 (Lejeune Papers, reel 10). On a four-point scale, Lejeune's grades were Spanish, 3.83; French, 3.75; English and history, 3.69; algebra and geometry, 2.73. (Grade Report of Naval Cadet J. A. Lejeune, Report of the Secretary of the Navy, 1885.)

16. Lejeune address to cadets of VMI, September 1936.

17. General Gerald C. Thomas, USMC, "John A. Lejeune," MS loaned to author; Captain John Craige, USMC, "Lejeune, A Fighting Man"; Colonel G. A. Taylor, USA, a tribute to the memory of J. A. Lejeune, November 21, 1942 (Lejeune Papers, reels 11, 12, 13).

18. Lejeune, *Reminiscences,* 38.

19. Report of the *Constellation,* August 27, 1885.

20. Report of the Superintendent of the Naval Academy, October 1, 1888; J. F. Kimball to Joe A. Simon, April 20, 1966.

21. Barnett, "Soldier and Sailor Too," 13.

22. John Lejeune to his cousin William Turpin, July 23, 1884, reveals that young Lejeune had a standing invitation to visit (Lejeune Papers, reel 1).

23. Remarks made by Lejeune as superintendent of VMI to the football team, October 15, 1936 (Lejeune Papers, reel 10).

24. Lejeune to sister, Augustine, May 24, 1885 (Lejeune Papers, reel 1).

25. Lejeune to Augustine, May 1886 (Lejeune Papers, reel 1).

26. Report of the *Constellation,* September 1, 1887; J. F. Kimball to Joe A. Simon, April 20, 1966.

27. Class standing from J. F. Kimball to Joe A. Simon, April 20, 1966.

28. Lejeune to Augustine, May 24, 1885 (Lejeune Papers, reel 1).

29. Ibid., March 15, 1885 (Lejeune Papers, reel 1).

30. Ibid., October 18, 1885 (Lejeune Papers, reel 1).

31. Ibid., April 3, 1885 (Lejeune Papers, reel 1).

32. Lejeune, *Reminiscences,* 56.

33. Captain Edward L. Beach, US Navy (USN), to Major General Lejeune, July 13, 1920 (Lejeune Papers, reel 3).

34. Report of the Board of Visitors of the Naval Academy, 1886. To determine class standing after six years of preparation, three-quarters of the final grade was derived from results of the first four years, the remainder from the comprehensive final exam plus each cadet's efficiency report from the two-year cruise.

35. Ovide had left the Catholic Church because of its opposition to the Masons.

36. Lejeune, *Reminiscences,* 50; Lejeune's address to fellow Masons, n.d. (Lejeune Papers, reel 9).

37. Navy Department to Lejeune, September 7, 22, 1888; January 14, 1889, Orders to Duty (Lejeune Papers, reel 13).

38. Noah Andre Trudeau, "An Appalling Calamity," *Naval History,* April 2011, 54–59.

39. John P. Dunning, "The Story of the Great Storm at Samoa," *St. Nicholas* 17 (February 1890). Dunning was an Associated Press reporter sent to Apia to witness a possible war between the United States and Germany. Instead, he was an eyewitness to the Great Samoa Typhoon of 1889. Rear Admiral L. A. Kimberly, *Samoa Hurricane* (Washington, DC: GPO, 1965), 3.

40. Lejeune, *Reminiscences,* 56; Report of the Bureau of Navigation, 1889, 1. The *Vandalia,*

commissioned in 1876, was 216 feet long and displaced 2,033 tons, with two engines of 1,200 horsepower each, providing a top speed of twelve knots. Her armament consisted mostly of obsolete muzzle-loading, smooth-bore cannon (Report of the Bureau of Construction and Repair, 1889, appendix 13).

41. Walter Millis, *Arms and Men: A Study in American Military History* (New York: Bobbs-Merrill Co., 1956), 127–50; Report of the Secretary of the Navy, 1889, 1–15; The USN had no armored cruisers or battleships and few steel cruisers and in naval power ranked behind Great Britain, France, Russia, Germany, Holland, Spain, Italy, Turkey, China, Sweden, Norway, and Austria.

42. Lejeune to Augustine, January 1889 (Lejeune Papers, reel 1).This was a sixteen-page letter.

43. "Lejeune Gets Welcome of a Hero in New Orleans," New Orleans *Item,* December 31, 1919.

44. Lejeune, *Reminiscences,* 61.

45. Trudeau, "Appalling Calamity," 55.

46. New Orleans *Item,* December 31, 1919.

47. Kimberly, *Samoa Hurricane,* 8; Report of Lieutenant J. W. Carlin, Executive Officer of the *Vandalia,* March 19, 1889, in Report of the Secretary of the Navy, 1889.

48. Lejeune, *Reminiscences,* 68–82.

49. Report of Naval Cadet J. A. Lejeune, March 23, 1889, to Lieutenant Carlin, commanding survivors, in Report of the Secretary of the Navy, 1889; Kimberly, *Samoa Hurricane,* 14.

50. A bowsprit is a spar that extends forward from the bow of a sailing ship.

51. Dunning, "The Story of the Great Storm," 16; Report of Commander D. W. Mullan of the *Nipsic,* March 21, 1889, in Report of the Secretary of the Navy, 1889.

52. Trudeau, "Appalling Calamity," 57.

53. Ibid.

54. Lejeune Report to Carlin, March 23, 1889; Report of Captain F. H. Farquhar of the *Trenton,* March 19, 1889, all in Report of the Secretary of the Navy, 1889. The *Trenton* was the largest and finest wooden ship in the USN, over 272 feet long and displacing 3,990 tons. Captain Farquhar's official report stated that the loss of the ship was due primarily to the location of the hawse pipes—holes in the ship where the anchors are slipped—where the water entered that extinguished the engines and flooded the ship. Ironically, a former captain of the *Trenton,* F. M. Ramsey, had referred the poor location of the hawse pipes to a naval board in March 1884. The board, headed by Admiral, then Captain, L. A. Kimberly, recommended "that the hawse holes be retained in their present position, as we find it impractical to work the chains on the gun deck without interfering with the guns," Report of the Bureau of Construction and Repair, 1889, in Report of the Secretary of the Navy, 1889, 494.

55. Quoted in Dunning, "The Story of the Great Storm," 22. Dunning interviewed Captain Kane and Admiral Kimberly shortly after the typhoon.

56. Report of Lejeune; Report of Carlin; Dunning, "The Story of the Great Storm," 25.

57. Lejeune, *Reminiscences,* 80.

58. Report of Carlin; Report of Lejeune.

59. Lejeune, *Reminiscences,* 82.

60. Report of Rear Admiral L. A. Kimberly, March 1889.

61. Quote from John Lejeune to the editors of the *Baltimore Sun,* April 7, 1939, to correct a printed error in a recount of the great typhoon disaster; Report of Lejeune.

62. Report of Kimberly; after great effort, the *Nipsic* and *Olga* were hauled off the shore and recommissioned.

63. Lieutenant Carlin to Admiral Kimberly, March 25, 1889, printed in Navy Report, 1889, appendix I.

64. Navy Department orders to Lejeune, March 25 and 27, April 13, 19, and 25, 1889, in Navy Report; Lejeune, *Reminiscences,* 83.

65. "Marine Corps Head Has Seen Revolts All Over the World," *Philadelphia Inquirer,* November 18, 1928, interview with Major General Lejeune, in Lejeune Papers, reel 10.

66. Ulm, "Lejeune, Composite of all Devil Dogs."

67. Commander Woodward to the Secretary of the Navy, October 12, 1889; Lieutenant Commander Hunker to the Secretary of the Navy, February 28, 1890, both in Navy Report, 1890.

68. A dygogram is a chart showing the horizontal variation in the magnetic force acting on a ship.

69. Senator R. L. Gibson to Midshipman J. A. Lejeune, June 22, 1890 (Lejeune Papers, reel 3); Lejeune, *Reminiscences,* 91.

70. Ulm, "Composite of All Devil Dogs"; Lejeune, *Reminiscences,* 92.

71. Report of the Bureau of Steam Engineering, 1891, 430–41, in Navy Report, 1891. While many naval officers accepted the Marine Corps as a necessary evil, they were not about to lose top academy graduates to it.

72. Lejeune, *Reminiscences,* 94–96. This incident reveals that John Lejeune followed the chain of command in his effort to change a military decision. This gives an early indication of the type of officer he was to become—a quiet, conservative officer who respected naval authority and went "by the book."

73. Orders to Duty (Lejeune Papers, reel 13).

3. JUNIOR OFFICER YEARS, 1890–1900

1. Colonel Commandant Charles Heywood to Lejeune, July 28, August 31, 1890 (Lejeune Papers, reel 3).

2. Joseph Cummings Chase, "Painting Marshall Foch and 'Other' American Generals," *The World's Work* 38 (May 1919): 40–57 (Lejeune Papers, reel 10).

3. Report of the School of Application, October 1, 1895, in Report of the Marine Corps Commandant, 1895; Clyde H. Metcalf, *A History of the United States Marine Corps* (New York: G. P. Putnam's Sons, 1939), 233–45.

4. Quoted from a talk Lejeune made at the opening of Quantico's MCS in 1922, in a letter from General Gerald C. Thomas, USMC (Ret.) to Joe A. Simon, May 3, 1966, in author's personal collection.

5. Col. W. M. Miller and Major John H. Johnstone, *A Chronology of the U.S. Marine Corps, 1775–1934* (Washington, DC: GPO, 1965), 97; John Lejeune, "The U.S. Marine Corps," *MCG* 8 (December 1923): 243–54.

6. Millett, Maslowski, and Feis, *For the Common Defense,* 241–47.

7. Ibid., 246.

8. Hattendorf, "Alfred Thayer Mahan and American Naval Theory," 51–67.

9. William Fullam, "The Organization, Training, and Discipline of the Navy Personnel, as Viewed from the Ship," *USNIP* 22 (1896); William Fullam, "The System of Naval Training and Discipline Required to Promote Efficiency and Attract Americans," *USNIP* 4 (1890); John G. Miller, "William Freeland Fullam's War with the Corps," *USNIP,* November 1975; Millett, *Semper Fidelis,* 137.

10. Quoted in Shulimson, "U.S. Marines in Panama, 1885," in Bartlett, ed., *Assault from the Sea,* 109.

11. A main contention of historian William R. Braisted was that naval officers helped establish a tradition of American naval participation in diplomacy which has been perpetuated without interruption to the present day. See Braisted, *The United States Navy in the Pacific, 1897–1909,* vii.

12. Shulimson, *The Marine Corps' Search for a Mission,* 61.

13. Millett, *Semper Fidelis,* 122.

14. Ibid.

15. Shulimson, *The Marine Corps' Search for a Mission,* 80–85.

16. Roark et al., *The American Promise,* 346–47.

17. Fullam, "The System of Naval Training and Discipline," 475; Miller, "William Freeland Fullam's War with the Corps," 38.

18. Fullam, "The Organization, Training, and Discipline of the Navy Personnel," 114.

19. Shulimson, "Charles G. McCawley, 1876–1891," "Charles Heywood, 1891–1903," and "George Frank Elliott, 1903–1910," in *Commandants, 97–114, 115–45, 146–62.*

20. Millett, *Semper Fidelis,* 126–28.

21. These progressive naval officers who wrote many articles about the curriculum of the Naval Academy and the future of the graduates wanted to find places in the naval establishment for as many Naval Academy graduates as possible. Articles in *USNIP,* March 22–April 10, 1879: "Naval Education," Lt. Cdr. Allan D. Brown, USN, 305–21; Lt. Cdr. C. F. Goodrich, USN, 323–44; Cdr. A. T. Mahan, 346–76; Professor J. Russell Soley, USN, Chair, "Discussion of the Prize Essay on Naval Education," 377–405.

22. Shulimson, "Charles G. McCawley, 1876–1891," in *Commandants,* 107; Millett, *Semper Fidelis,* 110–11; Shulimson, *Marine Corps' Search for a Mission,"* 49–50.

23. Millett, *Semper Fidelis,* 653.

24. Daugherty, *Pioneers of Amphibious Warfare,* 14; Schulimson, *The Marine Corps' Search for a Mission,* 101.

25. Heywood, *Commandants,* 117.

26. Captain Harry Allanson Ellsworth, USMC, *One Hundred Eighty Landings of United States Marines, 1800–1934* (Washington, DC.: History and Museums Division, Headquarters, USMC, 1974).

27. Schulimson, *The Marine Corps' Search for a Mission,* 186.

28. Lejeune, *Reminiscences,* 114–16; Lejeune to Augustine, March 2, 1909 (Lejeune Papers, reel 2).

29. Lejeune, *Reminiscences,* 101.

30. *Report* of the Commandant, 1891, 618.

31. Lejeune, "The Marine Corps, 1926," *USNIP,* October 1926; Report of the Bureau of Construction and Repair 1891, 324–25; *New York Times,* November 10, 1916.

32. Lejeune to Commandant Elliott, September 6, 1907 (Lejeune Papers, reel 3).

33. Bartlett, *Lejeune: A Marine's Life,* 41.

34. Report on Fitness of Officers, "J. A. Lejeune, 2nd Lieut., USMC, Comments by Commander R. B. Bradford, January 1, 1892," to CinC, Squadron of Evolution, January 16, 1892, RG 125, NARACP.

35. Lejeune to the Honorable Secretary of the Navy, copy to R. B. Bradford, Commander, *USS Bennington,* Montevideo, Uruguay, April 28, 1892, RG 125, NARACP.

36. Bartlett, *Lejeune: A Marine's Life,* 41. Quote from Heywood to Lejeune, June 8, 1891, entry 1, RG 127, NARACP.

37. Report on the Fitness of Officers, Lejeune by Bradford, January 1, 1892, to July 1, 1892, RG 125, NARACP.

38. Report on the Fitness of Officers, Lejeune by Bradford, July 1, 1892, to January 1, 1893. RG 125, NARACP.

39. Lejeune to Augustine, January 5, 1893 (Lejeune Papers, reel 1).

40. Lejeune, *Reminiscences,* 110.

41. Letter from General A. A. Vandegrift, USMC (Ret.), to Joe A. Simon, April 1, 1966.

42. A. A. Vandegrift as told to Robert B. Asprey, *Once a Marine: The Memoirs of General A. A. Vandegrift, Commandant of the U.S. Marines in WW II* (New York: Ballantine Books, 1966), 27–29.

43. Report of the Bureau of Navigation, 1893, 181–96; Heywood to Lejeune, July 25, 27, 1893 (Lejeune Papers, reel 3).

44. Heywood to Lejeune, July 13, 22, 1897 (Lejeune Papers, reel 3).

45. Lejeune, *Reminiscences,* 114–16.

46. Report on the Fitness of Officers, "First Lieutenant John A. Lejeune, Navy Yard, Norfolk, Virginia," by George Brown, Rear Admiral, USN, Commandant, Navy Yard, August 28, 1893, to May 31, 1897; Report on "Fitness of Lejeune" by Captain A. H. Farquhar, Commandant, Norfolk Navy Yard, Jan 1, 1897, to June 30, 1897, RG 125, NARACP.

47. Report of the Fitness of Officers, "First Lieutenant J. A. Lejeune, In Charge of Guard and Intelligence Officer for *Cincinnati,*" by Captain Colby M. Chester, USN, August 2, 1897, to February 1, 1889.

48. Report of the Secretary of the Navy, 3–16, 1898; Metcalf, *History of the United States Marine Corps,* 254–62.

49. Shulimson, *Marine Corps' Search for a Mission,* 184–87.

50. Report of the Secretary of the Navy, 1898, 3–16. Report of the Bureau of Navigation, 1898, 99–332.

51. Report of the Bureau of Navigation, 1898, 99–332 in Navy Report; Metcalf, *History of the United States Marine Corps,* 254–62; Vincent J. Esposito, *The West Point Atlas of American Wars* (New York: Fredrick A. Praeger, 1959), 155–56.

52. Daugherty, *Pioneers of Amphibious Warfare,* 30.

53. Shulimson, *Marine Corps' Search for a Mission,* 193–94.

54. Dion Williams, "Coordination in Army and Navy Training," *USNIP,* April 1922, 597–98.

55. Millett, *Semper Fidelis,* 135; Annual Reports of the Secretary of the Navy, 1898–1908; Daugherty, *Pioneers of Amphibious Warfare,* 31.

56. Daugherty, *Pioneers of Amphibious Warfare,* 30–31.

57. Lejeune, *Reminiscences,* 133.

58. Report of Lieutenant Charles N. Atwater, August 10, 1898, 652–57; Report of C. M. Chester, August 1898, 651, in Report of the Bureau of Navigation.

59. Report of Captain C. M. Chester, August 1898, 651, in Report of the Bureau of Navigation, 1898.

60. Chester's letter was reprinted in the *Marines Magazine,* n.d., in Lejeune Papers, reel 3. Other information compiled by the historical section of the USMC, June 24, 1955, and mailed to Joe A. Simon, April 20, 1966, in the author's personal collection; Report of the Operations off Puerto Rico, July, August, 1898, 18, Bureau of Navigation.

61. Report of Admiral Sampson to the Navy Secretary, April 28, 1898; Report of Captain F. E. Chadwick, CO of the flagship *New York,* April 28, 1898, appendix in Report of the Bureau of Navigation, 1898. All reports in Report of the Secretary of the Navy, 1898. "Men Were Cool When Under Fire," an Associated Press dispatch written April 29, 1898, by an unnamed reporter aboard the *New York* (Lejeune Papers, reel 3).

62. Chester to Secretary Charles Long, reprinted in part in "A Short Biographical Sketch of Major General John A. Lejeune," *The Recruiter's Bulletin,* July 1920, 9–10 (Lejeune Papers, reel 11).

63. Lejeune, *Reminiscences,* 138.

64. Lejeune to Augustine, April 1900 (Lejeune Papers, reel 1).

65. Lejeune to Senator Hugo L. Black, March 1, 1935 (Lejeune Papers, reel 6).

66. Lejeune to Augustine, February 19, 1899 (Lejeune Papers, reel 1).

67. The Naval Appropriations Bill of 1899 also authorized three more battleships and three heavy cruisers.

68. Lejeune to Augustine, February 19, 1899 (Lejeune Papers, reel 1).

69. Lejeune to Augustine, December 16, 1899 (Lejeune Papers, reel 1).

70. Lejeune to Navy Dept., October 28, November 6, 1899; Navy Dept. to Lejeune, November 1, 13, 1899 (Lejeune Papers, reel 3).

71. Navy Dept. to Lejeune, November 1, 13, 1899 (Lejeune Papers, reel 3).

72. Lejeune was compared to these officers by Captain Robert Asprey, "John A. Lejeune: True Soldier," *MCG,* April 1962, 32–41.

4. BUILDING A REPUTATION, 1900–1910

1. Daniel Joseph Costello, "Planning for War: A History of the General Board of the Navy, 1900–1914," PhD diss., Fletcher School of Law and Diplomacy, October 1, 1968, 1–23.

2. George Dewey, Admiral USN, President of Board, to Honorable Secretary of the Navy, General Board No. 51, Washington, DC, October 6, 1900, item 1975-40-10, RG 127, NARACP.

3. Ibid.

4. Report of the Commandant, 1901, 1249–57.

5. Ibid., 1902, 975–79.

6. Ibid., 1903, 1232–34.

7. Brian McAllister Linn, "William Phillips Biddle, 1911 to 1914," in *Commandants,* 67.

8. Heywood to Lejeune, June 30, July 2, 3, 20, August 7, 9, September 29, October 2, 13, 1900; Lejeune to Heywood, July 7, October 11, 1900 (Lejeune Papers, reel 3); Report of the Commandant (1901), 1253.

9. Robert Debs Heinl Jr., *Soldiers of the Sea: The U.S. Marine Corps, 1775–1962, (Baltimore, MD*: Nautical & Aviation Publishing, 1991), cover.

10. Heywood to Lejeune, November 10, 15, 22, 1900 (Lejeune Papers, reel 3); Report of the Bureau of Yards and Docks (1901), 168–69, in Reports of the Secretary of the Navy.

11. Letter printed in Report of the Commandant (1901), 1216.

12. Lauchheimer to Lejeune, February 3, 1902 (Lejeune Papers, reel 3).

13. John W. Ross, Surgeon, "Report of Medical Survey to Commandant of Navy Yard, Pensacola, Florida, September 23, 1902, on Lejeune, John Archer, Captain, USMC," RG 125, NARACP.

14. "Medical Record of Captain John A. Lejeune, June 22, 1903," by the Surgeon General, USN, RG 125, NARACP. Lejeune was on sick leave of absence from October 20, 1902, to January 8, 1903, in "Military Record of Captain John A. Lejeune," Adjutant and Inspector's Office, June 13, 1903, RG 125, NARACP.

15. Heywood to Lejeune, December 26, 1902 (Lejeune Papers, reel 3).

16. Heywood to Lejeune, August 3, 1903 (Lejeune Papers, reel 3).

17. Naval Appropriations Act of March 3, 1903, Report of the Commandant, 1903, 1226–27, 1240.

18. "Report on the Fitness of Officers, J. A. Lejeune, from August 16 to October 23, 1903," by J. C. Wilson, Commander, USN, in RG 125, NARACP.

19. MGC George Elliott to Lejeune, October 9, 1903; Wilson to Lejeune, October 23, 1903 (Lejeune Papers, reel 3); Lejeune, *Reminiscences,* 151.

20. Lejeune, *Reminiscences,* 152–53.

21. Heinl, *Soldiers of the Sea,* 160.

22. Orders printed in Metcalf, *History of the United States Marine Corps,* 292.

23. Information on the Panama situation from Edmund Morris, *Theodore Rex* (New York: Modern Library, 2001), 287–94; William Henry Harbaugh, *The Life and Times of Theodore Roosevelt* (New York: Collier Books, 1963), 194–205; Howard K. Beale, *Theodore Roosevelt and the Rise of America to World Power* (Baltimore: John Hopkins University Press, 1956), 101–8; Metcalf, *History of the United States Marine Corps,* 268–97; Report of the Bureau of Navigation, 1904, 484–87.

24. Report of Captain Francis H. Delano, senior officer present off Colón, November 10, 1903, Navy Report.

25. Report of MGC Elliott (1904), 1192–94.

26. Report of the Surgeon-General, USN (1905), 1207–8; Colonel W. C. Gorgas, USA, to Lejeune, May 5, 1910 (Lejeune Papers, reel 3).

27. New Orleans *Times-Democrat,* December 26, 1904.

28. Colonel W. C. Gorgas, USA, to Lejeune, May 5, 1910 (Lejeune Papers, reel 3).

29. "Marine Corps Commandant Here on His First Visit to Seattle," *Seattle Post,* April 19, 1923.

30. Rear Admiral J. B. Coghlan to Lejeune, March 8, 1904 (Lejeune Papers, reel 3).

31. Lejeune's daily reports, Panama, 1903–4 (Lejeune Papers, reel 15); Rear Admiral J. B. Pillsburg to Coghlan, March 12, 1904, Report of the Secretary of the Navy.

32. Lejeune to CinC, South Atlantic Squadron, March 28, 1904 (Lejeune Papers, reel 3); Report of Lejeune to Elliott, March 27, 1904 (Lejeune Papers, reel 15).

33. Regulations of the North Atlantic Fleet, issued May 26, 1903, paragraph 11, page 3, in General Records of the Department of the Navy, 1798–1947, RG 80, NARAW.

34. Lejeune to Sigbee, on *USFS Newark* at San Juan, Puerto Rico, August 15, 1904, Lejeune's daily reports in Panama (Lejeune Papers, reel 15).

35. Rear Admiral Charles D. Sigbee to Lejeune, September 24, 1904 (Lejeune Papers, reel 3).

36. Davis to Lejeune, December 21, 1904 (Lejeune Papers, reel 3).

37. Coghlan to Lejeune, 1904 (Lejeune Papers, reel 15).

38. New Orleans *Times-Democrat,* December 26, 1904; Report of the Surgeon-General, USN, 1905, 1207–8, 1904, 1166–67; Colonel W. C. Gorgas, USA, to Lejeune, May 5, 1910; Elliott to Lejeune, May 16, 1904; Report of the Secretary of the Navy, 1905, 1236; Rear Admiral C. F. Goodrich to Elliott, November 24, 1904; Second Endorsement of Goodrich letter; Commander G. A. Merriam to Lejeune, November 25, 1904; George W. Davis, Governor of the Canal Zone, to Lejeune, December 21, 1904; Rear Admiral J. B. Coghlan to Lejeune, 1904. All in Lejeune Papers, reel 3.

39. Lucien Young to Lejeune, August 8, 1904 (Lejeune Papers, reel 3).

40. Lejeune to Augustine, February 13, 26, 1906 (Lejeune Papers, reel 1).

41. Recommendations from Lejeune to Elliott, September 6, 1906 (Lejeune Papers, reel 3).

42. Major General Bennet Puryear Jr., USMC (Ret.) to Joe A. Simon, May 8, 1966, in the author's personal files. Puryear served as General Lejeune's assistant G-1, Second Division, in World War I, and on Commandant Lejeune's Headquarters Staff, 1921–25.

43. Elliott to Lejeune, May 7, 1906 (Lejeune Papers, reel 3).

44. Report of the Surgeon-General, 1906, 1040–46.

45. Quote from Lejeune, *Reminiscences,* 174; letter printed in Commandant Report (1906), 1086–87; Lejeune to Augustine, June 25, November 12, 1906 (Lejeune Papers, reel 1).

46. Elliott to Lejeune, February 25, 1907, March 21, 1907 (Lejeune Papers, reel 3).

47. Roosevelt to Henry Cabot Lodge, printed in Beale, *Theodore Roosevelt and the Rise of America,* 284; Harbaugh, *Life and Times of Theodore Roosevelt,* 285–87.

48. Braisted, *The United States Navy in the Pacific, 1897–1909,* 191.

49. Beale, *Theodore Roosevelt and the Rise of America,* 284; Harbaugh, *Life and Times of Theodore Roosevelt,* 285–87.

50. Colonel Eli K. Cole to MGC, "Subject: Encloses copy of lecture prepared for delivery at Marine Barracks, Philadelphia, PA, 19 June 1915," file 1975-10, 1820-40, RG 127, NARACP; Lejeune, *Reminiscences,* 175–76.

51. Ibid.

52. Braisted, *The United States Navy in the Pacific, 1897–1909,* 191–97.

53. Record of Proceedings of a Marine Examining Board convened at the US Naval Station,

Cavite, Philippines, in the case of Major John A. Lejeune, USMC, October 2, 1908; approved, November 12, 1908, Navy Department, Office of Judge Advocate General, RG 125, NARACP.

54. Cressman, "George Frank Elliott," in *Commandants,* 157.

55. Lejeune to Augustine, March 2, 1909 (Lejeune Papers, reel 2).

56. Cressman, "George Frank Elliott."

57. Millett, *Semper Fidelis,* 274–75.

58. Letters from Lejeune to Augustine, January 16, March 2, 20, April 5, 24, May 10, 1909 (Lejeune Papers, reel 2).

59. Cressman, "George Frank Elliott," 146–62.

60. The AWC was the Army's senior service college, the ultimate step in preparing promising lieutenant colonels and colonels for general officer status and high-level commands. See "The Army War College," *Army Reserve Magazine* 12, no. 3 (March 1966): 15.

61. Lejeune, *Reminiscences,* 188.

62. AWC Archives, 1909–10, vol. 9, Orange-Blue Problem, pt. 1, pp. 339–42 (Guam) and 343–75 (Alaska), US Army Heritage and Education Center, US Army Military Institute, Carlisle, PA.

63. Ibid., vol. 12, Orange-Blue Problem, pt. 4, US Army Military Institute, Carlisle, PA.

64. Lejeune, *Reminiscences,* 185–91.

65. General Thomas to Joe A. Simon, April 19, 1966. Copies in author's possession.

66. General Cates to Simon, April 2, 1966. Copies in author's possession.

67. Lejeune to Augustine, July 28, 1910 (Lejeune Papers, reel 2).

68. Ibid., June 7, 1910 (Lejeune Papers, reel 2).

69. Ibid., May 2, 1910 (Lejeune Papers, reel 2).

70. Ibid.

71. Senator Chamberlain to the Honorable George von L. Meyer, Secretary of the Navy, April 21, 1910 (Lejeune Papers, reel 3).

72. Lejeune to Augustine, May 2, June 7, 1910 (Lejeune Papers, reel 2).

73. Linn, "William Phillips Biddle," 163–73.

5. EXPEDITIONS AND THE ADVANCED BASE FORCE, 1910–1917

1. Lejeune to MGC Elliott, September 12, 1910; Elliott to Lejeune, September 21, October 20, 1910 (Lejeune Papers, reel 3); Report of the Commandant, 1911, 525; Lejeune, *Reminiscences,* 192.

2. "A Biographical Sketch of MGC John A. Lejeune," *Recruiters Bulletin,* July 1920, 10; MGC to CO, Marine Barracks, Navy Yard, New York, Inspection by MGC on May 9, 1912 (Lejeune Papers, reel 3).

3. Annual Report of Major Albert S. McLemore, Assistant Adjutant and Inspector, October 30, 1913.

4. Biddle to Lejeune, December 1, 1913 (Lejeune Papers, reel 3).

5. E. H. C. Leutze, Rear Admiral, Commandant Navy Yard and Station, Order 79, to CO, Marine Barracks, April 25, 1911; CO, Marine Barracks, to Commandant, Navy Yard, April 26, 1911; First Endorsement, April 27, 1911; Second Endorsement, May 1, 1911; Third Endorsement, May 2, 1911; Fourth Endorsement, May 3, 1911 (Lejeune Papers, reel 3). In a May 9, 1911,

letter to Augustine, Lejeune wrote, "The flag is once more flying over the Barracks" (Lejeune Papers, reel 2).

6. Lejeune, *Reminiscences,* 194.

7. Karmany to Lejeune, June 8, 1912 (Lejeune Papers, reel 3); David A. Shannon, *Twentieth Century America* (Chicago: Rand McNally, 1963), 130–31; Lynn Montross, *The United States Marines: A Pictorial History* (New York: Rinehart and Co., 1959), 94–95; Reports of the Commandant, 1907: 1281–82; 1909: 1034.

8. Metcalf, *History of the United States Marine Corps,* 324–32; D. B. Whitaker, vice president and general manager, Juragua Iron Company, Firmeza, Province of Oriente, Cuba, to Secretary of the Navy, December 26, 1912, in Lejeune Papers, reel 3; Lejeune to Augustine, June 24, July 8, 1912, in Lejeune Papers, reel 2.

9. Featured article in the *New York Herald,* n.d., 1912; Metcalf, *History of the United States Marine Corps,* 324–32.

10. D. B. Whitaker to Secretary of the Navy G. von L. Meyer, December 26, 1912; George Barnett to Lejeune, February 18, 1916, indicated that the letter was placed in Lejeune's official record (Lejeune Papers, reel 3).

11. "Taft Rushes Men and Ships to Cuba," *New York Times,* February 13, 1913; Arthur S. Link, *Woodrow Wilson and the Progressive Era* (New York: Harper and Brothers, 1963), 107–24; "Marines Starting for Guantanamo," *New York Evening Journal,* February 18, 1913; *New York American,* February 19, 1913; Norman Reeve, "Our Navy's Winter Base," *Leslie's Illustrated Weekly Newspaper,* May 1, 1913, 466; Lejeune to Augustine, February 7, March 14, April 7, 14, 1913 (Lejeune Papers, reel 2).

12. Issues of the *MCG,* January 1955 and September 1955, credit Lejeune with founding the Marine Corps Association. See also *MCG,* June 1955, 17; "Foreword: The Legacy of John A. Lejeune," *MCG* 46 (April 1962): 32; Heinl, "An Association Is Formed," *MCG* 47 (April 1963): 14–17. Lejeune expressed his unhappiness with Corps Headquarters in letters to Augustine, March 20, 1909; February 19, July 28, 1910 (Lejeune Papers, reel 2).

13. Lejeune, "The Mobile Defense of Advanced Bases by the Marine Corps," *MCG* 1 (March 1916): 1–18.

14. Millett, *Semper Fidelis,* 279.

15. Cosmas and Shulimson, "The Culebra Maneuver," 121–32.

16. MGC to Secretary of the Navy, April 10, 1913, file 1975-10, Headquarters USMC, General Correspondence, 1911–38, RG 127, NARACP.

17. Headquarters USMC to Lt. Col. John A. Lejeune, November 25, 1913 (Lejeune Papers, reel 13).

18. Costello, "Planning for War," 163–73; Cosmas and Shulimson, "The Culebra Maneuver," 127.

19. Fullam to Secretary of the Navy, "Establishment of Advance Base Outfit," May 1, 1913, in item 1975-10-15, RG 127, NARACP. See also Fullam to Secretary Josephus Daniels, June 23, June 27, September 22, 1913, in Linn, "William Phillips Biddle," 167–68.

20. President, General Board, to Secretary of the Navy, "Duties of Marines and their connection with Advanced Base Force outfits," July 2, 1913, item 1975-10-15, RG 127, NARACP.

21. Linn, "William Phillips Biddle," 170.

22. Braisted, *The United States Navy in the Pacific, 1909–1922,* 138.

23. Lejeune to Augustine, November 13, 1913 (Lejeune Papers, reel 2).

24. Ibid. Copies of Lejeune's letters of support are in Lejeune Papers, reel 2.

25. Ibid.

26. Lejeune to Augustine, December 13, 1913 (Lejeune Papers, reel 2).

27. The fleet train carried supplies, ammunition, and fuel for the fleet.

28. Chief Observer to CinC, US Atlantic Fleet, "Report of Chief Observer on Landing Operations by the Fleet on 21 January, 1914," January 23, 1914, in file 1975-80-30, RG 127, NARACP; Lejeune to Barnett, "Report of Maneuvers and Operations," January 31, 1914, in file 1975-80-20, RG 127, NARACP.

29. Cosmas and Shulimson, "The Culebra Maneuver," 130.

30. Lejeune to Barnett, "Report of Maneuvers and Operations," Case 10190 Supplementary, January 31, 1914; CO of three-inch Landing Gun Company to Lejeune, "Report on Joint Exercises," January 28, 1914; Rear Admiral Charles J. Badger, CinC, Atlantic Fleet to Barnett, CO, First Advance Base Brigade, "Instructions for Joint Exercises with Atlantic Fleet," January 17–24, 1914; Badger to Secretary of the Navy (Operations), "Advance Base in Vieques Sound Region," February 20, 1914; Barnett to MGC, "Report on Maneuvers and Operations," February 15, 1914; First Endorsement, Badger to Secretary of the Navy (Operations), "Report on Operations of Advance Base Expedition," Culebra, Puerto Rico, January–February 1914, April 5, 1914; Barnett, "Operation Orders No. 3," to Long; Barnett to Lejeune, "Aerial Scouts," January 9, 1914; Chief Observer to Badger, "Report of Chief Observer on Landing Operations by the Fleet" on January 21, 1914; Barnett to Secretary of the Navy, "Memorandum in Regard to Advance Bases," December 8, 1914. All in file 1975-80-20, RG 127, NARACP.

31. War Plan Orange is discussed at length in chapter 7.

32. Lejeune, CO, Second Regiment, First Advance Brigade to Brigade Commander, "Report of Maneuvers and Operations," January 31, 1914, file 1975-80-10, RG 127, NARACP.

33. Barnett, First Advance Base Brigade, to MGC, "Report on Maneuvers and Operations," February 15, 1914, file 1975-80-30, RG 127, NARACP.

34. Rear Admiral Charles J. Badger, CinC, US Atlantic Fleet, to Secretary of the Navy (Operations), February 20, 1914, no. 60-14-(4), A-Hs, RG 80, NARAW; Badger to Secretary of the Navy (Operations), First Endorsement, "Report on Operations of Advanced Base Expedition," Culebra, W.I., January–February 1914, April 5, 1914, no. 60-14-(4), A-Hs, RG 80, NARAW.

35. Josephus Daniels, *The Wilson Era: Years of Peace, 1910–1917* (Chapel Hill: University of North Carolina Press, 1944), 322–23.

36. Recorded in "Promotions and Fitness Reports of Lejeune, 1891 to 1916," RG 125, NARACP.

37. Lejeune to Augustine, February 20, 1914 (Lejeune Papers, reel 2).

38. Alexander, "Roots of Deployment—Vera Crux, 1914," 133.

39. Lejeune to Augustine, February 20, 1914 (Lejeune Papers, reel 2).

40. Jack Sweetman, "Take Veracruz at Once," *Naval History,* April 2014, 34–41.

41. Robert E. Quirk, *An Affair of Honor: Woodrow Wilson and the Occupation of Veracruz* (Lexington: University Press of Kentucky, 1962), 1–77; Lejeune, *Reminiscences,* 205–9; Link,

Woodrow Wilson and the Progressive Era, 107–24; Link, *Wilson, the New Freedom* (Princeton, NJ: Harper Torch, 1956), 347–416; Report of the Commandant, 1914, 469–70; Report of the Bureau of Navigation, 1914, 141–43; Alexander, "Roots of Deployment," 133–41.

42. Alexander, "Roots of Deployment—Vera Crux, 1914," 133–36.

43. Lejeune to Augustine, April 21, 1914 (Lejeune Papers, reel 2).

44. "Hot Fighting at Veracruz," *Brooklyn Eagle,* April 23, 1914; newspaper article by correspondent J. S. S. Richardson, n.d., 1914; Quirk, *An Affair of Honor,* 85–157; Arthur Rubl, "Fall of Veracruz," *Colliers* 53 (May 9, 1914): 6; Commandant's Report, 1914, 469–70; Report of the Bureau of Navigation (1914), 141–43; Metcalf, *History of the United States Marine Corps,* 298–304.

45. Lejeune, *Reminiscences,* 208.

46. Alexander, "Roots of Deployment—Vera Crux, 1914," 136.

47. Lejeune to Augustine, April 24, 1914 (Lejeune Papers, reel 2); Lejeune to Fletcher and Barnett, April 22–29, 1914 (Lejeune Papers, reel 3); Report of the Commandant, 1914.

48. Mahoney to Lejeune, May 2, 1914 (Lejeune Papers, reel 3).

49. Alexander, "Roots of Deployment—Vera Crux, 1914," 137–39.

50. Ibid., 138.

51. Sweetman, "Take Veracruz at Once," 41.

52. Lejeune to Augustine, August 30, 1914 (Lejeune Papers, reel 2).

53. Ibid., January 11, February 8, May 17, 1915 (Lejeune Papers, reel 2).

54. Alexander, "Roots of Deployment—Vera Crux, 1914," 139–41; Metcalf, *History of the United States Marine Corps,* 298–305; Sweetman, "Take Veracruz at Once," 34–41.

55. Alexander, "Roots of Deployment—Vera Crux, 1914," 140.

56. Sweetman, "Take Veracruz at Once," 37.

57. Lejeune, *Reminiscences,* 219–43.

58. Kenneth Condit, John Johnstone, and Ella Nargele, *A Brief History of Headquarters Marine Staff Organization* (Washington, DC: Historical Division, Headquarters, USMC, 1971), 8–9.

59. Ibid., 8.

60. Colonel L. W. T. Waller, Headquarters US Expeditionary Forces Operating in Haiti, Port-au-Prince, September 8, 21, October 13, 1915, to Colonel John A. Lejeune; Lejeune to Waller, October 1, 1915 (Lejeune Papers, reel 3).

61. Lejeune, *Reminiscences,* 228–29.

62. *Army and Navy Register* (Washington, DC), vol. 60, no. 1898 (December 2, 1916) (Lejeune Papers, reel 13).

63. Report of the MGC, 1915, 1916.

64. Lejeune, *Reminiscences,* 230–31.

65. Lejeune to Butler, December 19, 1916, Butler manuscript, GRC, and in Hans Schmidt, *Maverick Marine: General Smedley D. Butler and the Contradictions of American Military History* (Lexington: University Press of Kentucky, 1987), 97.

66. Lejeune, *Reminiscences,* 231.

67. Lejeune, "The Mobile Defense of Advanced Bases by the Marine Corps," lecture before

Advance Base School, Navy Yard, Philadelphia, May 21, 1915, Records of USMC, Office of the Commandant, General Correspondence 1913–38, file 1975-50, entry 18, RG 127, NARACP.

68. This list is necessarily restrictive, for there were other Marines advocating the amphibious mission. The men listed here, however, were more prolific in their writing, lecturing, and promoting the concept.

69. At this time the anticipated enemy was Imperial Germany.

70. Dion Williams probably hoped that Congress would fund strong defenses in the Philippines and at Guam.

71. Dion Williams, "The Defense of Our New Naval Stations," *USNIP,* June 1902, 181–94.

72. Williams, "Naval Reconnaissance: Instructions for Reconnaissance of Bays, Harbors, and Adjacent Countries" (Washington, DC: GPO, 1906).

73. Daugherty, *Pioneers of Amphibious Warfare,* 123–33.

74. Williams, "The Naval Advance Base," lecture at NWC, July 26, 1912, Historical Amphibious Files (HAF).

75. Millett, Maslowski, and Feis, *For the Common Defense,* 245–47.

76. Robert Henry Dunlap, "The Naval Advance Base," lecture at NWC, July 1911, Naval Historical Collection, Newport, RI; Dunlap, "The Temporary Naval Advanced Base, General Considerations," paper presented at NWC, 1912.

77. "Report of Eli K. Cole, On the Work of Installing the Naval Base Guns at the Entrance to Subic Bay," November 20, 1907, AWC, Problem Reports, AWC Studies and Committee Reports, Records of the War Department and General Staff, Serial 43, RG 165, NARACP.

78. See Daugherty, "Major General Eli K. Cole, USMC," in *Pioneers of Amphibious Warfare,* 100–104.

79. Cole to MGC, "Encloses copy of lecture prepared for delivery at Marine Barracks, Philadelphia, 19 June 1915," dated June 16, 1915, item 1975-10, 1820-40, RG 127, NARACP.

80. President, US NWC, to President, General Board, "General principles governing the selection and establishment of Advanced Naval Bases, and the composition of an Advanced Base Force outfit, a study made by Major John H. Russell, USMC," modified and edited by the NWC staff, December 10, 1909, HAF 768. John Russell, "An outline study of the defense of Advanced Naval Bases," October 22, 1909, NWC; "Notes on field construction work and guns for Advanced Naval Base" and "The preparation of war plans for the establishment and defense of a Naval Advance Base," June 14, 1910, as discussed by Daugherty, *Pioneers of Amphibious Warfare,* 246–50.

81. See "Discussion on a Plea for a Mission and Doctrine," *MCG,* June 1916, 188–96.

82. John Russell, "A Plea for a Mission and Doctrine," *MCG,* June 1916, 109–16.

83. Dirk A. Ballendorf and Merrill L. Bartlett, *Pete Ellis: An Amphibious Warfare Prophet, 1880–1923* (Annapolis, MD: NIP, 1997), 25–27.

84. Captain E. H. Ellis, USMC, "Naval Bases; Location, Resources, Denial of Bases, Security of Bases," 1914, in HAF 294, p. 7-B.

85. While most sources date Ellis's article as 1921, Ellis actually wrote it before the beginning of World War I. See Eli K. Cole to MGC, June 16, 1915, 39.

86. Lejeune, "The Mobile Defense of Advanced Bases by the Marine Corps," lecture.

87. Ibid., 1–9.

6. LEJEUNE, THE MARINE CORPS, AND WORLD WAR I

1. Roark et al., *The American Promise,* 796–97.

2. Lejeune to Augustine, April 25, 1917 (Lejeune Papers, reel 2).

3. President Woodrow Wilson, White House, to the Secretary of the Navy, May 27, 1917, section 1975-70, RG 127, NARACP.

4. Daniels, *The Wilson Era,* 150, 1917–23.

5. Lejeune to Augustine, August 9, 1917 (Lejeune Papers, reel 2).

6. Ibid., May 6, 1918 (Lejeune Papers, reel 2).

7. Cablegram from Pershing to Newton D. Baker, Secretary of War, enclosed in a memo from Baker to Secretary of the Navy Daniels, May 1, 1918, section 1975-70, RG 127, NARACP.

8. Lejeune, *Reminiscences,* 259–61.

9. Andrew Roberts, "A Bold New History of the Battle of the Somme," *Smithsonian Magazine,* July 2016, 1–14.

10. Ibid., 1–6.

11. Ibid., 10.

12. Ibid.

13. Lejeune, *Reminiscences,* 259–61.

14. Ibid., 261.

15. Ibid., 277.

16. Maj. Gen. James G. Harbord, Fourth Brigade, Marines, AEF, France, to Lejeune, July 12, 1918; Lejeune to Headquarters, Fourth Brigade, Marine Corps, AEF, General Order 16, July 26, 1918 (Lejeune Papers, reel 11).

17. Lejeune, *Reminiscences,* 284–85.

18. Lejeune to Ellie Lejeune Glennon, August 2, 1918, in the personal papers of the James Glennon family.

19. Lejeune, *Reminiscences,* 286.

20. Ibid., 293–95.

21. Millett, *Semper Fidelis,* 299–301.

22. Lejeune to Augustine, September 8, 1918 (Lejeune Papers, reel 2).

23. Ibid.; "St. Mihiel Operations—September 12–15, 1918, The Enemy's Situation Prior to Our Attack" (Lejeune Papers, reel 11); "2nd Division—Field Notes—At St. Mihiel," Records of the AEF (WWI), Organizational Records, box no. 8, RG 120, NARACP; Lejeune, *Reminiscences,* 312–35.

24. Lejeune, *Reminiscences,* 342–43.

25. Operation Report, 2nd Division (Regular), September 15 to October 9, including "Attack on MASSIF of BLANC MONT RIDGE and action in connection therewith," Lejeune to Hugh B. Myers, Colonel, G-3 (Lejeune Papers, reel 11); Field Orders, September 15 to October 9, 2nd Division, Historical Organizational Records, Records of the AEF Forces, World War I, RG 120, NARACP.

26. Lejeune, *Reminiscences,* 342.

27. Lejeune to Ellie Lejeune Glennon, November 14, 1918 (Lejeune Papers, reel 2).

28. Lejeune to Brig. Gen. Charles Long, October 19, 1918 (Lejeune Papers, reel 3).

29. Edward G. Lengel, *To Conquer Hell: The Meuse-Argonne, 1918, the Epic Battle That Ended the First World War* (New York: Henry Holt and Co., 2008), 255.

30. Container 1953, AEF Central File 201.6e, RG 120, NARACP, as published in Bartlett, *Lejeune: A Marine's Life,* 104.

31. Lejeune letter to Commandant of the Marine Corps, October 22, 1940, and Lejeune's officer qualification record, Headquarters Marine Corps, in Bartlett, *Lejeune: A Marine's Life,* 117.

32. Container 1953, AEF Central File 201.6e.e., RG 120, NARACP.

33. Bartlett, *Lejeune: A Marine's Life,* 117.

34. Lejeune, *Reminiscences,* 380.

35. See Edward G. Lengel, "Meuse-Argonne," *American Heritage Magazine,* Summer 2010, 30–39.

36. Operations Report of the 2nd Division, West of the Meuse, November 1–11, 1918, by Major General John A. Lejeune, Commanding, in Records of the of the AEF, Organizational Records, 2nd Division, box no. 31, Records of the AEF Forces, box 31, RG 120, NARACP.

37. Charles P. Summerall, CG, V Army Corps, to Lejeune, CG, 2nd Division, November 2, 1918 (Lejeune Papers, reel 11).

38. Lejeune, *Reminiscences,* 388.

39. Douglas V. Mastriano credits the Ninth Infantry Regiment commander, Colonel Robert O. Van Horn with the original idea to advance during hours of darkness. See Mastriano, *Thunder in the Argonne: A New History of America's Greatest Battle* (Lexington: University Press of Kentucky, 2018), 300–301.

40. Operations Report of the 2nd Division, West of the Meuse, November 1 to 11, 1918, by Maj. Gen. John A. Lejeune, RG 120, NARACP; Lejeune, *Reminiscences,* 392–93.

41. Operations Report of the 2nd Division, 11, RG 120, NARACP.

42. Edward M. Coffman, *The War to End All Wars: The American Military Experience in World War I* (Lexington: University Press of Kentucky, 1998), 348.

43. Coffman, *The War to End All Wars,* 353.

44. Lejeune, *Reminiscences,* 400.

45. Ibid., 399.

46. Maj. Gen. John A. Lejeune, Headquarters, 2nd Division, AEF, Germany, January 1, 1919, to the Officers and Men of the 2nd Division (Lejeune Papers, reel 11); Bartlett, *Lejeune: A Marine's Life,* 114; Lejeune, *Reminiscence,* 445; Millett, *Semper Fidelis,* 296–317.

47. Maj. Gen. John A. Lejeune, Commanding 2nd Division, AEF, to Lt. Gen. Hunter Liggett, Headquarters 1st Army, AEF, November 9, 1918; Liggett to Lejeune, November 13, 1918 (Lejeune Papers, reel 11).

48. Lejeune, *Reminiscences,* 413–15.

49. General Malin Craig, Chief of Staff, 3rd Army to CG, III Army Corps: Conditions of Elements of Command, November 22, 1918 (Lejeune Papers, reel 11).

50. Second Endorsement, Lejeune to CG, 3rd Army (through 3rd Army Corps, November 25, 1918 (Lejeune Papers, reel 11); Major General J. T. Dickman, CG, 3rd Army, AEF, to Chief of Staff, GHQ, January 14, 1919 (Lejeune Papers, reel 11).

51. Maj. Gen. Lejeune to Maj. Gen. Howze, March 29, 1919; Howze to Lejeune, March 31, 1919; Lejeune to Howze, April 1, 1919 (Lejeune Papers, reel 11).

52. Lejeune to Maj. Gen. Howse, CO, 3rd Division, Germany, April 1, 1919 (Lejeune Papers, reel 11).

53. Lejeune to Summerall, Germany, January 5, 1919 (Lejeune Papers, reel 11).

54. Harbord, GHQ, Office of the Chief of Staff, to Lejeune, June 26, 1919. In Lejeune's quest for greater recognition for the 2nd Division, see Lejeune to Gouraud, Commanding 4th French Army, January 6, 1919; Summerall to Lejeune, January 11, 1919; Lejeune to Summerall, January 16, 1919; Summerall to Lejeune, January 21, 1919; Leroy Eltinge, GHQ, to Lejeune, March 11, 1919; Pershing to Lejeune, March 26, 1919; Harbord to Lejeune, June 26, 1919; Lejeune to Secretary of Navy, September 6, 1919; Secretary of War to Secretary of Navy, October 2, 1919 (Lejeune Papers, reel 11).

55. Summerall, Headquarters 1st Division, Camp Zachary Taylor, KY, to Lejeune, Quantico, March 15, 1920 (Lejeune Papers, reel 11). There is no record in the Lejeune Papers of Lejeune's response to this letter.

56. Charles P. Summerall manuscript, edited and annotated by Timothy K. Nenninger, *The Way of Duty, Honor, Country: The Memoir of General Charles Pelot Summerall* (Lexington: University Press of Kentucky, 2010), 155.

57. Mastriano, *Thunder in the Argonne,* 332.

58. Operations Report of the 2nd Division, West of the Meuse, November 1–11, 1918, by Maj. Gen. John A. Lejeune.

59. Lejeune, *Reminiscences,* 406–7.

60. Millett, *Semper Fidelis,* 317–18; Lejeune, *Reminiscences,* 388–95, 406–7; Leo J. Daugherty III, "To Fight Our Country's Battles: An Institutional History of the United States Marine Corps during the Interwar Era, 1919–1935," PhD diss., Ohio State University, 2001, 3–4; E. H. Ellis, "Liaison in the World War," *MCG* 5 (June 1920), 135–41.

7. WAR PLAN ORANGE: THE MARINE CORPS AT A CROSSROADS, 1919–1920

1. See "The Geopolitics of the Pacific War" in Miller, *War Plan Orange,* 19–30; Millett, *Semper Fidelis,* 320.

2. The Tentative War Plan for use against Japan as proposed by the Planning Division, Office of Naval Operations, October 1, 1919, was deemed as unrealistic and filed as "superseded, for information only," by the Marine Corps's Division of Operations and Training, file 1975-70-1515, RG 127, NARACP.

3. Braisted, *The United States Navy in the Pacific, 1897–1909,* 191–215.

4. Miller, *War Plan Orange,* 77–132.

5. This conference is discussed in more detail in chapter 8.

6. See CNO to MGC, Function of Marine Corps in War Plans, January 23, 1920, item P.D., 198-7, RG 80, NARAW; MGC to CNO, Expeditionary Forces, March 8, 1920, item 1975-70, RG 127, NARACP.

7. Heinl, *Soldiers of the Sea,* 294.

8. Orders to Lejeune, 1892–1929 (Lejeune Papers, reel 13).

9. *Hearings before Committee of Naval Affairs of the House of Representatives on Estimates Submitted by the Secretary of the Navy,* March 2, 1920, Sixty-Sixth Congress (Washington, DC: GPO, 1920), 2013.

10. The purpose of this committee hearing was for Congress to determine the postwar size of the Marine Corps.

11. Admiral George Dewey, President of Board, to Honorable Secretary of the Navy, No. G.B. 51, October 6, 1900; Secretary of the Navy John D. Long, 1st Endorsement, Navy Department, Defense of advanced base in China in case of war by Marines, October 23, 1900, RG 225, NARACP.

12. *Hearings before Committee of Naval Affairs of the House of Representatives,* March 2, 1920.

13. Ibid.

14. In previous wars, such as the Sino-Japanese War of 1894–95, and the Russo-Japanese War of 1904–5, Japan had struck first without declaring war. See "Tentative War Plan for Use Against Japan," prepared by the Planning Division, Office of Naval Operations, October 1919. In section 1975-70, 1515, RG 127, NARACP.

15. *Hearings before Committee of Naval Affairs of the House of Representatives,* March 2, 1920.

16. Ibid.

17. Ibid.

18. Ibid.; Millett, *Semper Fidelis,* 654. It is unclear what Barnett meant by the statement that "the plans have changed materially since the Pacific Fleet went out." Probably Barnett was justifiably concerned that the manpower of 75,101 Marines in 1918 had dropped significantly to 17,047 Marines in 1920.

19. Coontz, CNO, to MGC George Barnett, "Function of Marine Corps in War Plans," January 28, 1920, file P.D. 198-7, RG 80, NARAW.

20. Ibid.

21. Ibid.

22. MGC to CNO, "Expeditionary Force," March 8, 1920, in item 1975-70, RG 127, NARACP.

23. Ibid.

24. Ibid.

25. Merrill L. Bartlett, "George Barnett," in *Commandants,* 181.

26. Josephus Daniels, *The Wilson Era, Years of War and After, 1917–1923* (Chapel Hill: University of North Carolina Press, 1946), 155–56.

27. Bartlett, "George Barnett," in *Commandants,* 187–89. Barnett's version of his dismissal is in "Soldier and Sailor Too," chap. 29.

28. Schmidt, *Maverick Marine,* 115.

29. Ibid., 115.

30. Lejeune to the Commandant, n.d., probably around 1940 or 1941, handwritten copy, (Lejeune Papers, reel 6, pp. 21–22).

31. Ibid., 22.

32. Ibid., 23.

33. Ibid., 24.

34. Dr. Cary T. Grayson to Lejeune, June 1, 1932 (Lejeune Papers, reel 6).

35. Ibid.

36. Schmidt, *Maverick Marine,* 115; from Barnett, "Soldier and Sailor Too," chaps. 20–31.

37. Dr. Cary T. Grayson to Lejeune, June 1, 1932.

38. Schmidt, *Maverick Marine,* 119.

39. Information from aides to Barnett who later became generals, William A. Worton and Clifton B. Cates, in Marine Corps University, Archives Branch, Alfred M. Gray Research Center, Oral History Collection, Quantico, VA.

40. Bartlett, *Lejeune: A Marine's Life,* 140; Lelia Montague Barnett to Lejeune, 1932, in Marine Corps University, History Division, Reference Branch, Biographical Files, Quantico, VA.

41. Schmidt, *Maverick Marine,* 119.

8. REINVIGORATION OF THE MARINE CORPS

1. Lejeune letters to Admiral W. S. Benson (Ret.), July 6, 1920; Colonel Dion Williams, July 9, 1920; Honorable Thomas S. Butler, Chairman, Committee on Naval Affairs of the House of Representatives, July 9, 1920. (All in Lejeune Papers, reel 3.)

2. *Naval Appropriation Bill, Marine Corps, Committee on Naval Affairs, House of Representatives, on Vocational Schools, Quantico, Virginia, Friday, March 5, 1920,* (Washington, DC: GPO, 1920). Comments of Josephus Daniels to Committee on Naval Affairs as related in enclosed letter of Smedley D. Butler to Daniels, January 13, 1920.

3. R. H. Williams, "Those Controversial Boards, *MCG,* November 1982, 1–8.

4. Quote from Lejeune in "Extracts from Testimony of the Major General Commandant before the Subcommittee of House Committee on Appropriations on the Naval Appropriation Bill, 1922," January 21, 1921, *MCG* 9 (March 1921): 85–111.

5. Ibid.

6. Record of Weekly Conference of the MGC, Tuesday, March 15, 1921. (All records of conferences of the MGC are in file 1395-30, RG 127, NARACP.)

7. Ibid., Tuesday, February 1, March 1, 1921.

8. Ibid., Tuesday, February 15, 1921.

9. Ibid., Tuesday, March 1, 1921.

10. Ibid., March 15, September 16, 1921.

11. March 15, September 16, 1921.

12. Record of Quarterly Conference, Friday, July 7, 1922.

13. "Extracts from Testimony of the Major General Commandant before the Subcommittee of House Committee on Appropriations on the Naval Appropriation Bill, 1922," January 21, 1921.

14. Record of Quarterly Conference of MGC, Friday, April 7, 1922.

15. Lejeune, *Reminiscences,* 476.

16. Record of Quarterly Conference of MGC, April 7, 1922.

17. Lejeune, *Reminiscences,* 461–62.

18. Lejeune to Paymasters Department; Commandants and Managers; Marine Barracks, Guantanamo Bay, Cuba; Foreign and Expeditionary; CG, Second ABF, San Diego, California;

all COs, July 17, 1920, entry 18, General Correspondence (1913–32), items 1395-20, 151-5-3530, RG 127, NARACP.

19. USMC Headquarters, Second ABF, San Diego, California, to Commandant, December 4, 1920, RG 127, item 1515-35-30, NARACP.

20. Conference of Section Chiefs, December 30, 1924, RG 127, item 1395-20, NARACP.

21. Record of Quarterly Conference, Tuesday, April 5, 1921.

22. Record of Weekly Conference, Tuesday, August 17, 1920.

23. Lejeune, *Reminiscences,* 460.

24. Major Matthew Ritchie, "Effective Leaders: The Importance of Relationships," *MCG,* September 2015, 63–65.

25. Record of Weekly Conference, Tuesday, March 8, 1921.

26. Lejeune to Theodore Roosevelt Jr., Assistant Secretary of the Navy, December 16, 1921, entry 18, General Correspondence, 1913–32, RG 127, NARACP.

27. Record of Quarterly Conference, Friday, January 6, 1928.

28. Brig. Gen. Logan Feland, "The Division of Operations and Training, U.S. Marine Corps," *MCG* 7, no. 1 (March 1922).

29. Condit et al., *Brief History of Headquarters Marine Corps Staff Organization.*

30. Ibid.

31. Capt. E. F. C. Collier, "The Executive Staff," *MCG* 8, no. 4 (December 1923): 255.

32. Lejeune to Honorable Thomas S. Butler, House of Representatives, July 9, 1920; Lejeune to Admiral W. W. Benson, USN (Ret.), July 6, 1920 (Lejeune Papers, reel 12).

33. Correspondence from the Officer in Charge to the Commandant, "Outline for course in instruction for Fourth Officers' Training School, May 20, 1919, item 1520-30-120, RG 127, NARACP.

34. Lejeune, *Reminiscences,* 98, 187.

35. MGC Lejeune's correspondence to all officers of the Marine Corps, September 16, 1921, section 1395-30, RG 127, NARACP.

36. Record of Monthly Conference of the Commandant, Friday, April 4, 1924; CO Marine Barracks, Quantico to Commandant, October 13, 1922, sections 1520-30, 1395-30, RG 127, NARACP.

37. CG, Marine Barracks, Quantico, to Commandant, Headquarters, USMC, Washington, DC, October 13, 1922; John J. McKelvey, *Handbook on the Law of Evidence* (St. Paul, MN: West Publishing Co., 1907); Lewis Hockheimer, *Criminal Law* (Baltimore: H. B. Scimger, 1911); George B. Davis, *The American Journal of International Law,* vol. 2 (New York: Harper and Brothers, 1916).

38. CG, Marine Barracks, Quantico, to Commandant, Headquarters, USMC, Washington, DC, October 13, 1922.

39. Ibid.

40. The Commandant to all officers in the Marine Corps, Headquarters, USMC, September 16, 1921 (Report of the Commandant).

41. The Commandant to CG, Quantico, June 21, 1924, section 1520-30, RG 127, NARACP.

42. Ibid.

43. Lejeune, Headquarters, USMC, to Division of Operations and Training, Washington,

DC, Memorandum for General Logan Feland, July 17, 1924; Lejeune to Feland, September 8, 1924, section 1395-30, RG 127, NARACP.

44. Lejeune, Headquarters, USMC, Marine Corps Orders, no. 39, series 1921, August 22, 1921, section 1395-30, RG 127, NARACP.

45. Lejeune to the Officer in Charge, Southern Recruiting Division, 601 United Fruit Building, New Orleans, January 13, 1922, section 1515-35-30, RG 127, NARACP.

46. Lejeune, *Reminiscences,* 464.

47. Monthly Conference of Commandant, Friday, April 4, 1924.

48. Weekly Conference of Commandant, Tuesday, March 15, 1924.

49. Quartermaster to Commandant, Headquarters, USMC, Washington, DC, June 1, 1925, section 1515-35-30, RG 127, NARACP.

50. Lejeune to Headquarters, USMC, Washington, D., January 11, 1923, section 1515-35-30, RG 127, NARACP.

51. Colonel John C. Beaumont to Lejeune, Headquarters, Washington, DC, March 7, 1927, section 1515-35-30, RG 127, NARACP.

52. Monthly Conference of Commandant, Friday, April 4, 1924.

53. Holland M. Smith, General, US Marine Corps (Ret.), and Percy Finch, *Coral and Brass* (New York: Ace Books, 1948), 57. There is some doubt among historians that Smith even wrote this book.

54. Vandegrift, *Once a Marine,* 66.

55. Condit et al., *Brief History of Headquarters Marine Corps Staff Organization,* 15–16.

56. Colin Michael Colbourn, "Esprit de Marine Corps: The Making of the Modern Marine Corps through Public Relations, 1898–1929," MA thesis, University of Southern Mississippi, 2009, 3–10.

57. Ivan Musicant, *The Banana Wars: A History of United States Military Intervention in Latin America from the Spanish-American War to the Invasion of Panama* (New York: Macmillan, 1990), 227.

58. Ibid.

59. Ibid.

60. Ibid.

61. Native guardsmen trained and officered by Marine enlisted men.

62. Musicant, *The Banana Wars,* 221–27.

63. Mary A. Renda, *Taking Haiti: Military Occupation and the Culture of U.S. Imperialism* (Chapel Hill: University of North Carolina Press, 2001), 161.

64. Dana G. Munro, *The United States and the Caribbean Republics, 1921–1933* (Princeton, NJ: Princeton University Press, 1974), 73–74.

65. Record of Conference of MGC, July 27, 1920.

66. Lejeune, *Reminiscences,* 466.

67. Ibid.

68. Robert Lindsay, *This High Name: Public Relations and the U.S. Marine Corps* (Madison: University of Wisconsin Press, 1956), 40.

69. "When Uncle Sam's Marines Play at 'War,'" Weekly Gravure Pictorial, *Nashville Banner,* Sunday, May 25, 1924.

70. Lindsay, *This High Name,* 37.

71. Captain John H. Craige, "Publicity," *MCG,* June 1929, 1–5.

72. Headquarters Memorandum, September 21, 1925; Headquarters *Bulletin,* no. 23, August 15, 1927, in Lindsay, *This High Name,* 38, 40.

73. Record of Quarterly Conference of the MGC, Friday, January 14, 1927.

74. Lindsay, *This High Name,* 39.

75. Record of Quarterly Conference of the MGC, Friday, January 14, 1927.

76. Major J. C. Fegan, USMC, Post Athletic Officer, Marine Barracks, Quantico, VA, "Athletics as Publicity," *MCG,* March 1923, 1–5.

77. Record of Monthly Conference of the MGC, Friday, December 3, 1926.

78. Record of Monthly Conference, April 18, 1924.

79. Record of Quarterly Conference, Friday, February 6, 1925.

80. Vandegrift, *Once a Marine,* 65.

81. Edwin Denby, "Men of the Mail Guard," November 11, 1921, in *Report of the Secretary of the Navy,* 1922, 824.

82. Hubert Work, Acting Postmaster General, *Report of the MGC,* October 10, 1922.

83. Lejeune, "Mail Guard Duty," *Report of the MGC,* October 10, 1922.

84. *Report of the MGC,* September 30, 1927, 1188, 1192.

85. Ibid.

86. Lejeune to Brig. Gen. Smedley Butler, December 7, 1926, in Butler Papers, Marine Corps University, History Division, Reference Branch, Biographical Files, Quantico, VA.

87. Ibid.

88. Record of Weekly Conference of the MGC, September 16, 1921.

89. Ibid.

90. Record of the Weekly Conference of the MGC, September 16 and n.d., October 1921; *Report of the MGC,* appendix 1: year 1921.

91. Ibid.

92. Ibid.

93. Record of Quarterly Conference of the MGC, July 7, 1922.

94. Ibid.

95. Ibid.

96. *Report* of the MGC, October 10, 1922.

97. Record of Conference of the MGC, September 18, 1923.

98. Report of the Commandant, September 26, 1924.

99. Dion Williams, "The Fall Exercises of 1924 Marine Corps Expeditionary Force," *MCG* 10 (June 1925): 1–17; Record of Monthly Conference of the Commandant, May 28, 1924; Report of the Commandant, September 30, 1925.

100. Lt. Col. Charles Neimeyer, USMC (Ret.), "Combat in Nicaragua: Effective and Unique," *MCG* 92, no. 4 (April 2008): 71–76.

101. Some of the aircraft used by the corps in the Caribbean were Curtis JN-4 airplanes known as the "Model T Ford" of the air. It was a two-seat biplane built by the United States as a trainer for World War I. The airplane had a Curtis OX-5 engine, 90 horsepower, a top speed of 75 miles per hour, with a ceiling of 6,500 feet.

102. Vandegrift, *Once a Marine,* 59.

103. Lejeune, *Reminiscences,* 483.

104. Ibid.

105. Colbourn, "Esprit de Marine Corps," 3–10.

106. The De Havilland DH-4B aircraft was a two-seat, single-engine biplane built by Great Britain. The US version was an observation and bomber aircraft with a 400 horsepower Liberty V-12 water-cooled engine. It was often called the "Liberty Plane."

107. Lejeune, Report of the MGC in Report of the Secretary of the Navy, 1062, October 14, 1920.

108. Robert Sherrod, *History of Marine Corps Aviation in World War II* (Washington, DC: Combat Forces Press, 1952), 22–25. According to Major Ross Rowell, Army pilots had practiced dive bombing at Kelly Field in 1923. The Army pilots credited its invention to the British pilots in World War I.

109. A throwback to the old Marine Corps mission as colonial infantry.

110. In Spanish-speaking countries, this is a military leader who sets himself up as a dictator or chieftain.

111. Lejeune, *Reminiscences,* 449; Roark et al., *The American Promise,* 791, 833; Record of Quarterly Conference, MGC, Friday, October 7, 1927; Record of Monthly Conference, MGC, Friday, March 3, 1928.

112. Record of the Monthly Conference of the MGC, June 9, 1928; "Testimony of the Major General Commandant before the Senate Committee of Foreign Relations," *MCG,* March 1928, 2–6; Neimeyer, "Combat in Nicaragua," 73; Sherrod, *History of Marine Corps Aviation in World War II,* 24–25; Report of the MGC, September 30, 1927, 1193.

113. The Vought 02U-1 Corsair was a 1920s biplane scout-and-observation craft ordered by the USN in 1927. It had a 400-horsepower Pratt and Whitney engine.

114. Millett, *Semper Fidelis,* 249; Record of the Monthly Conference, MGC, June 9, 1928.

115. Record of the Monthly Conference of the MGC, Friday, March 3, 1928.

116. Record of the Quarterly Conference of the MGC, Friday, October 7, 1927.

117. Lejeune, "The United States Marine Corps—Present and Future," *USNIP* 54 (October 1928): 859–61.

118. Background information on the American intervention in Nicaragua from Heinl, *Soldiers of the Sea,* 150–73; Millett, *Semper Fidelis,* 236–63; Record of the Conferences of the MGC, October 7, 1927; January 6, March 3, June 9, October 7, 1928; January 4, 1929.

119. General L. C. Shepherd Jr., USMC (Ret.) to Joe A. Simon, March 21, 31, 1966.

120. Manley R. Irwin, "Lejeune and Denby: Forging a Marine Corps Doctrine," *MCG,* February 9, 2004, 1–9.

121. Ibid., 3.

122. Ibid., 2.

123. Thomas G. Roe, Ernest H. Giusti, John H. Johnstone, and Benis M. Frank, *A History of Marine Corps Roles and Missions: 1775–1962* (Washington, DC: Headquarters, USMC, 1962), 4–5.

124. Address delivered by Lejeune at Philadelphia on the 151st birthday of the corps, November 10, 1926 (Lejeune Papers, reel 10).

125. *Marine Corps Manual* (Washington, DC: GPO, 1949), paragraph 24451.

126. Themes and Meanings, Critical Context, www.enotes.com/topics/ what-price-glory.

127. There is no record of a letter to Stallings by Lejeune.

128. Stallings to Lejeune, January 12, 1926, Lejeune Papers, reel 3.

129. There is evidence that Lejeune gradually convinced some senators to question supporting promotion by seniority. See Donald F. Bittner's article "John H. Russell, 1934–1936," in *Commandants,* 248–49.

130. Report of the Commandant, 1896, 589–92; Report of the Commandant, 1892, 629; New Orleans *Times-Picayune,* December 31, 1919.

131. In the following paper, Lejeune appeared very knowledgeable on the systems of promotion in all the military services, especially the Navy and Marine Corps: Maj. John A. Lejeune to Brigadier General Commandant, USMC, Headquarters, Washington, DC, "Suggestions in Reference to Personnel for Marine Corps Committee," September 6, 1906 (Lejeune Papers, reel 3).

132. "Suggestions in Reference to Personnel for Marine Corps Committee," September 6, 1906 (Lejeune Papers, reel 3).

133. Secretary of the Navy to Lejeune, September 15, 1920: "Examination for promotion of officers of the Marine Corps, reconsideration of, decision on," file 25521-405:1, RG 80, NARAW; Lt. Col. Donald F. Bittner, USMCR (Ret.), "John H. Russell," in *Commandants,* 248–49.

134. Record of Conference, MGC, January 4, 1929.

135. Ibid., December 2, 1927.

136. Ibid., December 3, 1926.

137. Ibid., May 11, 1928.

138. Ibid.

139. Ibid.

140. Ibid., January 4, 1929.

141. Ibid., March 1, 1929.

9. THE DEVELOPMENT OF AMPHIBIOUS ASSAULT, 1920–1929

1. Cosmas and Shulimson, "The Culebra Maneuver," 121–32.

2. Ellis, "Naval Bases," 7–13.

3. Lejeune, "The Mobile Defense of Advanced Bases by the Marine Corps," lecture, 1–9.

4. See chapter 7.

5. Lejeune served as a mentor to Smedley Butler, who performed well as a CO and administrator, but preferred the mission of colonial infantry over amphibious operations. Unfortunately, because he was a talented and brave officer, Butler was often self-destructive and later ruined his own career in the Marine Corps.

6. Lejeune, MGC, to CNO: Marine Corps Strength Available to carry out Part VII, War Portfolio, July 17, 1920, in item P.D. 198-12, RG 80, NARAW.

7. Minutes of the Joint Board, Jarvis Butler, Secretary, March 22, July 15, 1920, "determination of functions of U.S. Marine Corps in peace and war," Serial 96, RG 225, NARACP, 19–20.

8. Ibid., 21–22.

9. Minutes of the Joint Board, August 5, 1920, 24–25.

10. The MGC to the CNO, January 21, 1922, RG 225, NARACP.

11. Report of the Commandant, October 14, 1920.

12. Ibid.

13. Ibid.

14. Ibid.

15. Ibid.

16. Record of Weekly Conference of the MGC, December 14, 1920; Lejeune, *Reminiscences,* 462–63.

17. Fuller to Lejeune: Advance Base Plans, August 1, 1921, and Lejeune to Fuller, Advance Base Plans, August 3, 1921, in files 2515-75, 1975-10, 1840-65, RG 127, NARACP.

18. Lejeune to CNO: Detail of an officer to advise and assist in preparation of war plans, October 20, 1921, file 2515-75, RG 127, NARACP.

19. Smith and Finch, *Coral and Brass,* 56–57.

20. Ibid., 51.

21. Ibid., 50.

22. Record of Weekly Conference of MGC, December 14, 1920.

23. Braisted, *The United States Navy in the Pacific, 1909–1922,* 567–689; Robert Gordon Kaufman, *Arms Control during the Pre-Nuclear Era: The United States and Naval Limitations between the Two World Wars* (New York: Columbia University Press, 1990), 43–72; Millett, Maslowski, and Feis, *For the Common Defense,* 342–43.

24. Lejeune, Memorandum for the General Board: "Future Policy for the Marine Corps as Influenced by the Conference on Limitation of Armaments," February 11, 1922, General Board Subject File, 1900–1947, GB 434, RG 80, NARAW.

25. Lejeune, Memorandum for the Secretary of the Navy: "Effect on Marine Corps of Limitation of Armaments Conference," January 23, 1922, files 1395-40, 1455-20, 2385-25, RG 127, NARACP.

26. Lejeune, Memorandum for the General Board: "Future Policy for the Marine Corps as Influenced by the Conference on Limitation of Armaments," February 11, 1922, General Board Subject File, 1900–1947, GB 434, RG 80, NARAW.

27. Philip Rosen, "The Treaty Navy, 1919–1937," in Kenneth Hagan, ed., *In Peace and War: Interpretation of American Naval History, 1775–1984* (Westport, CT: Greenwood Press, 1984), 224–25.

28. Lejeune to Brig. Gen. Harry Lee, December 4, 1930 (Lejeune Papers, reel 3).

29. Frank Gibney, ed., *Senso: The Japanese Remember the Pacific War* (Armonk, NY: East Gate, 1995), 3–22; Paul Kennedy, *The Rise and Fall of the Great Powers: Economic Change and Military Conflict from 1500 to 2000* (New York: Random House, 1987), 206–9.

30. Hans G. Von Lehmann, "Japanese Landing Operations in World War II," in Bartlett, ed., *Assault from the Sea,* 195; Millett, "Assault from the Sea," 2.

31. Braisted, *The United States Navy in the Pacific, 1897–1909,* 11–15, 191. Braisted, *The United States Navy in the Pacific, 1909–1922,* 138. Army War College, 1909–10, vols. 1 and 9, Orange-Blue Problem (Guam, Alaska); vol. 12, Orange-Blue Problem (Samoa), Army War College Curriculum Archives, Military History Institute (AWWCA).

32. Ballendorf and Bartlett, *Pete Ellis,* 108.

33. Admiral Albert Gleaves, CinC, US Asiatic Fleet, *USS Huron,* Flagship, Chefoo, China, September 8, 1920, to the Secretary of the Navy, file P.D. 121-7, RG 80, NARAW.

34. Ibid.

35. Ibid.

36. Ibid.

37. George C. Thorpe, CO, Pearl Harbor, T.H. to Lejeune, October 19, 1922. In records of USMC, Office of the Commandant, General Correspondence 1913–38, entry 18, item 1975-10 to 1975-50, RG 127, NARACP.

38. Ibid.

39. Ibid., November 4, 1922.

40. Ibid.

41. Secretary Edwin Denby to War Portfolio List, Navy Department, Office of Naval Operations, March 18, 1921, in file P.D. 127-7, Op-12D, RG 80, NARAW.

42. Ibid.

43. Because of the Anglo-Japanese Treaty of 1902, the Orange and Red War Plan was based on a possible war between the United States and both Japan and Great Britain. The Anglo-Japanese Alliance ended for all practical purposes after the Naval Disarmament Treaty in 1921–22. War Plan Orange was the United States–versus–Japan plan which originated in 1906. The Green War Plan was for Mexico, from 1900 to 1918, to protect the oil fields in Mexico. See Braisted, *The United States Navy in the Pacific 1909–1922,* 13–15.

44. While terminology for the ABF and the MEF were both used at this point, the purpose of both forces was offensive warfare.

45. Lejeune to CNO, War Portfolio, April 26, 1921, file 1975-70, RG 127, NARACP.

46. Brigadier General Logan Feland, "Memorandum for the Major General Commandant," July 23, 1921, file AO-41-cel., RG 127, NARACP.

47. War Plans Files, AO-41-cel, 1921, RG 127, NARACP.

48. Ibid.

49. Maj. E. H. Ellis, "Advanced Base Force Operations in Micronesia," Operation Plan 712 J, HAF 165.

50. Ballendorf and Bartlett, *Pete Ellis,* 118–19; Millett, Maslowski, and Feis, *For the Common Defense,* 353–54.

51. A "walking barrage" required close coordination between the infantry and artillery. For amphibious landings, ships' guns would be necessary for close support. For many years—even during World War II—the fleet's cannon were unsuited for this role. Successful naval barrages did not occur until the supporting ships went from saturation shelling of an area to pinpoint shelling of actual enemy defensive fortifications.

52. Logan Feland, Memorandum for the Commandant, July 23, 1921.

53. Isley and Crowl, *The U.S. Marines and Amphibious War,* 4.

54. The "Cautionary Strategy" in Miller, *War Plan Orange,* 100–121.

55. Lejeune, MGC, to CNO: Lighters for Landing Expeditionary Force, 7th Endorsement, September 23, 1922, file 120-11, RG 80, NARAW.

56. Gallipoli was the Allied amphibious disaster in the Dardanelles in 1915 during World War I.

57. See Alexander Kiralfy, "Sea Power in the Eastern War," *Brassey's Naval Annual,* 1942, 150–60; and Liddel Hart, *The Defense of Britain* (New York: Random House, 1939), 130.

58. Clifford, *Progress and Purpose,* 27.

59. Lejeune to CNO: "Lectures," December 16, 1921, file 1975-70, RG 127, NARACP.

60. Robert H. Dunlap, "Lessons for Marines from the Gallipoli Campaign," *MCG,* September 1921, 1–6.

61. C. E. Callwell, *The Dardanelles* (Uckfield, East Sussex, UK: Naval and Military Press, 2005).

62. T. A. Gibson, "Eyeless in Byzantium," 83–96, in Bartlett, ed., *Assault from the Sea,* 142–53.

63. Michael J. Mortlock, *The Landings at Suvla Bay, 1915: Analysis of British Failure during the Gallipoli Campaign* (Jefferson, NC: McFarland & Co., 2007), 155, 159.

64. Record of Conference of MGC, September 28, 1923.

65. Ibid.

66. Ben Fuller to Lejeune: "Advanced Base Plans," Naval War College, Newport, RI, August 1, 1921; Lejeune to Fuller, August 3, 1921, RG 127, Items 2515-75, 1975-10, 1840-65, NARACP.

67. Record of Quarterly Conference of Commandant, April 7, 1922.

68. Captain Ralph Earle, USN, Control Force, US Atlantic Fleet, *USS Florida,* Flagship, to Lejeune, December 2, 1921; Lejeune to Earle, December 7, 1921, file 1975-35, RG 127, NARACP.

69. Captain Ralph Earle, USN, Control Force, US Atlantic Fleet, *USS Florida,* Flagship, to Lejeune, December 2, 1921; Lejeune to Earle, December 7, 1921, file 1975-35, RG 127, NARACP.

70. Cutts to Lejeune: "Report of Advanced Base Force operating with Control Force, U.S. Atlantic Fleet," January 9, 1922, to April 25, 1922, at Guantanamo Bay, Cuba, and Culebra, PR, July 20, 1922, in entry 39B, RG 127, NARACP. Naval ships' boats were wooden boats that came to a point in the front and rear. Generally motorized, the Navy had boats such as whaleboats, motor launches, rescue boats, utility boats, lifeboats, and so forth.

71. Report of the Commandant, October 10, 1922, 822.

72. Record of Conference of Commandant, September 28, 1923.

73. Ibid.

74. Dion Williams, "The Winter Maneuvers of 1924," *MCG,* March 1924, 1–10.

75. Eli K. Cole, "Preliminary Estimate of the Situation, Fleet Problem No. 3, February 15, 1924," entry 39B, Division of Plans and Policies, General Correspondence, 1921–43, RG 127, NARACP.

76. Basic Plan, Winter Maneuvers, Marine Corps Expeditionary Force, US Fleet Headquarters, Marine Barracks, Quantico, VA, December 15, 1923, Records of Training Exercises and Maneuver, 1914–40, RG 127, NARACP.

77. War Plans Files, AO-41-cel, 1921, RG 127, NARACP.

78. War Portfolio: US Marine Corps, July 23, 1921, included in HAF.

79. Notes Relating to Expeditionary Forces, at a Conference on Board the Flagship at Culebra, PR, by the CinC, US Atlantic Fleet, to discuss the Winter Maneuvers of 1924, Problem 4, Division of Plans and Policies, General Correspondence, 1921–43, RG 127, NARACP

80. Report and Comments on Landing Operations, Blue Forces, Culebra, Headquarters

USMC Expeditionary Force, Culebra, PR, February 5, 1924, entry 39 B, Division of Plans and Policies, General Correspondence, 1921–43, RG 127, NARACP.

81. Ibid.

82. Notes Relating to Expeditionary Forces, at a Conference on Board the Flagship at Culebra, PR, by the CinC, US Atlantic Fleet, to discuss the Winter Maneuvers of 1924, Problem 4, Division of Plans and Policies, General Correspondence, 1921–43, RG 127, NARACP.

83. Ibid.

84. Notes by the Observer, Summary of the Attack and Defense of Culebra with Observations and Conclusions, at a Conference Held on Board the Flagship at Culebra, PR, in Notes by the CinC, US Atlantic Fleet, to Discuss the Winter Maneuvers of 1924, Problem No. 4, RG 124, NARACP.

85. Ibid.

86. Report and Comments on Landing Operations, Blue Forces, Culebra, Headquarters USMC Expeditionary Force, Culebra, PR, February 5, 1924, entry 39 B, Division of Plans and Policies, General Correspondence, 1921–43, RG 127, NARACP.

87. Notes by the Observer, Summary of the Attack and Defense of Culebra with Observations and Conclusions, at a Conference Held on Board the Flagship at Culebra, PR, in Notes by the CinC, US Atlantic Fleet, to Discuss the Winter Maneuvers of 1924, Problem No. 4, RG 124, NARACP.

88. Report of the Commandant, 1924, 668.

89. Record of Monthly Conference, of MGC, Tuesday, December 2, 1924.

90. Dion Williams to Logan Feland, "Discontinue Marine Corps Schools for Maneuvers on West Coast, 1925," Headquarters, USMC, Division of Operations and Training, January 24, 1925, entry 39B, box 1, Records of Training Exercises and Maneuvers, 1914–40, RG 127, NARACP.

91. Record of Monthly Conference of MGC, December 2, 1924.

92. CinC, US Fleet to Commandant: Landing Places, Oahu, Hawaii, October 10, 1924, Enclosures (A) Topographic Map of Oahu, Hawaii, (B) Commander F. M. Gygax's report of landing places of Oahu, October, 1919, file 16-Bt-(0), RG 127, NARACP.

93. Dion Williams, "Blue Marine Corps Expeditionary Force," Joint Army and Navy Exercises, 1925, *MCG*, September 1925, 1–7; Leo J. Daugherty III, "Away All Boats: The Army-Navy Maneuvers of 1925," *Joint Force Quarterly* (*JFQ*), Autumn–Winter 1998–99: 107–13.

94. Secret Field Order No. 2, Blue Marine Corps Expeditionary Force, February 27, 1925, by command of Maj. Gen. Neville, written by Col. R. H. Dunlap, Chief of Staff (elaborate plan beforehand). In box 1, Records of Training Exercises and Maneuvers, 1914–40, RG 127, NARACP).

95. Major General Neville to Colonel R. H. Dunlap, Chief of Staff, Secret, Field Orders No. 2, Blue Marine Corps Expeditionary Force, Box 1, Records of Training Exercises and Maneuvers, 1914–40, RG 127, NARACP.

96. Williams, "Blue Marine Expeditionary Force," 1–7.

97. Williams in "Blue Marine Expeditionary Force" mentions that the Blue forces captured only Molokai as an advanced air base. Maj. Gen. J. L. Hines, Army chief of staff, in his article notes that Lanai was also captured. See Hines, "Grand Joint Army and Navy Exercise No. 3,"

lecture delivered at the AWC, Washington Barracks, DC, June 26, 1925, entry 39B, RG 127, NARACP.

98. Hines, "Grand Joint Army and Exercise No. 3," 2.

99. Ibid., 4. Hines and Admiral Robert E. Coontz were chief umpires at the maneuver.

100. Kenneth W. Condit and Edwin T. Turnbladh, *Hold High the Torch: A History of the 4th Marines* (Washington, DC: Historical Branch, USMC, 1960), 108–9.

101. Hines, "Grand Joint Army and Navy Exercise No. 3," 3.

102. Williams, "Blue Marine Corps Expeditionary Force," 7.

103. Ibid., 1–7; Daugherty, "Away All Boats," 107–13.

104. Hines, "Grand Joint Army and Navy Exercise No. 3," 4–5.

105. Ibid., 6.

106. Ibid., 11.

107. Report of the Commandant, 1925, 1223–24.

108. Colonel R. H. Dunlap, "Recommendations Based on Report of Critique on Joint Army and Navy Problem No. 3, by Officers of Marine Corps Schools," June 1 to 5, 1925, Division of Plans and Policies, War Plans Section, War Plans, 1915–46, RG 127, NARACP.

109. Monthly Conference of the MGC, November 4, 1927.

110. Ibid.

111. Dwight F. Davis, Secretary of War, to Secretary of the Navy: Detail of Infantry officers as students at the MCS, November 12, 1925, copy A.C. 210-65, MCS, RG 127, NARACP.

112. The Commandant to All Officers of the Marine Corps: "Policy and Rationale for Marine Corps' Officers Education," September 16, 1921, files 1520-30-5-70, AO-53-rac, RG 127, NARACP.

113. The CO, MCS, via the CG, Marine Barracks, Quantico, to the Commandant, December 10, 16, 1925, items 1520-30-100, RG 127, NARACP; 1st Endorsement from the CG, Marine Barracks, Quantico, to the Commandant, December 18, 1925, items 1520-30-100, RG 127, NARACP; Memorandum for the Commandant by the Director of Operations and Training, January 9, 1926, item 1520-30-100, RG 127, NARACP.

114. MGC to CO, MCS, Commanding General, MCS, files 1520-30-100, AD-37-kk, RG 127, NARACP.

115. Lejeune Papers, reel 11.

116. The Commandant to the CO, MCS, March 3, 1926, item 1520-30-100, RG 127, NARACP.

117. Ibid.

118. Commandant to Chief of the Bureau of Navigation via the CNO: Detail of Naval Officer on Staff of MCS, March 9, 1926, item 1945-35-35, 1520-30-100, RG 127, NARACP.

119. Clifford, *Progress and Purpose,* 36–38.

120. Lejeune to CNO: "Marine Corps strength available to carry out GREEN PLAN for present conditions," June 23, 1927, item SC 198-12, RG 80, NARAW.

121. Lejeune to the Navy Department: "Comments on the Marine Expeditionary Force in connection with the U.S. Fleet Maneuvers—Spring 1925," July 23, 1924, file SC 162-78:12, RG 80, NARAW.

122. Ibid.

123. While Lejeune preferred the term "MEF" over "ABF," he used both terms in his memorandum to Eberle in order for the Navy to understand that he was speaking about the corps's landing force. Senior naval officers at this time were obviously not that interested in a close relationship with the Marine Corps.

124. Lejeune to the CNO: "Recommends manner of designating Marine Corps units serving with the Fleet," March 22, 1926, SC 198-9:1, RG 80, NARAW.

125. Admiral E. W. Eberle to MGC Lejeune: "Recommends manner of designating Marine Corps units serving with the Fleet," SC 198-9:1, RG 80, NARAW.

126. For Report of Special Board of Policy by Lejeune, January 5, 1925, "Advanced Bases Including Marine Expeditionary Force for Shore Operations Essential to the Prosecution of the Naval Campaign," in Lejeune File at GRC.

127. Ibid.

128. Ibid.

129. Admiral E. W. Eberle, Senior Member, Joint Board, to the Navy Secretary: Revision of pamphlet entitled *Joint Army and Navy Action in Coast Defense,* February 12, 1925, SC Number 233-13, Serial 240, in RG 225, NARACP.

130. Secretary of the Navy to US CNO, CinC, US Fleet, Joint Board, Navy War College, Bureau Chiefs, the MGC, and others, February 19, 1925, S.C. 233-13, RG 225, NARACP.

131. Lejeune to the Navy Secretary: Revision of Pamphlet entitled *Joint Army and Navy Action in Coast Defense,* August 4, 1925, file SC 233-13, RG 225, NARACP.

132. Ibid.

133. *Joint Action of the Army and the Navy,* prepared by Joint Board (Washington, DC: GPO, 1927), 3, 12.

134. Ibid.

135. Lejeune, "The United States Marine Corps," talk delivered at NWC, December 14, 1923, in Lejeune file, GRC. Also printed in the *MCG* 8 (December 1923): 243–54.

136. Lejeune, "The United States Marine Corps," *Our Navy* 18, no. 8 (1924), copy in Lejeune Papers, reel 10.

137. Lejeune, "The Marine Corps," talk to students at the NWC, April 1925, partial manuscript in Lejeune Papers at GRC.

138. Ibid.

139. Lejeune, "The United States Marine Corps," *USNIP,* October 1925, 1867.

140. Ibid.

141. Lejeune, "The Marine Corps, 1926," *USNIP,* October 1926, 1961–62.

142. Lejeune, "The United States Marine Corps, Present and Future," *USNIP* 54 (October 1928): 860–61.

143. Ibid.

144. Annual Report of the General Board, September 24, 1920, RG 80, NARAW.

145. Record of Conference of MGC, January 4, 1929.

146. Naval ships' boats were not designed to rapidly land Marines in an assault against a fortified defense.

147. Richard Cutts to Lejeune, "Report of Expedition to Guantanamo and Culebra, operating with Control Force, US Atlantic Fleet, January 9, 1922 to April 25, 1922," July 20, 1922, 1–48, entry 39B, RG 127, NARACP.

148. Commandant to CNO: "Lighters for landing Expeditionary Force: Transport of artillery and motor transport with expeditionary detachments, 7th Endorsement," September 23, 1922, file 120-11, RG 80, NARAW.

149. Ibid.

150. Ibid.

151. Ibid.

152. Director of War Plans, C. S. Williams, to CNO (Material): Lighters for Landing Expeditionary Force, October 10, 1922, file 120-11, RG 80, NARAW.

153. Bureau of Construction and Repair to CNO, via Commandant, 9th Endorsement, October 25, 1922, file 120-11, RG 80, NARAW.

154. MGC to CNO, 10th Endorsement: Lighters for landing Expeditionary Force—Transport of Artillery and motor transport with expeditionary detachments, November 4, 1922, file 120-11, RG 80, NARAW.

155. Secretary of the Navy to the Bureau of Construction and Repair and to the Chief of Bureau of Engineering, 7th Endorsement, October 11, 1923, in file 120-11, RG 80, NARAW.

156. Eli K. Cole, Report and Comments on Landing Operations, Blue Forces, Culebra, Headquarters USMC Expeditionary Force, Culebra, Puerto Rico, February 5, 1924, entry 39B, Division of Plans and Policies, General Correspondence, 1921–43, RG 127, NARACP.

157. Lejeune, Report of the MGC, September 26, 1924.

158. Christie is best known for developing the suspension system used primarily in Soviet tanks during World War II, especially the Russian BT and T-34.

159. Frederick L. Wieseman, "Proper Design and Employment of a Marine Corps Tank for Landing Operations," lecture at MCS, March 1949, also cited in Isley and Crowl, *The U.S. Marines and Amphibious War,* 31.

160. Clifford, *Progress and Purpose,* 33.

161. Victor H. Krulak, *First to Fight: An Inside View of the U.S. Marine Corps* (Annapolis MD: NIP, 1984), 89.

162. Ibid.

163. Memorandum for the Chief Contractor: "Motor barges for landing troops and artillery," July 28, 1908, RG 80, NARAW.

164. Chief of the Bureau of Construction and Repair to Secretary of the Navy, MGC, CNO: "Lighters for landing expeditionary forces," May 23, 1925, file 120-11, RG 80, NARAW; MGC to Secretary of the Navy: "Lighters for landing expeditionary forces," July 7, 1924, file 120-11, RG 80, NARAW.

165. Chief of the Bureau of Construction and Repair to Secretary of the Navy, Bureau of Engineering, MGC, CNO, May 23, 1925: "Lighters for landing expeditionary forces," file 120-11, RG 80, NARAW.

166. MGC to Secretary of the Navy via CNO: "Lighters for landing expeditionary forces," June 23, 1925, file SC 120-11, RG 80, NARAW.

167. W. H. Standley, Director of War Plans Division, to CNO, July 15, 1925, file 120-11, RG 80, NARAW.

168. Harry W. Hill, Lieutenant Commander, USN, Naval Board, "Report on 50-foot Lighter for Landing Artillery," July 9, 1926; Reports by Alexander Galt, Alfred A. Cunningham, and Joseph Nettekoven of Tenth Regiment, Marine Barracks, Quantico to Commandant, July 21,

1926, RG 127, NARACP; Marine Board, "Report on 50-foot Motor Lighter and 50-foot Artillery Lighter," entry 39D, Division of Plans and Policies, War Plans Section, 1915–46, RG 127, NARACP.

169. MGC to Bureau of Construction and Repair, August 18, 1926, Report of Troop and Artillery Lighters, file 2500-17, RG 127, NARACP.

170. MGC to CNO: Marine Corps strength available to carry out GREEN PLAN for present conditions, June 23, 1927, item SC 198-12, RG 80, NARAW.

171. Louis McCarty Little, Director of Operations and Training: Disposition of Beetle Boats, September 19, 1928, to Lejeune, file 1994, RG 127, NARACP.

172. Little to Lejeune, November 21, 1928, file 2455-135-5, RG 127, NARAW.

173. MGC to CNO, November 27, 1928: Trials of 40-foot Motor Lighter No. 9700 for Expeditionary Forces, file 2455-135-5, RG 127, NARACP.

174. Lecture delivered by Major S. L. Howard to the MCS, Quantico, May 3, 1929, file 39D, RG 127, NARACP.

175. Photos of the "A" boat landing Marines taken in June and July 1931 are located in box 387, entry 18, number 2455-130-60, landing lighters, 1923–32, three files, RG 127, NARACP. A picture taken in 1935 at Quantico published in Clifford, *Progress and Purpose,* 52, shows Marines using the forty-five-foot artillery lighter to unload a five-ton tractor. The motor troop lighter "A" is in the background.

10. LEJEUNE'S LEGACY: THE MARINE CORPS OF THE 1930S

1. In a strategy research project completed as partial fulfillment for the requirements of the master of strategic studies degree, in 2008, Lt. Col. James T. Dillon, USMC, a student at the AWC, correctly noted that Lejeune possessed the strategic-leadership competencies as found in the AWC's *Strategic Leadership Primer.* (Dillon, "John A. Lejeune, the Marine Corps' Greatest Strategic Leader," US AWC, Carlisle Barracks, PA.)

2. Captain Michael Junge, USN, "Semper Huh?" *USNIP,* February 2013, 27–28. Junge is impressed by the Marine Corps's sense of identity: "Every Marine is a rifleman." Junge hopes to define for the Navy an equally impressive sense of identity.

3. Lejeune, *Reminiscences,* 115–16.

4. Record of Conference of MGC, Tuesday, August 17, 1920; Friday, July 7, 1922, and Friday, May 4, 1927.

5. Lindsay, *This High Name,* 90.

6. Lejeune, *Reminiscences,* 470–71.

7. Colonel R. S. Keyser, Headquarters USMC, to Major General John A. Lejeune, USMC (Ret.), Superintendent, VMI, Lexington, VA, February 15, 1935 (Lejeune Papers, reel 6).

8. Lejeune, *Reminiscences,* 484–85.

9. Lejeune to Senator Hugo L. Black, March 1, 1935 (Lejeune Papers, reel 6).

10. Merrill L. Bartlett, "John A. Lejeune, 1920–1929," in *Commandants,* 219.

11. John R. M. Wilson, "The Quaker and the Sword: Herbert Hoover's Relations with the Military," *Journal of Military History,* April 1974, 41.

12. Wilson, "The Quaker and the Sword," 43. The Kellogg-Briand Pact was developed in

1928 by American Secretary of State Frank Kellogg and French Foreign Minister Aristide Briand to promote world peace.

13. Wilson, "The Quaker and the Sword," 42.

14. Lejeune to Colonel J. C. Breckinridge, American Legation Guard, Peiping, China, June 27, 1930 (Lejeune Papers, reel 3).

15. Lejeune to Breckinridge, December 2, 1930 (Lejeune Papers, reel 3).

16. Lejeune to Brig. Gen. Harry Lee, Marine Barracks, Parris Island, SC, December 4, 1930 (Lejeune Papers, reel 3).

17. Ibid.

18. Ibid.

19. Interview with Col. James Glennon, USMC (Ret.), January 23, 2007.

20. Wendell Neville to Lejeune, February 25, 1930 (Lejeune Papers, reel 3).

21. Lejeune to S. D. Butler, Marine Barracks, Quantico, VA, April 21, 1930 (Lejeune Papers, reel 3).

22. Lejeune to Breckinridge, June 27, 1930 (Lejeune Papers, reel 3).

23. Neville to Lejeune, February 25, 1930 (Lejeune Papers, reel 3).

24. Memo 2753, Director, Division of Operations and Training, to Commandant, item AO-155-cel, February 1, 1930, item 1520-30-100, RG 127, NARACP.

25. D. C. McDougal, Director, Division of Operations and Training, to Commandant, October 19, 1931, in file 1520-30-100, RG 127, NARACP.

26. MGC to Commandant, MCS, February 5, 1930, items 1520-30-100 and 1530-30-100, RG 127, NARACP.

27. Brig. Gen. Refus H. Lane, Adjutant and Inspector, USMC, to Lejeune, May 24, 1932 (Lejeune Papers, reel 5).

28. Lejeune to Fuller, September 12, 1930 (Lejeune Papers, reel 3).

29. Lejeune to Breckinridge (Lejeune Papers, reel 3).

30. Lejeune to Harry Lee, Marine Barracks, Parris Island, SC, Oct 17, 1930 (Lejeune Papers, reel 3).

31. John R. M. Wilson, *Herbert Hoover and the Armed Forces: A Study of Presidential Attitudes and Policy* (New York: Garland, 1993), 78.

32. Fuller to Lejeune, September 18, 1930, and Lejeune to Fuller, October 1, 1930 (Lejeune Papers, reel 3).

33. Quote from Bartlett, "Ben H. Fuller," in *Commandants,* 228–29, from *Hearings before the House Naval Affairs Committee for FY 32,* 71st Congress, 3rd session, February 9, 1931.

34. E. A. Ostermann, Headquarters, to Lejeune, January 16, 1930; Lejeune to Ostermann, January 18, 1930 (Lejeune Papers, reel 3).

35. Brig. Gen. Refus H. Lane, Headquarters, to Lejeune, February 2, 1932 (Lejeune Papers, reel 5).

36. Ibid.

37. Lejeune to Honorable Burton C. French, House of Representatives, May 19, 1932 (Lejeune Papers, reel 5).

38. Lejeune to Lane, May 10, 1932 (Lejeune Papers, reel 5).

39. Ibid.

40. Lane to Lejeune, May 24, 1932 (Lejeune Papers, reel 5).

41. Brig. Gen. Dunlap, a close friend of Lejeune and a strong advocate of amphibious assault, was a rising star in the Marine Corps. Tragically he lost his life in an accident, May 19, 1931.

42. Lejeune to Senator Hale, May 20, 1932; Lejeune to Representative French, May 27, 1932; Lejeune to Lane, June 10, 1932 (all in Lejeune Papers, reels 5 and 6).

43. Senator Hale, Chairman, Committee on Naval Affairs, to Lejeune, May 23, 1932 (Lejeune Papers, reel 5).

44. French to Lejeune, June 1, 1932 (Lejeune Papers, reel 6).

45. Lejeune to Fuller, July 6, 1932 (Lejeune Papers, reel 6).

46. Wilson, *Herbert Hoover and the Armed Forces,* 76. Wilson's sources are "Memo for Chief of Staff," n.d., box 29, George Simonds Papers, Library of Congress; War Plans Division Memo, "Amalgamation of the Marine Corps with the Army," May 8, 1931, box 29, Simonds Papers, Library of Congress.

47. Information from *Lexington Gazette,* Lexington, VA, September 21, 1932, and Lejeune letters to Willie O. Bunch, November 13, 1934; Bryan D. Kaser, November 16, 1933; Grant Shepherd, February 3, 1934; H. R. Drummond, May 4, 1934; and Logan Feland, July 10, 1935 (Lejeune Papers, reel 6).

48. William Kamman, *A Search for Stability: United States Diplomacy toward Nicaragua, 1925–1933* (Notre Dame, IN: University of Notre Dame Press, 1968), 217–36.

49. Roark et al., *The American Promise,* 910.

50. Clifford, *Progress and Purpose,* 43.

51. Fuller to Berkeley, January 13, 1931, item 1520-30-100, RG 127, NARACP.

52. Dunlap to Fuller, January 19, 1931, item 1520-20-100, RG 127, NARACP.

53. Clifford, *Progress and Purpose,* 43.

54. Price to Berkeley, April 17, 1931, Gray Center, Quantico, VA.

55. Fuller to Berkeley, May 13, 1931, item 1520-20-100, RG 127, NARACP.

56. School Memorandum, by Command of Brig. Gen. Berkeley: R. H. Jeschke, Adjutant-Secretary, June 3, 1931, item 152-20-100, RG 127, NARACP.

57. Berkeley to Fuller, September 30, 1931.

58. Ibid., October 5, 1931.

59. Fuller to Berkeley, "Text for Landing Operations," October 20, 1931, item 1520-30-100, RG 127, NARACP.

60. Ibid.

61. Randolph Carter Berkeley, Arlington National Cemetery, www.arlingtoncemetery.net/berkeley.htm; Anthony A. Frances, *History of Marine Corps Schools* (Quantico, VA: Marine Corps Historical Library, 1945), 109.

62. Frances, *History of Marine Corps Schools,* 109.

63. James C. Breckinridge, "Some Thoughts on Service Schools," *MCG* December 1929, 230–34.

64. Richard Scott Moore, "The Legacy of J. C. Breckinridge," *MCG,* May 1984, 60–64.

65. Pedro del Valle, "Ship to Shore in Amphibious Warfare," *MCG,* February 1932, 11–18.

66. Pedro del Valle, "Boats in the Landing Attack," *MCG,* May 1932, 30–35.

67. Walter C. Ansel, "Naval Gun Fire in Support of a Landing," *MCG,* May 1932, 23–28.

68. Richard S. Moore, "Ideas and direction: Building amphibious doctrine," *MCG,* November 1982, 54.

69. Frances, *History of Marine Corps Schools,* 41.

70. E. B. Miller, "The Marine Corps: Its Mission, Organization, and Limitations," *MCG,* November 1932, 10–24.

71. E. B. Miller, "A Naval Expedition Involving the Landing of a Marine Expeditionary Force," *MCG,* February 1933, 33–36.

72. E. B. Miller, "Naval Support to the Landing of a Marine Expeditionary Force," *MCG,* May 1933, 32–46.

73. Daugherty, *Pioneers of Amphibious Warfare,* 237. Miller's work is located in HAF 40.

74. Clifford, *Progress and Purpose,* 44.

75. Frances, *History of Marine Corps Schools,* 44; Clifford, *Progress and Purpose,* 45; John H. Russell, "The Birth of the Fleet Marine Force," *USNIP* 72 (January 1946): 79.

76. Noble to Director, Marine Corps History (Washington, DC: Historical Division, Headquarters, US Marine Corps, April 3, 1971), cited in Clifford, *Progress and Purpose,* 46–47.

77. For a more complete story of the development of the manual, see Clifford, *Progress and Purpose,* 43–48; and, Frances, *History of Marine Corps Schools,* 44–50.

78. See chapter 9.

79. Moore, "Ideas and direction," 54–55.

80. In 1941 the Joint Army and Navy Board became the Joint Chiefs of Staff.

81. *Joint Action of the Army and the Navy,* 1927.

82. The following discussion on the landing manual is mostly based on the 1938 edition: Office of Naval Operations, Division of Fleet Training, *Landing Operations Doctrine, United States Navy, 1938* (*Fleet Training Publication* 167, Washington, DC: GPO, 1938), www.ibiblio.org/hyperwar/USN/ref/Amphibious/index.html.

83. Office of Naval Operations, *Landing Operations Doctrine, 1938,* 47.

84. Ibid., 67.

85. Keyser, Headquarters, USMC, to Lejeune, February 23, 1935 (Lejeune Papers, reel 6).

86. See Lejeune's comments about the use of automatic weapons against enemy aircraft strafing the landing boats in Monthly Conference, MGC, November 4, 1927. Similar information is included in Office of Naval Operations, *Landing Operations Doctrine, 1938,* 96.

87. See Office of Naval Operations, *Landing Operations Doctrine, 1938,* 174–75; Lejeune to CNO: Lighters for landing Expeditionary Forces, September 23, 1922, file 120-11, RG 80, NARAW.

88. The Higgins Boats and Amphibious Tractors carried from ten to twenty Marines.

89. See Office of Naval Operations, *Landing Operations Doctrine, 1938,* 82; Lejeune to Chief of Bureau of Construction and Repair, Navy Department, Third Endorsement, August 18, 1926, Report of Troop and Artillery Lighters, file 2500-17, RG 127, NARACP.

90. Office of Naval Operations, *Landing Operations Doctrine, 1938,* 180–83.

91. Heinl, *Soldiers of the Sea,* 302.

92. Lejeune to the Navy Department: "Comments on the Marine Expeditionary Force in

connection with the U.S. Fleet Maneuvers—Spring 1925," July 23, 1924, file SC 162-78:12, RG 80, NARAW; Lejeune to the CNO: "Recommends manner of designating Marine Corps units serving with the Fleet," March 22, 1926, SC 198-9:1, RG 80, NARAW.

93. Thomas Holcomb to Lejeune, November 7, 1933 (Lejeune Papers, reel 6).

94. Lejeune to Holcomb, November 10, 1933 (Lejeune Papers, reel 6).

95. Millett, *Semper Fidelis,* 335.

96. Ibid.

97. Proceedings of the Joint Board, February 9, 18, 1928, Memorandum for the Army Members, Joint Planning Committee, War Plan Orange, May 18, 1928; Memorandum for Admiral Hughes, June 12, 1928, item OP-12-CD, RG 225, NARACP.

98. Lejeune to Colonel Dion Williams, July 9, 1920 (Lejeune Papers, reel 12).

99. Leo J. Daugherty III, "John H. Russell, Jr.," in *Pioneers of Amphibious Warfare,* 243–67.

100. Congress passed the Marine Corps Personnel Act of 1934 (Public Law 263) that stipulated promotion by selection (merit) instead of by seniority.

101. Bittner, "John H. Russell," in *Commandants,* 246; personnel bill included in Report of the Secretary of the Navy, 1934, and Report of the Commandant, 1934.

102. Bittner, "John H. Russell," in *Commandants,* 246.

103. Vandegrift, *Once a Marine,* 79.

104. Bittner, "John H. Russell," in *Commandants,* 247.

105. Ibid.

106. Ibid., 248.

107. Ibid.

108. Schmidt, *Maverick Marine,* 123.

109. Millett, *Semper Fidelis,* 325.

110. Schmidt, *Maverick Marine,* 214.

111. Williams, "Those Controversial Boards," 98.

112. Schmidt, *Maverick Marine,* 213–14.

113. Butler to Lejeune, Western Union telegram, 18 Feb 1935 (Lejeune Papers, reel 6).

114. Schmidt, *Maverick Marine,* 213–14.

115. Telegram from Senator Park Trammell to Lejeune, February 13, 1935 (Lejeune Papers, reel 6).

116. Lejeune to Trammell, February 14, 1935 (Lejeune Papers, reel 6).

117. Lejeune to Black, March 1, 1935 (Lejeune Papers, reel 6).

118. Musicant, *The Banana Wars,* 157–235; Lejeune, *Reminiscences,* 220–25, 466–69; Millett, *Semper Fidelis,* 178–211; Renda, *Taking Haiti,* 158–63. There were some indiscriminate killings of innocent civilians by Marines, and a few guilty Marines were not punished.

119. Lejeune to Trammell, February 14, 1935 (Lejeune Papers, reel 6).

120. Ibid.

121. Keyser to Lejeune, February 15, 1935 (Lejeune Papers, reel 6).

122. Ibid., February 23, 1935 (Lejeune Papers, reel 6).

123. Senator Hugo Black to Lejeune, February 23, 26, 1935 (Lejeune Papers, reel 6).

124. Lejeune to Black, February 25, 25, March 1, 1935 (Lejeune Papers, reel 6).

125. Lejeune to Black, March 1, 1935 (Lejeune Papers, reel 6).

126. Lejeune to Senator Trammell, February 14, 1935 (Lejeune Papers, reel 6).

127. Ibid.

128. Ibid.

129. Thomas Holcomb to Lejeune, February 26, 1935 (Lejeune Papers, reel 6).

130. Keyser to Lejeune, March 2, 1935 (Lejeune Papers, reel 6).

131. Lejeune to Black, March 1, 1935. For a personal note, see the book by Russell's daughter, Brooke Russell Astor, *Footprints: An Autobiography* (Garden City, NY: Doubleday, 1980); Donald F. Bittner, "Conflict under the Dome: Senator Hugo Black, Major General Smedley Butler, and the Challenged Promotion of Major General John H. Russell," paper presented at American Historical Association, December 1984; and, Schmidt, *Maverick Marine,* 213–14.

132. Bittner, "John H. Russell," in *Commandants,* 248; and *Congressional Record,* 74th Congress, 1st sess., March 5, 1935, 2930–33.

133. Bittner, "Conflict under the Dome," 18.

134. Bittner, "John H. Russell," in *Commandants,* 249.

135. Bittner, "Conflict Under the Dome," 29; *Congressional Record*—Senate, March 5, 1935, 2946–49.

136. *New York Times,* March 5, 1935 (Lejeune Papers, reel 15).

137. Bittner, "Conflict Under the Dome," 31.

138. Clayton Barrow Jr., "Looking for John A. Lejeune," *MCG* 74 (November 1990): 72.

139. See remarks by Ulbrich in *Preparing for Victory,* 14, 16.

140. Ibid., 16.

141. Barrow, "Looking for John A. Lejeune," 72.

142. Ulbrich, *Preparing for Victory,* 27–28.

143. Ibid., 187.

144. Many naval officers were impressed with Britain's use of commando tactics in the war. Commandos, however, are not able to hold terrain. This was the role of Marine Corps infantry rifle battalions.

145. Millett, *Semper Fidelis,* 371; Vandegrift, *Once a Marine,* 182–85; Ulbrich, *Preparing for Victory,* 189–99.

146. Lejeune to the Navy Department: "Comments on the Marine Expeditionary Force in connection with the U.S. Fleet Maneuvers—Spring 1925," July 23, 1924, file SC 162-78:12, RG 80, NARAW.

147. Lejeune to Navy Secretary: Revision of Pamphlet entitled *Joint Army and Navy Action in Coast Defense,* August 4, 1925, file SC 233-13, RG 225, NARACP.

148. *Joint Action of the Army and Navy,* 1927.

149. Isley and Crowl, *The U.S. Marines and Amphibious War,* 86. In order to receive credit and public recognition for its service in World War II, the Marine Corps worked with these historians, offering them independent assessment and access to corps records unless the information was still classified as top secret.

SELECTED BIBLIOGRAPHY

PRIMARY SOURCES

Archival Sources

Army Heritage and Education Center, AWC, Carlisle Barracks, PA

AWC Archives, Lejeune, 1909–10. Attack and Defense of Guam, Samoa; Military Geography of Alaska.

Lejeune Papers, Louisiana State University Archives

Lejeune Papers, Manuscripts Division, Library of Congress

Attack Battle of Meuse-Argonne, 1918, reel 11.

Attack on Massif of Blanc Mont Ridge, 1918, reel 11.

Budget Crisis in Marine Corps, 1930–32, reels 3, 5, 6.

Commander, Marine Barracks, Brooklyn, 1912–14, reel 3.

Commendations, Spanish-American War, 1898, reels 2, 3.

Congressional Inquiry, John Russell, 1935, reels 6, 15.

Correspondence, World War I, 1918, reels 2, 3, 11.

Cuban Interventions, 1912, 1913, 1914, reels 2, 3.

Death of Wendell Neville, 1930, reel 3.

Dedication Ceremony of Lejeune Hall, Quantico, 1959, reel 14.

Lejeune Letters to Sister Augustine and Daughter Ellie Lejeune Glennon, 1882–1932, reels 1, 2, 3.

Lejeune's Injury, September 21, 1932, reel 6.

Occupation of Germany, 1918–19, reel 11.

Operations at Panama Canal, 1903–4, 1906, reels 3, 15.

Operations at Veracruz, Mexico, 1914, reels 1, 3.

Orders to Lejeune, 1892–1929, reel 13.

Promotion by Selection, 1907, 1920–35, reels 1, 3, 6.

World War I—St. Mihiel Operations, reel 11.

Marine Corps University, Archives Branch, Alfred M. Gray Research Center, Quantico, VA

Bittner, Donald F. "Conflict under the Dome: Senator Hugo Black, Major General Smedley Butler, and the Challenged Promotion of Major General John H. Russell." Paper presented at American Historical Association, December 1984, in Command and Staff College, Education Center, Marine Corps Development and Education Command.

Ellis, Earl. "Advanced Base Operations in Micronesia, Operation Plan 712J." July 23, 1921. Revised. HAF 165.

——. "Naval Bases; Location, Resources, Denial of Bases, Security of Bases." 1914. HAF 294.

History Amphibious File (HAF).

Lejeune, J. A. Report of Special Board of Policy, Amphibious Operations, 1925: "Advanced Bases including Marine Corps Expeditionary Force for shore operations essential to the prosecution of the naval campaign." Lejeune File, GRC.

——. "The Marine Corps." April 1925. Partial manuscript, Lejeune File, GRC.

Miller, E. B. "The Marine Corps in Support of the Fleet." In HAF 40.

Oral History Collection

Clifton B. Cates.

Edward A. Craig.

William A. Worton.

Interview Transcription: William A. Worton and Clifton B. Cates.

The Tentative Landing Manual, 1934. HAF 39.

Marine Corps University, History Division, Reference Branch, Biographical Files

George Barnett.

Smedley Butler.

John A. Lejeune.

National Archives and Records Administration, College Park, MD (NARACP)

Record Group 120 (Records of the AEF, World War I).

Lejeune's Participation with the 2nd Division in World War I.

Operations Report, 2nd Division West of the Meuse, November 1–11, 1918.

2nd Division, Field Notes at St. Mihiel, Records of the AEF, 1918.

2nd Division, Operations Report on Massif of Blanc Mont Ridge, 1918.

Record Group 125 (Judge Advocate General Records of the Navy).

Medical Records of J. A. Lejeune, 1882–1929.

Promotion Records of J. A. Lejeune, 1890–1920.

Reports on Fitness of Officers (re: J. A. Lejeune), 1882–1929.

Record Group 127 (Records of US Marine Corps).
Amphibious Maneuvers, 1922, 1924, 1925.
Amphibious Warfare Lectures by the Navy, 1921.
Cole, Eli. Fortifications at Subic Bay, 12 June 1915.
Correspondence with General Board of the Navy.
Culebra Fleet Maneuvers, 1901–3; January–February 1914.
Curriculum of Amphibious Operations in MCS, 1925–29.
Development of Lighters for Landing Expeditionary Force, 1922–29.
Dunlap, Robert. Critique of Joint Army and Navy Problem no. 3, 1925.
Early Development of *Tentative Landing Manual,* 1930–33.
Intelligence Reports—Pearl Harbor, 1922.
Lejeune, J. A. Effect on Marine Corps of Limitation of Armament Conference, 1922.
Marine Corps War Portfolio, 1921.
Operations Report in the Meuse-Argonne Attack, November 1–11, 1918.
Records of the Weekly, Monthly, and Quarterly Conferences of the MGC, 1919–30.
Tentative War Plan for Use against Japan, October 1919; War Plan Orange, 1920–29.
Record Group 165 (Records of the War Department, 1860–1952).
Report of Eli Cole. Subic Bay fortifications, November 20, 1907.
Record Group 225 (Records of the Joint Army-Navy Board).
Minutes of the Joint Board, 1920–29.

National Archives and Records Administration, Washington, DC (NARAW)
Record Group 80 (USN Records).
Attempts to Institute Promotion by Merit, 1920–29.
Development of Lighters for Landing Expeditionary Force, 1922–29.
Function of Marine Corps in War Plans, 1920.
General Board Subject File: Future Policy for Marine Corps as Influenced by Conference on Limitation of Armaments, 1922.
Intelligence Reports, China, 1920.
Intelligence Reports, Hawaii, 1921.
Minutes of the General Board of the Navy, 1900–1932.
Recommendation to Imbed MEF as Part of Fleet, 1924, 1926.
War Plan Green, 1927.

Personal Correspondence with Marines of the Period
Cates, General Clifton B., USMC (Ret.), to Joe A. Simon, April 2, 1966.
Glennon, Col. James, USMC (Ret.), Grandson of John Lejeune, with

Joe A. Simon, January 23–30, 2007.
Puryear, Maj. Gen. Bennett, Jr., USMC (Ret.), to Joe A. Simon, May 8, 1966.
Shepherd, General Lemuel C., USMC (Ret.), to Joe A. Simon, March 21, May 31, 1966.
Thomas, General Gerald C., USMC (Ret.), to Joe A. Simon, April 19, May 3, 1966.
Vandegrift, General A. A., USMC (Ret.), to Joe A. Simon, April 4, June 10, 1966.

Published Primary Sources

Annual Report of Major Albert S. McLemore, Assistant Adjutant and Inspector. October 30, 1913.

Ansel, Walter C. "Naval Gun Fire in Support of a Landing." *MCG,* May 1932.

Army War College, 1909–10. Vols. 1 and 9, Orange-Blue Problems (Guam, Alaska), vol. 12, Orange-Blue Problems (Samoa). AWWCA.

Astor, Brooke Russell. *Footprints: An Autobiography.* Garden City, NY: Doubleday, 1980.

Breckinridge, James C. "Some Thoughts on Service Schools." *MCG,* December 1929.

Captain Chester to Secretary John Long. Rpt. in part in "A Short Biographical Sketch of Major General John A. Lejeune." *Recruiter's Bulletin* (July 1920). Rpt. in *Marines Magazine,* n.d., in Lejeune Papers, reel 4.

Cole, Eli K. "On the Work of Installing the Naval Base Guns at the Entrance to Subic Bay." November 20, 1907, RG 165, AWC, Serial 43, Problem Reports, AWC Studies, and Committee Reports, Records of the War Department and General Staff, NARACP.

———. To MGC: "Encloses copy of Lecture prepared for delivery at Marine Barracks, Philadelphia, 19 June 1915." Dated June 16, 1915. Item 1975-10, 1820-40, RG 127, NARACP.

Collier, E. F. C., Capt. "The Executive Staff." *MCG* 8, no. 4 (December 1923).

Congressional Record. 74th Congress, 1st Session, March 5, 1935. Washington, DC: GPO, 1935.

Craige, John H., Capt. "Publicity." *MCG,* June 1929.

Daniels, Josephus. *The Wilson Era: Years of Peace, 1910–1917.* Chapel Hill: University of North Carolina Press, 1944.

———. *The Wilson Era: Years of War and After, 1917–1923.* Chapel Hill: University of North Carolina Press, 1946.

Del Valle, Pedro. "Boats in the Landing Attack." *MCG,* May 1932.

———. "Ship to Shore in Amphibious Warfare." *MCG,* February 1932.

Denby, Edwin. "Men of the Mail Guard." November 11, 1921. In *Report of the Secretary of the Navy,* 1922, 824.

Dunlap, Robert. "Lessons for Marines from the Gallipoli Campaign." *MCG,* September 1921.

———. "The Naval Advance Base." Lecture, NWC, July 1911. Naval Historical Collection, Newport, RI.
———. "The Temporary Naval Advanced Base, General Considerations." Paper. NWC, 1912.
Dunning, John P. "The Story of the Great Storm at Samoa." *St. Nicholas* 17 (February 1890).
"Extracts from Testimony of the Major General Commandant before the Subcommittee of House Committee on Appropriations on the Naval Appropriation Bill, January, 1922." January 21, 1921, *MCG,* March 1921.
Fegan, J. C., Major, USMC, Post Athletic Office, Marine Barracks, Quantico, VA. "Athletics as Publicity" *MCG,* March 1923.
Feland, Logan, Brig. Gen. "The Division of Operations and Training, U.S. Marine Corps." *MCG* 7, no. 1 (March 1922).
Fullam, William. "The Organization, Training, and Discipline of the Navy Personnel, as Viewed from the Ship." *USNIP* 22 (1896).
———. "The System of Naval Training and Discipline Required to Promote Efficiency and Attract Americans." *USNIP* 4 (1890).
Hearings before Committee of Naval Affairs of the House of Representatives on Estimates Submitted by the Secretary of the Navy. March 2, 1920, 66th Congress. Washington, DC: GPO, 1920.
Hearings before the House Naval Affairs Committee for FY 32. February 9, 1931, 71st Congress, 3rd Session. Washington, DC: GPO, 1931.
Hines, J. L. "Grand Joint Army and Navy Exercise No. 3." Entry 39B, RG 127, NARACP.
Joint Action of the Army and the Navy. Prepared by Joint Board. Washington, DC: GPO, 1927.
Joint Army and Navy Action in Coast Defense. Washington, DC: GPO, 1920.
Kimberly, Rear Admiral L. A. *Samoan Hurricane.* Washington, DC: GPO, 1965.
Krulak, Victor H. *First to Fight: An Inside View of the U.S. Marine Corps.* Annapolis, MD: NIP, 1984.
Lejeune, John Archer. "A Legacy of Esprit and Leadership," *MCG,* March 2016, 80–85. From Lejeune's speech to Army General Staff College, January 18, 1921.
———. "Mail Guard Duty." *Report of the MGC,* October 10, 1922.
———. "The Mobile Defense of Advanced Bases by the Marine Corps." Lecture before Advance Base School, Navy Yard, Philadelphia, May 21, 1915. Later published as first article in *MCG,* March 1916.
———. *The Reminiscences of a Marine.* Philadelphia: Dorrance and Co., 1930.
———. "Testimony of the Major General Commandant before the Senate Committees of Foreign Relations," *MCG,* March 1928, 2–6.
———. "The United States Marine Corps." Lecture to NWC, April 1925, Lejeune Papers.

———. "The United States Marine Corps." *Our Navy* 18, no. 8 (1924). Copy in Lejeune Papers, reel 10.

———. "The United States Marine Corps." Talk delivered at NWC, December 14, 1923. Lejeune file, GRC. Also printed in the *MCG* 8 (December 1923): 243–54.

———. "The United States Marine Corps, Present and Future." *USNIP* 54 (October 1928).

———. "The United States Marine Corps." *USNIP*, October 1925.

———. "The United States Marine Corps, 1926," *USNIP*, October 1926.

———. To Brig. Gen. Smedley Butler, December 7, 1926, in Butler Papers, Marine Corps Archives, Quantico, VA.

Marine Corps Personnel Act of 1934 (Public Law 263).

Miller, E. B. "The Marine Corps: Its Mission, Organization, and Limitations." *MCG*, November 1932.

———. "A Naval Expedition Involving the Landing of a Marine Expeditionary Force." *MCG*, February 1933.

———. "Naval Support to the Landing of a Marine Expeditionary Force." *MCG*, May 1933.

Naval Appropriation Bill, Marine Corps, Vocational Schools, Quantico, VA, Committee on Naval Affairs, House of Representatives, Thursday, February 26, 1920. Washington, DC: GPO, 1920. Comments of Josephus Daniels to Committee on Naval Affairs as related in letter of Smedley D. Butler to Daniels, January 13, 1920. Butler's letter is part of the comments by Secretary Daniels.

Office of Naval Operations, Division of Fleet Training. *Landing Operations Doctrine, United States Navy, 1938.* (*Fleet Training Publication* 167.) Washington, DC: GPO, 1938. www.ibiblio.org/hyperwar/USN/ref/Amphibious/index.html.

President, US NWC, to the President, General Board. "General principles governing the selection and establishment of Advanced Naval Bases, and the composition of an Advanced Base outfit, a study made by Major John H. Russell, USMC." Modified and edited by NWC Staff. December 10, 1909. In HAF 768.

Regulations of the North Atlantic Fleet. Issued May 26, 1903. Report of the Secretary of the Navy, 1903.

Reports of the Secretary of the Navy, 1888–1930. Includes Reports of the Commandant of the Marine Corps, Reports of the Bureau of Navigation, Reports of the Bureau of Construction and Repair, Reports of the Superintendent of the Naval Academy, and Reports of the Surgeon-General. Navy Reports, 1888–1930.

Russell, John H. "The Birth of the Fleet Marine Force." *USNIP* 72 (January 1946).

———. "General Principles governing the selection and establishment of Advanced Naval Bases, and the composition of an Advanced Base Outfit." December 10, 1909. In HAF.

——. "Notes on field construction work and guns for Advanced Naval Base." In Daugherty, *Pioneers of Amphibious Warfare.*
——. "An outline study of the defense of Advanced Naval Bases." October 22, 1909. NWC.
——. "A Plea for a Mission and Doctrine." *MCG,* June 1916.
——. The preparation of war plans for the establishment and defense of a Navy Advanced Base." June 14, 1910. In Daugherty, *Pioneers of Amphibious Warfare.*
Sledge, E. B. *With the Old Breed at Peleliu and Okinawa.* New York: Ballantine, 2007.
Smith, Holland M. "The Development of Amphibious Tactics in the U.S. Navy." *MCG* 30, no. 9 (September 1946).
——. and Percy Finch. *Coral and Brass.* New York: Ace, 1948.
Summerall, Charles Pelot. *The Way of Duty, Honor, Country: The Memoir of General Charles Pelot Summerall.* Edited and annotated by Timothy K. Nenninger. Lexington: University Press of Kentucky, 2010.
Tentative Manual for Landing Operations. Quantico, VA: MCS, 1934.
Trudeau, Noah Andre. "An Appalling Calamity." *Naval History,* April 2011, 54–59.
United States Marine Corps. *Small Wars Manual.* 1940. Rpt. New York: Skyhorse Publishing, 2009.
Vandegrift, A. A. "The Marine Corps of 1948," *USNIP,* February 1948.
——. as told to Robert Asprey. *Once a Marine: The Memoirs of General A. A. Vandegrift, Commandant of the U.S. Marines in WWII.* New York: Ballantine, 1966.
Williams, Dion. "Blue Marine Corps Expeditionary Force." *MCG* 10 (September 1925).
——. "The Defense of Our New Naval Stations." *USNIP,* June 1902.
——. "The Fall Exercises of 1924 Marine Corps Expeditionary Force." *MCG* 10 (June 1925).
——. "The Naval Advance Base." Lecture, NWC, July 26, 1912. In HAF 211.
——. "Naval Reconnaissance: Instructions for Reconnaissance of Bays, Harbors, and Adjacent Countries." Washington, DC: GPO, 1906.
——. "The Winter Maneuvers of 1924." *MCG,* March 1924.
Work, Hubert, Acting Postmaster General. Report of the MGC. October 10, 1922.

Manuscripts

Barnett, George. "Soldier and Sailor Too." Marine Corps University, History Division, Reference Branch, Biographical Files, Quantico, VA.
Fullam, William. To Secretary of the Navy: Establishment of Advance Base Outfit, May 1, 1913. In Item 1975-10-15, RG 127, NARACP.
——. To Secretary of the Navy, June 23, 27; September 22, 1913, RG 127, NARACP.

SECONDARY SOURCES

Books

Ambrose, Stephen. *D-Day: June 6, 1944: The Climactic Battle of World War II.* New York: Simon and Schuster, 1994.

Ballendorf, Dirk A., and Merrill L. Bartlett. *Pete Ellis: An Amphibious Warfare Prophet, 1880–1923.* Annapolis, MD: NIP, 1997.

Bartlett, Merrill L. *Lejeune: A Marine's Life, 1867–1942.* Annapolis, MD: NIP, 1996.

——. ed. *Assault from the Sea: Essays on the History of Amphibious Warfare.* Annapolis, MD: NIP, 1983.

Beale, Howard K.. *Theodore Roosevelt and the Rise of America to World Power.* Baltimore: Johns Hopkins University Press, 1956.

Bettez, David J. *Kentucky Marine: Major General Logan Feland and the Making of the Modern USMC,* Lexington: University Press of Kentucky, 2014.

Black, Jeremy. *Rethinking Military History.* London: Routledge, 2004.

Braisted, William R. *The United States Navy in the Pacific, 1897–1909.* Annapolis, MD: NIP, 2008.

——. *The United States Navy in the Pacific, 1909–1922.* Annapolis, MD: NIP, 2008.

Bullard, Robert Lee. *Personalities and Reminiscences of the War.* Garden City, NY: Doubleday, Page, and Co., 1925.

Callwell, C. E. *The Dardanelles.* Uckfield, East Sussex, UK: Naval and Military Press, 2005.

Cameron, Craig M. *American Samurai: Myth, Imagination, and the Conduct of Battle in the First Marine Division, 1941–1951.* Cambridge, UK: Cambridge University Press, 1994.

Clark, George B. *The Second Infantry Division in World War I.* Jefferson, NC: McFarland and Co., 2007.

Clifford, Kenneth J. *Progress and Purpose: A Developmental History of the U.S. Marine Corps, 1900–1970.* Washington, DC: History and Museums Division, Headquarters, USMC, 1973.

Coffman, Edward M. *The War to End All Wars: The American Military Experience in World War I.* Lexington: University Press of Kentucky, 1988.

Condit, Kenneth W., and Edwin T. Turnbladh. *Hold High the Torch: A History of the 4th Marines.* Washington, DC: Historical Branch, USMC, 1960.

Cronon, E. David, ed. *The Cabinet Diaries of Josephus Daniels, 1913–1921.* Lincoln: University of Nebraska Press, 1963.

Daugherty, Leo J., III. *Pioneers of Amphibious Warfare, 1898–1945.* Jefferson, NC: McFarland and Co., 2009.

Dyer, George Carroll. *The Amphibians Came to Conquer: The Story of Admiral*

Richmond Kelly Turner. Vol. 2. Washington, DC: GPO, 1971.

Esposito, Vincent J. *The West Point Atlas of American Wars.* New York: Fredrick A. Praeger, 1959.

Fleming, Walter L. *Louisiana State University, 1860–1896.* Baton Rouge: Louisiana State University Press, 1926.

Foner, Eric. *Forever Free: The Story of Emancipation and Reconstruction.* New York: Alfred A. Knopf, 2005.

———. *Give Me Liberty! An American History.* 3rd ed. Vol. 1. New York: W. W. Norton, 2012.

———. *Reconstruction: America's Unfinished Revolution, 1863–1877.* New York: Harper Collins, 2014.

Gibney, Frank, ed. *Senso: The Japanese Remember the Pacific War: Letters to the Editor of* Asahi Shimbu. Trans. Beth Cary. Armonk, NY: East Gate, 1995.

A Guide to American Battlefields of Europe. Washington, DC: GPO, 1927.

Hagan, Kenneth, ed. *In Peace and War: Interpretation of American Naval History, 1775–1984.* Westport, CT: Greenwood Press, 1984.

Harbaugh, William Henry. *The Life and Times of Theodore Roosevelt.* New York: Collier Books, 1963.

Hart, Liddell B. H. *The Defense of Britain.* New York: Random House, 1939.

Heinl, Robert D., Jr. *Soldiers of the Sea: The United States Marine Corps, 1775–1962.* 1962. Rpt. Baltimore: Nautical & Aviation Publishing, 1991.

Isley, Jeter A., and Philip A. Crowl. *The U.S. Marines and Amphibious War: Its Theory and Its Practice in the Pacific.* Princeton, NJ: Princeton University Press, 1951.

Jomini, Antoine-Henri. *The Art of War.* Restored ed. Kingston, Ontario, Canada: Legacy Books, 2008.

Kamman, William. *A Search for Stability: United States Diplomacy toward Nicaragua, 1925–1933.* Notre Dame, IN: University of Notre Dame Press, 1968.

Kaufman, Robert Gordon. *Arms Control during the Pre-Nuclear Era: The United States and Naval Limitations between the Two World Wars.* New York: Columbia University Press, 1990.

Kennedy, Paul. *The Rise and Fall of the Great Powers: Economic Change and Military Conflict from 1500 to 2000.* New York: Random House, 1987.

Lengel, Edward G. *To Conquer Hell: The Meuse-Argonne, 1918, the Epic Battle That Ended the First World War.* New York: Henry Holt and Co., 2008.

Lindsay, Robert. *This High Name: Public Relations and the U.S. Marine Corps.* Madison: University of Wisconsin Press, 1956.

Link, Arthur. *Wilson, the New Freedom.* Princeton, NJ: Harper Torch, 1956.

———. *Woodrow Wilson and the Progressive Era.* New York: Harper and Brothers, 1963.

Locklin, D. Phillip. *Economics of Transportation.* Homewood, IL: Richard B. Irwin, 1960.

Mastriano, Douglas V. *Thunder in the Argonne: A New History of America's Greatest Battle.* Lexington: University Press of Kentucky, 2018.

Menn, Joseph Karl. *The Large Slaveholders of Louisiana, 1860.* New Orleans: Pelican Publishing Co., 1964.

Metcalf, Clyde H. *A History of the United States Marine Corps.* New York: G. P. Putnam's Sons, 1939.

Miller, Edward S. *War Plan Orange: The U.S. Strategy to Defeat Japan, 1897–1945.* Annapolis, MD: NIP, 1991.

Millett, Allan R. *In Many a Strife: General Gerald C. Thomas and the USMC, 1917–1956.* Annapolis, MD: NIP, 1993.

———. *Semper Fidelis: The History of the United States Marine Corps.* Rev. and expanded ed. New York: Free Press, 1991.

Millett, Allan R., and Jack Shulimson, eds. *Commandants of the Marine Corps.* Annapolis, MD: NIP, 2004.

Millett, Allan R., and Williamson Murray, eds., *Military Innovation in the Interwar Period.* New York: Cambridge University Press, 1998.

Millett, Allan R., Peter Maslowski, and William B. Feis. *For the Common Defense: A Military History of the United States from 1607 to 2012.* 3rd ed. New York: Free Press, 2012.

Millis, Walter. *Arms and Men: A Study in American Military History.* New York: Bobbs-Merrill Co., 1956.

Montross, Lynn. *The United States Marines: A Pictorial History.* New York: Rinehart and Co., 1955.

Morris, Edmund. *Theodore Rex.* New York: Modern Library, 2001.

Mortlock, Michael J. *The Landings at Suvla Bay, 1915: An Analysis of British Failure during the Gallipoli Campaign.* Jefferson, NC: McFarland & Co., 2007.

Munro, Dana G. *The United States and the Caribbean Republics, 1921–1933.* Princeton, NJ: Princeton University Press, 1974.

Musicant, Ivan. *The Banana Wars: A History of United States Military Intervention in Latin America from the Spanish-American War to the Invasion of Panama.* New York: Macmillan, 1990.

Neilson, Keith, and Elizabeth Jane Errington, eds. *Navies and Global Defense: Theories and Strategy.* Westport, CT: Praeger, 1995.

Newman, Roger K. *Hugo Black: A Biography.* New York: Pantheon, 1994.

Parker, Geoffrey. *Cambridge Illustrated History of Warfare: The Triumph of the West.* Cambridge, UK: Cambridge University Press, 1995.

Quirk, Robert E. *An Affair of Honor: Woodrow Wilson and the Occupation of Veracruz.* Lexington: University Press of Kentucky, 1962.

Renda, Mary A. *Taking Haiti: Military Occupation and the Culture of U.S. Imperialism.* Chapel Hill: University of North Carolina Press, 2001.

Riffel, Judy, ed. *A History of Pointe Coupee Parish and Its Families.* Baton Rouge: Le Comité des Archives de la Louisiane, 1983.

Roark, James, Michael Johnson, Patricia Cohen, Sarah Stage, Alan Lawson, and Susan Hartmann. *The American Promise: A History of the United States.* Boston: Bedford/St. Martin's, 2005.

Rodrigue, John C. *Reconstruction in the Cane Fields: From Slavery to Free Labor in Louisiana's Sugar Parishes, 1862–1880.* Baton Rouge: Louisiana State University Press, 2001.

Ross, Steven T. *American War Plans, 1890–1939.* London: Frank Cass Publishers, 2002.

Schmidt, Hans. *Maverick Marine: General Smedley D. Butler and the Contradictions of American Military History.* Lexington: University Press of Kentucky, 1987.

Sherrod, Robert. *History of Marine Corps Aviation in World War II.* Washington, DC: Combat Forces Press, 1952.

Shulimson, Jack. *The Marine Corps' Search for a Mission, 1880–1898.* Lawrence: University Press of Kansas, 1993.

Stallings, Laurence. *The Doughboys: The Story of the AEF, 1917–1918.* New York: Harper & Row, 1963.

Strahan, Jerry E. *Andrew Jackson Higgins and the Boats that Won World War II.* Baton Rouge: Louisiana State University Press, 1994.

Taylor, Joe Gray. *Louisiana: A History.* New York: W. W. Norton & Co., 1984.

Townshend, Charles. *The Oxford History of Modern War.* Oxford, UK: Oxford University Press, 2005.

Tunnell, Ted. *Crucible of Reconstruction: War, Radicalism, and Race in Louisiana, 1862–1877.* Baton Rouge: Louisiana State University Press, 1984.

Ulbrich, David. *Preparing for Victory: Thomas Holcomb and the Making of the Modern Marine Corps, 1936–1943.* Annapolis, MD: NIP, 2011.

Vadal, Gillis. *Rethinking Southern Violence: Homicides in Post–Civil War Louisiana, 1866–1984.* Columbus: Ohio State University Press, 2000.

Venzon, Anne Cipriano. *From Whaleboats to Amphibious Warfare: Lt. Gen. "Howling Mad" Smith and the U.S. Marine Corps.* Westport, CT: Praeger, 2003.

Wilson, John R. M. *Herbert Hoover and the Armed Forces: A Study of Presidential Attitudes and Policy.* New York: Garland, 1993.

Winters, John D. *The Civil War in Louisiana.* Baton Rouge: Louisiana State University Press, 1963.

Articles and Book Chapters

Alexander, James H. "Roots of Deployment—Vera Cruz, 1914." In Bartlett, ed., *Assault from the Sea.*

"The Army War College." *Army Reserve Magazine* 12, no. 3 (March 1966).

Assmann, Kurt. "The German Invasion of Norway, 1940." In Bartlett, ed., *Assault from the Sea.*

Barrow, Clayton Jr. "Looking for John A. Lejeune." *MCG* 74 (November 1990).

Bettez, David J. "Lejeune's Lieutenants: Smedley Darlington Butler and Logan Feland." *MCG,* November 2014.

Cosmas, Graham A., and Jack Shulimson. "The Culebra Maneuver and the Formation of the U.S. Marine Corps' Advance Base Force, 1913–14." In Bartlett, ed., *Assault from the Sea.*

Cressman, Robert. "George Frank Elliott, 1903–1910." In Millett and Shulimson, eds., *Commandants,* 97–162.

Daugherty, Leo J., III. "Away All Boats: The Army-Navy Maneuvers of 1925." *JFQ,* Autumn–Winter 1998–99.

"Foreword: The Legacy of John A. Lejeune." *MCG* 46 (April 1962).

Gibson, T. A. "Eyeless in Byzantium: The Tragedy of Ian Hamilton." In Bartlett, ed., *Assault from the Sea,* 142–53.

Hagan, Kenneth J. "The Apotheosis of Mahan: American Naval Strategy, 1889–1922." In Neilson and Errington, eds., *Navies and Global Defense.*

Hattendorf, John B. "Alfred Thayer Mahan and American Naval Theory." In Neilson and Errington, eds., *Navies and Global Defense.*

Heinl, Robert D. Jr. "An Association Is Formed," *MCG* 47 (April 1963).

Hittle, Lt. Col. J. D. "Jomini and Amphibious Thought." *MCG,* May 1946.

Irwin, Manley. "Lejeune and Denby: Forging a Marine Corps Doctrine." *MCG,* February 9, 2004.

Junge, Michael. "Semper Huh?" *USNIP,* February 1913.

Kiralfy, Alexander. "Sea Power in the Eastern War." *Brassey's Naval Annual* (London), 1942.

Lengel, Edward G. "Meuse-Argonne." *American Heritage Magazine,* Summer 2010.

Linn, Brian McAllister. "William Phillips Biddle, 1911 to 1914." In Millett and Shulimson, eds., *Commandants.*

Miller, John G. "William Freeland Fullam's War with the Corps." *USNIP,* November 1975.

Moore, Richard Scott. "Ideas and Direction: Building Amphibious Doctrine." *MCG,* November 1982.

———. "The Legacy of J. C. Breckinridge." *MCG,* May 1984.

Neimeyer, Charles, Lt. Col., USMC (Ret.). "Combat in Nicaragua: Effective and Unique." *MCG* 92, no. 4 (April 2008): 71–76.

Ritchie, Matthew. "Effective Leaders: The Importance of Relationships." *MCG,* November 2015.

Roan, Richard W., Major, USMC. "Roebling's Amphibian: The Origin of the Assault Amphibian." Command and Staff College, Education Center, Marine Corps Development and Education Command, Quantico, VA. www.globalsecurity.org/military/library/report/1987/RRR.htm.

Roberts, Andrew, and Simon Norfolk. "A Bold New History of the Battle of the Somme." *Smithsonian Magazine,* July 2016.

Ruhl, Arthur. "Fall of Veracruz." *Colliers* 52 (May 9, 1914).

Shulimson, Jack. "The U.S. Marines in Panama, 1885." In Bartlett, ed., *Assault from the Sea.*

Stewart, R. A. "The Japanese Assault on Timor, 1942." In Bartlett, ed., *Assault from the Sea.*

Sweetman, Jack. "Take Veracruz at Once." *Naval History,* April 2014, 34–41.

Von Lehmann, Hans G. "Japanese Landing Operation in World War II." In Bartlett, ed., *Assault from the Sea.*

Williams, R. H. "Those Controversial Boards." *MCG,* November 1982, 98.

Wilson, John R. M. "The Quaker and the Sword: Herbert Hoover's Relations with the Military." *Journal of Military History,* April 1974.

Wright, Edward. "Better Than When They Came." *USNIP,* August 2015.

Newspapers

Amodio, Joseph V. "Fast Chat with Sir Maurice Mickelwhite—Better Known as Michael Caine." *McClatchy Tribune News,* May 28, 2009.

"The Army War College." *Army Reserve Magazine* 12, no. 3 (March 1966).

Craige, John H., Captain, USMC. "A Fighting Man Who Led the Corps." Interview, *New York Times,* February 24, 1929.

"Hot Fighting at Veracruz." *Brooklyn Eagle,* April 23, 1914.

Lejeune, J. "John Lejeune Recalls Carpetbag Reign of Terror." New Orleans *Times-Picayune,* March 12, 1939. Times-Picayune Historical Archives (online).

———. "Lejeune Reviews V.M.I.'s Century of War, Peace." New Orleans *Times-Picayune,* May 7, 1939. Times-Picayune Historical Archives (online).

———. "Louisiana's Fighting Marine Tells His Life Story." New Orleans *Times-Picayune,* March 5, 1939. Times-Picayune Historical Archives (online).

———. "Major General John A. Lejeune Tells How a Boat and Some Books Influenced His Choice of a Career." New Orleans *Times-Picayune,* March 19, 1939. Times-Picayune Historical Archives (online).

———. "Rigorous Training at L.S.U. Recalled by Lejeune." New Orleans *Times-Picayune,* March 26, 1939. Times-Picayune Historical Archives (online).

"Marines Starting for Guantanamo." *New York Evening Journal,* February 18, 1913.

New Orleans Times-Democrat, December 26, 1904.
New York American, February 19, 1913.
New York Times, November 10, 1916.
Reeve, Norman. "Our Navy's Winter Base." *Leslie's Illustrated Weekly Newspaper,* May 1, 1913.
Ruhl, Arthur. "Fall of Veracruz." *Colliers* 52 (May 9, 1914).
"Taft Rushes Men and Ships to Cuba." *New York Times,* February 13, 1913.
Ulm, A. H. "Lejeune, Composite of All Devil Dogs." *New York Times,* February 15, 1925.
"When Uncle Sam's Marines Play at War." Weekly Gravure Pictorial. *Nashville Banner,* May 25, 1924.

US Marine Corps Publications

Condit, Kenneth, John Johnstone, and Ella Nargele. *A Brief History of Headquarters Marine Corps Staff Organization.* Washington, DC: Historical Division, Headquarters, USMC, 1971.
Ellsworth, Captain Harry Allanson. *One Hundred Eighty Landings of United States Marines, 1800–1934.* History and Museums Division, Headquarters, USMC, Washington, DC, 1974.
Frances, Anthony A. *History of Marine Corps Schools.* Quantico, VA: Marine Corps Historical Library, 1945.
Gayle, Gordon D. *Bloody Beaches: The Marines at Peleliu.* History and Museums Division, USMC, Washington, 1996.
Johnson, Edward C. *Marine Corps Aviation: The Early Years, 1912–1940.* Ed. Graham A. Cosmas. History and Museums Division, Headquarters, USMC, 1977.
Miller, Colonel William, and Major John H. Johnstone. *A Chronology of the United States Marine Corps, 1775–1934.* Historical Branch, G-3 Division, Headquarters, USMC, Washington, DC, 1965.
Nalty, Bernard C., and Ralph F. Moody. *A Brief History of U.S. Marine Corps Officer Procurement, 1775–1969.* Historical Division, Headquarters, USMC, Washington, DC.
Roe, Thomas G., Earnest H. Giusti, John H. Johnstone, and Benis M. Frank. *A History of Marine Corps Roles and Missions: 1775–1962.* Washington, DC: Headquarters, USMC, 1962.

Theses and Dissertations

Colbourn, Colin Michael. "Esprit de Marine Corps: The Making of the Modern Marine Corps through Public Relations, 1898–1929." MA thesis, University of Southern Mississippi, 2009.

Costello, Daniel Joseph. "Planning for War: A History of the General Board of the Navy, 1900–1914." PhD diss., Fletcher School of Law and Diplomacy, 1968.

Daugherty, Leo J., III. "To Fight Our Country's Battles: An Institutional History of the United States Marine Corps during the Interwar Era, 1919–1935." PhD diss., Ohio State University, 2001.

Dillon, James T., Lt. Col., USMC. "John A. Lejeune, the Marine Corps' Greatest Strategic Leader." US AWC, Strategy Research Project, Class of 2008, USAWC, March 15, 2008, Carlisle Barracks, PA. Submitted in partial fulfillment of the requirements of the master of strategic studies degree.

Simon, Joe Arthur. "The Life and Career of John Archer Lejeune." MA thesis, Louisiana State University, 1967.

———. "John Archer Lejeune and the Development of Amphibious Assault in the United States Marine Corps." PhD diss., Lancaster University, UK, 2015.

INDEX

Note: The abbreviation JAL refers to John Archer Lejeune. Italic page numbers refer to illustrations.